DATE

# Mr. Skylark

# Mr. Skylark

## JOHN BENNETT
## AND THE
## CHARLESTON RENAISSANCE

# Harlan Greene

THE UNIVERSITY OF GEORGIA PRESS    ATHENS AND LONDON

Published by the University of Georgia Press

Athens, Georgia 30602

© 2001 by Harlan Greene

All rights reserved

Designed by Sandra Strother Hudson

Set in Centaur with Fairfield Display by G&S Typesetters

Printed and bound by Maple-Vail

The paper in this book meets the guidelines for permanence
and durability of the Committee on Production Guidelines for
Book Longevity of the Council on Library Resources.

Printed in the United States of America

05  04  03  02  01  C  5  4  3  2  1


Library of Congress Cataloging-in-Publication Data

Greene, Harlan.

Mr. Skylark : John Bennett and the Charleston renaissance /
Harlan Greene.

p. cm.

Includes bibliographical references (p.    ) and index.

ISBN 0-8203-2211-3 (alk. paper)

1. Bennett, John, 1865–1956.    2. Authors, American—
20th century—Biography.    3. Charleston (S.C.)—Intellectual
life—20th century.    I. Title: Mister Skylark.    II. Title.

PS3503.E5475 Z68 2001

813'.54—dc21

[B]          00-053640


British Library Cataloging-in-Publication Data available

The silhouette drawings appearing
throughout the book are by John Bennett and are reproduced
courtesy of the estate of John Bennett.

In memory of

OLIN B. JOLLEY, M.D.

1963–1996

*the gallant hearted*

# Contents

# Introduction

ON THE LAST DAY OF 1956, the *Charleston (S.C.) Evening Post* published a tribute to the recently deceased John Bennett. Having excoriated him nearly fifty years before, the paper now set out to refashion the past. He "came to Charleston," the editor wrote, "liked the city, found that liking . . . reciprocated, and became as devoted a Charlestonian as any native ever has been." It followed with praise for his character and his works: "As a friend and an associate, he was held in deep personal esteem. It was a delight to converse with him, a privilege to be a member of the circle in which he moved. He lived to a ripe old age," the article concluded, prophesying that "the memory of him will live even longer."[1]

In truth, this seemed to be the case back in 1956; for less than a month before his death, his children's book *Master Skylark* had been named one of the "100 Best Books from All Time."[2] It is "easily one of the nineteenth century's premier children's works of historical fiction," claimed one scholar; another wrote, "If this period had produced no other books than those of John Bennett, still it would be . . . notable."[3]

Articles about his gifts and accomplishments appeared in the next few months; as the opera *Porgy and Bess* went around the world as a goodwill ambassador for the U.S. State Department, Bennett's role in its creation and staging was noted often. *Bartlett's Familiar Quotations* continued to feature quotes from both his prose and his poetry, and books and articles based on his research continued to appear over the years. Yet, as I grew up in Charleston (I was three years old at Bennett's death), his name was heard less and less.

He was not totally forgotten, however. (That came later.) As a child, I enjoyed visiting the old deteriorating mansion that housed the public library (which he had worked to found, and in whose overgrown garden he had handed out diplomas to children for summer reading). The children's room was named for him, and all around its walls pranced silhouettes from his Newberry-nominated *The Pigtail of Ah Lee Ben Loo.* The children's librarian (who to me seemed ancient and always in black) was Janie Smith, whom Bennett had known as young and girlish. Just a few blocks north stood the Charleston Museum where I (and other Charleston children) looked with awe at many of the objects Bennett had prompted the museum to collect. (Both of these institutions are now in new buildings that no longer recall his contributions.)

I was an avid reader and decided to become a writer. To see how it was done, I began reading authors who had lived in Charleston and employed the city in their works. I read DuBose Heyward, Robert Molloy, Josephine Pinckney, Katherine Drayton, Mayrant Simons, Ludwig Lewisohn, and Harry Hervey. Bennett, I came to realize, had known them all; and they, in turn, had all praised him. Then I read his *Madame Margot,* a strange hypnotic and hallucinatory trance of a prose poem; when I put it down, I blinked at the mundane world dizzily.

In high school and college, there was no mention of any of these writers. Like many small cities, Charleston both distrusted and bragged about its local heroes; while it paid lip service to the past, it nevertheless forgot it. In some survey courses there were mentions of Charlestonians William Gilmore Simms and Henry Timrod, from the nineteenth century. We were taught that no truly good writer had ever come from Charleston; this ultimately made all Charleston writing suspect. (In creative writing classes in the early 1970s, I was ridiculed for writing about Charleston instead of other more interesting things.) At the College of Charleston, a professor to whom I confessed my interest in Bennett assumed that I was speaking of the British novelist Arnold Bennett.

Like her, scholars and literary historians dismissed Charleston, as if embarrassed by it. They relegated the city to a footnote even in histories of the Southern literary renaissance, that flowering of letters between the world wars starting with minor Charleston poets and ending up with the major Mississippian William Faulkner. (Faulkner's stepson, Malcolm Franklin, had married a Charlestonian and was living here; to him, my college class went to pay tribute.) New critics, with politics and tastes far more liberal than those of the past, had too easily conflated the works that had came out of Charleston with the tourist label stuck on the city. To outsiders the city seemed old, always looking nostalgically to the past and the Civil War. With its still mostly segregated ways, it was an easy target for dismissal as a backwater; all who had written in the pre—Civil Rights era were tainted with the label, too. The one possible exception seemed to be DuBose Heyward, whose slender claim to fame was based on his authorship of *Porgy*, on which American icon George Gershwin had based the opera *Porgy and Bess*. (The novel was considered racist and forgettable, and the opera, although staged at La Scala, had yet to be produced at the Met.)

One day while doing research for county historian Elias Bull, I wandered into the South Carolina Historical Society. Going through a gothic pointed arch, I came across a shelf full of Heyward's works; rather grandly I congratulated the director, Mrs. Granville Prior (who as a girl had won poetry prizes funded by Bennett), on the completeness of the collection. As diminutive as Faulkner's Miss Rosa, she smiled up at me and said graciously, "We have his papers, too; would you like to catalog them?"

That was one of the turning points of my life, and the true origin of this biography; on Saturdays for about a year or so in the early 1970s, I started going through the papers of John Bennett's protégé DuBose Heyward; they had already been rough sorted by Helen McCormack, once head of the Gibbes Art Gallery, an organization helped and encouraged by John Bennett. I prided myself on my generosity and found none of my basic assumptions challenged. I knew Heyward was the only important Charleston writer. I knew that he had known John Bennett, and everything I ran across on Bennett rang true: he was not from Charleston (and so, as local reasoning went, was not important); he wrote children's books set in other times; he was interested in Negroes and their way of speech and their beliefs. He was a kindly white-haired gentleman who was nice to everyone, and everyone I met (Laura Bragg, a friend of Bennett and once director of the Charleston Museum; Elmina Eason of the Library Society, on whose board Bennett had served; Mrs. Robert N. S. Whitelaw, widow of the director of the Gibbes Art Gallery; and Bennett's own daughter Susan) grew excited and said how much they had admired and liked him. They vowed he was always gracious and kind, with never a cross word for anyone, truly the kiss of death to a youngster interested in secrets and unknown things about Charleston literary history as I was then.

In time, I came to work at the historical society under the fine directorship of Gene Waddell. Gene gave me the opportunity to catalog all the papers of the Charleston writers in the fireproof building; as an archivist I got a firsthand opportunity to witness the difference between the writers and what literary historians had said of them. All of us interested in the field owe Gene a debt of gratitude for acquiring the papers of Josephine Pinckney, Julia Peterkin, Herbert Ravenel Sass, and more of John Bennett's.

While fortunate to have worked on all of those collections, I was most engrossed with Bennett's—for their volume, if for no other reason. They comprise over thirty linear feet of correspondence, scrapbooks, photographs, clippings, typescripts, galleys, mounted silhouettes, and manuscripts, spanning the century from the 1860s to the 1960s. If my body often cramped as I hunched on the floor sorting stacks and stacks of papers, my mind certainly didn't. It whirled with the sheer magnitude of the panorama suggested by the documents (surely one reason no one had ever attempted to "do" him), and I fell under his spell. Here indeed was the kindly old man, like a grandfather I had never had, and I was charmed by him. Like a good novel, his papers transported me backward in time; I was entranced by his idyllic Midwestern and mid-nineteenth-century childhood, his young-adult romanticism, his authorial brilliance, and his accomplished artwork. Too, he was a member of Charleston society, and a promoter of young talent. Sorting through his papers, however, I also found other John Bennetts: there were traces of a bitter, suicidal young man, feeling sacrificed by his family; a cynic and drug addict; someone the Charleston newspapers called dirty and disgusting, unfit to entertain proper white ladies; a man who said unkind things behind other's backs; who made excuses for his failures while wallowing in self pity; and an elitist with prejudices against Jews and blacks.

At first I felt guilty finding these "other" Bennetts. But then I began to realize, almost with skin prickling, that all of them had been waiting for me or, if not me exactly, then someone like me. A true Victorian with a large house at his disposal, Bennett seemed to have saved every scrap of paper that had crossed his desk; he also deliberately transcribed letters he thought important, eventually keeping carbons of nearly all his correspondence. Long before my birth, he had been anticipating me, someone to whom he could plead his case; instead of explaining to contemporaries his motivations and reactions to things, he started doing so on sheets of paper and making notes in margins for someone to unearth.

I, of course, found this fascinating and took to heart the advice he had given to DuBose Heyward and other writers: write about what you know, he had said. Now that I had gone through his papers, I knew a lot about people in Charleston in the 1920s. And now I was writing, too. Bennett had known the true-life Charlestonian on whom I was basing a novel. He had encouraged and documented him, as had Miss Bragg, who spoke of him to me. Out of adulation and gratitude then, I decided to write Bennett's biography, not the worst reason, perhaps, to prompt such a work, but certainly not the best (there are too many books on too many shelves attesting to the sterling nature of too angelic characters from history). By the early 1980s I had stitched together an adulatory work nearly entirely in Bennett's own words, salvaged from his own letters and autobiographical writings. In it, I quickly and guiltily noted those few qualities of his that were less than perfect.

Fortunately, my life changed. I published my first novel, got more responsibility at work, fell in love, and left Charleston; I said good-bye to John Bennett and his biography. But periodically over the years, some scholar would ask me a question, and I'd rediscover Bennett. Like the aftermath of a brutal crime, I'd open a closet and see boxes containing vital pieces of him, labeled "beliefs," "early works," "important things." I started looking back over my notes, and with maturity I saw that here was not just a subject worthy of adulation but a man and writer of great interest and even importance. Here was an author of at least one children's classic, a trailblazer in the study of Gullah, the language of the coastal South Carolina blacks, an oral historian who had saved black folklore from vanishing, a promoter of talent the likes of DuBose Heyward and Hervey Allen, and a man integral to many cultural movements that had left their stamp on the country and the city. Thomas Beer, dismissing the mauve decade of the 1890s, had had to make sullen tribute to Bennett; others, whether they acknowledged him or not, built on his earlier works and unpublished research. He had helped nearly every person and institution in an important American city for nearly half a century. He was a key player of a time and a place scholars were turning to more and more frequently to explore. For Charleston, we are now acknowledging, did not just shape America in the colonial, slaveholding, and Civil War eras; its influence has extended into the twentieth century as well, artistically and culturally if not politically. The early decades of the twentieth century in Charleston saw the birth of the historic preservation movement, a new way of depicting the African American in art, and a serious new way of documenting African American history. All appeared here around the time that the city lent its name to a dance that epitomized the earth-shattering and decadent decade of the 1920s. For a brief moment, many eyes turned to Charleston and were mesmerized by what they saw, and the one who had a finger in all these different movements, who observed it from both inside and out simultaneously, and who recorded it with some objectivity—was John Bennett.

How could scholars and authors have missed him, I wondered. Certainly it had to do with the way earlier scholars and social critics had dismissed Charleston as upholding the old school and being all of one piece. It had to do, too, no doubt, with the vastness of his papers—a mountain of documentation daunting to anybody with a deadline. I think that his age also played a part in his oblivion. He lived past ninety; those who remembered Bennett spoke of the old gentleman. It was that kindly white-haired image of the man smiling and nodding at everyone that slipped into history. The fact that he was white and of the patrician class, writing on African American subjects, also made him suspect, someone a bit dangerous to explicate in an era of political correctness.

It's encouraging to see these old attitudes changing—a shift Bennett, ironically enough, remarked upon his arrival in Charleston at the end of the nineteenth century. Academics, historians, and critics no longer have to explain their attraction to someone who lived and wrote in a South that was staunchly old-fashioned and segregationist. Susan Williams has done a masterful job in her biography of South Carolina's Pulitzer Prize—winning novelist Julia Peterkin, a white aristocrat who, like Bennett, wrote of poor blacks. (Bennett was intrigued by her and noted her mastery.) Jim Hutchisson has given Bennett's protégé, DuBose Heyward, critical scrutiny, and Ralph Melnick has produced a massive two-volume biography of Ludwig Lewisohn, who arrived in South Carolina from Berlin as a child, tried at first to assimilate in Charleston society, and eventually became a novelist (praised by Freud), a Zionist, and a faculty member at Brandeis University. (Bennett, though chastising him for his behavior, always acknowledged his genius, and Lewisohn admired him.) Louise Allen has written a biography of Laura Bragg, the first woman director of a science museum in this country, who came to rely on Bennett for his expertise; Bennett, however, had trouble with her as a "modern woman," something that troubled his relationship with writer Josephine Pinckney, whom the fine scholar Barbara Bellows is now documenting. (Despite his personal conflict with Pinckney, Bennett eventually acknowledged her artistry.) The pendulum has swung back; the "Charleston school," once dismissed in favor of the Fugitives and Agrarians, is once again sparking critical interest, and many of their works are being republished.

All this makes the moment auspicious for a study of John Bennett. His writings and his achievements are worthy of discussion—yet he did more than achieve certain remarkable things. For with a flair for language, a passion for justice, and a keen eye, he wrote down what he saw and felt; he was an eyewitness to much of what occurred in Charleston in the first four decades of the twentieth century. "It's odd that a city so proud of its history should know so little of it," he once wrote in a newspaper piece on the church bells of Charleston.[4] There were so many half-truths, misconceptions, clichés, and outright errors on the subject (as there are these days about the Charleston literary renaissance itself) that he felt obliged to set the record straight. So as an old man already in his seventies, he climbed steeples, went through recently discovered manuscripts in the courthouse, researched contemporary records, and entered into correspondence with people around the county to find out the fate of the church bells taken from Charleston during the Civil War. Like a lot of his research, it was left mostly unpublished at the time of his death in 1956.

When Bennett did his research, many spires were still empty. But in the last few decades congregations have repurchased and rehung bells in their buildings. No longer silent, they ring out a new song of time and history. Similarly, with decades of silence on him behind us, now it's time to hear from John Bennett again.

As mentioned previously, John Bennett's papers are so voluminous that, if desired, one could "write" an autobiography about him in the first person. I have chosen to use his words (when I could be sure they seemed to reflect the true version of things, which was nearly most of the time) for a number of reasons. First, he wrote so well and distinctively that I thought there would be no better way to get him before the public and, since many of his works were never collected or are out of print, this would offer readers access to materials otherwise beyond reach. Besides, the truth as one perceives it has a life of its own. Much of his writing was formal and meant to be read by an audience, while other comments and asides expressed on bits of paper and backs of envelopes were stream-of-consciousness. In nearly all of his personal writing, he employed dot ellipses, using . . . between thoughts and sentences; in most cases the ellipses employed here, however, are editorial. I have periodically corrected some of his obvious typing mistakes. The choice of words are his, the errors mine entirely.

Many people helped me in writing this work. I'm happy to acknowledge the assistance of the past and present staffs of the South Carolina Historical Society and the financial assistance of the Charleston Scientific and Cultural Educational Fund, which allowed me to travel to Chillicothe, Ohio, and to acquire photocopies of correspondence and papers in other research libraries. My friends have been very helpful and encouraging, and my colleagues, many of whom I now count as friends, were very generous with their comments and thoughts on Charleston and Charleston personalities. Many thanks are due to Susan Williams, Steve Hoffius, James Hutchisson, Barbara Bellows, Anne Blythe Meriwether, James B. Meriwether, Louise Allen, Jennet Robinson Alterman, and Robert Cuthbert. Jonathan Ray, my beloved, merits special attention. John Bennett, the grandson of the subject of this biography, has been unfailingly gracious in working with me and allowing me access to his grandfather's published and unpublished writings. His death at an early age removes a gracious presence from the city.

# Prologue

AUGUST 1941 was hot in Charleston.

The three-story wooden house at 37 Legare Street stood silently in the glare and heat. The few tourists out fanning themselves, mopping their glowing foreheads, turned from it to admire the famous Sword Gates across the way. After they left, a shimmering mirage of heat rose in the street. As the day progressed, the sun rose higher; the temperature and brightness increased. People stayed in or headed for the beach. "Oleander Time" in Charleston meant fewer visitors; those who came usually had business at the bustling Navy base beyond the city limits.

That was the case with a young man named Millard Brand, who had come to visit an ailing family member there. Brand had recently published a novel and wanted to visit other writers in the city. Mrs. Tillinghast at The Book Shelf on King Street suggested he see John Bennett; and that was also the name given him by Tom Lesesne, editor at the local paper.[1]

So the young man went unannounced to the tall, thin house on Legare Street. He rang and was let in. Mr. Bennett would be down in a minute, the maid told him. Above his head, in the upper reaches of the silent, dark, hot house, Brand could hear someone stirring. Then silence; someone coming down steps. The door opened, and in came a smiling, evenly featured, white-haired man in a light-blue shirt. Magnified by the lenses in his gold glasses, his bright blue eyes glimmered overlarge but friendly. He extended his hand, and Brand told him why he had come.

The old man was kind, offered him a seat. He asked about Brand's work and answered his queries about other writers in the city. No, he said, in answer to the young writer's question; he had been born not in Charleston but in a town far away, Chillicothe, Ohio.

Brand thought that puzzling; he could name many other famous writers he knew were from Charleston—there was DuBose Heyward of *Porgy* fame;

Hervey Allen of the bestseller *Anthony Adverse* had lived here, too, hadn't he? And there were others, a couple named Ripley, a poet and novelist named Pinckney. And didn't Dorothy Heyward just have a play on Broadway?

This old man had not published a book since the 1920s; still, everyone had named John Bennett as the writer to meet. He had wanted to be artist, the old man said, but became a writer accidentally.

The young man listened and, after some refreshments and a glass of tea, took his leave. Bennett thanked him for coming and vowed to look up his book; the visit had tired him.

Later, in his third-floor study, Bennett looked at the mess, the piles of papers, prints and clippings, and the old-fashioned typewriter on his desk. He picked up the typescript and tried to get back into the scenes he had been working on when the buzzer had sounded. He closed his eyes and tried to see the scene he was working on, and it rose before him, again, shimmering in his memory.

He had begun *Buckhorn Johnny* decades before, even before he had come to Charleston. In it he was telling the story of the "chain of seemingly broken . . . but always connected links" that had brought his father to Ohio nearly one hundred years before.[2]

PART ONE

# Spring

## CHAPTER I

# Buckhorn Johnny

THE STORY BEGINS with the birth of John Bennett's father, John Briscoe Bennett, in Shephardstown, Virginia (later West Virginia), on October 10, 1821, to Margaret Lorena Beale Evans of Harper's Ferry and Thomas Swearingen Bennett, a descendant of the Bennetts in Jamestown in 1607 and of the Swearingens, among the original Dutch settlers of New Amsterdam.[1]

John Briscoe Bennett never met his own father, however, for Thomas Swearingen Bennett died on September 17, 1821, three weeks before his son's birth. The grieving family gathered around the squalling infant included a sister, Elizabeth, a brother, Thomas, and his mother, who had had a difficult delivery. "But for [her cousin and physician] John Briscoe's unmeasured devotion and skill, she undoubtedly [would] have died, and the boy with her. Therefore she named him John and he was so baptized John Briscoe."[2] His sister, Elizabeth, died soon after this, and there was even more grief in the family.

Despite the sorrows, John Briscoe and his older brother seemed destined to grow up Virginia planter gentry. But on October 23, 1826, just after his fifth birthday, their mother remarried; the groom was the handsome, dashing, slightly disreputable Hilary Talbot. Talbot did not like his stepsons, and they, especially the elder Thomas, did not love him; they felt Talbot took their idolized mother away too often. Indeed, for several years after their mother's remarriage, the boys were farmed out to various relatives as the young couple passed their time in Baltimore, Washington, and Richmond.[3]

In the first years of her second marriage, Margaret Talbot gave birth to two daughters, Rebecca Smith in 1827 and Laura Cornelia in 1829. As Hilary Talbot gambled and lost more of his wife's money, they traveled less and returned more often to Shephardstown. Her sons were happy to have her back but unhappy to be around the cold, condemning Talbot. Their half sister Rebecca died in 1830. The following year their mother delivered a son, but Lyttleton Savage died almost immediately. Talbot was crushed, but the Evans and Bennett families did not feel much sympathy for him. It was not just that he was chilly toward the Bennett sons, but through his drinking, high-life, and squandering habits he had seriously reduced his wife's fortune. Addicted to gambling, he once bet the family's store of firewood, and when he lost it, the whole family spent a miserably dark and cold Christmas.

The word that had come down to John Bennett of this grandmother of his (often called "Pretty Peggy") was that she was proud and beautiful. To believe that her handsome husband had ruined her and the future of her children was too much; she could not tolerate the family's tacit understanding of that, or their pity. To save herself and her pride, she sold much of what was left of her belongings, cut family portraits from their frames, rolled them up, and took her two sons, daughter, and ne'er-do-well husband west in a covered wagon. They left quickly to avoid the Asiatic cholera that had broken out in Harper's Ferry.

Moving west, they traveled the Cumberland Road through a variety of small towns, including Chillicothe, then a bustling gateway to the west. In Chillicothe, the family met up with some distant cousins, the Jameses, and rested for a few weeks. Before Hilary Talbot could borrow money and cause further embarrassment, Margaret moved them on.

The family dropped south through Louisville, then west to St. Louis. Reaching St. Charles, Missouri, they sold their wagon and everything else, keeping one horse. (Or so John Bennett wrote in his manuscript. In real life it appears the family was actually not so poor: Talbot drove a barouche; one slave, Aleck, followed in a jersey wagon with his wife; and another slave and his wife brought a freight wagon.)[4]

No matter their economic status, life on the frontier was rough for these pampered and unprepared Virginians who saw themselves as aristocrats. With the last of the cash, Hilary Talbot purchased a tavern. The structure had a large raftered room with a huge fireplace for the public and a "private parlor," above which was the family's dormer quarters. In the public and private rooms, Talbot consorted "with the scum of westward drift [including] blighted gentry, discredited politicians, evasive cashiers . . . horse-traders, and . . . petty criminals looking for lands where laws were lax. . . . With these disreputable acquaintances he gambled and drank. . . . Their quarrels were loud . . . vulgar, bawdy and blasphemous."[5]

Disgusted with one particular outburst, Margaret stalked out one day but Talbot ran after her; "when tipsy he was irritable, when drunk, he verged on brutality." With face flushed, eyes watery, clothes in disarray, and "his cravat ends . . . loosely thrown over his shoulders," he shouted, "You're coming down again to entertain my friends!"[6]

The frequency of such behavior and the meanness of her life made their mark on her, while the continued slide into poverty upset the sullen Talbot and triggered angry, self-pitying bouts of drunkenness. He blamed everyone for his downfall and focused mostly on the oldest male in the house, Thomas. In Virginia he had "paid little attention to his step-sons, whom he strangely miscredited with mediocre intelligence."[7] But now he turned on them with a vengeance. And Thomas, in his mid-teens, was not above talking back. After one particularly violent confrontation, Thomas quickly ran off; he never came back. (This was the version Bennett wrote in his novel; it seems likely, however, that Thomas left the family earlier.)

This act of flagrant disobedience and defiance made Talbot angrier; his drinking increased and his behavior became wilder and more erratic. He lunged at the demons he imagined, screaming obscenities at his wife and children. Shaken by so many tragedies and changes in so few years, Margaret fell prey to the cholera that had been shadowing the westward-bound emigrants. (In some versions of the tale, it is tuberculosis, too long untreated.) Her death in 1834 at the age of thirty-eight left the children at the hands of an abusive, violent drunk; they clung to each other, wide eyed, as Talbot drank himself into a coma, racked by fevers. He died a few weeks later, leaving John Briscoe and Laura orphans, bereft.

The boy managed to get his stepfather buried and then assumed care of his half sister, getting her meals and keeping her washed and dressed. But eventually neighbors caught on to their orphan status. The result was an early lesson for John Briscoe in the ineffectual efforts and casual betrayal of adults (something which would later haunt the writings of his son). Years later, John Briscoe Bennett would tell his children what happened next, and they'd listen round-eyed and horror-struck, picturing Roman Catholic nuns coming for Laura and carrying her off but leaving the boy to fend for himself.[8] Distraught, the young boy hired himself out for odd jobs, stole food, and begged; in St. Charles he visited his mother's grave daily. As he sat there, his conviction grew that everything would be lost if he stayed in the Missouri Territory.

The Mississippi River was frozen when he crossed it. In Louisville, he traded his horse for a ride on a river steamer that took him up the Ohio River to a frontier trading post. At Hanging Rock, the skinny boy, begging for food, was directed to the nearby Buckhorn Furnace ironworks, where he found a job. For two years he worked as the assistant to the cranky store-keeper who ran the general store; the man was both a bully to and somewhat in awe of this planter's son, whom he suspected of putting on airs. As sort of a pet to the men who labored in the iron works, he earned the nickname "Buckhorn Johnny."

Life in the iron works was coarse; there were no schools, women, or any other children. One day after work, John Briscoe stole into the attic above the shop and came upon an abandoned trunk containing the first books he had seen in years. There had been books in Virginia, and even some back in St. Charles; the boy was intelligent and "avid for learning." [9] Every day after that, he sneaked upstairs to read. He was so carried away one day that he failed to latch the door, and the suspicious shopkeeper caught him. He hurled John Briscoe downstairs, saying he paid him not to read but to work; he forbade the boy to ever read again and nailed the copy of Don Quixote to the wall.

The nail stayed in place for months; but one day, hearing terrible shouts, John Briscoe ran into the office. There, in a scene Bennett perfected in his manuscript, the boy found his boss frantically trying to get rid of a rodent that had run up his pants. The man pled for help and the boy jumped to the task, cannily extracting a promise first. After he got the mouse out of his employer's pants, his boss begrudgingly kept his word; sullenly, he took the nail out of the wall, giving John Briscoe the chance to finish Don Quixote.

Such reading had its effects. Bennett's son acknowledged later, "I have never known a man who had and consistently used a finer vocabulary of clean, concise, explicit English or could write it more simply or charmingly in personal correspondence. Yet he had small education . . . practically none but the use and constant reading of good and standard books. Such gifts of language, as I have . . . I believe I get from him." [10]

By the time John Briscoe had exhausted all the books in the gentleman's trunk, he approached his boss's supervisor; he was transferred to a store owned by the same firm in Chillicothe. Arriving at the bustling town about 1836, a sense of déjà vu must have overcome him. He stopped in front of a familiar-looking building and realized he had been in Chillicothe before—

with his mother, Thomas, and Laura years before on the trek west. He found the cousins with whom he had stayed, and they told him of his brother Thomas's whereabouts; he had made it back to Chillicothe, too, and his mother's cousin had taken the boy to Rapid Forge "to be reared as an iron man, under the tutelage of the forge-master, Gus Marshal, an able and educated man." [11] In Chillicothe, then, these orphan sons of Virginia gentry found home and family at last.

In 1838, the family put John Briscoe to work in the store of James P. Campbell; he stayed until 1841, when at the age of twenty he went down the Mississippi to make his fortune in New Orleans as a commissions merchant. His fabulous visions of wealth and advancement failed, however; he returned to Ohio and embarked on a new business venture in nearby Circleville.

But he failed in that, too, and returned to Chillicothe, where he tried his best to leave behind his history of lost wealth, false starts, and missteps. He put on a jovial face and seemed to all "a handsome, dashing, popular young man." [12] Cocky and confident, John Briscoe Bennett formed a partnership in a dry goods business with his brother Thomas and a financial backer, Judge Owen T. Reeves. At the relatively late age of twenty-seven, Bennett proposed to and married the nineteen-year-old Eliza Jane McClintick, daughter of James and Charity Trimble McClintick.

The bride's father (who spelled his named differently than other family), was a merchant and farmer who served as an associate judge of the Ross County Court. (His warrant for his judgeship had misspelled his name and so he kept it.) His wife, Charity, was the daughter of John Trimble, fuller, of nearby Kinnikinnick. [13]

Eliza Jane Trimble, their daughter, born November 26, 1829, was a shy young girl, unassuming and meek, almost too meek to say what she wanted in life. "There was a strain of Quaker blood got into her veins some way," her son said later of her, "and the *quiet* of it all came to her, as well as the [qualities of the] . . . old-fashioned Quaker names, Patience, Mercy, Faith, Charity and Truth." [14] Elsewhere he said Eliza Jane was "gentle, patient, unassuming, simple of heart, tender, tolerant and wise," [15] "the salt of the earth," [16] obviously the prototype for the "gentle woman with a sweet, kind face, and a little air of quiet dignity" he was to describe in his novel *Master Skylark*. [17]

After their marriage on March 2, 1848, the young couple moved into a gray, two-story brick house with wide windows and doors at 76 West Second Street, built for them by Eliza Jane's parents. To get ahead, John Briscoe borrowed money and in 1850 bought out a rival dry goods establishment. He was reaching his stride when a fire broke out in downtown Chillicothe on April 1, 1852. It burned most of the business district to the ground and reduced all of his uninsured stock to ashes.[18]

Having watched his store burn, John Briscoe, like his mother before him, tried to salvage what he could of the financial wreck. Like her, too, he was proud and independent, too proud apparently, to ask for help. Family lore had it that being honest to a fault (a trait that would also bedevil his son), John Briscoe vowed to pay back all his suppliers and lenders no matter the cost. So in his pride he came to handicap his children the same way he had been: all were affected and shadowed by grave events before their births.

In the 1850s and early 1860s, John Briscoe and Eliza Jane Bennett experienced "poverty, but not [the] ugliness nor the hopelessness that breaks the spirit of the poor. Hopelessness," their son claimed, "came later. And dumb endurance."[19]

Nine babies were born to Eliza Jane in these years, but the first three died of diphtheria and scarlet fever, none reaching their fourth year.[20] Alice, the first to survive, was born in 1855 and was almost immediately followed by a boy and another girl, who also died young. (Alice herself would become a hypochondriac, perhaps encouraged unwittingly by parents who feared for her life.) The next child after Alice to survive was Henry Holcomb, born December 5, 1863, the shining star, the eldest son and favored in the family. On May 17, 1865, just barely a month after the end of the Civil War, John Bennett was born. A second girl, Martha Trimble, born September 26, 1867, rounded out the quartet.

Looking over his sons and daughters, John Briscoe vowed that they would not be robbed of their early childhood years as he had been. He and Eliza Jane would do their utmost to keep their children from cruelty, unhappiness, and want. And in this they succeeded. They gave their children safe and secure, even idyllic, childhoods. All, especially John, would look back on these times, like exiles from Eden, with fondness, regret, and astonishment.

CHAPTER 2

# *Yore*

AS AN OLD MAN, John Bennett would take Charlestonians to task for casting an unnatural, haloed glow over their city's antebellum past. All such romanticizing was foolish and sentimental, he laughed. But it was not a rule he applied to himself. He once asked himself, "The Valley of my Youth: Was it really so beautiful or was it only a dream?"[1]

He answered that it *was* that beautiful. The idea of an idyllic childhood was something he'd allow no one, not even himself, to doubt. In minute detail, he could render and remember all of it. The names and faces of his childhood friends and their families; Chillicothe's houses, stores, and dusty streets; and the shining, bending Scioto River under the sycamore trees all rose up in his mind as utter and clear as photographs.

This ability he attributed to the fact that he had been visually oriented from birth. "I drew in with my first breath that deep delight in the shape of things which becomes the love of drawing," he wrote. "When I was a very little boy, sick or well, summer or winter, I would rather draw than . . . play. . . . I would rather draw than eat, and was late to many a meal in consequence."[2]

One of the memories he lingered over centered on

the sweet and gentle face of Gottlieb Wiedler, a German book-keeper, drawing swans and grenadiers on ribbon paper behind the counter of my father's store.

That wonderful swan was beyond me; the grenadier I mastered with a thrill of honest pride.

When stringency caused our removal from the private dame-school to . . . public school, there, almost at once, I won unexpected distinction.

One boy could draw a bird. Another had a trotting horse deeply scratched into his slate which became white and clear on running one's slate pencil around it.

I could draw neither horses nor birds, but I could draw a soldier, and, seeing nothing to equal that occupation, I drew a slateful. . . .

The boy behind me was observed by the teacher staring . . . over my shoulder. . . . "He's drawing a picture," said he.

"Are you drawing a picture in school time?" she asked.

"Yes, ma'am," I answered proudly.

"Bring your slate here," she said.

I arose from my seat in triumphant pleasure . . . proudly I exhibited my . . . row
of pie-faced grenadiers, each precisely like all the others, acquired by sedulous effort
from the old book-keeper, Gottlieb Wiedler.

"You have done those during school-time?"

"Yes, ma'am." [ . . . ]

"You may remain in at recess," she said, "and draw another slateful!" [ . . . ]

With a happy smile I resumed my seat. . . .

I was so happy at being permitted to draw . . . I believed it to be the actual
reward of an uncommon excellence that I was not compelled to go out into
the . . . rough horse-play and petty bullying of small new boys then customary in
the schools.

The principal of the school [Mr. Dowd] came in. "What has this little
boy done?"

"He draws pictures on his slate in school hours."

"Indeed?"

"I have a slateful of soldiers, Prussian soldiers; would you like to see them?" I
asked eagerly.

Mr. Dowd was human. [He perceived] my total unconsciousness of offense, my
serenely innocent content.

Next morning I was heavily pumped on by two big boys, for being immaculately
clean, and sent to Mr. Dowd's room, drowned and sobbing, where for some interior
reason impossible for me to define, I won new distinction by refusing to name my
oppressors.

I cannot recall the look on his face, nor the looks of those culprit lads; my row
of soldiers I can still see; and Gottlieb Wiedler's sweet and gentle face (sweeter than
all the votive paintings in the cathedrals of Europe) drawing swans and Prussian
grenadiers on ribbon paper for two enchanted small boys, my brother and me.[3]

Like a musical prodigy hearing music in his head, this pudgy little boy
called "Dumpling" beheld visions that were fantastic and grotesque—like
those on a paper fan kept in the family pew in Chillicothe's Walnut Street

Methodist Church.[4] It had dragons and tiny Chinese men on it, and on Sundays he sat so silently entranced by it that his family first thought him devout, a religious mystic.[5]

During the week it was quite a usual thing to see the stocky, stodgy blond-haired boy with plump, pale cheeks standing on a chair as he leaned over the table. "Jack," as he was called to distinguish him from his father (his Sunday-school teacher Diantha Cooke started it), "Jack," his family would ask, "what are you doing?"[6] He'd smile and hold up the pages from journals he was copying—pages with the illustrated initial letters of Thackeray, the drawings of John Tenniell, and the satirical cartoons of Thomas Nast. (Nast's 1870 drawing of "Death on a Skeleton horse with a torn dark banner in his hand" in *Harper's Weekly* burned itself so vividly into his consciousness that he was able to recall it vividly seventy years later.)[7]

Asking for paper and ink, he'd copy them out and ask to see the line drawings in his father's copy of William Rowlandson's *Dr. Syntax in Search of the Picturesque* and John Leech's drawings in *Punch*. Then he discovered silhouettes. The black designs on startling white pages offered a way of drawing and not drawing, of delineating and suggesting, and set his imagination free (and his fingers twitching, so much so that he later said he itched "like scabies" to get to work.)[8]

He got scissors and black paper immediately; but his hands were fleshy, his fingers plump, and he had a hard time cutting; but he kept at it, finally, with happiness, compelling his heavy hands to "delicacy . . . and [succeeding in] the cutting and mounting of almost lace-like and intricate paper silhouettes."[9] His penchant became so well known in Chillicothe that family friend Hedwig Krause traveling abroad sent him back a set of silhouettes from Germany.[10] The silhouettes of Paul Konewka were so thrilling that right then and there he vowed to try to match or better this artist he felt to be the "Prince of Silhouettists."[11]

The boy's knack of seeing shapes and visualizing was further enhanced by John Briscoe Bennett's vivid storytelling. As the boy listened, there came in his mind a fusion, a melding of image and telling which came to characterize his writing; he'd have to see scenery and people first in his own mind's eye before he could render them. (And this in turn later gave his fiction a very visual quality.)

Delighting in the books once denied him, the elder Bennett read to his children; he favored standards like Ingoldsby's *Legends* and Chaucer's *Canterbury Tales* and read them to his children at night as they gathered at his feet on cushions and hassocks. The tales were bulwarks against the darkness, faintly punctured by flickering coal-oil wicks, dimmer (but far cheaper) than kerosene or gas. Eliza Jane allowed no "more than a taper" in the house's long hallway.[12]

He preferred his mother's reading voice in the darkness but liked his father's comfortably Victorian choice of stories. He wanted more in the morning, pestering his parents for stories as insistently as an insect buzzing around them; and they, just as similarly, waved him away. Adults had things to do other than read stories.

He found a solution in Peter Dunn, the stable boy who worked for the neighboring, better-off Poland family. Full of the tales he had heard as a child in Ireland, Dunn promised to share them with the children when his chores were finished. So John and Henry Bennett and all the Poland boys (Will, John, Walter, Nick, and Charlie) eagerly helped him carry wood and water, pull down hay for horses, and carry corn to the bin. Then Peter would sit, and the children would ring themselves in a circle around him and listen to the folktales he told, many touched with that sense of homesickness and longing that later would tinge most of Bennett's own writing. When he ran out of those, he began in on a series of new ones, tales of "Ala-bama" and the forty thieves and the marvelous but mangled words "Open See-Same!" which is how Dunn pronounced it. The children of the "West End" of Chillicothe sat "suspended between wonder and delight" at the fireside in winter and on the horse block in front of the Polands' house in the summer twilight.[13]

As he sat listening to stories with his friends, the two became intricately and inevitably linked; he'd never outgrow his love of stories or friends and would show, in the coming years, an equal genius for each.

Once they learned how to read, the boys he befriended began ransacking their parents' libraries for books like Charles Dickens's *Oliver Twist* and *David Copperfield* or Bulwer Lytton's *Last Days of Pompeii*, which they read aloud to each other, one reading, the others listening.

In this way, they went through the complete Sea Tales of Marryat found in George Tyler's father's library, which they read in the back yard. As the trees heaved in the breezes like the sea on which they imagined themselves,

Bennett, reading fastest and with the most feeling "became official reader to the . . . club." One day, "some perverse or mischievous inspiration put it suddenly in to my mind to replace the dull spot by improvising an exciting incident . . . casting it into language . . . as closely like that of the story as possible." Peeping over the edge of the book, he saw boys in rapt attention around him. This secret power was thrilling and, he confessed, was later "one of the potent things which turned me to the writing of fiction."

Undetected for weeks, he kept on improvising, until he was undone by "one of the Poland boys surreptitiously reading the . . . story before we assembled, . . . which was forbidden by the bylaws of the club. In the midst of one of my most successful flights of improving fancy he called out, 'That's not so; that's not what the story says! I read it yesterday.'"[14]

He had to cease; and the Poland boy was punished, too, for all took the club, the FBS, whose full name they promised never to reveal, and its bylaws seriously. In fact, Bennett was so intensely loyal that as late as 1921, at the age of fifty-six, in naming for *Who's Who* the "exclusive clubs" to which he belonged, he listed straightfaced, with no other explanation, "The F.B.S."[15]

It might have been the swearing-in ceremony to the FBS that had prompted them to go to a photographer with the remains of local murderer Percy Bowsher, whom doctors in town had exhumed to study; the boys posed, grim and serious, waiting for the flash to fix their image for posterity before taking the bones back before they were reported missing.[16] The members of the FBS then ran to the banks of the Scioto River, which ran through Ross County:

There at the logs [Will Poland] and I went swimming one year until after Thanksgiving; and there on the west bank, from drift wood, we built ourselves a shelter, a roofless log cabin, which other . . . boys burned down. But they did not discover our hiding place in the big hollow sycamore, in which we . . . could crawl, where we kept minor canned goods, and crackers and salt and pepper. . . . We dubbed that tree "The Castle" and carved a label on it, a cryptogram [something he would use years later in his novel *The Treasure of Peyre Gaillard*].[17]

Determined to convince others that no one could have ever been happier than he, Bennett wrote a description of that era for the Chillicothe paper in the 1920s, creating a world as impossibly happy as the one he imagined in his fable *Madame Margot:*

The sun didn't burn in the afternoons beneath the shade of those great green trees; the ancient scum of Dog Days didn't faze us; and two of [us] . . . regarded it as a sacred duty to climb to the top of every large tree between the Snag and the foot of the High Bank. . . . Our vests were white with the dust of the sycamores.

Spring came earlier there; and autumn lingered longer; and sycamore leaves were a little more golden-brown there, too; the cottonwoods came like moveable scenery between the big trees and beaches.

Many's the day I have been caught there with all the . . . West End gang, and soaked by a sudden thunderstorm. . . . And many's the windy afternoon, when the west-wind whistled shrill, we emerged from the water into the wind, to find our shirt [sleeves and] tails tied in knots [by other boys] . . . for us to chew out while . . . "goose-flesh" made every small hair stand like quills upon the fretful porcupine.[18]

Cold, chilled to the bone, Bennett ran back to the square gray house on West Second Street where his family waited and everything seemed wonderful, safe and secure, and impossibly happy. But, of course, it was not. The family was poor and emotional stresses were already appearing, but John Briscoe and Eliza Jane worked to keep it from the children. And Bennett himself later conspired to keep up the pretence. Although he confessed some of his childhood agonies to himself, he never shared them with others. It was only to stray sheets of paper that he admitted that his childhood had not been perfect.

It had begun to fragment as early as 1870 when his elder brother, Henry, went off to the "dame school" down the street from the Bennetts, befitting their genteel, if poor, family. John could not stand being left behind by "Harry," as he was called, so he followed his brother to Miss Anna Welsh's; she kept a school for children just down the street.[19] The next day, and the next, he went back.

Perhaps his parents thought it harmless, or maybe even helpful, giving Eliza Jane more time with the baby, Martha, and the eldest, Alice, who was exhibiting some emotional problems. The result was that since the boy was there, he was allowed to stay. He was big for his age, and looked so much like his brother that "most people took my brother and me for twins, and reckoned our development and ability accordingly." Two years ahead of him in maturity, dexterity, and mental development, Harry thus outshone his younger brother. Bennett felt inferior "and toiled terribly to equal the accomplishments of my older class mates. . . . My brother danced through the printed page and had the text at his finger-ends, while I still could not say the multiplication table of seven-times-seven." [20]

If his parents had realized this and tried to prevent it, they would have encountered Bennett's own refusal to stop. He was "stubbornly determined and persistent"; strong-willed, articulate, and unswayed by argument, he followed Henry every day, despite the fact that he was behind, or maybe even because of it. He would not give up, even though he was considered "dull" and "mastered school work with great difficulty." "I was constantly laughed at and discouraged . . . any unusually dexterous feat I undertook with the deep-rooted sense that I should fumble it somewhere." [21]

But he kept going back to disprove this opinion of himself. Making failure worse was the heavy expectations John Briscoe Bennett placed on his children; they had to go to school and do well—not just for themselves, but also for him. His children understood instinctively that they were to vicariously make up for all John Briscoe's early privations. So it could have been for such reasons that, as an older man, Bennett once acknowledged the thread of sadness running through his youth. "Even in my boyhood, which, estimated by usual standards, was idyllic, my happiest summers were tinged . . . by [an] unsatisfied longing for something unknown and never found, nor ever since," he confessed, acknowledging "a vague unsatisfied yearning for something out of reach." [22]

He hated admitting that he had a terrible jealousy of Henry, who "could outrun, and outjump, out wrestle and out throw me two times out of three, and never failed, boy-fashion, to tell me so . . . with such ready speech that I was no match at all for." These feelings "embittered . . . [his] earlier childhood and drove him to success. Compelled by "an eradicable streak of the most damnable tenacity," he worked long and hard to get better. [23] Beginning innocently enough, this trait ossified into a lifelong pattern: like his father before him, working against his own comfort to pay off a debt and erase the supposed blot on his honesty and integrity, so the boy, beginning a project, would refuse to give up, often passing into an exhausting, obsessive frenzy until he finished. If to no one else, he had to prove his worthiness, his superiority over Henry, to himself.

"Henry could out-run me," he saw, "but I could make a better wooden gun." And: "Henry filled the woodbox more quickly and with a dexterous celerity I could not match; but I piled it higher and filled the box more deeply than he ever did." This stubborn persistence and willingness to work without flagging (as well as his plump, phlegmatic look, perhaps) earned him the nickname "The Dutchman," a tribute not just to his obstinacy but also his descent from Gerrit van Sweringen, his ancestor of New Amsterdam.[24]

His father saw himself in his son and encouraged him. "Brag was a good dog," John Briscoe would tell him, as they sat on the porch in the afternoon sunlight. "But Hold-Fast was better." "Slow and sure and thorough." The boy was so moved that he always kept a stuffed dog by his desk; it was still by his side in Charleston when the pinned maxim, "Every dog shall have its day," finally fell apart.[25] Even more importantly, he put his father's words into the mouth of Queen Elizabeth in a pivotal scene in *Master Skylark*, a book that can be read as a key to his childhood.

To surpass Henry, the boy began to concentrate less on school work, focusing instead on what he could do best. Just as he had willed himself to learn to cut silhouettes, so he taught himself taxidermy with books in the town library; to win popularity, he mounted "the deceased pets of disconsolate friends, rare ornithological specimens and a galaxy of owls for the libraries of gentlemen of literary tastes."[26]

And once, on a lark, he carved an Indian's pipe in the shape of a bear's head from sandstone and secretly deposited it by the Scioto River for other boys to discover. He watched with amusement as it was found; adults displayed it in a shop window on Paint Street on a piece of velvet. His bemusement turned to fright, however, when townsmen proposed to take plaster casts of it to send to the Smithsonian Institute, and sell it for a large sum of money. Before anything serious developed, he confessed his trick; "the pipe instantly disappeared from exhibit," but "the claim that I had made that 'curious relic' was denied with some heat until . . . from another chunk of sandstone from the Main Street Ravine I cut a[n] exact duplicate."[27]

The merchant boosters and historians, feeling foolish for being duped, were angry at him, assuming it deliberate. His reputation as a "smart aleck" and troublemaker was growing; and one winter day, running from school, he proved it when he jumped on an ice floe on the frozen Chillicothe canal. "The cake gave one quick flop and I was in the canal, head and ears. I went under . . . my head and hands came up through the broken ice."

Henry threw out his long bookstrap. "I caught it . . . and held on . . . while he pulled me though the water to the bank. . . . I scrambled out, soaked to the skin." [28] It was so cold that his clothes froze to him. His teeth were chattering by the time he got home; his mother panicked when he caught pneumonia, something frightening in a household that had known numerous infant deaths.

For weeks his life hung in the balance, thanks to his silliness. "I was in bed ten months, part of that time so weak and sick that I could not so much as turn my head from side to side on my pillow." [29] (This was to be the cause, he felt, of his later sufferings from hay fever, sinuses, and even weak eyesight. But it is clear that it was only through such symptoms, whether psychosomatic or not, that he got pampering and sympathy.) Alice had already found this out and was well on her way to becoming the self-declared, long-suffering invalid of the household. As they had to Alice, so his parents gave into their sick boy, too, pampering him. If it was stories he wanted, they all took turns reading to him. Listening, he lay looking up at the ceiling, and the cracks in the plaster began to assume the look of rivers and boundaries on a map; he spoke of the creatures and ceilinged nations of his imaginings, and, like the Brontë children with their imagined world of Glass Town, he made up stories about them to his parents and siblings. John Briscoe then brought a real map in. As the boy grew better and read the books brought him, he began to put pins on the map to show all the far-off places the stories he read "took" him.

After a year of bed rest, he was allowed to move about, but still his parents feared for his health; his mother would not let him overtire himself, so he was pampered and kept out of school, making an excuse for his continued academic failing once schooling was continued. He languished for a long while in this self-fulfilling state of lassitude and idleness; "it was two or three years before I was really well again." [30] In and out of school he continued to play with the Polands; their father, the major, owned a building occupied by a trade school; once it failed, owing him money, he seized upon its contents, taking home a small printing press and installing it in his carriage house loft for his sons. So the Polands and the Bennetts and the other children in the neighborhood soon taught themselves the "Black Arts."

"No better opportunity was ever afforded boys," Bennett felt. [31] So impressive was the newspaper they printed (*The Little Messenger*, they called it) that the real newspaper in town commented favorably on it. To entertain everyone, Bennett volunteered to take over *The Little Messenger* once school began again and he rejoined his friends, now in high school. This version, in manuscript, was called *The High School Detective;* from its masthead, an all-seeing eye looked out.

"More and more ideas, amusing and ridiculous, came [to me] with the dull idling months in which my class-work fell away to lowest levels," he later confessed. In fact, "So many fancies crowded into my head, that although I had always hesitated to write because my brother wrote with such facility . . . I was driven to [do so] for the entertainment and amusement of my friends." He contributed "sketches in prose, short stories and verses, illustrated with drawings in pen and ink"; included, of course, were puerile stories, often at a disliked teacher's expense.[32] It was consolation; but it was simultaneously a disguised cry for help.

But the boys loved it; passing it from hand to hand, they broke out laughing. The teachers and principal, however, declared it mischief and were quite upset when they discovered it. It showed disrespect, and they believed it proved the boy smart after all, underscoring his bad grades and making his failure seem pointed, almost deliberate.

That was the final straw. "My idleness, my poor standing in my classes, my constantly being accused and suspected of being engaged as a principal offender in every form of mischief and annoyance cropping out . . . led to my leaving the High School, where, as the phrase had it, 'I was doing no good.'"[33] And so at the age of seventeen, he was punished for not fitting into the pattern adults expected of him, a predicament that would eventually bedevil his fictional children.

It was a terrible embarrassment for him and his family. (He'd long feel its sting, finally admitting, "I have all my life as deftly as possible concealed my lack of education by continuous and persistent accumulation of oddly-assorted knowledge . . . gained by association with men, literate and illiterate, by constant wide-ranged reading, and by working hard.")[34]

As a teenager, the failure was impossible to hide. John Briscoe and Eliza Jane were already worried over Alice. She seemed strangely unsuited to the world, and could not make her own way, or even help bring in money by doing tasks suitable for ladies of her day. She volunteered for church work, did sewing around the house, but would not separate from the family.

And now Jack was being difficult, too, and a disappointment.

He even let his father down one day in his own "dogged thoroughness." John Briscoe had asked him to help out at the hardware store; though he went in willingly enough, he soon tired of the task, finding work in the counting room "drab and tedious." He left the task "to go swimming with the gang." When he came back, his father stood sadly in the store's doorway.

"I had thought if I gave the job to you, that it would be done," John Briscoe said, shaking his head. "That was all," but that apparently was enough. "That mild rebuke burns [and] stings in recollection still more than half a century later," [35] he recorded sadly.

At the time, it stung worse; he realized that he had not only failed to make up for his father's earlier sorrows but had actually added to them. It pained him to the core and made him feel worthless, especially when compared to successful Henry. Childhood, so unusually idyllic as it was for Jack Bennett, was typical enough in the swiftness with which it passed.

CHAPTER 3

# The Black Arts

THE FAMILY now faced a dilemma. What to do with Jack to punish him but also further his education? They put the boy to work in the family store but also sent him to a private academy in Chillicothe where Mr. Poe, the proprietor, promised to teach him accounting. To atone for his past behavior and to prove his worth, Bennett acquiesced and did well at both school and work. All went well until Poe caught pneumonia and died, closing the academy.

A sort of paralysis then beset the dazed family. John Briscoe seemed to be able to do nothing about it; Eliza Jane deferred to him, used as she was to loss. Not able to bring about change themselves, they accepted it in the guise of a godsend. "Call it luck, what you will, or pure chance" (Bennett said later), but local businessman Oliver B. Chapman approached John Briscoe Bennett. Having just bought the county's one weekly newspaper, the *Ross County Register,* he was on the lookout for reporters who could stay sober. (Most, according to the custom of the day, "got drunk as lords every Saturday night and as often as someone set them for drinks during the week.")[1]

Attending the Walnut Street Methodist Church, where he approvingly watched the young Jack Bennett appear every Sunday to pump the church organ and earn his fifty cents, Chapman heard the boy needed employment and perhaps remembered that Bennett and his friends had been congratulated by the paper for knowing how to run their own presses, compose type, and edit. He seemed the perfect candidate.

There is no way of knowing if John Briscoe knew the type of work his son would be doing and with whom he would be associating. If he did, and still agreed, it would have been due to need, not vindictiveness. Jack needed to help support the family, and since he had gotten in trouble for being a "journalist," this solution offered an elegant form of justice.

There is no record left of how the teenager himself felt, but later there would be suggestive echoes in his writing. In his first book, *Master Skylark*, he'd show Nick Attwood, his boy hero, running away to escape an apprenticeship arranged by his father; and in his second book, the eponymous hero, Barnaby Lee, would cry out to his missing father, asking why he had abandoned him to a crew of drunks.

That Sunday in church John Briscoe Bennett and Oliver Chapman came to an agreement; they shook on it. On June 4, 1883, a few weeks after his eighteenth birthday, Jack Bennett reported to the office of the *Ross County Register*.[2] His duties included reporting the news and helping set type—fishing the letters out of boxes, and setting them in forms by hand. He must have been excited by the prospect, for he had loved working on *The Little Messenger* with his friends in the loft of Poland's barn, and now he was to be paid two dollars a week for his efforts. He was young, willing, strong, and intelligent, brimming with optimism and high spirits; but he found the real-world, spittle-fouled newspaper office and the men working there a shock.

One of the other journalists in town who helped him out was Charles Lummis, who'd become well known for his prolific writings on the west, California, Native Americans, and the Spanish.[3] But most of his co-workers were an indifferent, hardened, cynical lot.

The worst, perhaps, was a "curbstone . . . gambler, patron of cheap bars, companion of the least desirable of the underworld, friend to no man, [and] the unfeeling ruin of as fine a newspaper man as ever did excellent work from Washington to St. Louis, but held no good position long from the unfortunate and untimely fatal habit of . . . becoming foolishly inebriated on very important assignments."[4] He was there on Bennett's first morning, glaring up through red eyes, at this fresh-faced, guileless apprentice.

The apprentice introduced himself; the man, hung over, grunted. Bennett kept his distance but watched him from the corner of his eye, and soon accorded him a grudging respect. Here, he realized, was "a man who could write anything brilliantly, from an important session of the United States Senate to a wedding in high life, a battle in the red light district, or a dog fight on Mt. Pisgah. But 'Doc,' as we called him, could not resist drink. When slightly intoxicated, he was the most brilliant and fascinating conversationalist I ever knew, and for the sake of his own enjoyment, [another] running mate got him drunk for the mere pleasure of hearing him talk." The boy thought that cruel beyond belief, since "every drunk ended in a blind and terrible spree for weeks."

"When I first knew Doc, and felt his genial charm and unresentful kindness, I ventured on a day when he was sad and sober to ask him earnestly why, in God's name, did he not quit the stuff? 'Why should I?' he replied, carelessly roused from gloom and laughing. 'I like it. It gives me a sense of superiority and brilliance beyond all bounds. And then, you must know, I can quit whenever I want to; and shall as soon as I see that it is hurting me.'" [5]

The boy might have believed this, being as romantic and gullible as he was; or, due to his own family's involvement, he may not. For although no one mentioned it, the Bennett family was afflicted with the same curse. Melancholia (even then starting to be called depression) and alcoholism (not just in his father's stepfather, Hilary Talbot, but in the Bennett line itself, perhaps in his father, and definitely in his brother Henry) menaced the family.[6] Nowhere is there a hint of it in the massive amount of papers he left, but a family member eventually orally admitted it, and it does offer a believable explanation for some of the older Bennett's subsequent behavior.

As Jack tried to reform Doc, he became a drone at work; he saw his best friend Will Poland and his brothers and the rest of the West Second Street gang going swimming, jumping out of the sycamores in the river, lazing on banks, and courting young ladies in buggies while he, doomed daily to his realm of ink, grease, and tobacco spit, worked around language so foul that he blushed upon hearing it; this of course just goaded the men to curse all the more, as they laughed at his naiveté and innocence.

Every day he trudged to the office, which seemed to him a descent into an underworld of stygian gloom and unrelieved darkness. Going home, the stench of tobacco and grease clung to him; he had to scrub and scrub to get free of it.

That summer he learned a lot; the season eventfully passed and burned itself out like a fever or an illness. As autumn colors flared and the horizon seemed blue with smoke, he felt anxious to get back on track. On October 10, 1883, his father's sixty-second birthday, the *Ross County Register* noted that "John Bennett has decided to sever connections with the Ross County Register and will attend School of Design in Cincinnati." Since he liked to draw, and needed a profession, it made perfect sense to become an illustrator and support himself by doing what he loved best. He enrolled at Mat Morgan's School of Design on November 1, 1883.[7]

The school was expensive for the poor family; and it cost too much for him to live in Cincinnati, so he commuted daily from nearby Maplewood.

In class, he "opened my eyes to what drawing is, and increased my lifelong love of making pictures in one manner or another." [8]

He had nearly finished his first year when, in March 1884, the Ohio River flooded. In Cincinnati, this caused havoc; there were riots and the school closed early. But as he made his way home, he could hardly check his excitement. His teachers said he had talent; so he planned to redeem his failure and get his life back. He had decided to go east and study illustration at the best place then in the country—the Art Students' League in New York City.

## CHAPTER 4

# Cold Courage

## Famous to Myself

IN CHILLICOTHE, things had not gone well with the Bennett family. At an age at which many of his friends were slowing down, John Briscoe could not. The house given him at his marriage was mortgaged; with debts from the April Fool's fire mounting, he was caught in a downward economic spiral, from which he could not figure out how to extricate himself.

Eliza Jane was resigned and would do whatever was necessary but could provide no solutions. Known earlier for her dry Scottish wit, now she rarely laughed but hung her head defeated, having sacrificed "her own beauty and ease" almost too willingly.[1] She could, at least, take comfort in the fact that they had kept the news from Jack.

When he rushed in, excited about sharing his plans, he stopped short. Only as an old man did he ever recall that scene. "I'm sorry, son," he reported his father flatly telling him, "but you must get something to do. I can no longer afford to send you away to learn an artist's business."[2] The absence of any comment on his own emotions speaks volumes and suggests the anger he felt at his father for making him give up his dreams (and perhaps his guilt over feeling that). For it was not just that the Art Students' League was out of the question; he had no chance now of even going back to Morgan's School of Design in Cincinnati. Someone had to help support the family.

That "someone" could not mean Martha, the youngest, just seventeen, bright, and conscientious. She was so giving, she would have deferred her plans (as an old woman she'd say that keeping her brother happy was the one last aim left in her life), but she had her heart set on going east to get a degree so she could teach.[3] She'd eventually attend the adjunct college for women at Harvard, Radcliffe.

Nor could they turn to Alice, the eldest, because "Alice of the loving heart and tortured mind" was, in the family's parlance, "shaken by an irremediable nerve disorder" in which she suffered from things "never to happen and her own timidity."[4] She sang in church and musicales, visited friends and family, sewed and baked at home and went to neighborhood teas, but foremost in her consciousness were her illnesses, both feigned and real. Not even a suitor who courted her for over a decade could intervene; she'd never forsake her invalid status to marry.

So help was to come from the sons, but not Henry. He, who had always performed well in school, was currently enrolled at Kenyon College; his future beckoned brilliantly. Jack's childhood had been poisoned with comparisons to the stellar Henry, and now it "continued a jealous and . . . envious regard on my part." (It would not be until years later that the rift would mend, and Bennett realized that "my older brother was deeply attached to me [and] loved me with all his generous and valiant heart.")[5]

Now, however, there was only anger and envy. Seeing it was he who would have to stay home and help the family, he seized upon the idea, realizing now he could prove to Henry that he, Jack, could be a hero, too. He'd show him; he'd show the world, but most of all, he would really show himself. In his anger and hurt pride and youthful self-aggrandizement, he set out to martyr himself even further by vowing to never show his true feelings. He'd refuse to admit the truth of how much it hurt, while pretending to be cheerful for his father and his family. Stray thoughts and notes, however, would occasionally betray his faux stoicism; and absent and failing fathers (and dead or ineffectual long-suffering mothers) would come to dominate his writings. In his story "His Father's Price" (ca. 1895), for instance, he'd posit a stalwart and loving father bringing about near tragedy for his son. This medieval yeoman endangers his own life with his honesty, as John Briscoe Bennett hurt his family in his stubborn need to pay others who had put their faith in him. In the story the yeoman's son gets in trouble for displaying his father's similar integrity; they are eventually both redeemed, but in the real world the resolution was not so happy.

Next, in *Master Skylark*, Bennett would create a boy running away to escape his father's demands; he'd escape to be a successful artist. And years later, as an adult in Charleston, when he'd come to serve as a father figure to younger struggling writers, he'd ostensibly and very graciously give up his career for theirs; but he would complain of it bitterly—and secretly—to his family.

"Adversity frequently makes a man wise," he noted at the time, "but it does not make him rich, and seldom makes him happy." [6] Thus he abandoned his dream of the New York Art Students' League.

Summer settled in, school let out, and thunderstorms broke the intensity of the heat and washed the dust from the thick-leafed trees. Bennett resigned himself to the season's fated heaviness; he walked the streets, hands shoved deep into his pockets, dejectedly looking for work instead of starting off to New York City.

He disliked newspaper work, but went immediately to the office of the *Ross County Register.* There were no openings; but he heard rumors of a new paper coming to Chillicothe, not a weekly but a daily, to be run by the grocer Rufus Putnam. Bennett went to see him, and Putnam hired him on May 4, 1884, at three dollars a week. [7] "I had no option," Bennett wrote dramatically. "The old song, 'Root, hog, or die,' had not yet been forgotten." [8]

He was among familiars again; Doc, apparently having been fired from the other paper for drinking, was now working here. If the boy secretly nursed the idea that he could soon be on his way to the Art Students' League, he promptly relinquished it as he saw his job threatened immediately. Putnam had expected his brother John, a successful newspaper man, to act as supervisor of the *Chillicothe News.* But President Grover Cleveland appointed John as consul general of Hawaii, leaving no one, certainly not the grocer, to lead; and no one in this town of 12,000 knew how to proceed with a daily paper where before there had only been weeklies.

Knowing they would be out of jobs if the paper failed, the staff directed itself. Bennett not only reported but also solicited patent medicine advertisements and business announcements. At the courthouse he abstracted real estate transfers and probate court proceedings; he told of births, deaths, and marriages; and filled space with the minutes of city council meetings, baseball scores, and anything else he could turn into copy. Just as he and co-workers put the press to bed, it was time to start again.

All the deadlines and rushing frenzy could have seemed glamorous to some, but Bennett, not there by choice, bitter about it and believing himself wronged, saw it differently. Not for a moment, he said later, did he believe that either he or his coworkers were real journalists; "we were . . . just a few tolerably intelligent young fellows . . . earning a precarious living . . . by the sweat of our brows, journalism be damned." What "a reporter needed . . . was then known as cheek or brass." A journalist had to be crass, tough, hard, and callous; he had to barge in on the tragic and unseemly, ignore terror, angst, sadness, or suffering, and focus in on what the public wanted to read. Bennett was too young, just twenty and too sensitive for that; as for cheek, or brass, "I did not have it." [9]

He was shy and well behaved, helpful and conciliatory. More inclined to turn his face away from shameful events and tragedies and offer remedies than report on them unfeelingly, he'd lose time helping, offering advice, staying with distraught folks at accident scenes, finding doctors or lawyers before returning. Back in Chillicothe, he'd head for the office, a large barn-like space jammed with tables and chairs and littered with spittoons, cigarette stubs, and pipe dottles, to dash out his story. Then Putnam would dispatch him to "go out quick, find Doc or Willy or Eddie and tell 'em for Godsake get their stuff in, we're late and the press is waiting." [10]

Out on the street, he'd run back and forth, asking everyone if he or she had seen the other reporters; he'd check saloons and barns and brothels. Finding them drunk or passed out in allies, he'd drag them back to the office. "More than once I rode herd upon uncertain steps and assisted in unraveling from broken notes and vocal recitations the [half-done] preparation of the lead article as Doc hiccoughed . . . Willy belched, and Ed looked as solemn as an owl, writing nothing, saying nothing, paralyzed with beer." Often he'd find a coworker senseless, rifle his pockets, and write the story himself from the jumbled, pencilled bits. Then "up the rickety back flight of tobacco spittled stairs" he'd run to set type, fishing letters of the alphabet, one by one from their boxes, assembling words, headlines and columns. As he labored, "streams of profanity ebbed and flowed like the tide among the richest sewerage of the city, as every muscle [of every employee] was strained to make the e-box last . . . out the afternoon edition." [11]

The press, cantankerous, too, "consisted of two or three footpower 'kick it yourself' jobbing presses, all of which generally had something the matter with their rollers." "The thick, rich, characteristic smell of printer's ink and a sweet undercurrent of chewing tobacco drifted from every compositor's stand" as they sent the forms down greased tracks from the composing room overhead. Once, an entire form containing a whole page of set type spilled "down the slide. The rattle of the descending rain of type cast a deadly paralysis on the entire shop. No one spoke for an actual minute." Then the foreman began swearing and everyone scrambled for letters of the alphabet and began frantically resetting the page.

"One morning, instead of using yellow soap to grease the stairway slide, an ingenious youth greased the slide with limburger cheese; it was, when the room warmed up, very much like an attack by a . . . polecat."[12]

With such conditions and a drunken, cavalier, and nonchalant staff, there was much hilarity on the paper, but Bennett, too stiff, too unhappy, could not join in it. He took all the failures seriously; a perfectionist, he thought the paper "looked like a patchwork quilt," its errors, misstatements, and misspellings making him wince.[13] (He'd feel the same thing when mistakes appeared in *The Year Book of the Poetry Society of South Carolina* in Charleston.) He also worried about the staff and their drinking, Doc especially.

One day he took him aside and asked, anxiously, "Why in the name of all that is holy, and all that is dear to you, why don't you stop [drinking]?" Doc looked startled. Then he "turned to me with a twisted face and tragic glance, and said, 'By God! I can't stop it if I would.'" He went off with a bitter laugh.

The events that followed soon after were tragic. "Proud and sensitive . . . he fell to sleeping in the back-room of mean saloons, or could he still stagger far enough, to sleeping in his sister's stable." Not surprisingly, he got sick. "He recovered from typhoid fever to die of tuberculosis. . . . He faded out like a waterless flower . . . and he looked like a wistful charming boy." Or so said the wistful charming John Bennett, who longed to be back to his own boyhood himself. For after Doc's death, Bennett found himself further adrift. "I had no mentor, no kindly critic, [usually] only angry men, indignant women, and angry subscribers . . . furious about WHAT I said, and not . . . the WAY in which I said it."[14]

He took guilt and responsibility onto himself. And many, remembering the "smart aleck" who had duped the town fathers with a carved Indian pipe, were more than willing to believe he had done it. One time, "I printed a small, inconspicuous item . . . which made three men, individually and separately, and each of his own instinct . . . leave town by the first train out, after they had seen the paper," he bragged; but more often than not, people did not abscond or turn the other cheek, but came into the office, upset, demanding retractions and threatening to beat up the staff if they did not get them. It became a fairly common occurrence, but "if I said I paid no attention to threats [or] . . . took no notice of what men said, I should be a cheerful liar. . . . Yet had I worried overmuch about the ungodly beatings promised me I should never have slept. . . . I was not then," he admitted, "and never have been a bold man; I have a cold courage, more mental stubbornness than physical valor." [15]

This cold courage stood him well over the coming years as his unhappiness and depression grew along with the family's poverty. "My hat was full of holes," and his shoes were so worn that one day he walked home in his stocking feet, having worn through the leather soles. [16]

While the Poland boys and others wore the latest styles, he made his previous summer's straw hat look new by holding it in sulfur fumes and bleaching it with lemon and salt. When the white thread of worn seams peeked through, he inked them black. On the surface he seemed the same, neat and tidy, boon companion Jack Bennett, but to himself he complained bitterly.

"I conceive of myself as resembling Friedrich Nietzsche," he noted grandiloquently as he looked back on these years at the turn of the century. "I shall be famous," he believed, "not for what I have done, famous, not to the world . . . but in my own heart, to myself, famous for what I have endured, the hardness I have met and borne, the dullness met, the misunderstanding, pedantic, bigoted ignorance and coarseness which I have been forced . . . to associate with [in newspaper work] and yet above which I have risen in the end." He was impressed with himself and knew he had a role to play in the universe. "It has from some unknown, remotely guessed at purpose pleased God that I should not fall victim to . . . Philistine dullness or be worn . . . by a hard struggle." [17] He suffered nobly as if he knew there was an audience aware of and moved by it.

He told everyone he had given up his dream of going to the Art Students' League, but in fact he had not. He still held to his ambition and practiced it on the job, drawing "in court and out, exaggerated caricatures of eminent lawyers, criminals and culprits; we produced a gallery of local celebrities" in the paper via chalk plates. But somehow he could not admit that the job brought any benefit, so he complained that in this practice of drawing, he "saw all the vice, nastiness, petty crime and all the disillusionment I ever wanted to see." [18]

To counteract that, to get his equanimity back, and to try to recapture a bit of that idyllic childhood feeling, he'd take off an occasional Saturday afternoon with his best friend Will Poland (getting his paycheck docked) to swim or go horseback riding through the hills of Ross County ("the hills of Ross," he romantically called it); he'd come back, wind-burned, color in his cheeks, his head reeling and heart pumping with the beauty of the world, his constant antidote to depression and overwork.

One hot and steamy Memorial Day, instead of attending a local politician's speech, he absconded with Poland to the Scioto River. They jumped in, lying on their backs, watching the light come down and dapple them. Later that afternoon, with a deadline looming, he and Poland sat around in the reportorial room, smoking cigars, with their feet up. Second-guessing the politician's oratory, they concocted a talk of clichés and bombast and capped it with flourishes of fine-sounding nonsense. Then they sprinkled it with descriptions of crowds cheering and mobs bursting into whistles and stamping feet; satisfied, they passed it up to be printed and then went to sleep. The next morning, when the paper appeared, the local politician came in to buy extra copies for constituents; he congratulated the reporter for reporting on the capstone of his career.[19]

Working with him and on other papers in Chillicothe and surrounding towns in these years, many people were drawn to Bennett. Among their number were Herbert Dawley, future designer of the Pierce Arrow automobiles and proclaimed inventor of the "claymation" figures used in early horror movies; Billy Ireland, who'd become one of the most popular political cartoonists in the Midwest; and Burton Stevenson, who, starting as a paper boy, later produced a boy's magazine carrying Bennett's first serial.[20] Stevenson went on to author numerous books and edit such volumes as *The Home Book of Verse, Home Book of Modern Verse, Home Book of Quotations, Home Book of Shakespeare Quotations,* and *Home Book of Biblical Quotations.* He'd also create the American Library in Paris.

Bennett also befriended many townsfolk, and, wanting to be liked, he appealed to them, knowing "that high or low, rich or poor, there was nothing in God's world so interested a man as himself and his own interests; and that all . . . were gratified to see their names in print in the columns of our paper." But this he refused to say was cynicism or flattery; he was needy and "wanted men to like me for myself, not alone for what I said of them" in the paper. "And gradually I believe they came to see that . . . I was not assuming what I did not feel, but was truly interested in them and their affairs."[21]

So there were things to be liked about newspaper work, despite his constant complaining about it. In 1886, at the age of twenty-one, he was offered a promotion to the position of local editor and took on the extra responsibility and salary, his father having lost his store entirely now. Bouts of self-loathing and self-pity overcame John Briscoe Bennett; it is possible he gave into drink, but this is speculation only.

"It makes me very sad . . . to hear you speak of 'failure,'" Bennett wrote his father. "Cash counts, God knows, and we'd like our share; but cash is not everything. . . . If you had faltered or given it up, it would be another thing. . . . The winner is he who keeps his soul and never turns his back."[22]

As if he could not bear to meet the eyes of his wife and children, the elder Bennett took to the road working as drummer, or salesman, traveling through six states in the Midwest, trying to earn a bit of money. "I am very sorry that it has seemed neglect . . . because no letter from me reached you while you were on the road," Bennett wrote his father testily. "I had no idea when you simply mentioned . . . 'Morehead, Saylorsville,' etc., that that was the list of places you would send me for mailing points. . . . I was afraid you would construe silence on my part as a lack of interest . . . and from the way you speak of being 'left out in the cold' . . . I conclude that you *have* so construed it."[23] His father wanted to feel sorry for himself, as the younger man was also doing quietly; but Jack would not allow it, trying instead to cheer his father up. "I think everyday, 'I must work hard to day, that Father may find some new credit in the life he has left in my hands,'" he wrote him; he also told his father he worked so "Mother may take some pleasure yet in what I can do." He propped his father up further by declaring that "I find in your life-history so much to admire and cherish that to the day of my death I shall keep it bright in memory, and never forget."[24]

Ostensibly holding out no hope for his own happiness but working, he said, for that of others, he buried himself in work; it became harder when a group of politically connected businessmen in town decided to launch a newspaper of their own. "Perhaps their employees were tempted by their paychecks," Bennett mused; "their editors were brilliant and experienced . . . none better in all that end of the state. Our employees were working for an employer whom they neither greatly respected and certainly did not love; but for him, as the underdog, they worked . . . like trojans; they cursed, reviled and worked their hearts out." Not to be bested was their aim, for they all knew Chillicothe could only support one daily. "We either won or lost everything."[25]

Without the staff or the time, Bennett and his coworkers never planned an issue in advance; this made their ragged sheet look spontaneous; the competition's product was formal and studied, and the editors hobbled themselves by never printing anything the *Daily News* had printed first; it also "drew a line on their social page, and announced nothing below a certain grade of local society. With us no man was too poor or too lowly to have his place in the news of the day; no one was too rich or great to escape criticism; no party or business could buy our support.

"Every pleasant mention brought us a new subscriber; every denunciation attracted new attention; an increasing subscription list brought new advertising; increased advertising brought new profits; and increased profits enabled new presses and greater facilities."

It was "at times very exciting . . . and in struggling to beat my competitors . . . with . . . quickness, accuracy and completeness . . . something very like a prize fight . . . in which the man who struck the blows soonest, straightest and hardest and took his punishment longest . . . won." But still he could never forget that he "had never planned to be a writer or a journalist; I became one by chance; call it destiny, fate, fortune, misfortune, what you will. I became a writer from necessity, not by choice."[26]

But a writer he was now, and a successful one; for the rival press went down. There was a great noisy celebration in the office, with lots of drinking no doubt, when the other editors acknowledged defeat. But it was back to work the next morning.

And now to keep up the level the paper had achieved, Bennett drove himself punishingly. "I rose at 4:30 A.M. and got to bed . . . at midnight. . . . There were no trolley cars, busses, or taxis, not even a bicycle."[27] He walked wherever he went.

Yet hope flared suddenly when he fell in love. He became involved in a "desperately passionate attachment to a young girl whose immediate family were among my nearest friends. It was . . . futile and . . . distressing . . . and kept my life troubled for seven years. We were at one time actually engaged to be married, had exchanged tokens binding; but at long last, after much and mutual misery, the attachment came to nothing but wreck and something of disgrace for both parties."[28] This happened as he worked as the local editor, and the heartache over it, on top of years of general depression and overwork, led to something like a breakdown or at least a crisis; perhaps he was finally compelled to show others how badly he felt.

At one point, he said it stemmed from reporting a bit too facetiously on the wedding of a daughter of a prominent Chillicothe family.[29] (Perhaps the same to whom he had been engaged.) But elsewhere, he made himself sound noble by attributing what happened to his honest evaluation of a new real estate development, advising the public against it; the backer of the development, he told a friend in Charleston, went to his boss.[30] In January 1889 Jack Bennett was fired unceremoniously after five years of hard, demanding work. Needing to escape what he felt as disgrace, he left Chillicothe.

There were no jobs for reporters on the *State Journal* sixty miles away in the capital, Columbus, but Bennett went there anyway. The only job he could find was collecting overdue subscriptions; although it brought in just half of what he needed to pay for the apartment he rented above a black-owned restaurant in Rich Street, he nevertheless took it. He was then on the lookout for something else.

CHAPTER 5

# *"The Fragrance of Success"*

AFRAID OF GAMBLING on a new occupation, Bennett stuck with what he knew best. Since he could not get a job with one press, he decided to try them all; he'd support himself through freelance writing.

Having been faced with white space at the *Daily News*, he had begun producing long descriptions of local events, scenes, or vignettes and writing up local history, jokes, and stories. The pieces he had written had been noticed by editors of the larger newspapers looking through other publications in search of material for their Sunday supplements. They reprinted Bennett's work and paid him to be a "stringer," reporting on news in his part of the state. He planned to pull on those connections when he moved to Columbus. He also immediately dashed off a sentimental prose piece of tough men banding together to help a child and called it "How the Church Was Built at Kehoe's Bar"; it was bought by the *Home Journal* in Washington, D.C. (other than journalism, the first piece of fiction he sold). He was promised an astonishing fourteen dollars for it. "I felt fame and fortune were at the door." [1]

He also fell back on his drawing skills, submitting designs to contests; he soon won five dollars (over a week's wages) for a commercial logo for the Midland Accident and Insurance Company. [2] To double his chances and practice his art, he started to attach drawings to his stories.

He had been doing something similar for years—adding drawings to letters he sent to friends. Fred Dunlap of Chillicothe, a professor of chemistry at the State University, realizing Bennett was in town and looking for work, showed an illustrated letter of his to the editors of the university fraternity annual, *The Makio*. They made Bennett a proposition, and he accepted his first job as an illustrator, artist of *The Makio* edition of 1889. Since university rules expected staff to be students, Bennett obligingly attended chapel every day he worked.

Another Chillicothe friend, George Smart, the son of a newspaper man, told Bennett of a comic weekly named *Light* (formerly called the *Owl*) that was asking for jokes and drawings. Bennett sent over one of his illustrated comic strips. His work was clear and humorous and precise (similar to Palmer Cox's phenomenally popular Brownies, the little creatures that had begun to appear in 1883). Bennett visited the editor's office next. Within three weeks, Opha Moore offered Bennett a position on this journal, which billed itself "the only five cent colored cartoon paper in the world."[3]

Bennett began July 19, 1889, at ten dollars a week, becoming in one bold, swift move a well-paid professional illustrator. It was an astonishing feat for Jack Bennett who, in the words of Moore, "existed down in Chillicothe and gyrated around Columbus and cultivated dyspepsia and liver complaint and the idea that he was not long for this world."[4]

If this sudden shift of fortune seemed too giddily amazing to be true, it *was*. For with no warning, *Light* suddenly went bankrupt, jolting Bennett unceremoniously back into unemployment. He waited around for something else to turn up in Columbus. As he started to run through his funds and still could find no other work, he had to swallow his pride and ask for his old job back, as if the whole episode in Columbus had never happened. But just after starting back at the *Daily News* in Chillicothe, he heard again from *Light*, resurrected in Chicago now and under new management.

"What will you take for all your time?" the editor wired him.

"What will you give?" he telegraphed back.

"Thirty dollars a week for drawing and text."[5]

He gasped at the extravagance, two and half times what he was making. Could he stay at home in Ohio, he asked, and send it all in the mail?

When they acquiesced, he was ecstatic, never realizing that he was being radically underpaid for his work. So he left the *Daily News*. Everything he sent from the upstairs room on West Second Street, which the family called "the Roost," they printed: verses, prose paragraphs, comic drawings and strips.[6]

He was getting thirty dollars a week from *Light* and more and more money for his sale of features to Ohio's metropolitan Sunday supplements. And his drawings were appearing all over the country. (Over the years, his uncopyrighted drawings would resurface in other publications, some of his early art work still appearing decades after his death.)[7] He started saving for the Art Students' League. It could only be further good news, he felt, when editor Phil Darrow wired him a train pass to come up to the Windy City.

On his way up the stairs to the office, however, he had misgivings as he "met a tall, good-looking, slender fellow [coming down] with a Remington type-writer in his hand."

"The paper's defunct [the man said] and this is all I could carry off. You'd best go up and see if there is anything . . . for what is owing you." There was not. Tables, chairs and filing cabinets were too awkward to carry. So there was only fear and worry to take back with him to Chillicothe, where he soon fell into a deep gloom and depression, "a period of desperation, the most difficult of my life." Refusing to go back to the *Daily News,* Bennett wrote: "I was at wit's end for a living and had not two brown pennies to rub together."[8]

To earn money, he worked as a taxidermist, painted scenery for theatrical troupes, played guitar in an orchestra, and furnished music for private entertainments. He drew window advertisements and contributed freelance articles to publications such as the *New York Journalist, Printer's Ink,* and *Art in Advertising.* He devised designs for the Logan Sarsaparilla Company and for Galbraith's Catarrh Cure. It was nerve-wracking—not knowing from week to week what he would be doing next—but he kept at it. "Through seven hard years of unremitting work and uncertainty, I scrambled up inch by inch, step by step."[9]

Whether it was psychosomatic or not, in these years on his own in Chillicothe Bennett again exhibited effects of stress. His eyes bothered him, and he was plagued by hay fever and allergies. The times were frequent "when I sat at my typewriter grinding out gems of wit and humor, pathos, poetry and piffle, a handkerchief at either side of the machine and half-blind two thirds of the time with sneezing."[10] Even being near open windows beset him with symptoms, and he sneezed and gasped for breath. As a solution he took cocaine, then an easily available over-the-counter remedy and present in many patent medicine products. Although it brought relief, it had unanticipated side effects; he found himself caught up in cycles of euphoria and the ensuing fallow periods of lethargy, depression, and apathy. He experienced loss of appetite, weight, sexual drive, and sleep. This made it harder to concentrate, which affected his earning capabilities. "Darn your old cocaine bottle," one friend, a journalist named Jack Appleton, eventually wrote.[11]

To break the habit, Bennett went north to the clear air of Mackinac Island, a resort for the wealthy and health-conscious in Lake Michigan. There he rented a room in an attic in someone else's vacation cottage and struck up a slight acquaintance with another literary man, Booth Tarkington.

Free from hay fever, with thoughts as clear as the air and unmoored from his past and the emotional demands of his family, he looked back at his life and tried to devise a plan for change. He saw that if his work improved, he could sell more of it for higher sums; and with his savings, he might be able to go study art in New York. He saw, ironically, that if he became a better writer he'd have a chance at becoming an artist.

At Mackinac in the early 1890s he began experimenting, sparing no effort to advance his broken education, improve his style, and expand his vocabulary. Still having the basic visual orientation of his childhood, he first had to see in his mind's eye what he was trying to convey; with an image firmly in mind, he'd then build it with words; and once he saw it, his readers could, too.[12]

To get better still, Bennett, like a painter copying the works of masters, started mimicking other writers of the gilded area, including the popular poets Ella Wheeler Wilcox, James Whitcomb Riley, Lizette Woodworth Reese, and Bret Harte.

Like many of them, he employed sentimental verse for his poem "The Dead Pussy Cat," written in a child's dialect. Though maudlin and bathetic, it achieved a bit of success; newspapers around the country reprinted it, and Bennett used it in a short story he wrote.[13]

As he continued to learn, he continued to use children to examine the world; he invested the commonplace with grandeur and tragedy, employing simple language and often dialect to render emotions both authentic and heartfelt. Nonsense and jest came easily as well, and these efforts have aged better. All, nevertheless, were just ways of making money.

Something that changed his attitude to his work was an offhand comment from Charles Graham Dunlap, of the English Department of Kansas State University, who had known Bennett as a boy in Chillicothe. Coming across a piece of Bennett's in a paper, Dunlap wrote to "warn" him that if he didn't watch out, he'd soon find himself writing good English.

He was thunderstruck, as he had been upon discovering silhouettes. He had believed it impossible for someone who had failed out of school to aspire to be literary; but he had just been praised by an academic. For "the first time the idea had occurred to me that I might possibly do something better than newspaper work."[14] Where, he wondered, might he send his poetry, jests, and artwork?

He thought of *St. Nicholas Magazine;* it had been a constant companion of his childhood, the Bennetts having been one of the first subscribers when it appeared in 1873 under the editorship of Mary Mapes Dodge, author of the perennial children's classic, *Hans Brinker and the Silver Skates.* What the then eight-year-old Bennett discovered was that Dodge did not aim to be didactic, but to entertain; and she did so by using the best writers of the times, including Longfellow, Whitman, Howard Pyle, Kipling, and Louisa May Alcott. Mixed in with verse and fiction were articles on science and technology, biography, and how to make and do things. (Later, the forum for children, "The St. Nicholas League," would give children such as Ring Lardner, Stephen and Vincent Benét, Cornelia Otis Skinner, Babette Deutsch, Elinor Wylie, Bennett Cerf, and Edmund Wilson their first experience of publishing.) For reasons such as these, the magazine would gain the reputation of being the best children's magazine ever published, prompting Henry Steele Commager to call it the magazine in which "majors wrote for minors."[15]

Bennett liked the idea of writing for children, bringing up, as it did, memories of his own childhood, which seemed happier and brighter the more depressed he got. In 1891 he nervously sent *St. Nicholas* "The Barber of Sari Ann." The poem was accepted. Heartened, he began to send on other things—songs, doggerel, ballads, and verse; more often that not, he sent along drawings to accompany them, mostly his deftly cut silhouettes. He sent so much and they bought so often, that within a year or so, it seemed that nearly every issue had a small contribution by John Bennett.[16] Although rejections still came, they were less frequent; the staff encouraged him. When stories were declined, they came back with words of praise from the editorial office; and technical suggestions for improvement of his drawings came from Alexander Drake, head of the Century Company's art department, which eventually bought *St. Nicholas.* Such advice made its mark on Bennett; others noticed the improvement. In 1892 Ed Flynn of the *Cincinnati Commercial Gazette* was so impressed with a poem of Bennett's, called "In a Rose Garden," that he refused it. It was too good for newspapers, he said, and should be sent "higher up."

Bennett dutifully copied out the verses which were a bit of a consolation to a desperate young man; the poem owed its origins to the failed love affair that so tortured him in 1884:

> A hundred years from now, dear heart,
> We shall not care at all

It will not matter then a whit,
The honey or the gall.
The summer days that we have known
Will all forgotten be and flown
The garden will be overgrown
Where now the roses fall

A hundred years from now, dear heart,
We shall not mind the pain
The throbbing crimson tide of life
Will not have left a stain
The song we sing together, dear
The dream we dream together here,
Will mean no more than means a tear
Amid a summer rain.

He carried on in this vein for two stanzas more.[17]

The poem went the rounds of literary magazines, all the major ones rejecting it until Stone and Kimball paid four dollars for it in 1894 and published it on October 1, 1895, in their distinctive *Chap Book*.

Although technically not good verse, people liked its fin-de-siècle attitude; it was a great success. Over the years, with its name changed to "A Hundred Years from Now," the poem appeared again and again in magazines and newspapers. Two composers, Carrie Jacobs Bond and Neal McCoy, set it to music, and it was recorded on disc at least once, bringing Bennett thousands of dollars in royalties.[18] Poetry anthologies, distinguished and popular, wanted it. Charles Dudley Warner used it in his *Library of the World's Best Literature*, and it also appeared in *The Best Loved Poems of the American People*, first published in 1936, forty years after the poem's first appearance. (The book is still in print.) It brought Bennett much praise and at least one lifelong friendship—with Charlestonian Yates Snowden, who read it first and then sought out Bennett.[19] It passed into folk consciousness, many knowing about and able to paraphrase it but ignorant of who wrote it; people constantly wrote to the long running "Queries and Answers" department of the *New York Times Book Review* about its authorship. It became so well known that eventually *Bartlett's Familiar Quotations* came to include it.[20]

Bennett felt "urged on by the fragrance of success, dimly felt; . . . I disliked the newspaper world where it paid best, in cities; I could not contemplate being driven again to go into that field, if I could possibly make a living elsewhere." So he kept on writing, suffering various illnesses, becoming more and more "famous" to himself. "I had hay-fever all summer and dyspepsia the rest of the time; in fact life was pretty rough . . . sledding."[21]

In 1892, at the age of twenty-seven, Bennett served as cartographer for the Peabody Museum's prehistoric mounds field expedition in Ohio (an ironic task for someone accused of faking ancient relics). In the same year his illustrations for Warren K. Morehead's *Primitive Man of Ohio* received mostly appreciative reviews.[22]

A publication on Ohio authors in this era called him one of the most talented men in the Buckeye State,[23] and in a profile in the New York City *Journalist* he noted, "I am determined to succeed if my health will hold out." He said that "if hard work can bring any degree of success," he would have it. "I would rather be known by my work—as a hard worker— . . . than anything else."

As if realizing the improvement in his writing, he changed his professional name, ceasing to sign his work "Jack" and assuming the more dignified "John."[24] (But it was a hard habit to break; for accompanying the quoted 1893 article was a photograph of a very short-haired, full-cheeked young man captioned "Jack Bennett, of Chillicothe.")[25]

It must have been an old image, for in the summer of 1892 he caught cholera at Mackinac; recovery was slow, and the next summer he did not want to go back; so in 1893, still weak and thin, he accepted an invitation to visit Jack Appleton, the journalist who had warned him about cocaine. That revived his spirits, but once he returned to Ohio he grew depressed, and confessed in a letter that he felt "like the ashes left from a first class fire" due to the past ten years of hard work and disappointment.[26]

He was so despondent, he turned back to cocaine to lift his spirits; he lost even more weight and became so apathetic that he could no longer take interest in art, writing, affairs of the heart, or even of the flesh.

He told Appleton that

I met a girl last night whom a mutual acquaintance ruined a year or so ago . . . I couldn't take her home, for she hasn't any; so I took her to the first assignation house I could find, and got her warm and dry and gave her some wine, and drank some myself, and heard her story out from end to end, with some of the letters she still carries around with her. And I damned the fellow feebly, which did her no bit of good; and I gave her the value of a couple of meals, which will do her more good than they will me. . . . And the poor devil wanted to return my so-called kindness with her whole heart in the only way she could, and cried because she thought I was angry with her when I didn't accept. And I a poor, damned physically exhausted wreck that couldn't have accepted her offer if I would!

I didn't preach reform, for it will come out in the wash, and I didn't recommend; but I saw that she was fixed for one quiet, comfortable night, so much at any rate, and kissed her and let her kiss me, and then I came home, and it's a damned funny world!

At home, he told Appleton,

I have shut up all my drawers and put away my books and works-stuff, and am doing nothing—only longing for Spring to come . . . though I know that as soon as Spring comes, the season I love most of all, I shall begin sneezing and gasping as usual. I think God lost the pattern if he cut me out intending me to fit in anywhere at all in this damned world of His.

I do not want to be wakened again into the fight; but I suppose I shall have to somehow. Year after year, I have grown more and more unwilling to the work and now I find myself honestly heartsick with it.

He hinted at thoughts of suicide.

A darkened intellect, some folks call it. It is a mistake; my intellect is just as bright as ever; I see everything as clear and some things a great deal clearer [than before]; and yet [it] may be . . . that I AM in the dark. . . . You know it is easier to see that way, than looking into the dark from the light.[27]

In the darkness he found himself wondering if he could "make [his] mind do the work . . . [laid] out for it."[28] Never before had he been so frank; perhaps it was due to the fact that he did not see Appleton every day—for they lived far apart; it was a friendship kept up through correspondence. Even so, such dark frankness was uncharacteristic; Bennett kept the letter for awhile in his desk, debating whether or not he should send it.

"I think . . . the strongest incentive to . . . go forward in the face of unsurmountable obstacles is our honest and . . . honorable desire to fulfill the hopes of our families and friends," he thought, "and not to fail their expectations." He also believed there was "honest manhood in refusing to sink in the common slough of despondency." [29] After much thought, he crumpled the letter up but, perhaps as a way of being famous to himself, nevertheless kept it.

"Our wishes, more often than our reasoning powers, are the sources of our deepest convictions," he saw.[30] He kept up his façade of cheerfulness, but the mask began to slip; by the time he accepted another invitation to visit Appleton and his family he was in crisis.

CHAPTER 6

# A Transcendent Word

It's impossible to know how much he was exaggerating when, thirty years later, Bennett described his arrival at Jack Appleton's, for just as he used only bright colors in recalling his childhood, so he cast his young adulthood in almost unrelieved blackness.

When he got off the train in the West Virginia mountains, he said observers remarked to each other, "He has come too late." He was thin, dark-eyed, hollow-cheeked, and cadaverous. His host was appalled.

"'Old top,' said [Appleton] long afterward, 'you were one of the poorest bets. When I first met you at the station and gave you . . . the once-over, you may remember I urged the driver to push on nor spare the [horse] leather. Why? My dear and disreputable friend, I thought you would pass out before we reached the hotel!'"[1]

Severely underweight due to his cocaine addiction and depression, Bennett held onto others for physical, but never emotional, support. "Like all discouraged young things, I was a black pessimist; all the dolls were stuffed with sawdust and the earth a flop, eternity one everlasting stretch of . . . negation, and mankind . . . vultures, . . . thieves and . . . proverbial liars."[2]

But he had come to West Virginia at the Appleton's insistence nevertheless, all the while keeping up his façade of cheerfulness. He waited for the reason for the invitation to be revealed; Jack Appleton said he had admired Bennett's writing and wanted to meet face to face the man with whom he had been corresponding. But Bennett felt Appleton and his parents, owners of the Salt Sulphur Springs hotel, surely must want something else. "What in the heck did they expect to get out of the venture?" Keeping his thoughts to himself, he watched, amazed, as Appleton and his parents, "took me . . . fed me . . . lent me gay companionship, horses, amazing understanding and corrective courage [just] for the unmentioned sake of a kindly and genuine humanity."[3]

He stayed all summer at the large rambling structure that sported porches and rocking chairs with views to green hillsides, mountains, valleys with springs. People walked along the paths, "took the waters," assembled in the large dining rooms for meals, and met in parlors for games, visits, and letter writing. It was the refuge of mostly Southern families who had been coming since before the Civil War to mingle, present their marriageable daughters, recover health, and get breaks from the coastal heat. South Carolina writer Louisa McCord, for instance, had come here in the 1850s, argued her secessionist views, and snubbed the visiting President and fellow guest Millard Fillmore.[4]

In this idle world, Bennett felt free from his enervating routine of work and worry. He became a young man of leisure, reading, eating, taking naps, and socializing. He played guitar and sang. Before going to bed at night, he looked up at the stars and then slept, soothed again by the beauty and rhythm of the natural world.

Sometimes in the mornings and afternoons this "pair of Jacks," Appleton and Bennett, talked languidly;[5] they told each other tales of their pasts and shared and criticized each other's writings. They played cards, read, walked the hills, or went riding. Bennett wrote his sister Martha in Chillicothe of his happiness and success. "I have gained a pound or two," he told her, confirming the fact that he was radically underweight.[6] And to his father he confided that he was now up to 132 pounds after several weeks of gaining a pound a day. "That is encouraging."[7] "*The A[ppleton]s are my kind of people!*" he went on. "Kind, genuine, unaffected and well-informed, up to date and delightful."[8] This was as close to the South as he had ever come, and he was intrigued too by their black servants, whose dances he watched and who took to him immediately.

One afternoon, he went out along Peter's Creek on his host's horse, Don Quixote. As he looked at the mountains, a line of poetry sprung in his mind:

> These are the hills the Lord hath made,
> That man may fear him, unafraid.

"A storm had, but a moment before, broken into blinding thunderous rage and gone booming down the ranges, and on the great blue shoulders of the mountain lay the brilliant, stormy sun, strangely and almost unreally bright."

He had an epiphany, realizing he had come through his own personal storm and had emerged from a spiritual darkness. "I realized that I had attained a certain measure of sound health, strength, and what was better, peace."[9] And he thought of more verse:

Up through the gateway of the skies
Their purple slopes of peace arise
Like sunlit paths to paradise.

"Where Paradise is . . . there was no geographic knowledge. . . . But peace at heart is near it, and for those bright few months, I had . . . peace, and made a friendship that has never changed, with the bravest, calmest people I have ever met." Back at the hotel, he conjured more lines, and as he grew stronger the unfinished lines hung in his mind. He stayed on at Salt Sulphur Springs after the guests left, alone with the Appletons and their son, "the most gallant hearted boy I have ever known." He had put on forty pounds, "but better by far, I had found unaltering friends."[10]

The poem, which he called "The Magnificat of the Hills," was finished before he left and published eventually in 1894 in the *Independent*.[11] Like "In a Rose Garden," it was reprinted and anthologized numerous times over the years, helping him earn the nickname of the "James Whitcomb Riley of Southern Ohio." While never entirely disowning his poems, he did recognize their limitations. "If men liked or were moved by them it was for their simple sincerity . . . and their basic honesty of feeling [and] not for their poetical excellence of which, indeed, they have little," he admitted, quickly declaring, "I am under no delusion about them."[12] The poems expressed a personal view: "I like my verse mixed with high spirits and courage, just as life is at its best."[13]

His times at Salt Sulphur Springs were his happiest. After his first visit in 1893, he came back almost annually with his brother and some of his pals from the FBS. It was a return to the unspoiled world of his childhood before he had gone off to school and come into an envious relationship with Henry. He and his brother made up,[14] and together, with other friends, took inspiration from Howard Pyle's Robin Hood and his Merry Men: "We played at Sherwood Forest and the greenwood tree, and masked our friendship under the old familiar titles." Bennett was Little John; Henry was Will

Scarlett; other friends such as Joe Taylor and Will Poland were Robin Hood and Friar Tuck. "That was our play—to cover deep and genuine things with the light air of make believe." [15]

"We had among us what Friendship is to the Orient," he wrote. It was "a transcendent word" to them. All were young artists, some wanting to write, others paint; all "worked together with immense pleasure and mutual benefit . . . hailing each piece of good work with mutual unselfish cheers . . . and rejoicing over every sale." It was "with these three men [Henry Bennett, Joe Taylor, and Jack Appleton] and in those few years," Bennett wrote, "[that] I shared . . . more of the intense moments . . . I have ever shared with others either before those golden days or since." [16] As a team, they called themselves "The Cheerful Idiots," literally unfurling a three-colored flag with a fool's head on it and the command, "Cheer Up."

"As a newspaper worker I became a harsh and pessimistic realist," Bennett admitted, but "as a creative writer in the company of companions such as few men have ever had, I was hopelessly and well-nigh incurably romantic." [17]

The guests at the Salt Sulphur Springs reaped the rewards of their high spirits. One summer when unending rains and the death of a young girl brought on a general depression, the Cheerful Idiots presented a spoof of *Uncle Tom's Cabin*, a work still regarded with suspicion and disgust south of the Mason-Dixon line. Simon Legree was played by the gentlest soul present; Eliza, the escaping slave girl, was played by John Bennett, sporting a moustache. "The ice in the Ohio was simulated by a row of wooden soap boxes attached to a rope . . . agitated offstage by a stout boy. . . . While she perched on an 'ice block' there came floating from somewhere upstream a guitar, which she at once rescued . . . and employed to accompany herself in . . . a fine female baritone." Uncle Tom ended his days peacefully in Cincinnati, and Little Eva was not dead at all: that was "a false rumor maliciously circulated by abolitionists." [18] Over and again with such nonsense, they presented amateur theatricals at the Inn.

Later, "each lingering evening at about ten o'clock, [the cheerful Idiots or "easy streeters," as they sometimes called themselves] climbed the steps to the rooms of Colonel and Mrs. Appleton to lounge a while on the queer old chairs, the soft divan, and the wickerwork 'easies.'" As some had once listened to the stable boy Peter Dunn, now the men sat "listening to the Colonel's reminiscences of the [Civil] War and Mrs. [Appleton's] recollection of the troubled days just after when they came from Boston and had to sleep with revolvers under their pillows and . . . a gattling gun under the front hall stairs." [19] From Colonel Appleton, Bennett heard of Charleston, where he had served with the regiments of "colored troops" who had led the assault on the city from James Island in 1863.[20]

Bennett would never forget the Appletons' (or any friend's) kindness. Years later (Christmas 1911), he'd dedicate to Jack Appleton, his "dying but dauntless friend" [21] wasting away with multiple sclerosis, his most famous poem (which would decorate his bookplate, usher in the Charleston Literary Renaissance, and appear in Bartlett's *Familiar Quotations*):

> We are all but Fellow-Travelers
> Along Life's weary way.
> If any man can play the pipes,
> In God's name, let him play.

"That's my motto, if I have a motto." [22]

It was here at Salt Sulphur Springs that Bennett and his friends tried for success; and he referred to this era as glowingly as he did to his childhood in Chillicothe. "We wanted something we had not yet found, something perhaps which was not there; [but which we] . . . set out to find, each in his own way . . . in work and play, in love, [and] in . . . achievement of honest work well done. . . . In prose, verse, drawing, painting, in line and in color, and in unselfish . . . friendship . . . [we] found our golden days.

"In the pitiful, magnificent madness of youth we loved, romanced, dreamed, worked and played . . . we had our try at it, . . . our fling. Wanting so much . . . [we aimed for] work done as well as our skill could make it . . . something that would last, a little while . . . 'just for fun.'" [23]

After leaving Kenyon College, Henry Holcomb Bennett drifted from job to job, perhaps having been spoiled by success that had come too early; he also had problems with alcohol. But he eventually found himself, following in his younger brother's footsteps, finding newspaper work back in Chillicothe and, like John, publishing works in *St. Nicholas*. He would find his niche, and be hailed as one of America's best patriotic poets, for his 1898 verse, "Hats Off the Flag Is Passing By." [24] Henry would eventually admit, "The Dutchman was right after all; thorough's the way." It "warmed my heart and thrilled me through," Bennett confessed, hearing it.[25] Joe Russell

Taylor, wanting to be an artist, painted and drew and eventually became dean of the English Department at Ohio State University. Jack Appleton, author of a few books of poetry, saw his promise sputter and fade as he wasted away.

Of all of them, John Bennett came closest to success. With the Cheerful Idiots at Salt Sulphur Springs in the summer of 1895, he hearkened back to another time of good fellowship—the Elizabethan era of Ben Jonson, Christopher Marlowe, and William Shakespeare. He used it for a children's story he hoped "would last, a little while . . . just for fun."

CHAPTER 7

# *Master Skylark*

THE CHILDREN'S STORY Bennett worked on at Salt Sulphur Springs owed its origins to many things: Bennett's life history, Chillicothe, his sister, and *St. Nicholas* magazine. Ever since first being accepted in 1891, Bennett had been contributing more often to the magazine. His correspondence with editor Tudor Jenks and Alexander Drake of the art department was very encouraging. Once with a gap to fill, the editors wrote, asking if he had anything on hand to send in.[1] Anxious to please, he immediately dashed off a poem, "The Knight, the Yeomanne, and the Fair Damosel." If the verses were suitable, he wrote back, he would send along the accompanying silhouettes.

"Verses accepted," the company wired.

"I drew all day; I drew all night"; he made the deadline for mailing the silhouettes.[2] The relationship flourished. Editor Mary Mapes Dodge and her prim assistant, William Fayal Clarke, requested first refusal of all Bennett's works, eventually telling him, "We are desirous . . . that you should feel identified with *St. Nicholas*."[3]

Encouraged, Bennett wrote a short story in 1895 called "His Father's Price." The time he chose was medieval England, but the theme was more contemporary and closer to his heart. It is a tribute (and yet also a chastisement) of a son to his father. They both suffer for their stubborn courage, honesty, and integrity. Studded with archaic language (which required footnotes) but marked with an authenticity of time and sentiment, it was accepted immediately (although not published until May 1896 in an issue that also contained a poem by Henry Holcomb Bennett). The work brought Bennett high praise from the editorial offices, and he started on another tale set in the same time period, which he titled "1327" but never finished.

Bennett sent a copy of "His Father's Price" to his sister Martha Trimble Bennett. He always sought her critical advice because she had good ideas and because he, the high school dropout, was both proud of and somewhat in awe of her scholarship. Like Alice and Henry, she did not marry;[4] in 1894–95, in her late twenties, she was at Radcliffe College pursuing a graduate degree in English.

In the past, they had discussed medieval and Elizabethan England. Reacting to "His Father's Price," she wrote, "I have a plan for a story or an idea for a situation which strikes me as a new and interesting field for a short story. If you like the idea, I will gather a little 'local color' while I am here, and we can talk it over this summer. Let me know what you think of it. It may not strike you as useable; but to me it is a singularly attractive setting." He read on and realized at once that she was right.

"[As] you know, the 'Children's Company of Players' were recruited from all parts of England, partly, at times, by force. Wouldn't it be a good idea to have a little Eliz[abethan] fellow kidnapped and made into a choirboy in London, to act in the plays? He could be summoned to the court and there play before [Queen] Elizabeth—perhaps speak the prologue and be noticed by her—I could give you a few points on it."[5]

It was April 1895 when her letter reached him. He was engaged in the stressful grind of freelance writing, which brought about a period of sleeplessness. A night or two after reading his sister's letter, as he lay tossing and turning in his childhood bed, he heard the clock in the Ross County courthouse strike 2:00 A.M.. Knowing that he would probably not sleep, he cast about for the most pleasant thing to think about.

He turned to his sister Martha and her recent idea. "I began to revolve its plot and structure mentally; I found myself having an unexpectedly delightful time; the topic waked my imagination, and called up a period always brilliantly enjoyable to me. Plot and characters began to wake, and a background [rose] from the subliminal."[6]

He pictured a lad of about eleven running away from his father's demands, as perhaps he himself had been tempted to run away from Chillicothe. Instead of art school, the boy wants to leave Stratford to see a troupe of actors in nearby Coventry. Going without his father's permission, the boy and a friend suddenly behold a wondrous sight—a "Master Player" who is also on his way to Coventry; he has been separated from the troupe, having spent the previous night in Stratford jail for insulting the Master Bailiff. The player overhears the little boy defending the honor of Will Shakespeare; the boy is related to the actor/dramatist by his mother's kinship to Anne Hathaway. Delighted by the lad's defense, the Master Player offers to take him to Coventry with him. As they travel together, the boy sings a song he learned from his mother. His voice is so entrancing, it gives the Master Player an idea. "I'll do it," he soliloquizes, "I'll have it out of Master [Bailiff] Stubbes and canting Stratford town! . . . I'll do it—I will, upon my word, and on the remnant of my honor!"[7] The little boy does not know what he means, but the plot has begun to assert itself.

The Elizabethan setting and language came naturally to Bennett; for years he had been carrying notebooks around with him (so much so the Cheerful Idiots called him "Old Notebooks" one summer at Salt Sulphur Springs).[8] In these he recorded "curious and sparkling bits of information . . . [on] the unregarded corners of life centuries ago, particularly . . . the days of Elizabeth."[9] And from his father, who always had a ready quote, he had learned an appreciation of Shakespeare.

Many knew such things, but bringing Shakespeare into the plot, albeit tangentially, was Bennett's idea, not his sister's. A century later it was quite common to employ historical characters such as Sigmund Freud or Stanford White in bestselling works, but the idea of including and representing them realistically was unusual in the 1890s. Bennett would always be ahead of his time; this would often lead to his being castigated by publishers and the public, but at this point he succeeded brilliantly.

As he tossed and turned in bed, bits of remembered lore from his notebooks and his reading flooded up. April in Chillicothe became April in England; he imagined "the piping of birds in white-thorn hedges, the hollow lowing of kine . . . and the long rush of the river through the sedge beside the pebbly shore."[10] Suddenly there were more and more ideas.

"These progressed so fast, and imagination sped so pleasantly . . . that I dared not let them escape. I rose, closed my doors against disturbing the house, lighted my lamp, took pad and pencil, and began to set out a skeleton plot, scenario and cast of characters. These took form and shape so rapidly that I wrote all night, sketching in several scenes in the rough. By morning the story had so taken form that I saw at once not a simple short story, but [the] possibility of a book."[11]

Bennett went on with his chores around the house, taking care of his parents, tending to his "for-order" writing; but all the while he kept his mind on his project like a tune hummed under his breath. The project seemed to develop by itself. He came up with a name for the boy: Nick Attwood, "Nick" having been a friend of his who had lived across the street, and

"Attwood" from cousins in the family.[12] Gaston Carew, the Master Player, owed his name to the Gaston family of Chillicothe;[13] and though Bennett never acknowledged an origin for the surname Carew, perhaps it came from the name of Walter Raleigh's son. Carew's psychological profile could have evolved from tales John Briscoe Bennett told of his stepfather, Hilary Talbot.

Nick sings with great success in Carew's play in Coventry; then he is told he is being taken home but slowly realizes that he and the players are heading, not to Stratford, but toward London. Carew, in need of money, and wanting to punish Stratford for jailing him, has hit upon the idea of using the boy in his troupe for his Skylark's voice. Bennett had chosen the title by May 8.[14]

The tale, in his mind's eye, developed not just chronologically but psychologically as well. At first, he portrayed Nick excited to be with Carew— how could he not be? Carew treats him wonderfully, continually telling him, "I love thee, lad." Only slowly does the boy come to see that he has been kidnapped and, through Carew's clever psychological manipulation of him, he is being kept from returning to his family.

He tries to flee but is captured, tricked, and taken to London. His character grows, and he is shown to have more depth, as he becomes homesick for his mother yet nevertheless intrigued by the glamor and excitement of the big city. Back home, Nick's father believes that Nick has deliberately run away instead of being kidnapped. Simon Attwood disowns his son, and that is why no one sets out to look for him. This situation drives the plot but also very cannily allows children to enjoy Nick's pleasures in London, without having Nick (or his readers) feel guilty or remiss for deserting or hurting the family. This complex and contradictory situation may also shed some light on Bennett's own feelings when he dreamed of being an artist while kept back against his will in Chillicothe. (And indeed, his father would come to question Bennett about Simon Attwood, seeing glimpses of himself in the character; Bennett would reply that it was "pure nonsense. . . . I . . . have . . . too much pride . . . to so caricature . . . my own blood kin.")[15] He shows Nick longing for home yet nevertheless enjoying London, perfecting his art—as perhaps Bennett himself may have longed to follow his dream—instead of staying at home, a slave to duty.

He endowed Nick with some of his own childhood memories and conflicts, while the hero/villain Carew seemed to evolve magically. He's not entirely evil (that is the role of his second in command, his groom Gregory Goole); he's plagued with regret and remorse and his love for the boy, resulting in a typically adult hypocrisy, which Nick, as a boy, cannot fathom in the least. Carew is trapped between the remnant of his honor, upon which he constantly swears, and his need for money, which he is not amassing entirely for himself but for his motherless daughter Cecily.

To round out Carew, Bennett visualized him and gave him real-life qualities of those he knew. Carew's trick of opening and shutting his eyes, for instance, came from Wash(ington) Hall, Chillicothe's policeman who fancied himself rather like Louis Napoleon.[16]

So intriguing did Carew become that a generation later the critic Thomas Beer would call him the book's crowning achievement in his work *The Mauve Decade*, a send-up of the 1890s era. (Whistler's comment that "Mauve is just pink trying to be purple" serves as the book's epigram and sums up its gleeful and malicious look at the decade of the nineties.) Although he'd sneer at nearly all children's stories in popular magazines and call Nick Attwood a sort of pale Little Lord Fauntleroy, Beer would relent and admit that Nick does become real when he starts showing his love for his mother and his homesickness. Grudgingly allowing that, Beer nevertheless believed that children's attraction to the dishonorable Carew accounted for the book's popularity.[17] Whether or not that is true cannot be gauged, but Carew *is* the truly superior creation of the tale, the person whose villainy and heroism create most of the tension and drive the action.

Inspired by a tale that seemed to tell itself, and believing that vitality in literature comes not from "novelty of approach but in honesty and authenticity," Bennett continued to look at his townsfolk and to ransack his old notebooks.[18] More and more of his known and remembered worlds surfaced into the imaginary one he was creating. Reginald Birch, the artist who'd win mothers' hearts and young boys' disgust with his rendering of the suit of clothes in Frances Hodgson Burnett's *Little Lord Fauntleroy*, was commissioned to illustrate *Master Skylark* and told Bennett, "You visualize scenes and characters so vividly that anyone with a draughtsman's fancy, reading your text, sees at once the vision you have attempted to record, and finds its depiction easy."[19] He'd also illustrate "His Father's Price" in *St. Nicholas* (Bennett would only do drawings for his poetry and pieces of whimsy). Asked later in life which of his illustrations he considered his best, Birch would reply, "not *Fauntleroy*, but *Master Skylark*."[20]

It was not just vision Bennett brought to his tale but revision as well. "There is not a page of Master Skylark which was not rewritten again and again, not one less than three or four times, some even thirty times, until . . . the result was the best I could do."[21] Again, it was his Dutchman's persistence; he had to prove his story's worth to himself. When he couldn't sleep, he wrote late at night; and when he grew tired, he walked the streets at dawn, retrieving and writing on the back of July 4 excursion bills on the morning of the fifth. He also used the backs of Century Company rejection slips. Then, as the height of summer and the hay fever season approached, he went off to Salt Sulphur Springs as he had been doing the past few years. There he worked on his manuscript, encouraged by the other "Cheerful Idiots."

Having Nick in London now, Bennett allowed him the sights of the town, losing him in the fog of the Thames and also in the perplexing mists of human behavior. In London Nick is taken up and petted by Carew's daughter Cecily, who, having seen only her father's good side, loves him blindly. Nick cannot understand this and finds himself causing pain to Cecily by frankly airing his unhappy feelings about her father.

Carew enrolls the boy in St. Paul's choir, where he is trained to act and sing, and for this Carew is paid handsomely. He counts the boy's earnings out into separate piles, rhyming, "One for me, and one for thee, and two for Cecily Carew," showing his divided loyalties in his figuring.[22]

In London, it is the common folk who cheer Nick and toss him coins when he sings (as commoners cheered Jack Bennett in his newspaper days in Chillicothe.) The boy sings from his heart; his songs are joyful and buoyant but touched with longing for his mother. The bandy-legged Gregory Goole, with malevolent leer, grizzled cheeks, and a piratical ribbon in his ear, prevents him from escaping to his kinsman William Shakespeare, whose theater is near the river.

At Christmas Nick and the rest of the St. Paul's boys are ferried by river (as Martha Bennett suggested) to Queen Elizabeth; he and a boy named Colley sing a duet of the coming of spring that hushes the assembly. Moved by its beauty, Queen Elizabeth offers them positions as pages in her court; the orphaned Colley accepts eagerly, but Nick says he cannot stay in such a place.

"Thy comrade hath more wit," the queen answers Nick angrily.

"He hath no mother," Nick replies; "I would rather have my mother than his wit."[23]

Elizabeth, stung into remembrance of her own dead mother Anne Boleyn, is touched; she says he is no fool after all but is like a stubborn dog for resisting all her badgering. As Bennett's own father had told him, she says to Nick, "Brag is a good dog, but Hold-fast is better."[24] So Elizabeth sets him free; he's going back to his mother, she thinks, but it's really back to Gaston Carew.

Realizing the importance of this crucial scene, Bennett knew it had to be good. So, he only sketched it in on his race to the tale's conclusion. With Nick back from St. Paul's, Carew now has no opportunity for cashing in on Nick's singing. Like Hilary Talbot, he grows depressed, drinks, and takes up gambling. He inadvertently stabs and kills a man for cheating at cards, and he is whisked off to prison.

The fracas gives Nick an opportunity to escape—and he finds his cousin, Will Shakespeare. The playwright, busy with seeing to the printing and staging of his works, promises to take the boy back to Stratford. Shakespeare then hears that Carew is in prison. He has asked for the boy, so Nick is taken to the dismal, chilly place where, chastened and apologetic, Carew begs Nick to look after Cecily; then Carew asks for Shakespeare.

Nick goes for Cecily but finds she has been kidnapped by Gregory Goole, who plans to ransom her back to Carew for all of the money he made from Nick; Goole does not know where it is hidden. Nick tricks Cecily away from Goole in a mob scene of London apprentices vowing to make her May Queen (a nice irony here, since it was on May Day the year before in Stratford that Nick ran off to see the play in Coventry).

Nick takes Cecily to find Will Shakespeare, but the playwright, confused by the boy's disappearance, has already left for Stratford. Nick and Cecily make their own way through small towns, charming the common folk with their singing. They arrive in Stratford and Nick, seeing his father, runs to him. But Simon Attwood is too angry and too proud to take him back. Cecily, ignorant of her father's imprisonment and his sentence to hang, cries out that her father is better after all.

Now Shakespeare and his men intervene. They convince Attwood that the boy was kidnapped against his will and that he kept trying to find his way home. Attwood apologizes and says he'll take his boy back and the girl, too, though his business has failed and they are facing poverty. Again Will Shakespeare intervenes.

Being a good friend, he tells how he obeyed Gaston Carew's summons to prison. Carew told him where the money Nick made was hidden; Shakespeare turns it over to the family and furthermore asks Attwood to act as his agent and occupy the large house in Stratford he has just purchased. In one move, Nick's father is shown that art, as represented by his wife's playwright cousin and his son, can be practiced by those worthy of respect; moreover, art's returns can save a family from poverty. Thus, on a number of levels, Bennett neatly resolves the story. There is a happy ending; children readers have been allowed to picture a wonderful adventure, free of parents, through no fault of their own; and Bennett depicts his own wish coming true: a boy who follows his artistic impulse manages to save his family, which is exactly what Nick and Carew's creator was hoping. For, with the encouragement of his friends at Salt Sulphur Springs, Bennett began to think again of taking up his old dream. Could he, he wondered, finally leave Chillicothe for New York and study at the Art Students' League? Now that his writing was going well, he might be able to use its proceeds to study drawing.

Tempting him further were a number of things. He had come to a crucial point on May 17 of that year, his thirtieth birthday—"when a man is old enough to have had experience and to have demonstrated his ability, and young enough not to have yet begun to slow down." [25] His sister Martha no longer needed his support; with her splendid education she could be an independent woman in an era that did not have many: having taken honors in English at Radcliffe, she'd teach first in Ohio and then move to Massachusetts, where she'd head the English department of the girls' preparatory school, Dana Hall in Wellesley. Brother Henry was now home in Chillicothe, in a secure job with a newspaper. He and Alice could take care of their parents. So maybe now it was his turn to leave.

Alexander Drake, head of the Century art department, had been encouraging him to do so for years; Drake had asked Bennett what type of training he had received. When he found out Bennett had little to none, he was amazed. With such natural talent, he should definitely get schooling. [26]

*Master Skylark* seemed the key. Looking it over, and reading it aloud that summer in Salt Sulphur Springs, Bennett saw it was good. But it was only two-thirds done; he had an ending, but the climactic scenes like Carew in prison and Nick singing before Queen Elizabeth were merely sketched in. Thus, in the fall of 1895, he and his hero Nicholas Attwood were in the same situation; both had a rough past behind them and an ending in view. Both were facing an unwritten climactic scene of how to reach their dreams. Gambling, Bennett sent his unfinished manuscript off to *St. Nicholas.*

It was first read by Samuel Austin Chapin, who passed it with a strong recommendation to Mary Mapes Dodge. Chapin wrote her that if the missing parts could be filled in, the serial was bound to be a success. Dodge agreed and, according to Bennett, this was the first time in the history of the magazine that a serial was accepted for publication before it was finished. Six hundred dollars was the price mentioned for it,[27] but the price was to rise higher eventually.[28] It was enough to tide him over, so he went to New York.

He left in late 1895 or early 1896 and found the metropolis overpowering. The effect the city had on him was both frightening and inspiring. To filter out his unhappiness, he focused his attentions on succeeding in the Art Students' League; he enrolled immediately, beginning a process that would take two to four years to finish; one did not earn a degree.

Anyone could begin at the League by just showing up and taking the preparatory class, for which one paid monthly fees. Only after instructors approved could one advance to the antique class, which Bennett achieved quickly, winning permission by April 6, 1896, and being allowed in by the thirteenth.[29]

Here he found himself in a large room filled with statues and plaster casts; students were told to draw arms and legs before advancing to full-figure drawings. He and his classmates were only treated to live models once every other week; in composition class, the instructor would announce a monthly theme. All worked on a drawing and sat by nervously as, on judgment day, the instructor passed, dispensing comments; at this monthly concours, usually one student, the one judged creator of the best drawing, would "transcend" to the third and highest level—the "life class." Here students were treated to live models every day; when one was deemed proficient, the "degree" conferred was just membership in the League; this distinction was enough to earn one a job as a full-time illustrator, a dream that had lured all the hundreds of students to New York City.

Most of those enrolled were in their early twenties, "young men with hopeful expressions and hopeless pockets," as a graduate of this era termed them; they were "apt to let their hair grow long like musicians and football players." The women, however, wore high collared dresses and pulled-back hair and followed "the strictest decorum"; among them were a few "old maids [the class] . . . called 'the white cats' all the blood in their faces having been worked away by years of study." [30] Students from all over the country attended, usually about six hundred on any given day, about twelve hundred individuals a year; Bennett stuck out because of his age and because of his talents. His teachers found him completely ignorant of the basic rudiments of drawing, yet he could somehow "fairly paint with a pen." [31]

"Some says I am clever," he wrote his father of it, "some says I'm a genius—I says I'm a Jack of All Trades and get there just the same." [32] To combat his homesickness, he wrote home often, still feeling out of place in the bustling, anonymous city. He was forced by circumstance and dwindling funds to move from one apartment to another, calling himself "the loneliest young fellow in the western hemisphere." [33] In a boarding house on West 55th Street, with no water in the pipes and holes in his mattress, he said his teeth "fairly chattered with loneliness." [34]

But with his outgoing, unassuming ways he made friends at the League. He and other students shared lunches together and much "jolly companionship." [35] There were balls and monthly parties. Two of his friends were Valentine Kirby and Rollin Kirby (no relation), whom he and the other students called Big and Little Kirby. [36] Worried over Bennett losing weight, the Kirbys bought éclairs, which they placed in his apartment.

Like Bennett, Rollin Kirby had come from the Midwest in hopes of changing his life, but at the end of his first year he received an ominous letter from his father calling him back. Kirby, in a panic, appealed to Bennett who, in his eyes, was someone his father would respect due to his published status and his contract with *St. Nicholas*. So Bennett, borrowing some of the rhetorical flourishes he had used to embellish the speeches of the orator he did not actually hear, wrote the boy's father and convinced him to allow young Kirby to stay in New York City. There he continued his studies and eventually won Pulitzer Prizes in 1922, 1925, and 1929 for his political cartoons. [37]

Bennett also made friends with the staff of the Century Company, once he mustered up his courage to visit their august offices. It was not easy for "an awkward, shy, uncertain fellow, shrunk to an atom in the sophistication of a great city." [38] The first time he approached the building he lost heart and turned away, circling Union Square. But then he went in, crossed the lobby, swallowed hard, and screwed up enough courage to take the elevator up to the "fatal floor." Every face of every doorman and copy boy he encountered assumed a look as "fierce as an Assyrian door-guard."[39] As soon as Bennett entered the office and sent his name forward, Tudor Jenks, sitting at his desk, sipping lemonade and eating peanuts, waved him in.

Jenks, after taking a degree in law, had gone to Paris to study art. Returning to New York, he had become a writer instead and was as famous for his dozens of children's books on history, literature, and patriotic subjects as he was for his witty conversation and improbable antics. Jenks smiled as Bennett introduced himself.

"Well, well, well," Jenks said, looking him up and down. "So this is Jack Bennett, from Chillicothe." He narrowed his eyes. "Well, well. Why I had confidentially expected to have you come stalking in the room with your sombrero and leather chaps on and two guns tied down to your pants-leg, demanding revenge for the latest insult in tones of fire and wrath. And here, why you're just as mild mannered a man as ever scuttled a ship or cut a throat. Sit down, let's analyze the situation."[40] Bennett gasped, sat, and accepted a peanut. They became friends instantly. Tudor Jenks would eventually help edit *Master Skylark* and doodle his trademark nonsense drawings in the margins.

When not engaged at the League with his own artwork, Bennett spent time writing and researching Elizabethan England in the New York Public Library. He drove himself to exhaustion, reaching a point when he felt he could not go on. He asked Martha to step in and collaborate with him, but she knew him, she said: she had faith in his ability to finish it himself.

After much self-doubt, Bennett did finish, turning in a revised draft of the manuscript by March 24, 1896. It still had spots that troubled him—especially the key scene of Nick singing before Queen Elizabeth. "I had written that scene over and over again, worse each writing: and more wooden and lifeless; it had no thrill, no charm, no nothing."[41] He summed it up more succinctly elsewhere, stating, "I write and write and too much of what I've writ is rot."[42]

To take his mind off his failure, Bennett went with friends from the Century Company to hear the Australian coloratura soprano, Nellie Melba, sing. For such an unsophisticate, sitting in the darkness of the Metropolitan Opera House, listening to Donizetti's *Lucia di Lammermoor*, was a marvelous experience. All he wanted to do was soar with her and forget everything, but suddenly, as Melba sang "the mad scene . . . with harp and flute obligato in the orchestra, the thing came spinning out of the big black place where such things abide, and just as I wanted it."

He grabbed a pen and "wrote around the edge of my program, and was beginning to write on my white cuff, when a young woman sitting next [to me] tore a bunch of leaves out of a small notebook and silently handed them to me, evidently thinking me a reporter . . . in a jam. I wrote as Melba sang, and afterwards found what I had written that afternoon was exactly what I wanted for Nick's singing before the Queen, voice, harp and flute . . . together."[43] At the end of the performance he looked for the woman to thank her, but she had disappeared.

Having begun on a sleepless night in Chillicothe, the story was finished in a New York opera house. Better than he had thought it could be, he wanted to renegotiate the terms with *St. Nicholas.* "Saturday I made up my mind . . . that I would ask one thousand dollars for it," he told his family. "I did so Monday . . . and it was given without a kick. Mrs. Dodge said many very nice things . . . and Mr. Clarke is to reserve all rights for me, . . . for he thinks there are good possibilities . . . for . . . the stage."

Lest his family back home not realize what this meant, he told them, "They have never paid one thousand dollars for anybody's first serial before this . . . unless it was one . . . of someone already famous." He also told them that "Tudor Jenks has begun to cultivate me in earnest. . . . A man who has sold his first serial to 'St. Nicholas' for one thousand dollars is worth cultivating."[44]

Exhausted and thrilled, Bennett went home to recuperate from his busy year and visit his family. A letter came from the Century Company, however, requesting some changes in his manuscript. Nick and Cecily's trek home to Stratford worried William Fayal Clarke, Dodge's assistant. "He niggled over inessentials, hesitated over decisions, and shrank from innocent situations. . . . He suggested a chaperon for Nick and Cecily Carew . . . lest someone suggest an impropriety in the association of those two children."[45] Bennett refused, allowing the children to make their way safely home without the aid of adults, who had caused most of the problems.

As originally written, they arrived back home in Stratford at a feast that had been prepared for Shakespeare. "And then, when the boy's mother came to where he was, the while of that long, bitter year, was nothing anymore to Nick." [46] So Bennett had originally ended his manuscript; but the Century Company, again unwisely, requested more, saying it stopped too abruptly.

Bennett thought a bit. "I remember I walked from my mother's room where I had been sitting, into my own; my old Remington no. 2 sat on the table by the wall under the bookcase; I sat down, and after a moment's thought, wrote the ending passages as they stand [a long maudlin tribute to mother's love]. What I wrote was to my mother put in Nick Attwood's mouth.

" 'There,' I said to my sister, 'if that will do, they may have it. I will write no more.'

" 'It will do,' she replied. And it did." [47]

*Master Skylark* ran as a serial in *St. Nicholas Magazine* from November 1896 until October 1897 and was immediately published afterward to catch the fall trade. The public, having enjoyed it in the magazine, now rushed forward to catch it in book form; they were urged on by the critics. The reviewer for the *Chicago Tribune* complimented Bennett's work in its "delineation of character and its portrayal of the romance of the Elizabethan Age"; [48] the *Boston Daily Advertiser* called it "one of the best published this season" and indulged in prophecy, stating that " 'Master Skylark' is certain to be widely read and deserves success." [49]

Another commented that, "Although written for children, 'Master Skylark' appeals in a remarkable manner to the mature mind. . . . Mr. Bennett's book is a rare and delightful treat; as a study of England in the times of Queen Bess and some of her famous subjects, it is valuable as well as entertaining, and as an example of pure literature, it is a brilliant piece of work." [50]

It is. Humor, erudition and psychological insight distinguish it; and much of the writing is delightfully sly. Characters constantly paraphrase the playwright or toss off his own words so aptly that one hardly notices. Bennett suddenly found himself famous for his storytelling skills, his visual knack, and his precise scholarship.

He had conjured up Stratford and London successfully and accurately in names of streets and placement of buildings; people and clothing and ways of life that had bad been gone for nearly three centuries appeared new and vivid. He had, in fact, done his research so well that Shakespearean scholars could find little fault with it. One German Shakespeare scholar did note that the jester, Will Armin, who appears briefly, had died before the reign of Elizabeth. Bennett had known that but had included him anyway.

Another error was pointed out only by a descendant of the manager of the troupe that played with Shakespeare. Contemporary documents had called him Jack Condell; Bennett did as well. But when a family member wrote Bennett to say he had been baptized Henry, he had it amended in later editions.[51]

The other mistake, another deliberate anachronism on Bennett's part, was his use of the phrase "As fast as you can say Jack Robinson," which had not yet appeared in common usage. Bennett kept waiting to be called on it, but no one did.[52]

Nor were there any complaints about the story. Read today by the great-grandchildren of the original readers, *Master Skylark* still entrances. "It is a story of human emotions, principally of love—the love of Nick Attwood for his mother, the love of Gaston Carew for his daughter. It is also a story of courage and fidelity, as well as of greed and faithlessness and cruelty, antithetical qualities often found in the same person," Alice Hogan wrote for the paperback edition bringing the book to children in the 1960s. In Canada, the book appeared in a school edition, complete with questions and thoughts for discussions.

"In addition to all its other attributes," Hogan wrote, "*Master Skylark* is, finally, a first rate adventure story—dramatic, exciting, suspenseful, well-constructed, with quickly shifting scenes, laced with practical philosophy, as well as beauty."[53] "Master Skylark is easily one of the nineteenth century's premier works of historical fiction," wrote another scholar long after Bennett's death.[54] If the period had only produced it, other literary historians noted, it would have still been notable. "*Skylark* remains unsurpassed. It is exuberant with the abundant life, exultant with the creative work, delicately responsive to the sense of beauty which made the Elizabethan age glorious. It is crowded with characters and events, but never confusing; filled with details, but never exhausting. It is written with a sensitivity that makes the reading of it an experience to be coveted, And through it all breathes the spirit that is uniquely forever England."[55]

Soon after its appearance in America, *Master Skylark* crossed the Atlantic. It was published in England and translated eventually into German, Dutch,

Portuguese, Braille, Russian, and Polish. Edition after edition was printed until it became the bestselling children's work the Century Company ever published.[56] It was dramatized so many times Bennett lost track, and in 1916 was staged over the world to celebrate the three hundredth anniversary of Shakespeare's death. In later years, it was to be heard on the radio and sold to the movies. Eventually the American Library Association was to recommended it; it would be called a milestone in American literature, would make the One Hundred Best Children's Books list,[57] and would be included in *Peter Parley to Penrod*, the list of the best and most collectible American children's books considered to be classics.[58] And what perhaps is most telling is that one hundred years after it first appeared, *Books in Print* still lists it. Upon its publication, Bennett and *Master Skylark* became synonymous; he had a name now in New York, in Ohio, and among children all over the country. After years of struggling, he was a success at last. So well known was *Skylark* that Dodge and the Century Company cannily encouraged him to quickly follow up its success with another book; they'd promote it heavily, they promised, and publish it first as a serial in *St. Nicholas*.

Bennett felt he couldn't let the opportunity pass. Casting about for an idea, he quickly decided to write a tale of another heroic boy, a boy born to riches in Virginia but who lost them, his mother, and the rest of his family in Missouri; he'd struggle against odds and complete his rites of passage in Buckhorn Ironworks, where he would be known by the name of Buckhorn Johnny. If *Master Skylark* was the tribute of a boy's love to his mother, this new one would honor his father, John Briscoe Bennett.

"Just you hold your horses . . . until . . . I get 'Buckhorn Johnny' builded into the best little tale of the Scioto Valley that ever shall be written," he wrote his father. "It is a story worth the telling."[59]

But the Century Company disagreed. When staff heard of Bennett's plans, they were less than enthusiastic. They felt it was too different, "that no one would be interested in the midwest." If he wanted to do an American story, they wanted one that would appeal to the same readers of *Skylark*, so they suggested one approximately contemporary with it and "possessing the same style and atmosphere."[60]

So if he couldn't write his father's life, he'd do the next best thing. Growing up, his father had praised him for his stubborn persistence by calling him a Dutchman, based on their descent from Gerrit van Sweringen, the sheriff of New Amstel (now Dover, Delaware). So Bennett decided cockily to write of the Sweringen line of his father's family. It was about as close to Skylark's era, in the United States, as one could get.

He had to do research, for unlike his previous familiarity with Elizabethan England, Bennett knew little of the history of Dutch New Amsterdam. But here he was, fortunately, in New York City. He began spending day after day at the New York Public Library, beginning not just a new book but a lifelong fascination with research and history. To master the time period and get his tale told, he knew that he had much hard steady work ahead of him; it meant, he realized with a sinking heart, that to keep writing, which offered him the best way to make a living, he'd have to give up drawing at the Art Students' League. "I did so under protest and with inward regret, feeling something fatal in so doing."

It was hard. "But one must make one's way as chance offers fair opportunity"; his need was both great and "immediate to follow up the critical victory of 'Skylark.' I laid my drawing aside. . . . It seemed chance. It was Fate, I guess." [61]

He felt uneasy, and the thought was bittersweet. "Yet I shall always do a little drawing in one way or another," he noted to a new friend. "I love the very shape of things in the world," he said, "and trying to reproduce them is a passion for me." He told his correspondent how it had been that way ever since he had first won attention and was "'kept in' at recess, on my first day of public school for filling my slate full of soldiers instead of with stories." [62] It was fate at play again, for it was to the person who would shape his future that he was telling his past. He was writing to a young girl from South Carolina named Susan Smythe.

PART TWO

# Summer

CHAPTER 8

# *"I Am Glad People Like Me"*

THEY HAD MET in the summer of 1894 at Salt Sulphur Springs; taking off to read, he stumbled, hunter and fawn, upon a girl "patiently and with indomitable courage drinking nauseous iodine water, at an unfrequented spring house, a little Greek Temple in a vale." [1]

She looked up; Susan Smythe, just a "slip of girl" with large hazel eyes, about sixteen years old, was visiting with her parents from Charleston, South Carolina. Having been raised strictly, she knew only to speak on certain things, especially with young men, even though he was significantly older than she at twenty-nine. As guest of the inn's owners, however, he was intriguing—one of the most popular young men on the premises. With his serene, regular features, fair hair, blue eyes, and polite way of speaking, he was handsome and interesting. They spoke a bit, perhaps about the book he was reading, and then he left. Later, on one of the walks, in a dining room or lobby, he met her parents. Augustine Smythe was a tall handsome man with graying, curly hair and blue eyes. Having fought for the Confederacy, he was now a man of circumstance and substance, a state senator and attorney; his striking aristocratic wife Louisa McCord was the daughter and namesake of South Carolina's preeminent antebellum female writer, who had visited the Springs in the pre-war years championing the cause of the South. If her daughter had been at the inn the season the Cheerful Idiots had presented their farce on *Uncle Tom's Cabin*, one wonders what she would have thought of it—and him. In 1853, McCord had published a scalding review of Harriet Beecher Stowe's book. "Over this, their new-laid egg, the abolitionists . . . have set up so astounding a cackle," she wrote. "It is very evident . . . they think the goose has laid its golden egg at last." But she found it "an old addle[d] thing, whose touch contaminates with its filth." [2]

That was water under the bridge in the 1890s, he hoped, as was the fact that cousins of Bennett's had occupied Lang Syne, the McCord family plantation, during the Civil War.[3] Not realizing this, Mrs. Smythe smiled along with her husband at the personable young man. The major soon commissioned two watercolor paintings and paid, also, for a drawing of the initials of their daughter Susan.[4]

After the Smythes left, Bennett and the major corresponded. Bennett "wrote a good letter," and Smythe, impressed and well-connected, passed two of Bennett's to the local press; the editor obligingly printed them verbatim on November 25, 1894, under the heading "Charming Letters from an Artist at the Old Salt." "The Champagne in the Atmosphere of the West Virginia Mountains Babbles in Every Line and Sparkles in Every Phrase," the headline ran infelicitously.[5] In closing, Bennett had noted, "My health is excellent; thanks for Miss Susan's wishes for it." He was chagrined when he read the published version the major sent him; for in this Victorian era of shielding women, a lady's name, it was thought, should appear in print only twice: to announce her wedding and then her death. "If Miss Susan can forgive the proof-reader who left her name [in]," he wrote, "I can certainly forgive the funny combination of circumstances which resulted in my appearing as a shining light in epistolary art."[6]

The Major and Mrs. Smythe showed their approval of Bennett by allowing him to correspond with their daughter. So he wrote "Miss Smythe" rather self-consciously—as if he knew his letters were being read. (Such, in fact, was the practice in the Bennett family, one member passing a letter to another.) It was very formal, a sort of question-and-answer match going on across the distance; once when he asked Susan her opinion of his art, she answered that it was "rather a hard task to give a poor unpracticed *polite* person who never speaks her mind."[7]

Under the formal veneer of their letter writing, they were getting to know each other, Bennett feeling freer after a while to call her "Miss Susan" and finally "Miss Suzy." The tone he achieved was jocose and courtly, and she wrote back noting how everyone at the inn had liked him. "I am glad people like me," he told her once. "Upon my word, I think I would rather have it put on my tombstone just plainly so: 'Men loved him everywhere,' than 'He did this or that.'"[8]

But he had done something; he was now well known for *Master Skylark*; children (and adults) in Charleston loved it; Edwin DuBose Heyward, or "DuBose" as all called him, a friend of Susan's nephews, seven years younger than she, liked the book tremendously. As an adult he'd say, "I turn to it today with the same thrill I experienced then."[9]

Bennett and Susan's relationship continued in letters over the years; they met again face to face when the Smythes visited New York City while he was there writing. She was now nineteen, and their correspondence had matured too. "I shall . . . take the pleasure of calling upon you," he wrote her frankly;[10] and he also frankly shared with her the difficulties he was having writing his new book.

He had thought its composition would be easy; he had confidently promised the manuscript to the Century Company and *St. Nicholas* by March or April 1898. But very soon he was telling Susan Smythe (if not his editors) that the book was taking "generations to finish"; he was, however, resigned to it, explaining solemnly that "I was meant to be a slow, painstaking, cautious, careful workman, and know no other way."[11] Although that certainly was true, the real reason for the slow pace was that he did not know where his story was going.

Having started the book with no definite scenario or plot in mind, only with the idea of employing New Amsterdam as a setting and his ancestor Gerrit van Sweringen as a character, he inevitably bogged down. So instead of writing, he spent his time researching the times and atmosphere. If he found something of interest, he used it. As a result, the story spread out like a spill in various directions, instead of running directed in a channeled narrative stream. He worried, despaired, and developed health problems; he suffered from hay fever, other ailments, and allergies; he complained of "excruciating headaches . . . for a period of twelve months or more . . . relieved only by dangerous . . . drugs," a reference to cocaine most likely, which he again started using.[12]

Another health problem was a case of "gas poisoning" he contracted in one of the cheap, unventilated apartments he occupied in New York City.[13] In 1898, summering at Mackinac, he consulted Doctor Maria Norris, who recommended he find a warm place to winter; the Smythes lived in a warm place and had told him to visit them if he ever came their way.

Bennett wrote the major, asking for the recommendation of a good boarding house. Hospitable and eager to please, Smythe kept sending him ideas; they exchanged something like nine letters in a week. Finally, he invited Bennett to come stay with them for awhile and pick a place himself. "Just take any hack," he wired. "Tell the driver to drive to Lawyer Smythe's."[14]

All Bennett knew of Charleston was what Colonel Appleton, who had fought to take it in the Civil War, had told him—and that as a young boy, he had known an irascible and cantankerous old man, a Grimke family member, from Charleston. So, arriving at the poor-looking station on November 10, 1898, he felt neither confident nor happy.[15]

The station was "the shabbiest I had ever seen"; and the hack he hired "was a worn out conveyance with the horse on the verge of death; [its tattered] harness looked like a fish net."[16] With great trepidation, he sat back. But when the driver tugged on the reins, Bennett stopped doubting. The place was poor, still locked in a depression and alienation that had begun even before the Civil War. But the beauty of the blight overwhelmed him. "We drove into a maze of houses, tenements, [and] shacks with strange flowers hanging over the walls." He saw tall thin houses and great stuccoed mansions, marked by "pathetic beauty and faded grace."[17] Everything was damp-stained; stucco peeled, and the colors, collaborations between man and the atmosphere, shimmered iridescently. The city, like Venus, or Venice, could have just risen from the sea.

But Charleston, steeped and stained in the past, had become bitter, like tea. The place was "hopelessly behind the times to the mind of a northern man," but he nevertheless was charmed by the city's "slow pleasant atmosphere . . . [with] an ancient gentility 'on its uppers.'"[18] Having been founded in 1670, Charleston was a full century older than the country; whole neighborhoods survived from earlier eras; people could not afford the new styles, nor did they like them; early on, the city had seemed to cherish its past and looked backward toward it.

He was mesmerized by the African Americans selling flowers and cakes, while others he passed pushed carts of shrimp, vegetables, and fish. "To hear a street vendor making an oratorio of 'sweet potatoes, ten cent a peck, I got 'em fresh, I got 'em sweet' . . . gives a story telling feeling."[19] He had known a family of African Americans in Chillicothe; Bill Abrams there was an expert on fruit trees. And he had attended one of the very first concerts of the Fisk Jubilee Singers when they sang in Chillicothe in 1870. At Salt Sulphur Springs, he had befriended the servants and had written fondly and a bit stereotypically of them to his family.

But none of this had prepared him for Charleston's black majority, whose folk reminded him of European peasants and images in medieval paintings. They had marvelous evocative faces, some poignant with humility, others twisted "grotesque as gargoyles" with age and suffering.[20] The blacks seemed to speak a language all their own; he could pick out words that sounded like English every now and then; they stuck out like broken bits of china might in the alluvial mud of marshes he was passing. All conspired to give him the feeling that "he had entered a world of which he knew little or nothing, of which strive as he might, he should know nothing or little, and to which he was [to be] forever a stranger and an alien."[21] Disorienting as it was, all seemed to be approached at an oblique angle, down an alley, through a door that took you to a porch, instead of inside; the houses, narrow end to the street, looked back, shyly, regretfully, or flirting.

Henry James, on a visit to Charleston in a few years, would come up against the same wall of feeling; peering through a door to a long gallery or porch, called piazzas in Charleston, he would think of Italy and wonder if he had not glimpsed the past, like water evaporating, shimmering before it disappeared.[22]

"The piazzas and iron porticoes . . . the wrought iron fences, with great gates and walls of stucco . . . the dark live-oaks, sweet bay hedges and palmettos" mesmerized Bennett,[23] as did the "strange macabre loveliness" of the scene; he wanted to find out what lurked beyond "the stuccoed walls, the whispering jalousies shrouding unknown interiors, glimmering with light" and wander into "the pathless courtyards, labyrinthine inlets, covert lanes and outlets."[24] But he felt he would get lost, as one could in a jungle or the casbah of a Moslem city.

He was in somewhat of a trance then as the hack pulled up at 31 Legare Street, a white house set back behind a wrought-iron fence from the unpaved street. With its two levels of porches across the front and its generous front yard, it had the air of a country house that had been swallowed by the city. Standing at the door of this "quaint old home built before the revolution, [under] palmettos and great vines hanging in tops of tall elms" stood Mrs. Smythe, "a handsome old lady with a Roman nose and piercing dark eyes," and Susan, smiling shyly, coyly beside her.[25]

Susan Smythe remembered the scene a bit differently; she later recalled "a young man in a blue cloth suit who . . . entered . . . the . . . gate, and advanced with rapid steps towards the front door. His intention of ringing the bell, and . . . having a few minutes to . . . think what to say, was frustrated

by the lady of the manor, who appeared as if someone had pulled a string."
Right behind her appeared, "a most forward young lady." [26]

"You are very welcome," they said and whisked him in.[27]

The time he spent with the Smythes, their friends, and extended family
passed like a feverish, fast-paced dream. Constantly introduced and congratulated as the author of *Master Skylark,* he found himself treated like a
celebrity. "To be a writer is shibboleth in the south," he noted to others, and
had been that way, he felt, "even from the days of their own forgotten [poet
Henry] Timrod." [28] Writers were bragged of to outsiders, to show that culture had flourished there once, but they were not respected or supported.
(Henry James would notice the same thing; the only book of note to come
out of the South in a generation was *The Soul of Black Folks,* he believed; white
Charlestonians must have found this insulting.) [29]

Just a few months before, however, another writer, a friend of Henry
James, had visited. Owen Wister, having grown up in Philadelphia, was
related to many Charlestonians by his descent from the English actress
Fanny Kemble and the South Carolina planter Pierce Butler. Wister and
his wife had honeymooned there in April 1898 and had been welcomed by
many of the old families. "Of Charleston people I will not speak," he'd say
in a few years, noting that they were charming and that he shared their belief that the amendment enfranchising the blacks had been a big mistake.
He also castigated his friend President Theodore Roosevelt for having appointed William Crum, a black man, to the head of the customs house in
the city.[30] Bennett did not have such rigid ideas on race, but he agreed with
Wister at how astonishing everything was, from the weather (it was warm
still in November) to the time they sat for meals (a big one in the middle
of the day, a light supper in the evening). He was struck too, by the whites'
way of speaking. Charlestonians still "pronounced as their great grandfa-
thers did"; he himself spoke so differently that they called him "an interesting beast . . . the Negroes like to watch me talk. . . . They said I moved my
mouth so funny." [31]

He, in turn, was intrigued with how the blacks themselves spoke, and
asked many questions about their patois while his own accent was dismissed
as "vulgar." [32] When he tried to tell the Smythes and their friends that it
was their accents that were odd, they disagreed. To prove him wrong, they
"noted every word . . . that I did not pronounce as they did" and ran to the

dictionary; but "the dictionaries they used were Sheridan, Walker and Johnson, printed in the eighteenth century. There wasn't a modern dictionary in the place outside the Charleston Library [Society] and it had an English Dictionary, the Oxford; Webster's, [judged] a Yankee dictionary, was held in supreme contempt."[33] It was so delightful, but also a bit a disturbing. For although charming and cordial, these Southerners were still unreconstructed and disliked many things he held dear.

His host, Augustine Smythe, had spent time during the war, stationed in St. Michael's church, a white, chaste, colonial church whose slightly cracked bells were the voice of the city; they "play hymns all day long on Sundays, and it sounds passing sweet through the bright sunshine," Bennett wrote of them.[34] From this vantage point, the major had watched shells from the federal fleet out beyond Fort Sumter fall into the deserted neighborhoods south of Calhoun Street.

A full generation later, Charlestonians still spoke of "the war" (as if there had never been another) as not just a recent occurrence but the defining moment of their history. They did not celebrate the Fourth of July (Bennett's favorite holiday, in which he and his friend Will Poland delighted) and never flew the U.S. flag, for which his brother Henry had written his most famous poem. It was rarely seen in Charleston except on federal buildings, like the customs house and U.S. Post Office. And these Charlestonians avoided, being examples of federal authority. "There were old ladies still in Charleston who always stuck George Washington stamps upside down on envelopes [a sign of distress]" to demonstrate their anger and inability to take defeat gracefully.[35]

Their aversions were not just reserved for the government and its symbols. "Most strangers were not welcomed," he noted. "Tourists were not wanted; their riding about town was resented; what business had they to stare at private residences and peer into private yards?" As "people from the steamers rolled through the streets, the children ran out to the front calling, 'Yankees.'"[36] Owen Wister, in his novel *Lady Baltimore*, would note the same thing, as would Henry James, who'd visit in 1905 and describe Charleston in *The American Scene*.

Bennett was exempted from this treatment, for he had friends to take him about the city. The poor unfortunate "who came to Charleston in those days without an introduction might knock his heels on the curbstone till doomsday," Bennett wrote. "He never met anyone of the old Charlestonians, never saw the inside of their homes; he would sneak around like a stray cat if he chose; he simply didn't exist." But Bennett did; on a visit to a neighbor of the Smythes, "a very charming woman told me that in her girlhood it had been her delight when Yankees passed her premises, to heave a brick over the fence at them, hoping to hit their heads."

Comments such as these gave Bennett pause. "A watch was kept on me, curious and keen." [37] He understood that his behavior was being judged, as was perhaps the whole state of Ohio, and his hometown Chillicothe. At home, he had approached all social levels equally. So in Charleston he treated all, black and white, old family or not, with equal courtesy.

And all responded, even the children. Bennett was for many of them, such as Sam Gaillard Stoney, the Major and Mrs. Smythe's eight-year-old grandson, "the first honest-to-God walking, talking Yankee" they had even seen. As such, they wanted to hate him for the misdeeds of Abraham Lincoln, General Grant, and especially William Tecumseh Sherman, whose marauding troops had burned plantations on the outskirts of the city. But the author of *Master Skylark* understood children; he did not talk down to them but treated them as peers, told them stories, and to their astonishment turned "lumps of clay into animal statues." [38]

But not all Charlestonians were won over so easily. Behind the garden gates, down those piazzas Bennett passed and into which Henry James peered, many shook their heads and gossiped against the Smythes, "who [they said] had done a very venturesome thing inviting a damned Western Yankee to visit in their home without investigating [him first]." [39] Bennett caught Susan Smythe "peeping through the dining room shutters . . . on the night of her father's dinner [for me] to see how I bore myself." [40]

He must have done well; for within a week, "all the gentlemen who had met me [that night] came to call: Judges, lawyers . . . the President of the College of Charleston, two professors, and an author of a history of [South] Carolina." Even "the Mayor called with his carriage and took me for a drive." Others asked him to dine and use the Yacht Club; he was feted by old families like the Rawlinses and the Pinckneys. At the Charleston Club, his victory was complete. Could he, members asked, consult on a damaged painting? Consenting, Bennett found himself standing in a circle of somber old men shaking their heads in front of a ripped painting of Cupid and Psyche.

How was it damaged, he asked, thinking perhaps it might have been bayoneted in the war; by fixing it, he thought he could amend relations. The men looked at each other uneasily, finally admitting Cupid had been damaged by the popping of a champagne cork![41]

At the end of his ten days with the family, Bennett packed up his belongings and told his hosts, "I must remove to my new . . . lodgings and get to my winter's work." The family urged him to stay, but Bennett was firm. "Well," Major Smythe said, "at least you can consider this home your home while in the city . . . come in at any time [and] if you want a library, use mine."[42]

Bennett replied that he would; he'd catalog and rearrange its contents, and in a few months, his life would change in that library. But first he had to tend to the book he was writing.

## CHAPTER 9

# The Story of Barnaby Lee

BENNETT MOVED a few blocks away to a boarding house at 18 Meeting Street, a house built by Thomas Heyward, signer of the Declaration of Independence. In this "low-ceilinged [room] . . . hot with a little, one-eyed cyclops of a stove and bright with two uncurtained windows full of the cloudless sunshine," he settled down to write.[1] Every morning he went for a walk on the sea wall; on the Battery, one could meet Charlestonians as they took the air and look across the water to the ruins of Fort Sumter, the symbol of the city. On his visit, Henry James would recall how two of his brothers had nearly died participating with Massachusetts Regiments in the siege of the city.[2] In the afternoons Bennett stayed in with his manuscript, traveling back to another place and time. Every now and then he took a break to investigate the back alleys of town that had intrigued him upon arriving. He struck up conversations with blacks, listening to their accents, stories, songs, and beliefs, jotting down a few notes, wondering if they might be of use eventually. He wanted to learn and see more, but he made himself return to his boy hero, Barnaby Lee.

For this tale "contemporary to *Master Skylark* and possessing the same style and atmosphere," he followed many of the tactics and themes he had in *Skylark*.[3] He again set it in April, but seventy years later and across the Atlantic. *Skylark* had begun with players coming to Stratford. Now he presented an English rogue ship entering the harbor at New Amsterdam. The English crew under John King are little better than pirates. They do not honor the Dutch claim to this part of the new world; instead, they sail by the city.

Aboard the ship is a reluctant, abused cabin boy named Barnaby Lee, who has been pressed into service against his will, just as Nick Attwood had been kidnapped by Gaston Carew. Again like Nick, this sixteen-year-old lad, with the look of "a thoroughbred" to him, becomes a vehicle for some of Bennett's own feelings.[4] His "apprenticeship" is due to his father's disappearance and death back in England just as he and his son were to embark for Maryland. Barnaby's cry seems to echo Bennett's own feelings at having been abandoned and apprenticed to drunks when he first worked as a news-paperman in Chillicothe. "Oh Daddy," Barnaby blurts out in agony, "why did ye never come back?"[5]

As the ship bypasses the city without tipping its flag or paying to trade with the Iroquois, a hot-headed Dutchman, Gerrit van Sweringen, known as "the Man from Troublesome Corner" or by Bennett himself as "the man Peter Stuyvesant wanted to hang but couldn't," commandeers a ship and gathers volunteers.[6] They come upon the English as they are landing up-stream. Van Sweringen and his men attack and bring the crew and their booty back to New Amsterdam.

Barnaby is not among them, however, for van Sweringen's surprise at-tack has given him the chance to flee. Free, on land, and happy, Barnaby sets south for Maryland, the place his father was taking him. He walks and walks; lost and hungry in the wilderness, he stumbles into a marsh and nearly drowns, perhaps recalling Bennett's own near drowning back in Chillicothe.

Dorothy, daughter of Gerrit van Sweringen, hears the boy's screams. She parallels the role played by Gaston Carew's daughter Cecily. (Both are said to be of French descent, as well.) As if determined to let there be no more parallels, Bennett pointedly tells his readers that Barnaby cannot sing.[7]

Out sailing with Dirk Storm, who is quite content to let the English boy drown, Dorothy argues to save Barnaby. She shames Dirk and saves Barnaby, whom they take back to New Amsterdam, where Dirk and Dorothy's argu-ment is taken up by others. The men want to imprison him for being En-glish. But the women, Dorothy's mother and Peter Stuyvesant's wife in par-ticular, cry that he is ill and intervene. Frau Stuyvesant takes the boy home to take care of him personally.

In *Skylark*, William Shakespeare and his friends step into the story. Here, Peter Stuyvesant, a less famous historical character, and Gerrit van Swerin-gen (and his daughter, in real life named Elizabeth) come in; as if to com-pensate for their being less well-known, Bennett gives them a greater role to play in the story.[8]

He introduced his ancestor van Sweringen because he thought it would be amusing; he became something of an alter ego for this mild-mannered man from Chillicothe, who deferred to nearly everybody. Van Sweringen, on the other hand, did exactly as he pleased no matter what his family or the times wanted of him. (Bennett would later write another work on another Sweringen forebear who bucked the rules of civilization: Marmaduke van Sweringen left his early life to become Bluejacket, a Shawnee chief. Bennett would also give his own son the middle name "Sweringen" to "keep his memory green.")

Once he let the character into the tale, Bennett could not stop Sweringen. "[H]e walked right into the book," he said, "and just did as he pleased." [9] "This introduction of a subordinate character, who at once takes for himself the lead of affairs in the story and almost sets the hero in second place is an interesting venture in literature," he proclaimed in a brochure he wrote for the Century Company [10] to be sent to members of the Sweringen family. [11] To Susan Smythe, however, he summed it up more truthfully. "Think of it! Barnaby Lee had nothing at all to do with the story, and was just dragged in by the heels because it had to be a children's story and a boy was necessary. So I made Barnaby Lee necessary." [12]

So with Barnaby to entertain the children, Bennett developed van Sweringen along the lines of Carew in *Master Skylark*. Unlike the latter, however, Bennett portrayed van Sweringen heroically, believing that "brave deeds by brave men are good things for boys to be told." He believed heroes "encourage emulation and imitation; and before heroism of the soul is to be reached, there is heroism of the body." [13]

His sister Alice sent him some research notes on their ancestor; he himself had been pleased to find traces of him in his lonely research vigils at the New York Public Library. There he had discovered that van Sweringen had gone to Maryland to discuss the return of runaway apprentices; and in return, Maryland commissioners, arguing a disputed boundary, had come to see him.

With this bit of true history, Bennett found a way to work Barnaby back into the plot and make him integral to the story. After Barnaby is rescued and put to bed by Frau Stuyvesant, van Sweringen and Stuyvesant meet to think of a pretext for van Sweringen to go on an espionage mission for the Dutch colony to its southern neighbor, Maryland. Barnaby, asleep in the Dutch bed, wakes and inadvertently overhears their secret meeting, and van Sweringen gets an idea. Here is an escaped apprentice from a ship originally bound for Maryland; he can pretend to be doing his legal duty of returning him while ferreting out other desired information.

As he prepares to leave, Frau Sweringen and Frau Stuyvesant argue with their men, saying the boy was enslaved. They quote the Bible, asking for mercy and his release; but the men quote the Scriptures, which demand a cold justice. Barnaby is buffeted by forces he can't control and is to be sacrificed for political expediency, perhaps mirroring a way Bennett felt being sacrificed for the benefit of his family.

They set sail for Maryland, where van Sweringen first meets with Governor Charles Calvert's rude cousin, Philip, a fictional creation with no basis in history; readers have just seen Calvert conspiring with the ship captain John King, who has told Calvert that the boy he has been hiding for him disappeared in the scuffle with the Dutch and is presumed drowned in New Amsterdam. For some reason, Philip is pleased with this news; then his cousin, the governor, returns and meets with van Sweringen, who explains that he has come to return the boy.

Charles Calvert is intrigued by Barnaby, who claims to be the son of a gentleman, Henry Lee of England, who had been killed for his loyalty to Charles II. This Philip overhears, realizing that this is the boy of whom he has just spoken of to John King. Philip does his best to kill the boy the next morning when the hair-triggered van Sweringen, a true-life trait, gets upset over a trifle and challenges the governor to a duel (fiction entirely). Charles Calvert and Gerrit van Sweringen meet, and as the duel begins Philip jumps in with his men; Barnaby is wounded trying to protect Sweringen.

Grateful for the boy's heroism and shamed by his previous willingness to have sacrificed him, van Sweringen takes Barnaby back north as a member of his family; in New Amsterdam the boy is nursed by Dorothy. Echoing John Bennett's wonder at the generosity of the Appletons, Barnaby cannot understand such kindness by anyone not family.

Just as Barnaby finds peace, van Sweringen dashes off to fight the Mohicans, and the English lay siege to the Dutch city. Again, a father is absent in a time of crisis. The siege is a vivid set piece; Bennett sustains it for several chapters, delineating the day-to-day anxiety of the townsfolk, bringing the contemporary times to life, and weaving historical fact and fiction together vividly.

"All night above the stream and across the bay the lights of the English fleet waved and nodded like dizzy stars," he begins. "All night long, above the never-silent troubling of the water, the ship-bells rang the watches, sharp, thin and brassy clear. All night the red windows of New Amsterdam stared through the darkness at the enemy; and in his room, until gray dawn, Peter Stuyvesant went up and down like a wild beast in a cage, and beat his fists together in despairing rage and shame."[14]

The surrender of the city brings grief to Barnaby; among the victorious English is John King, who sues in court for the return of his escaped apprentice. The case is being heard when Governor Calvert arrives to reveal what he has found out about Barnaby's past. He has discovered that John King's ship was filled with the belongings of Henry Lee, and there were hundreds of acres of land in Maryland awaiting him. These his cousin Philip Calvert seized, hearing of the legal owner's death and relinquishing the vessel to John King on the condition that the boy never be seen again.

How Calvert discovered this back in Maryland is presented in an awkward flashback, showing the trouble Bennett had with structure and plotting. It could have been cut easily, but Bennett was apparently loathe to lose some of the book's most vivid writing, as he described a thunderstorm and doom coming simultaneously for Philip Calvert:

For a while he [Philip Calvert] sat beneath the trees smoking uneasily and watching the stars. . . . He arose and came quickly up to the house, and, entering, went swiftly from room to room, peering furtively into each, then back to the hall to look out.

A fitful glimmer came and went along the hills, of summer lightning dancing in the south. . . . There was no thunder as yet; a hush lay upon the remote uplands, and a silence upon the valley. . . . "Here," he said coming to the door where the servants were sitting together, . . . "why don't somebody make a sound? . . ."

So they made up a sound among them desultorily . . . but it had not aim or purpose, and as soon as he was gone, died away. He looked back once or twice as if he would rather have lingered there for the sake of company . . . but . . . his uneasiness drove him on through the house like a moth, from candle to candle. . . .

As he came to the landing where the stair turned to the right he suddenly paused, and for a moment listened: there was the sound as if some one were rolling a heavy table to and fro in one of the rooms below. Then, boom, boom, boom, the sound resolved itself into a sullen, hollow rumble, beyond the walls. "There it comes!" he said. . . .

The air was close; the midges danced around the candle-flames. He opened the window-lattice and looked out.

Along the low hills the clouds came . . . up like a billowing mountain range. As he watched them slowly heave across the green, uncanny sky . . . suddenly, far off, he heard again the rumble of thunder. Then all the world was suddenly still. "It's coming," he said uneasily. . . .

As he drew the lattice, a chill drop of rain struck and spattered upon his cheek— and just for a moment, as through the opening of a door comes a burst of music and laughter, and then is shut away, he heard through the stillness the beat of a horse's hoofs, cut-a-thump, cut-a-thump, cut-a-thump, coming on through the darkness; and then the sound was gone. Down rushed the wind through the tree-tops. The grass at the roadside bowed and sprung again before it. The house shook. The elm beat against the gable. For an instant nothing could be heard but the furious tumult of the gale. Far off he heard a great tree fall somewhere within the forest, a riving, splintering, startling sound. Then nearer, louder, sharper-beating than before, he heard the drum of a horse's hoofs, seeming to race with the break-ing storm. . . .

Through the roar and rush and the sweep of the wind he could hear the dull beat of that great, racing stride, coming on through the darkness and the storm: cut-a-thump, cut-a-thump, cut-a-thump. It seemed to be coming nearer and nearer. . . .

He crossed himself, for, as he spoke, there came a blinding flash of light. . . . Then followed a peal of thunder which made the very foundations shake; with a sudden-rising whiff of the wind out went the lights. . . .

Clasping his hands upon his breast, Philip Calvert . . . heard the muffled thump of feet as the footman sprang out of bed, and a swift snipping of flint and steel; a wavering thread of light came swiftly down the hallway. On the heels of a parley came a rattle of chains. He crept to the landing and peered down across the balus-trade just as Johnson shot back the last bolt, and threw the door wide open.[15]

There Governor Calvert stood, with his men, to confront him. After that meeting, the Governor took off the next day to New Amsterdam; there, Barnaby, now rich, is convinced to return to Maryland with him.

He is out of harm's way now, but lonely; Calvert, however, has also con-vinced the van Sweringens, having lost all their possessions to the English, to come too, a fact of historical accuracy. Van Sweringen is now sheriff here. Barnaby is befriended by them in a deus-ex-machina turn: his father in En-gland had not been killed after all—only wounded, it is revealed—and now reappears. (Only with fairy-tale endings, it seems, can fathers be ex-pected to do their duty.)

It is van Sweringen, however, who ends the story. His descendants, the author says, "are scattered through many a State and many a Territory. It may be that you who peruse these pages have in your vein a spark of the heat and fire that stirred his heart." [16]

It took years and countless drafts of the manuscript to get to this ending. "Having at first no sense of the story as a whole, I had no comprehension of the particles of its structure," Bennett confessed.[17] He was making it up as he went along in Charleston in the fall of 1898 and the winter of 1899.

Unlike *Skylark*, whose plot sprang to mind almost full blown and whose characters came alive instantly, Bennett had a much more difficult time with this brainchild, Barnaby Lee. "Like the only child of inexperienced parents, each infant chapter seemed the most important in the world, and like the only child [was] humored in every fanciful whim, was spoiled by over-indulgence, and needed a deal of . . . [discipline] before it took its place into the little world I was . . . blindly [and] aimlessly endeavoring to create." [18]

As spring appeared in Charleston, Bennett had to flee the pollen to avoid his debilitating allergies. He went to Mackinac Island and wrote much of the novel in the McIntire and Hamilton cottages.[19] Since he was so late delivering the manuscript, he was worried that his publishers might be angry. But they were willing to wait. "The Century Company then composed of old fashioned gentlemen of grace and courtesy, was consideration itself, and never referred to the terms of our contract." [20]

It was not until September 1899, nearly a year since first coming to Charleston, that he finally finished the first draft on Mackinac Island. He sent it to his family in Chillicothe to read, and then set to work revising it, ironing out the inconsistencies in tone, point of view, and style. His sister Martha (to whom he'd dedicate the book) helped him with these points and in breaking the long draft into chapters and paragraphs. It took a year to do it all, a year he spent in Mackinac, Charleston, and Chillicothe.

He finished it in June of 1900 and personally delivered the manuscript to the *St. Nicholas* offices. Mary Mapes Dodge was just on the verge of leaving for her summer vacation, but she postponed her departure and stayed up all night to read the story.

She was smiling when Bennett came into her office the next morning. She told him she "considered *Barnaby Lee* a stronger and better told historical romance than *Master Skylark*," a shrewd assessment; for it *is* technically more of a romance, more tied down to actual historical events, and it does encompass many a more dramatic incident. She called it *"fine, broad, strong, magnificent!"*[21] The praise was wonderful, but the price she named for it was not.

He would not settle for that, he told her, suddenly displaying the cheek and brass he had earlier lacked. Telling her that he was a man "whose great painstaking care and . . . personality . . . made his product worth more [in quality] than its quantity," he demanded $5,000 for the work.[22]

Mrs. Dodge said firmly that was impossible; and she rose to leave. So, Bennett noted,

I readjusted myself like a reasonable man and I . . . set my figure at $4,000 for the serial rights; 10% for my royalty on the first 5000 copies; 15% on the rest. And there I stuck. . . .

Mrs. Dodge excused herself—said she must see the President. President Scott, Mr. Chichester the Treasurer, Mr. Ellsworth the Secretary and Mrs. Dodge were closeted in the president's office. I think it was half an hour—Mr. [Albert Bigelow] Paine and Mr. [Tudor] Jenks looked in at me, sitting there alone, and told me to stick to it, whatever I asked, and make them come to it. "They are having a mighty big pow-wow!" said Jenks. Then hearing them coming, he fled, and I was descended upon by the whole of the Century Company embodied in Mr. Scott, the President. I was as cool, as calm, as courteous and smooth as my own old Gerrit van Sweringen. We fought it out for an hour or more; but I stood by my colors like a mule.

"We have never paid so much for any *St. Nicholas* serial," objected Mr. Scott.

"That has nothing to do with this case; you have never bought *this* story," said J[ohn] B[ennett].

"It will establish an unusual precedent," said the Century Company . . . .

"I am here to establish a precedent," said I flatly.

We fought some more, but I would not come down—and the Century Company had to come up.

"Think of it, they [will] pay more for 'Barnaby Lee' than they ever paid for any serial in St. Nicholas. . . . I offer it to you all as the spoils of your loving and hardworking boy," Bennett crowed to his "Dear Father and dear people" back in Ohio.[23] To his family he offered it, but he had stood by his colors for the sake of Susan Smythe; he told her this in person as she and her parents, on their way to Europe, passed through New York City.

*Barnaby Lee* ran as a serial in *St. Nicholas* from November 1900 to October

1901; questions regarding the story came from as far away as Russia.[24] It appeared in book form in 1902, handsomely stamped with the beaver and windmill symbols of New Amsterdam, bearing the two-tone illustrations of Clyde O. Deland. As handsome as *Master Skylark*, the book, like Bennett's first, also made the *Peter Parley to Penrod* list of one hundred classic American children's books.[25] As for *Skylark*, critics praised him for his straightforwardness and vigorous storytelling, the vitality of his writing, and the way he appealed to both young and mature readers.[26]

"Your colonial men and women and your scenes of New Amsterdam are as vivid as Mr. Deland's ships, windmills and fascinating interiors," wrote one critic, addressing the author directly. "Your book is good work—honest, careful, worthy."[27] The *New York Commercial Advertiser* commented on its "unusual literary merit"; and Bennett was claimed as a native in the Charleston press.[28]

It sold well, and in 1916 it was filmed by the Edison Company, which, not liking the finished product, never released it. It was published in England, Canada, and Australia and was dramatized for school children. In the 1920s Bennett was approached by the editors of a pulp magazine to revive his swaggering van Sweringen and make him the subject of adventure stories.[29] The story would later be broadcast over the radio in the 1940s and '50s. Although unfailingly popular, and still available in print over fifty years after its first appearance, *Barnaby Lee* nevertheless failed to capture the popular imagination as had *Master Skylark*.

In his first book, in its pivotal scene, Bennett had unwittingly created a metaphor that explained it. Before Colley and Nick sing for queen Elizabeth in *Skylark*, performers present "a masque of Summer-time and Spring." Dancers first do a "sprightly galliard and . . . nimble jig for Spring" and then "a slow pavane, the stately peacock dance, for Summer-time." *Skylark* is all spring innocence of a talent in first bloom; *Barnaby Lee* is fuller and darker and denser, a maturer work but less appealing. In the masque, "Spring won. The English ever loved her best."[30] So did the reading public; they liked the summery *Barnaby Lee* but championed the springlike *Master Skylark*.

Bennett, not surprised, had anticipated this. As early as 1899 he had told Susan Smythe, "My book in someways will not touch *Skylark*; how could it? *Skylark* was out of my heart, and this has been very much out of my head."[31] But, ironically enough, this product of his head allowed him to follow his heart. For it was "on the strength of mutual affection (as I have always believed) and the financial returns from *Barnaby Lee*" that made him feel fit to marry.[32] For that, he had argued with the Century Company over money, even though Susan had written, "I have always thought it a false pride when a man will not marry a girl until he can support her as her father does."[33] But, obstinate as he was, Bennett had to prove his worthiness not just to Susan but to himself.

## CHAPTER 10

# "Love in Its Fullness, Replete"

SOME TIME after his November 1898 arrival in Charleston, Bennett realized he had feelings for Susan. Each evening after he moved to his boarding house, he "longed to come to # 31 Legare St.—and . . . when I came and you were not there it was not . . . satisfying . . . the evening seemed empty without you." [1]

But the thought of sharing his feelings with her was nerve-wracking. The class system existed more strongly in Charleston than in Chillicothe; the Smythes seemed to inhabit a rarified aristocratic atmosphere. But he determined, nevertheless, to ask for her hand in marriage and went to Legare Street one day in early February. "I am glad you . . . 'feel used to . . . and do not mind' me," he wrote in a note, adding, "I am willing to take you as I find you. I shall . . . drop in today . . . to see *you.*" [2] Doing so, he was told she was in the library.

She looked up and smiled as he came in, but did not stop darning socks she had stretched over gourds from the garden. A cat dozed in her lap; busts of John C. Calhoun, George McDuffie, and Langdon Cheves, defenders of the South, looked down on him from their brackets. Bennett said hello and lapsed into silence; she went on with her sewing.

Then they both looked up at the same time and laughed; he looked away and she looked back. She suddenly had a presentiment why he, usually loquacious and easy, was now tongue-tied and nervous. "Color surged up her cheeks, ran along her temples and played at the roots of her hair." [3] She got up.

"I must go, Jack," she whispered.

But he also stood, and "words came . . . in a torrent. He hardly knew what . . . words his tongue chose"; stuttering and blushing, he tried to convey his feelings.

"Please don't! Please don't!" she whispered . . . [and] repeated his words. . . . "You love me? Love me? Love me? You? . . ."

"With that she swayed, suddenly dizzy. . . . Sudden and vast the outlook swept before her: life . . . death, hope, joy . . . grief . . . and the anguishing sense of love in its fullness, replete."[4]

"I am a very ordinary girl," she believed; unsentimental, she was uncomfortable with this naked show of emotion. Her one idea was to flee.[5] But before she could, Bennett reached. Could—did—she return his feelings?

"Oh I don't know!" she cried in an anguished voice. . . . "I . . . I . . . I am terrified."[6] She ran from the library. And he, looking up at the gaunt death-masks on the shelves, also ran, back to his room at 18 Meeting Street.

When he arrived there, he grew angry at himself. "Pray start a list of ancient fools and write me down upon it," he wrote her on the fourth of February.[7] But it was too late; the damage had been done. On the sixth, her father summoned him.[8]

"Your father and mother need you," he wrote Susan some time after that and another interview with her. Obviously, she was unsure of her feelings. "This is your place, and I was wrong in thinking to take you from it," he soon wrote her. "There is nothing so dangerous as forced or false sentiment," he continued, thanking her for her honesty.

"I am a man, not a coward. Just deal with me as such. I shall feel . . . more true to everyone concerned, your father and mother, whom I honor and admire, and my own dear, troubled people, to whom I shall be going." He vowed to be her "poorer lover" and "better friend."

"I shall not be over for dinner; most probably not for tea; I shall be writing letters home and to my sister, Martha, and digging into the story [of *Barnaby Lee*]. . . . I shall be over during the week. Just now I am pulling myself together. . . . This . . . is all I have to say." He finished the letter, "Yours very sincerely and gratefully," but did not sign it.[9]

In a few days she went off to Savannah, as earlier planned, to visit family. Ironically, her sister Hannah was engaged to be married and was visiting her fiancé's family. Bennett stayed in Charleston and continued with his writing, occasionally visiting those he had met through the Smythes. He found a genial host in the older Captain Thomas Pinckney, the father of the future novelist Josephine Pinckney, born in 1895. One wonders if Bennett could have told this little girl, then about three, some of his famous stories and nurtured in her a love of storytelling. The household was literary and well connected; Bennett met the novelist John Fox and George Howe, a nephew of Woodrow Wilson, at the Pinckney's; at the same time, the critic and editor Hamilton Mabe was also visiting the city.

The Pinckneys and their guests, knowing nothing of his anguish, talked of literature, expressing their disdain for current writers such as Hall Caine and Thomas Hardy. Charlestonians favored Tennyson, Shakespeare, and Browning and welcomed Bennett into their company.[10]

Affecting a calm he did not feel, Bennett wrote letters to Susan in Savannah trying to regain their firm, friendly footing; he also told her of his expectations for *Barnaby Lee*. "Hope is like chickweed; it never quite gives up," he wrote her on March 5;[11] but it was more than his manuscript making him hopeful. Two days later, knowing she was due home soon, he wrote asking "if I may come to call upon that evening without undue intrusion upon your family or yourself."[12]

An invitation to tea was issued. It was either then or soon after, in a moment alone, that she accepted his proposal of marriage. "Miss Susan Smythe is one of the finest girls I have ever seen north or south," he crowed, "and I think that just as soon as I get my pile made, and my ship unloaded, I shall marry her, providing she agrees. So if you see any ships going around unclaimed please catch one for me and keep it safe until I come home."

It was only to himself and Susan that he dared utter these things because they decided to keep their engagement secret; "the completion of my story is the day when I announce our engagement to the Bennett family," he wrote her, signing himself as "your boy."[13] In one of his previous letters to her, he had morosely complained that "nothing generous or beautiful or freely given [is for] . . . me."[14] But now the world was different. A changed man, he went to see Major Smythe.

The older man's blue eyes were shining as Bennett told him about waiting till he got a firmer footing from the sale of *Barnaby Lee*; the major nodded and asked about his family.

"The fact that my people's quality was to be questioned had not until that moment occurred to me." Bennett looked perplexed; but the major, understanding, tried to put him at ease. "I can enquire, but . . . perhaps," he said graciously, "you yourself can give me entirely satisfactory information regarding them?"

"Indeed, Major," said Bennett, "I can think of nothing. . . . My mother's brother was forty years chief counsel for the B[altimore] and O[hio Rail-road]. . . . That's the single thing [that] comes to me!"

Smythe was not totally assured; so Bennett, perhaps remembering his alter ego Gerrit van Sweringen triumphing over the pirate John King, had an idea.

"It occurs to me, however, . . . that one of my father's cousins was hanged."

The major's kind . . . face fell. . . . "Perhaps," he said, "it was not as bad as it sounds."

"Perhaps not; . . . they hanged him, and the charge . . . was piracy."

The Major's . . . face fell further. . . . "But that could be explained?"

"I don't know," Bennett replied.

The man in question was John Yates Beall, hanged on Governor's Island by the U.S. Government. He held a commission from Jefferson Davis, however, and had been tried for his activities on behalf of the Confederate States Navy.

"I think that alters the case!" [Major Smythe] said and laughed. . . .

"I thought it might," said [Bennett], "but one can never tell."

He shook my hand, laughing merrily—he had an infectious laugh.

Major Smythe said he would write a lawyer he knew in Chillicothe about the Bennett family.[15]

The letter came back, attesting to the family's worth; the secret of their engagement leaked out. Congratulations poured in. Mrs. Appleton of Salt Sulphur Springs said she had known they were in love when she had seen them together; "may it not have been so, and we two 'children' not realized it?" he asked his fiancée.[16] Back home the Bennetts were thrilled, but in Charleston some raised their brows. He might be a nice individual, they thought, but he lacked connections and ancestry, being an "Ohio Yankee."[17]

Bennett might have been aware of this, possibly prompting his use of genealogy as a close for *Barnaby Lee*. Instead of just ending with the close of the tale, he went on, "It may be that you who peruse these pages have in your veins a spark of the heat and fire that stirred his heart," he wrote of van Sweringen. "His descendants are scattered through many a State and many a Territory."[18]

No doubt, he and the Smythes let it be known that there was now a descendant in Charleston (later he'd inform everyone that the head of the state department of education, a Sweringen, was descended similarly). It was a way of showing that he was descended from settlers who came to New Amsterdam and Maryland even long before Charleston had been founded in 1670.

It was important to let Charlestonians know about him, since it seemed decided from the start that Susan would not go to Ohio but he would stay in Charleston. "Your father and mother need you," he had already acknowledged to her. "This is your place, and I was wrong in thinking to take you from it."[19] Charlestonians were like hothouse flowers, too exotic to transplant. In their secure world, everyone, old families and African Americans, knew their place. In comparison, Bennett was rootless, being just the first generation in Chillicothe. And Susan, younger and the "weaker vessel" in the Southern and Victorian codes of the day, had never spent much time elsewhere and was still very much integrally linked to her family.

Bennett himself was free; his older siblings Alice and Henry could care for their aging parents in Chillicothe. And besides, Bennett liked the idea of sacrifice; it fit his view of himself and his duty and was another way he could show his love for Susan. There was some tearing at his heart, however, for he loved his hometown. Only one Charleston friend, Yates Snowden, would understand; he'd concede Chillicothe as Bennett's "mother" and Charleston his step-mother. Most other Charlestonians, however, assumed that there was no other place on earth to compare to their native city and expected all others to agree.[20]

For many reasons then, Bennett decided to stay. It would be pleasant to move to a city that knew you only as a successful writer, a place that had no idea of your past sadness and long-suffering family. Here he could become the famous person many Charlestonians thought him to be. So a changed man, engaged to be married, he left Charleston in the spring. Continuing to write *Barnaby Lee* in Ohio and Mackinac Island, he also kept writing Susan, and she him: she passed on greetings of friends inquiring "most tenderly after 'Mr. Skylark' . . . as well as sympathizing most sincerely with 'Mrs. Skylark.'"[21] He wrote her of his doings and his family.

"We are all busily reading [of the] Re-Union in the Associated Press," Bennett wrote her after perusing the coverage given to the national gathering of Confederate veterans then convened in Charleston. "It is the first thing read in the Bennett house when the . . . paper comes. I think they all feel a sort of proprietary interest in Charleston now—an interest by proxy." The city was so festooned with Confederate banners that he asked Susan "if you would not put up just one five-cent 'Old Glory' in the stable-shed for me." Knowing she wouldn't, he consoled himself by singing "The Battle Hymn of the Republic" continuously.[22]

She wouldn't accept his views on that subject, and instead showed him her spin on things. "I saw two Yankees, of a most pronounced and remarkable type, stop in front of the Whaley[']s [house]. They looked at it for some time, cocked their heads . . . critically . . . [and] walked around and around it carefully." Seeing her, one man "took off his hat politely, and with a smile, said, 'Beg pardon, but is that a *Club*-house or a *private* house?' I hastened to assure him that it was Mr. Whaley's private residence," she wrote, reserving most of her scorn for those Charlestonians who did not live modestly. "We have been gloating ever since," she wrote. "Think of having one's home taken for a club house," she laughed, condemning the Whaleys for looking rich and conspicuous; "it is as bad as the Roger's [sic] 'lunatic asylum' on Wentworth Street"—a huge second-empire brick pile, four and one-half stories high, built after the Civil War, with money raised from business dealings.[23] That was not the Charleston way of doing things, Susan believed, and she kept writing her fiancé, further indoctrinating him in the ways of the city. When Bennett wrote her of attending a social gathering where women wore revealing dresses and people drank, she wrote back, saying that "the girls in Charleston do not dress in the fashionable way; they still keep their self-respect." As for drinking, she told him, "that unless you wish to, you need never come in contact with that sort of thing in Charleston."

"There are houses where you can find plenty of it," she said, specifically mentioning the Simonds, the Trenholms, and the Dawsons. "But I have never been to . . . any one of them . . . and don't intend to."[24] Andrew Simonds was married to Daisy Breaux of New Orleans; in her lavish new house on the Battery, she would soon scandalize the city. The Trenholms' wealth came from blockade running. And Mrs. Dawson was not from Charleston; her husband, an Englishman and a Catholic, had been editor of the *Charleston News and Courier* but was murdered by a doctor whom Dawson angered. The doctor was acquitted; Mrs. Dawson would soon leave the city for France, where her son would settle permanently.[25] Susan and her family disapproved of all of these families, noting that "When *we* give a dance we never have any wine but sherry or madeira; and at my coming-out dance the average amount of wink drunk was less [than] a glass apiece. . . . Say what people may, it does keep a check on a young man for the girl he is with not to take a glass of wine."[26]

Learning of Charleston's ways by letter was fine, but in May of 1900 (and again in June the next year) he joined Susan and her married sister, Louise (called Loula or Lou), and her husband, Sam Gaillard Stoney Sr., at Medway, a Stoney family plantation on the Back River to get a closer feel for the old ways of life cherished by the city. Although only about twenty miles or so from Charleston, it took a day on bad roads, a bateau, and a river steamer to reach Medway. There was no electricity, gas, or indoor plumbing in the tumbled old brick house whose Dutch gable had fallen out in the 1886 earthquake. Despite its desolation (or because of it, really) the house was occupied most of the year by a cousin, a Major Dwight Stoney, a Confederate veteran, and his "body servant," Davey, whose presence kept poor neighbors from pillaging the property.[27]

The place, in its wildness, fascinated Bennett; he watched deer come right up to the walls to feed; pines had grown up in the gardens; swamps had engulfed rice fields. The house glimmered like a ghost, and time seemed as dark and stagnant as the black pools of water under the cypress trees. "Harry says I rhapsodize," Bennett wrote, describing the place, "but . . . the Lord God Almighty built this earth of rhapsodies. . . . All a man has to do is look, see, and feel. . . .

"It is the pathos and sadness that hangs over everything in this land that wrings me closest [to] the heart. . . . The wreck of once-noble mansions, the tragedy of lost estates haunt you everywhere. At times the sense of desolation where once the very ground sprang beauty is exquisitely painful." Especially appealing were "the great, unbroken silences, the tender gentleness of broad sunshine, the hoary mysterious stillness of the huge live oaks . . . draped in gray, trailing, faintly washing moss. . . . And to hear suddenly, far off in the great, gloom-haunted break . . . a man's shrill, high natural falsetto voice strike up a . . . negro hymn . . . is more than I can assay."[28]

Besides the physical beauty of the place, he was also taken with its history. This may have been colored by his affections for Susan and his desire to belong; but he had been intrigued ever since first stepping off the train in

1898, and now he was developing his own relationship with the land, the lore, the setting.

Susan, at the same time, was getting to know his family. There were trips to the Bennetts in Chillicothe. The betrothed spent Christmas 1901 in Ohio and returned to Charleston to attend the St. Cecilia Ball in early 1902. Bennett's siblings Martha, Henry, and Alice came to town as his wedding neared; his mother had to stay back home to care for their father, who was ailing. Spring reached its peak; the bushes and trees and vines were festooned with blossoms when on April 2, 1902, family and guests filled the Second Presbyterian Church (nearly five hundred names were on their list) to witness an Ohio Yankee achieve the impossible by joining the ranks of the local gentry.

Some thought it not quite right; and, as if to confirm it, another person from "off" (which meant any place not Charleston) who had married a local shocked the city the very next week. Daisy Breaux, originally from New Orleans, married to Charlestonian Andrew Simonds, had been doing her best to rise in a town that did not take kindly to social climbing. (Susan had referred to the Simonds as one of the bold party-giving families; invited there, she went to another function instead.)[29] The Inter-State and West Indian Exposition, a trade fair and sort of small world's fair, was outside the city limits in these years, bringing numerous celebrities to town, Owen Wister among them. He had returned with his young family, his wife being Pennsylvania's representative to the exposition's women's building.[30] Wister had helped lure his friend, President Theodore Roosevelt, to Charleston; the word was put out (perhaps due to the lack of any coming in) that the president was too busy to accept private invitations to entertainments.

Daisy Simonds, however, was determined to snag him. She stopped the president when he came ashore at the river gardens after touring the harbor; in her employ, she said, was an old servant, born a slave, whose last wish was to meet the representative of the Federal Government that had set him free. Pleased to be able to grant such a request in a town where many despised his more enlightened view of African Americans, Roosevelt acquiesced and accompanied her to her grand-white confection of a mansion with its soaring columns, balconies, and fountains, next to more chaste and severe houses from earlier centuries. But when he entered, he saw no servant but instead a long table, with dinner guests waiting.[31]

Roosevelt stayed to dine, giving Simonds the opportunity to brag of his visit over the years. Although she tried to keep her hoax a secret, word got out, and she was pointed out as a warning to others who might want to advance in society too rapidly. (Years later she successfully prevented Wister, with the threat of a lawsuit, from writing of the event in his biography of the president.) She'd write her own memoirs, glossing over the event; but her greatest contribution to Charleston literature would be her house, which, as a guest lodge, would house many famous writers and be depicted in their writing.[32] Bennett would have reason to see Simonds as a warning soon; and he would refer to her slyly over the years.[33]

He knew nothing of the fracas at the time, however, as he was honeymooning at Woodburn plantation, a Smythe family property at Pendleton, South Carolina, near the mountains. Susan had summered there for years, and in the cool basement she and her sisters had been taught domestic chores and cooking. Her mother had neglected other parts of her education, however. Susan, "even though reared on a farm," knew nothing of sex.[34] Fretting, not knowing what to do, Bennett treated her like a child and spent much of his time wandering the thousand acres, sightseeing. He became intrigued with the children of the black servants who sang and played on pipes cut from bamboo.

It made a piquant, almost timeless sound, and he went to the fields and a church to listen to their singing. (He'd write of a sermon he heard in Anderson county).[35] The spirituals he listened to convinced him again of the unusualness and beauty of the South, and struck a chord in his memory. He recalled his attendance at one of the first concerts of the Fisk Jubilee Singers, a chorus of black singers, who sang rather stylized and operatic versions of such things.[36] The songs he heard in South Carolina were simpler, more authentic, more African, and he found them very moving.

As a sort of hobby, Susan Smythe and her sister Hannah McCord Wright had been collecting spirituals, Hannah transcribing the lyrics and Susan sketching the music on her violin.[37] Bennett now joined their collaboration, and he invited the children of Woodburn Plantation to sing for him, paying them twenty-five cents, the wage for a whole day chopping wood. This amazed the children, usually shy of strange white men, and they warmed to him.

One young woman of about twenty who worked for the Smythe family met Bennett then; preparing her autobiography thirty-five years later, she'd write, "When I worked in the laundry for Mrs. Smythe, you had me come up to the corner of the fence under the shrubbery and sing Negro Spirituals. I have . . . held the memory of this particular incident sacred." By this time she was a woman of accomplishment; Jane Hunter, whose brother Winston Harris (called Dang) taught Bennett how to carve his own pan pipes, founded the Phillis Wheatley Association, a training center for young black women in Cincinnati; she'd tell others of her experience of having sung for the author of *Master Skylark* in *A Nickel and a Prayer*, her autobiography.[38]

Happy with the spirituals he recorded, fired by this idea of their collaboration, but still perplexed about how to tell his naive wife about sexual intimacy, Bennett brought Susan back to Charleston on April 28, 1902. They immediately moved into a rented house at 14 Friend Street (now 48 Legare Street), a block and a bend in the street away from her parents. One entered the lower-level piazza from a door at the street and walked down to the entry, which opened to a stair hall. There was one room on either side of the hall; a kitchen and dependencies straggled along, like ducklings, to the back of the lot. The house had a red tiled roof, a garden of violets, plums, and figs, and here, Bennett wrote, Susan "is never anything but cheery . . . so that she is most excellent company for morbid and melancholy me."[39]

He had, with the help of the family physician, explained the facts of life to his wife; his life was complete and all was well, except for John Briscoe Bennett, his father. Now over eighty, the elder Bennett was failing and spent his days in his chair, "watching the changing colors of the evening sky and repeating, as he watched the fading light, passage after passage of his beloved poets which dwelt upon the beauty of the world."[40]

John Briscoe Bennett died March 23, 1903, not quite a year after his son's wedding; the younger Bennett raced to Ohio, only to arrive after the ceremony on Cemetery Hill. He had no time to mourn or linger, for he had to return immediately to Charleston, where Susan was due to deliver their first child. Jane McClintock Bennett was born on May 11, 1903; she was named for Bennett's mother Eliza Jane McClintick, something, Bennett realized, his father had not lived long enough to see.[41]

Saddened, Bennett renewed his vow to tell his father's story. In that tale, he'd erase the sadness; in the book, his father would always be young, triumphant, and on his way to success. Like the photographs of low-country

African Americans he was now taking, he would "fix" John Briscoe Bennett forever in time and keep his memory "green" in *Buckhorn Johnny*, the book he had abandoned for *Barnaby Lee.*

He resumed the manuscript where he had left off but had to put it down almost immediately again. For just after her granddaughter's birth, Eliza Jane Bennett fell ill. Bennett raced back to Chillicothe to nurse her. He had married, lost his father, and become a father himself in just two years, and now, nearing forty, was witnessing "life, birth, death, hope, joy . . . [and] grief." He, too, was feeling "the anguishing sense of love in its fullness, replete." [42]

## CHAPTER 11

# Charleston's Adopted Son
# and His Treasure

WHEN BENNETT RETURNED from Ohio, it was already summer—time for the old families to leave for the mountains of North Carolina, the West Virginia springs, or the nearby beach. But he, Susan, and their infant daughter, Jane, stayed in the heat. Although they had lived in their Friend Street home for just over a year, they were already moving, south around the corner, two doors up from Susan's parents, to a three story "single" house at 37 Legare Street. "The great green barn," Bennett would call the place that would, over the years, become synonymous with creativity and hospitality in the city.[1] The move brought him closer to the strongholds of Charleston's society.

Eager ever since his engagement to prove himself worthy of Charleston, he had already produced his first local publication, not counting the two newspaper articles published before he moved south. (The first had been his letters the major had printed in the *News and Courier*; another, "An Old Fashioned Mecca," about South Carolinians and their visits to White Sulphur Springs and Salt Sulphur Springs, had appeared in 1895.)[2]

In 1902, to raise money for the local chapter of the United Daughters of the Confederacy (which Susan's mother would chair, as national president, the next year), Bennett designed and saw through press "A Souvenir Calendar."[3] It featured his purplish-hued photographs of Charleston sites, many of which he overpainted to blot out anachronisms or highlight details lost in the printing. Accompanying the images (a new idea for the city just waking to the tourist trade of the West Indian Exposition) were snippets of the city's history. Making history, too, was his inclusion of at least two spots associated with African American history.[4] It was not something Daisy Simonds would have done, for nowhere did Bennett's name appear.

Despite his self-effacement, many in town began to recognize his growing interest and expertise, and, thinking that as a writer he had no real job (an attitude that made him angry), a few asked for his help. Paul Rea, director of the Charleston Museum, made him an honorary curator. The institution had a glorious, if hazy, past, for no one knew its founding date; and to face its future, it soon moved from the College of Charleston to an auditorium built for the Confederate veterans convention Bennett had followed back in Chillicothe. (Both sites—the College and Thompson Auditorium—were featured in his calendar of 1902.) After the move, he'd work to fill its new galleries, convincing his mother-in-law to donate her carriage and advertising for a stuffed Carolina parakeet, recently extinct, in his native Chillicothe.[5] Perusing old newspapers, he'd find and pass on to the museum news of its movements in the 1820s.[6]

An even older cultural institution, the Charleston Library Society, founded in 1748, asked for his help; he was elected a trustee as early as 1903. One of his tasks was to read "doubtful" books to decide if they were fit for general circulation in this genteel private lending library.[7] (In the 1930s a young Citadel cadet would watch him climb the steps to the building for which he had raised funds and designed the carved lettering over the doorway; in the large airy room, he'd sniff the air and ask if what he smelled was not the odor of sanctity.)[8]

In this city of amateurs and dabblers he was looked up to as an ambassador of the greater world. On the third anniversary of his wedding, the local paper printed his assessment of the works of Barton Grey, the pseudonym for the local poet George Herbert Sass, whose works Bennett had mooned over as a "moody and sentimental boy" back in Ohio.[9] Now, ironically, they met, and Bennett was paying him tribute (which he would do again in *The Library of Southern Literature*; he'd come to help Barton Grey's son, too).[10] Obviously, Bennett was being accepted, despite the fact that he surprised people by refusing to wear a jacket in the city's subtropical heat; he was one of the first of his class to appear publicly in his "vivid" blue shirt-sleeves (earning him the nickname "The Blue Man"); he was also one of the first men in town to appear hatless in the street.[11]

He was sought out by many for his cheer, polite bearing, dignity, and authority. Needing help with a novel, Thornwell Jacobs, a native of Clinton, South Carolina, and founder of Oglethorpe College in Atlanta, wrote Bennett for criticism.[12] And Edwin Augustus Harleston, a descendant of black and white Harlestons, looked up to him. Harleston was an undertaker by profession but really an accomplished portrait painter; he'd eventually serve as the first president of Charleston's NAACP. Harleston would report happily to his wife Eloise that Mr. Bennett had nodded to him on the street.[13] Bennett was also one of the few in town with kind words for another marginalized Charlestonian: meeting Ludwig Lewisohn in the Library Society, Bennett spoke words of encouragement to "the gifted Jew."[14]

The appellation would have upset Lewisohn; for, in hopes of fitting into Charleston society, he had all but denied his Jewish roots. But just as Bennett was constantly identified as an Ohio Yankee and Daisy Breaux was pegged as an interloper from New Orleans, so Lewisohn, despite attending the Catholic cathedral and Methodist Church, was considered a Jew by others in the city. Charleston was the home of many old Jewish families dating from before the American Revolution, and although they and their religion were respected, Jews (especially those foreign born) were not accepted socially.[15] Bennett, like many others, had some mild, stereotypical anti-Semitic views.[16]

As a young boy, Lewisohn had emigrated with his parents from Berlin; they moved to Charleston after a few bleak years with cousins in Saint Matthews. He attended the College of Charleston, where he was refused entrance into a fraternity due to his Jewish origins. But he was so taken with the charm and languid beauty of the city that, like Daisy Simonds, he wanted to belong and thought, like Bennett, that by mastering the city's past he might be welcomed into its present society. Possessing a brilliant mind (but a short, plump body and Semitic face that matched stereotypical views of Jews) and wanting to be a writer, Lewisohn had looked back to Charleston's traditions for encouragement; he researched the nineteenth-century writers who had flourished before the Civil War; he published a series of articles in the *News and Courier* that he longingly called "Books *We* Have Made" (emphasis added).

The ladies of the Library Society cataloged his newspaper series, but they disdained his later writings. In his novel *The Broken Snare*, autobiographical *Upstream*, and then in *The Case of Mr. Crump*, his masterpiece, he'd speak of sex and women all too frankly; nevertheless, in his books he'd depict Charleston with tenderness and longing. As if to prove his manners, Lewisohn, like Owen Wister in his forthcoming novel *Lady Baltimore*, would not name the city. (Wister had planned to, but Henry James, feeling that to call the city by its name would be too glaring, convinced Wister to mask her identity.)[17] Despite the line drawings in his novel clearly delineating Charleston, Wister changed the town's name to "Kingsport"; and Lewisohn followed suit, using the name "Queenshaven" in most of his works depicting the city.[18]

Lewisohn kept trying to breach the walls of the social elite, into which Bennett had married. Lewisohn himself would marry tragically a number of times—the first time to a much older woman who made his life so miserable he parodied her in his novel *The Case of Mr. Crump*, which could at first only be published in Paris due to its frankness and risk of libel.[19]

But Charleston, in a way, did value Lewisohn. Several gentlemen, having civic pride in his brilliance, paid for his schooling at Columbia University. He later went to teach at Ohio State University, where Bennett believed he treated friends of his shabbily.[20] Lewisohn would succeed as a writer, scholar, cultural and literary critic, as well as Zionist; he would be acclaimed (by the likes of Sigmund Freud and Thomas Mann) in New York, Vienna, Paris, and Tel Aviv but garner only faint praise in the city that first inspired and then condemned him.[21]

Bennett watched Lewisohn over the years, reporting on his actions and gossiping on his failings, while he himself began to fit in. Being older, well-married, and possessing a handsome presence and charm that Lewisohn lacked, Bennett was welcomed into many social circles. He served on committees and helped artists who were struggling—all rewarding and satisfying, but which did not make him any money. He was uncomfortable accepting the Smythes' largesse; he wanted to make his own living.

"I had married," he wrote "on the expectation of continuing to write for *St. Nicholas*."[22] He had been offered a position in its editorial office, but declined that to continue his writing. "Mrs. Dodge . . . and I were planning a series . . . on Shakespeare's plays, similar to Lamb's *Tales from Shakespeare* but from a different angle . . . [and] Mrs. Dodge proposed to collect all my short stuff [his silhouette tales] from *St. Nicholas*" and publish them in book form, giving him income.[23] This had been discussed as early as 1901, but William Fayal Clarke vetoed all those ideas after he took Mary Mapes Dodge's place at her death in 1905. He also turned down Bennett's projected sequel to *Master Skylark*. "He did not even ask for my proposed sketch plot," Bennett countered testily a generation later; it was to be based on the book's most successful character, Gaston Carew, who, it would be revealed in the sequel, "on the intercession of Will Shakespeare and Benjamin Jonson was not hanged, and instead was pardoned by Queen Elizabeth on condition that he leave the country."[24] Then "by the exhibit of smartest courage [Carew would be] . . . permitted to return to London, through . . . the agency of that rare old man, Old John Churchyard."[25] This would bring a reunion of Carew and his daughter Cecily (and revive a seemingly dead father like Barnaby Lee's). Though the Century Company was not interested, Bennett turned to it periodically over the years, having mentioned it first to his father in the summer of 1896.[26] He eventually told the story to a class of girls at Dana Hall, where his sister Martha, who had provided him with *Skylark's* original premise, taught.[27] He did not totally relinquish the idea of a sequel until the 1920s when, in his fifties, he admitted to having lost the necessary "lyric Elizabethan feeling."[28]

Not being able to resuscitate Gaston Carew, he wanted to revive his father's story; but again there was no financial interest by the Century Company in *Buckhorn Johnny.* Without Dodge around to champion his cause, this lack of interest by *St. Nicholas,* which had been the vehicle of all his successes, was frightening.

So Bennett began to consider writing on other subjects—the things he had found fascinating about the South Carolina low country. None of the locals were. Barton Grey had written classic elegies; and a genteel lady writer, Annie Hay Colcock, had written a novel set in Europe (*Her American Daughter;*) her *Margaret Tudor,* set in Spanish St. Augustine in the era of the colony's founding, would soon appear. Local attorney Theodore Jervey was castigating blacks and denouncing reconstruction in his novel *The Elder Brother.* No one, other than William Molen, who wrote poems celebrating things such as the new post office and a company's new brand of ice cream, seemed to be making good use of the "capital" of the low country. (Molen was something of a joke to the local citizens; but Bennett shared his interest in the current scene.) In 1903, not long after his honeymoon, Bennett lectured the Federation of Women's Clubs in Charleston on the topic "Spiritual Songs of the Old Plantations." He reported on how he had collected them, one woman telling him God had spoken the words of her song. Possessing a good voice, he also sang a few. And, according to the *News and Courier,* which featured his speech prominently, he "drew attention to the similarity of musical forms to the ancient Greeks, the Scotch and the Afro-Americans." He compared the cane pipes cut by the "colored boys" to the syrinx or panpipes of ancient times. "Passing along the country roads at night playing on these pipes, the ragged negro boy might pass for a faun of old," Bennett said; "the 'Spirituals' are the only real folk songs this country has ever produced," he concluded definitively.[29]

Many in the audience no doubt were skeptical, preferring to think of them as "Songs of the Charleston Darkey," as Jane Screven Heyward, Du-Bose Heyward's mother, would style them in a pamphlet she'd issue to catch the tourist trade in a few years. But Bennett was fascinated. He sent off to New York a manuscript of over 150 songs he and his wife and his sister-in-law had collected, but there found only prejudice and disinterest. One publisher told him that his true-to-life moving and eerie transcriptions did not fit in with the public's symphonic and sophisticated concept of what they should be. "We published many years ago the volume entitled [Fisk] Jubilee Songs," the editor wrote back. "We can go no further."[30] He was asked if he cared to add a few of his to the anthology; he declined politely.

"I suppose Mrs. Bennett and I were too early in the field to receive recognition," he wrote sadly (to Jane Hunter) in 1939.[31] A generation later, Society for the Preservation of Negro Spirituals concerts would be the rage, and it would be quite common to find folklorists, WPA folk-tale recorders, slave-life transcriptionists, and linguists carrying their primitive equipment around the low country. (One would even record Bennett's voice as typically "American.")[32] "Mother and I . . . started the interest here," he told his family in later years.[33]

At the turn of the century, interest in African American culture was nearly nonexistent; only a handful of people understood what Bennett was doing. One was Booker T. Washington of Tuskegee who wrote to consult his collection of spirituals; Washington was possibly looking for something cultural his audiences could take pride in—or perhaps he was looking for texts that students at Tuskegee could sing. Bennett wrote him back amiably and also later lent his whole collection to Tudor Jenks, who passed it to a friend, who later gave advice on the South and blacks to her son, Owen Wister.[34] Thus it seems likely Bennett inadvertently influenced Wister's *Lady Baltimore*, which would appear in a few years.

Disappointed by the disinterest in spirituals, yet still wanting to gain a name for himself and fame for his adopted state (as well as make money), Bennett began a Wilkie Collinsesque mystery. What the English novelist had done with the mysterious and atmospheric novels *The Moonstone* and *The Woman in White*, Bennett now tried to do for the low country. He concocted a story centering on the death of Reverend Ansel Seahurst. To it he grafted some Edgar Allan Poe elements, natural perhaps, since Poe's "The Gold Bug," set on nearby Sullivan's Island, was then one of the few well-known stories in American literature that took Charleston as a setting. From it he had appropriated the ideas of ratiocination (thinking logically and rationally) and a cryptogram; he went Poe one better, however, by making his a double cryptogram. He called his story "The Labyrinth" and sometimes "The Apostle of Beauty," having written 145 pages by September 1904. He changed his tale's name when he read Henry James's comment on man being torn between twin demons of imagination and observation. He christened it "The Twin Demons" then; (Collins in at least one of his novels, *What Sheila Said*, also employed twins). He planned to have the mystery of Reverend Seahurst's death solved by two detectives: one scientific, the other intuitive, each needing the other to decode life, death, and their many mysteries. He was pleased with its progress, but had to stop after losing his way in its labyrinthine plotting.[35]

He shelved the story for awhile but kept the setting, using the Carolina low country for a few short stories. In 1904, the *Criterion* published "Tudo & Crook Fang: The Story of a Desperate Fight Between a Cooter [turtle] and a Moccasin," illustrated with his own drawings. And in December of that year, in the same magazine, he published a tale of Brer Rabbit in "A Carolina Christmas Story."[36] He also published a story about a Negro sermon in *Harper's* in 1906.[37]

This marked his first extended use of Gullah, the language of the local blacks, which often baffled visitors to the city; for it differed not just from white speech but also from the language spoken by blacks in other Southern states, as popularized in the dialect stories of Georgian Joel Chandler Harris. The talk of the coastal blacks featured bizarre pronunciations, contained seeming gender, case, and tense inconsistencies, and employed cryptic vocabularies of unknown etymologies. It could seem totally incomprehensible and not at all related to English to someone not acquainted with its peculiarities. In his article, Bennett used musical notation to demonstrate the tune patterns and cadence of the speech, and ended his piece with a postscript, noting that "ridicule of any sort is utterly outside the writer's purpose." In the note, he also demonstrated the fact that he was already familiar with W. E. B. Du Bois's *The Souls of Black Folk*, published just a few years before in 1903.[38]

Ever since arriving he had been intrigued by Gullah, asking questions about it of whites of his class. They, however, seemed more interested in criticizing his Ohio way of pronouncing than in taking seriously his questions of how and why the blacks spoke the way they did. It's just bad English, they told him. This he did not believe, but the insistence of their dismissive replies taught him to stop asking; he turned a keen ear and listened intently, realizing that blacks who had never met used words similarly, with some standardization of word order, case, gender, and vocabulary.

And there was something else intriguing: although they might dismiss its intellectual meaning, often whites in town treated Gullah as a distinct language, perhaps unconsciously; white children raised by their black nannies, called dahs, spoke it with their dahs and with black children, but switched to standard English when with white adults. Some whites also used Gullah to tell dialect stories (as DuBose Heyward's mother would soon do to raise money from the tourists coming to the city; in the process she'd unwittingly give her son the name of his most famous novel and character, Porgy).[39]

Fascinated by all the interplay, Bennett took notes and augmented his "field research" by searching out all the books on language, Africa, and early Southern history he could find in his father-in-law's home and in the Charleston Library Society. As he progressed, he tried to get others excited about his project; but African American culture was viewed as inferior, debased, and unworthy. Although she had worked to transcribe spirituals, Susan did not think as he did; being a busy mother, she was less in awe of him now and took on her expected role as champion of local beliefs. So Bennett quietly stopped talking about what he was doing, even as he persisted in his observations and studies. Like picking up the music and singing by ear, he also picked up the speech; in fact, he taught himself Gullah so well that he, too, began to tell dialect stories. Among those who listened was his young nephew, Sam Gaillard Stoney Jr. As an adult Stoney would unwittingly include one of his uncle's invented stories as an authentic tale from the oral tradition in *Black Genesis*, a collection of Gullah creation tales co-authored with Gertrude Matthews Shelby.[40]

Bennett was becoming so intrigued with Gullah that he amassed vast stores of notes, eventually compiling numerous scrapbooks on the subject.

He pasted in observations, clippings, and abstracts from published sources on Gullah subjects such as vocabulary, place of origin, and word etymologies. He started reading everything he could find from earlier times to see if other observers had commented on it (the earliest description and transcription of Gullah he found was from 1794). This led him to the colonial newspapers, which he began to read in the Charleston Library Society; he reasoned that if he could ferret out the geographic origins of the slaves advertised and auctioned in Charleston, he could deduce where their language had its beginnings. He was so captured by this mystery that he began to look for a way to use Gullah not just in his nonfiction but in his fiction, too. The opportunity came unexpectedly, as he joked with Susan's sister, Loula, and her husband, the parents of the young Samuel Gaillard Stoney.

In 1905, Stoney's father bought out all the other heirs' interests in Medway, the old family plantation on the Back River that Bennett had visited and rhapsodized over at the turn of the century. Along with the property came a trunk of papers documenting all the various owners and tracts. "These papers were delivered to the Stoney's house in Charleston at 101 St. Philip Street."[41] Knowing his interest in local history, Loula and Sam invited Bennett over to examine them. When they pried open the lid, they discovered "mouldering documents . . . tied in bundles with rotten ribbons, . . . the oldest [ones], engrossed on parchment . . . in almost perfect condition [while] those . . . on cheap, [acidic] machine-made paper . . . had already rotted. . . . In others the ink had eaten away the paper . . . leaving strange little rows of stencils . . . through the yellow sheets."[42] From among the pile, Bennett " picked up a . . . map, torn in two, having a large star particularly marked upon one portion, with some indecipherable notes across the back. 'Just the sort of thing for a story of buried treasure,'" he said to Mrs. Stoney.

"I dare you to write one," she laughed.[43]

Bennett laughed back. But when he took up his "The Twin Demons" manuscript again, he remembered. That story still had its problems and, as he put it down again, the thought of the treasure map now intrigued him.[44] He went back to Poe and to his family, taking structure from the author and characters from the Smythe and Stoney clans. "The Gold Bug" is told by a nearly anonymous narrator, and so Bennett followed, creating a narrator (whose name "Buck Guignard" is only revealed on the title page) who has been witness to many of the events he has just seen.

Since the trunk and map documenting Medway had given him the idea, Bennett used it as his setting, changing the name of Back River to Blue Hill and the plantation to Indigo House: "It is a quaint old edifice, Indigo Mansion House," Guignard tells of it, "two centuries old, its wall stained all possible colors by the dampness and by time, the ferns growing in the . . . old green plaster and in the cracks of the hooded chimneys. Its roof is of cypress shingles, blue with age, with deep valleys and gutters . . . as if it were an old castle . . . or a reverend minster-tower. Nothing remained of the old Dutch gables but a crumbling edge of precipitous wall, and nothing of the minster but the bats . . . among the rafters."[45]

After setting the scene to make Blue Hill look like Medway when Bennett first saw it, Guignard begins with the intertwined histories of it and the Gaillard family, "those happy hearts who built the old house."[46] Instead of Sam Gaillard Stoney owning the site, the owner in Bennett's version is Tom Gaillard. His wife is Marie Louise, called Lou (just as Sam Stoney's wife was Louise, called Loula or Lou). Tom, Lou, their children, and various cousins are trying to eke out a living on the plantation in the 1890s when they receive a letter from a Yankee cousin who has lost his health and has been ordered south (as had Bennett himself). The Gaillards, rich only in family connections, invite this unknown cousin of theirs to visit immediately.

In his way of coming to town, in his intense brooding, his melancholy ways, and fascination with local history, the Yankee Jack Gignillatt (pronounced Gin-lat) is remarkably similar to the Yankee Jack Bennett. Thus, although he was using a new setting, Bennett was nevertheless continuing an older pattern. In the England of *Master Skylark*, he had employed Shakespeare; then his ancestor Gerrit van Sweringen had walked into and taken over his story set in New Amsterdam, *Barnaby Lee*. Now in the Carolina low country, Bennett put himself into the story. "Writers must amuse themselves," he said of this book's beginnings.[47]

As in *Skylark*, the story came quickly. "Jack had not been in Blue Hill two weeks before we all felt as if we had known him half our own lives and all of his," Guignard tells us. "Indeed, I confess, the young fellow was irresistible . . . unfailingly courteous . . . comprehending . . . simple of heart, . . . [and] frankly sincere."[48] It's such a true and conceited portrait of Bennett himself that one can almost hear the family laughing in the background. In fact, Bennett later confessed that "to amuse the family while the book was in process . . . I used to read the various incidents and episodes aloud to the household at Capt. Stoney's on summer evenings as I completed the chapters."[49]

Paralleling true life, Bennett's alter ego Gignillatt falls in mostly with his young cousin, Jeanne, who bears more than a passing resemblance to Susan Smythe. (Indeed, one illustration in the published text is an unretouched photograph of her.) Bennett had first met Susan in a small Greek-like temple at Salt Sulphur Springs; similarly, Gignillatt first sees Jeanne, standing "against the light, tall, slender, and straight, lovely as a Greek Caryatid."[50]

Gignillatt and Jeanne look over the house, and he, somewhat of a mathematician and surveyor, realizes there is a room secreted in its staircase. He and Jeanne find a hidden door and go up the hidden interior staircase. They discover a trunk of papers similar to the one opened by the Stoneys. Among all the plats and maps are old letters and diaries, which are reproduced verbatim in the text—complete with odd eccentric spellings and gaps where the papers have ostensibly disintegrated and fallen apart.

From the documents, Jack and Jeanne (and the readers) follow the travails and triumphs of the French emigrants, the Gaillards; in the first years of the colony, they make a fortune raising indigo. But when the area erupts into anarchy during the Revolution, Peyre Gaillard, the family patriarch, and his trusted servant, Judas Gay (similar to the slave Joop in Poe's "The Gold Bug"), flee. Gay single-handedly buries the treasure in the wild and mysterious Pompion (pronounced "Punkin") Swamp and shows his master the burial place. (Susan wrote to John about Pompion Hill Chapel—and how to pronounce it—before they were married.)[51] Gaillard maps the place and notes swamp landmarks on it. Then he tears the map in half; one part he keeps and the other he gives to Judas. Thus the one half, which is all that survives, is similar to the document Bennett pulled from the trunk.

He had based the story on a legend of the Drayton family; it told of the patriarch ordering his mustee (half-Indian and half-Negro) servant to bury the family silver to keep it from the marauding British. In that version, the owner died and, when the war was over, the servant refused to tell where the treasure was buried since the woman to whom he was devoted could not claim it, she being the daughter of the second wife and disinherited by law of primogeniture. As he approached death, however, the servant relented and called for his mistress. She had died long before, but her similar-looking niece came in her stead to hear his confession; she could not understand a word he said, however—it was gibberish to her. So the Drayton treasure remained lost, although apparently a similar silver cache was found while Bennett was writing the book.[52]

In his tale, Bennett fashioned events a bit differently; Peyre Gaillard, the owner of this family's treasure, is hanged by Tories; his slave Judas Gay, mad with grief and his "reversion" to barbarism by his frightening experiences in the morbid swamp, manages to return and hand over his half of the map. He tries again and again to tell the surviving Gaillards what he knows, but no one can understand his mad ramblings.

After the Revolution, some family members search for it. But since they become rich, this time rising high on the tide of rice, the lost wealth is not necessary. Stray family members seek it, each suffering something like a curse in their obsession. When the Civil War ends, however, the family is utterly ruined and in dire poverty. To make matters worse, just after Jack Gignillatt arrives, a usurious moneylender named Geake shows a forged mortgage he holds on Indigo House and threatens to foreclose and evict the family.

They despair, but cousin Jack Gignillatt rises to the bait and audaciously claims that he will find the treasure and save the family, just as Nick saved his family in *Skylark* and Bennett saved his back in Chillicothe. Other than his Dutchman's stubbornness, Gignillatt has only Judas Gay's half of a map with odd jottings on the other side, and the nonsensical mix of syllables handed down the generations from Judas; his words are: *"A rumble souf wid a parasol at noon f'om Monday Goole's to Hongry Jane's; bile de can souf-wes' wid a leak in the pan, tanny-go, sanny-go."*[53]

In setting up this situation, Bennett borrows heavily from "The Gold Bug." Legrand, its main character, is of a rich Southern family faced with reversals of fortune; in his intensity in trying to solve the cryptogram he discovers on a piece of paper, he is manic and melancholy. The same holds true for Gignillatt, whom the cousins watch as he locks himself up in his room. Furthermore, Gignillatt, like Legrand, comes to realize that neither the jottings on the back of the map nor the odd jumble of words handed down from Judas Gay are nonsense. Thinking rationally and logically, Gignillatt solves the written cryptogram as Legrand does (even referring to the Poe story). Deciphering the verbal cryptogram, which consists of the twisted language of Judas Gay, is the more compelling mystery; and it is Bennett's creation entirely.

In "The Gold Bug," Legrand wonders if the message is in English or Spanish; he assumes English, so that makes its decoding easy. But Gignillatt, like Bennett, knows more and has no such luxury. He realizes that Gullah, Judas Gay's slave language, comes from not one vocabulary but many— archaic English, French, Portuguese, Spanish, and African. Thus in Gignillatt's untwisting of the seemingly nonsense phrases of Gullah, Bennett places his fascination with the dialect in the center of the mystery.

The importance and true nature of Gullah is something only he and his alter ego Gignillatt see. (Gullah is even one of the inside jokes in the book. The narrator mentions a dowser named Israel Manigault, "no relation to the preacher of that name."[54] To most it would mean nothing; but Bennett is tipping his hat to J. Palmer Lockwood of Charleston, who gave Gullah "Darkey Sermons" under the name of Rebberand Israel Manigault.)[55] Since coming to Charleston, Bennett had been told there was neither rhyme nor reason to Gullah and that it was bad English spoken by ignorant blacks; similarly, the Gaillards have dismissed Gay's twisted black's speech as "imbecile jargon." "He who has no Greek pronounces Greek . . . unimportant," Bennett answers the whites of Charleston through his fictional mouthpiece.[56] In this way he is showing Charlestonians that he knows more than they do; he can decipher what they cannot read. Only Bennett and Gignillatt, the non-natives, unblinded by prejudice, can see to the true meaning of things. They are like Poe's detective in "The Purloined Letter," who can see what in plain sight others miss.) Suddenly, Jeanne, guided by her cousin Jack, has a breakthrough and realizes the importance of Gullah. (This is a dream, a wish only, for in real life Bennett wanted his wife to, but they would argue about Gullah and its importance for years.) Here there is an echo of his earlier mystery manuscript, for the cryptograms require the twin demons of imagination and observation to decode them. Jack provides the scientific observation, and Jeanne helps to decode it instantly "in a flash" with her intuition.[57]

The words now decoded are these: *A rumbo* (a Portuguese sailing term), southward *par la sol* (by the sun) at noon, from *monticule* (a hill or knoll) to *un gros chene* (a large tree) *par thes cannes* (by the canes—bamboo), southwestward to *le pin du roi* (the king's oak—a measuring landmark) at an angle of *cing e'quarante* (forty-five degrees). With these clues, they run to dictionaries and see on the map that a line going "due north from the great oak tree on the (cane) ridge . . . and another northeast from the Kings Tree, through

Pompion Swamp" will eventually cross each other. Here, on the Monticule du Jude, or Judas's knoll, the treasure will be buried.[58] Thus despite the galaxy of exotic characters and a very romantic setting (for Bennett's prose is as lush as the low country and as dense and overworked as the greenery itself), this cryptogram and its unraveling are the most compelling pieces of the story. Other than that, there is nothing much else going on; the historical narratives of the loss of the treasure and the attempts to find it are interesting; yet there is no character development, no one struggling against odds, traits that distinguish *Master Skylark* and *Barnaby Lee*. True drama is lacking. It is a tour-de-force about the use and the deconstruction of language that carries the tale.

In Poe's narrative the treasure is found first, and then Legrand backtracks to explain the code and how he broke it. In Bennett's tale, Jack Gignillatt and Jeanne Gaillard break the code and then bring in the family to find the treasure. They break into two teams (again showing the earlier influence of "The Twin Demons"): with the two starting points from the two different halves of the map, and knowing the angles and degrees supplied by Judas Gay, they start off.

The chapters treating the treasure's recovery from Pompion Swamp are wonderfully textured and poetic, sustained page after page at a fever pitch; it's appropriate that language is used dexterously in a story where untangling language is the key. "Swinging their brush-hooks, the negroes dashed into the thicket," Bennett begins,

and we plunged into the waste of rushes; . . . as we went the canes grew higher and higher and became so interlaced by vines that there was no thoroughfare save along narrow paths trodden by wild creatures. . . .

We passed old indigo fields ridged with almost obliterated furrows; the earth shook like a jelly-bag; advance constantly became more difficult; here and there wrecks of ancient causeways and rice-field banks faced with mildewed brick lent solider footing; black pools impeded our progress; fallen trees and rotten logs gave insecure support . . . [as] we came to the edge of the great swamp, a region of dreary terror. . . .

For hours we struggled forward. . . . It was into a region indescribably dreadful and desolate.

Densely thicketed, dim and gloomy at any season, the growth of spring's fresh foliage . . . deepened the darkness. Twilight, huddling and melancholy, gathered among the shadowy trees. No matter what the hour, always, here, it seemed the end of the day. Where, by momentary vistas along black canals, we obtained imperfect views . . . dismal lakes as dark as ebony . . . added a deeper sense of gloom. Beyond these dark lakes . . . trees, young a century ago, shot chiseled and voluted trunks. . . . In every direction, as far as the eye could reach, the vast bulks of immense trees arose . . . choking with their interlocking roots the courses of dark water, and . . . precipitously furrowed by their own straining upward growth. Vast and sombre as the swamp had been though which we had already passed, what lay behind us was radiant compared to that which stretched before.[59]

Cutting one's way through the lush language, one hardly notices that these chapters, like the swamp itself and similar chapters in *Barnaby Lee* describing the storm and Philip Calvert, actually slow down the pace of the story. "I don't believe your fairy tale for an instant," a minor character tells Gignillatt as they set out, but he is so mesmerized by its vivid telling that he states, "I'll go with you till you drop."[60] This may be the reader's feeling, too.

Finally, the two teams meet. On a knoll rising from the swamp (Judas's Knoll, they call it, or the Monticule de Jude, both early working titles for the story) Gignillatt and the Gaillards fell a tree. Within its hollowed-out heart, an old footprint (that of the slave Judas Gay), still (improbably) fresh in the mud is revealed. As they dig, Jack Gignillatt reveals that he once worked with archaeologists funded by the Peabody Museum. In real life, Bennett himself did the same thing; the experience helped him describe the condition of the disturbed soils and the corroded wooden chest they find. (Poe, illogically, described his century-old boxes as fairly intact.) All the treasure is taken back to Indigo House where it is weighed and tallied; values are assigned to each piece, something Poe included but Bennett expanded.

In an odd way, where the story is most fabulous Bennett is most realistic; he worked with Tiffany and Company to find out what years of being buried would do to specific pieces of silver and jewelry, and to get a true value of their worth, he described the whole lot to a Charleston firm, James Allen and Company, to appraise them, piece by piece.[61]

This type of manipulation of fact and fiction and playing with real and imagined stories was not as common in 1906 as it is in today's "stories based on fact." Many readers expected the boundaries between fact and fiction to be kept intact and so would have trouble with the story, but this was a plus, the author felt. To keep the story appropriate for children, he concentrated most on the treasure and its recovery, just hinting at Jack Gignillatt's and Jeanne Gaillard's future relationship, as he had Nick and Cecily's and Barnaby's and Dorothy's. As in these other stories, Bennett planned for his book to appear first in *St. Nicholas* before being issued as a book. Happy with what he foresaw, he set off to New York with his manuscript when he finished it.

When William Fayal Clarke, Mary Mapes Dodge's successor, read it, however, knowing of a hole in the Century Company's adult list, he suggested oddly that Bennett change his children's treasure tale to an adult adventure and love story and have it published right away by the Century Company, bypassing *St. Nicholas* entirely. Bennett declined, but Clarke insisted; it was to be an adult book or not issued by the Century Company. Anxious to keep his name before the public, four years having now elapsed since the appearance of the book form of *Barnaby Lee,* and feeling a loyalty to the company, Bennett was torn. He told Clarke he'd think about it.

Mulling it over while walking the streets of New York, he went back and forth; he did not like being rushed into things and he felt it was really a children's story. He had put in little lectures on water tables, mapping, and surveying, in keeping with the tenor of *St. Nicholas;* nevertheless he saw that the change would mesh many of the things he had been thinking about the past few years. He had wanted to make his new relations and their circle proud of him; and he had wanted to show the world the beauty and history of Charleston and the low country. He saw now, too, that without Dodge as his champion, he might not succeed as he had with *St. Nicholas.* It was an opportunity to move off in a new direction, coalescing all his new hopes and dreams in his adopted city. With some misgivings, he agreed to Clarke's idea.

"To make the book an adult one," as Clarke directed him to, "I interpolated some not badly done, but quite intrusive love making towards the middle of the ms to appease the romantic." [62] He did this by adding a chapter where Jack and Jeanne meet at night accidentally on the old, elaborately carved Indigo House staircase. As they stand there alone, love, "The Unbidden Guest," like a vagrant, unsuspected breeze, enters the story. In keeping with the blend of realism and romance, he based the scene on his proposal to Susan in her father's Legare Street library. Remembering and enshrining it, Bennett achieved one of the high spots of his career, creating a tender scene where his book's characters finally struggle in real-life situations.

The chapter worked wonderfully well as a set piece, but when he got to Chillicothe and reread the whole text, Bennett saw to his dismay that the "Unbidden Guest" had brought some unexpected repercussions along with it. The whole story, other than that chapter, was told by the narrator, but Jack and Jeanne's meeting on the staircase is unwitnessed. The book was now in galleys, the publication date announced; he did not have time to change the point of view to omniscience. Thinking quickly, Bennett worked out the solution of allowing Guignard's version to stop and be interrupted with inserts, which, he noted on the title page, were "arranged by John Bennett." [63]

It was an awkward solution, and indeed one reviewer would call him on it, noting that the love interest seemed to be thrust haphazardly into the text, violating the predominant first-person telling.[64] The rewriting in galleys, and the hurried shifting of the novel from a children's story to an adult's apparently also caused other problems. There is a confusing scene change on page 123 of the published text, and the running chapter titles at the top of the pages do not agree with the title at the chapter's beginning.[65] Used to being a careful rewriter and reviser, Bennett had no time to catch these things; the printer's proofs came back to him so fast, in fact, and he was so close to the publishing date that a July 12 *New York Tribune* article on agricultural conditions in Texas could be included, in a recast and re-attributed form, in his book, which was for sale in stores in October.[66] Getting to that finish was as frenetic as a horse race.

When the book appeared, he collapsed but had a good time recuperating. For nearly all the reviews were glowing. "A Tale of Genuine Wonder," was the verdict of the *New York Sun.* The *Norfolk Landmark* called it the "best story of the unravelling of a cryptogram since Poe's Gold Bug." The Brooklyn *Eagle* pronounced it "splendid." [67]

Ludwig Lewisohn wrote Bennett, envious of the achievement; [68] and George Wauchope, a professor of English at the University of South Carolina, called it (in the *Charleston News and Courier*) the best South Carolina novel ever published, a slap at *Lady Baltimore*, which was selling much better than Bennett's book and had appeared a few months earlier, in July 1906.[69]

Charleston was now in the public eye—despite the fact that Wister had called Charleston "Kingsport" in his novel and Bennett did not center his tale in the city itself but nearer Georgetown, to the north. People could nevertheless take pride in Bennett. Critics hailed his lush language as evidence of a poet working in prose and praised him for giving glimpses of untold stories, "of open windows and of corners with people around them."[70] The *New York Times* applauded his giving a standard tale "new dress of skillful and unique contrivances, cleverly woven together, full of human interest,"[71] while Lyman Abbott and Hamilton Mabe, of the distinguished publication *Outlook,* called it one the important books of the season: "the marvel of it is that it is told with such simplicity and produces so strong an impression of verity."[72]

In fact, so truthful did the book appear that many readers, unused to Bennett's blending of factual and fictional techniques and unheedful of the Latin epigrams from Horace and Phaedrus warning of the book's fictional theme, took it literally; they thought the story real.[73]

Bennett had dedicated the book to the Stoneys, and as soon as the book appeared the Captain and his family began to receive mail and visits from those who not only claimed relation and descent from Peyre Gaillard but also demanded their share of the treasure. Others instead wrote to advise the Stoneys how to invest their money.

A few apparently even believed that more treasure must still be buried; twenty-five years later, someone unknown, guided by the illustrations—which were mostly photographs of actual settings—dynamited a huge cedar tree on nearby Parnassus plantation, believing the tree in the illustration to be the one on the map where treasure would be found instantly.[74]

Indeed, these uncredited illustrations (all by Bennett) added to the general air of verisimilitude pervading the story. The cover design of Judas's oak was based on Bennett's idea (but rendered by a commercial artist); and the frontispiece, based on Medway, "to further the scheme of the book . . . was prepared to represent an old engraving, supposedly lithographed by an old time French artist" but was done by none other than the author himself.[75]

For a picture of the hero Jack Gignillatt, Bennett offered an unretouched photograph of his brother-in-law, Augustine Smythe. (Locally, the *Sunday News [and Courier]* recognized the truth and on November 25, 1906, commented on it.) A close-up of Jeanne is a photograph of a house guest visiting from Virginia, while a distant shot of "Jeanne under Judas' Oak" is Susan Smythe Bennett at Parnassus. (Several reviewers noted the disappointing nature of the images, and wrote cruelly that the hero and heroine, not as handsome as the book described them, deserved each other in their lack of comeliness.)[76] Judas Gay, the slave, is really a retouched image of Bill Abrams, whom Bennett knew in Chillicothe; Abrams did double duty, serving also as the basis of the image of "Daddy Pompey" in Bennett's 1904 "A Carolina Christmas Story."[77] The book, according to Bennett, was also printed in England—from the American sheets by the London *Times*—to break publishers' monopolies.[78]

Although he received nearly unstinting praise for *The Treasure of Peyre Gaillard*, the author himself knew it had its limitations. The novel, he acknowledged, "has some excellent high points in it, [but is] more truly a tour de force . . . made necessarily unequal in texture . . . when altered to suit a publisher's desire. . . . The story is not as well-woven, nor as compacted as I should have made it had I aimed at adult readers from the first; hence its 'spottiness.' Parts of it I have never bettered."[79]

He was right; in *The Treasure*, Bennett reached a sustained lyricism he'd never match again in his career. But after this book, his career would be entirely different. He had begun *The Treasure of Peyre Gaillard* as a lark, a children's story, and a tribute to his new family; it ended up as an adult tale based on serious African American and South Carolina history.

The opportunity to alter it had come by chance, but he had seized it willingly. And once he did, he never looked back. Except for a book republishing previously printed stories, all his subsequent works would be for adults, all on historical and Negro themes. All, like *The Treasure*, would employ deft combinations of realism and romance, of true-life characters blended with fictional ones in exotic and eccentric settings.

It appears that he was quite conscious of what he was doing; for a close reading of the text reveals that Bennett believed he truly had found a treasure in the fertile soil of the Carolina low country, and that he had been led here, like Gignillatt, following the footprints and language of blacks. These discoveries were of such great value that Charlestonians would lionize him for their discovery, he knew. So secure was he, in fact, that he could not resist indulging in prophecy. "This young 'lion' of the moment, the celebrity of a day, will be loved by a State and its people a few years later along," one of the Gaillard cousins decrees of Gignillatt/Bennett. "Mark my word, *ma chère*; he is one of the coming men. We conceit ourselves, you know, that he is a typical Carolinian for all his foreign birth."[80] A "typical Carolinian," his fictional cousin asserts, is a "Huguenot in lofty, proud relentlessness of purpose; an Englishman in loyal frankness and intrinsic common sense; a

Scot in . . . steadfast austerity, [and] a . . . Dutchman, obstinate." [81] Bennett claimed all these specific lines of descent in his own family tree. [82]

So, decoding the manuscript the same way Gignillatt did the cryptogram, one easily deciphers what Bennett is declaring in *The Treasure of Peyre Gaillard*. He is staking a claim to the area's rich lore and is vowing to unearth and restore it to those whose legacy it is. And for this, "in a few years along," as the cousins decree, he expects not just to be thanked but to be lionized. For discovering this treasure, he'd surpass those new arrivals like Ludwig Lewisohn and Daisy Simonds; Charlestonians and South Carolinians would accept him totally. This he knew would happen soon, and maybe had already.

CHAPTER 12

# *"A Brilliant . . . Execution"*

BENNETT WAS RIDING A CREST of emotion and expectation at the end of 1906: not only had he just published a book, but it looked like he might be launching a dynasty. *Peyre Gaillard* appeared in October 1906, and on the first day of the new year Susan presented him with a son. They named the boy John Henry van Sweringen Bennett; like Jane McClintock Bennett, four years older, this child bore Bennett names entirely. John Bennett III, his son would call himself eventually, if not literally correctly.[1]

Bennett vowed to support his son as his own father had failed to do him, but it would not be with income from *The Treasure of Peyre Gaillard*, he realized. Unlike all his previous works, it was not selling well, nor had he been given a large advance for it.[2] After exhausting the first edition, the Century Company ordered no more printings; Bennett acquired and stored the printing plates, hoping for a local edition eventually.[3]

"The critics . . . seem kind, but timid," he determinedly wrote his brother-in-law, Augustine Smythe (who had posed as Jack Gignillatt for the book's photographs), two weeks after his son's birth. "Excuse my wrath, but it waxes toward divine exasperation after twenty-four years of bitter perspiration and pencilling to have men hesitate, and palter, and spit white cotton froth, when one knows himself . . . to be a master of his craft. If I'm conceited, let it pass; I'll prove it true, some day, before or after the worms have played tag among my bones."[4]

He tried to prove it immediately and bolster his claim as interpreter of all things Charleston with a magazine article for *Harper's;* the editors asked for a series on "Negro Superstitions and Voodooism in the Carolinas," but they were not as interested in accuracy as he. "They pushed me unreasonably, and advertised the series to begin before I could possibly get my materials in shape, so I just choked off that hopeful breath too eager in its exhalations."[5]

He did manage, however, to get a piece in the *South Atlantic Quarterly*. In 1908, it published a two-article series, apparently the first scholarly article on Gullah as a language. He showed it had its own logic and rules, which he gave examples of, and he offered some African word etymologies; it was not just bad English spoken ignorantly. In Charleston, it barely made an impression; and then the magazine went out of business.[6]

But no matter; for he was at work on another subject he hoped would bring him renewed prestige. To announce it and to test the waters, he wrote a letter to the *New York Times* on 22 January 1907, just a week after his melancholy comments to Augustine Smythe. In his letter (published January 26) Bennett commented that some critics of *The Treasure of Peyre Gaillard* had chastised him for a turn his plot had taken, punishing the villainous Geake, who held the forged mortgaged on Indigo House. (This might have been a ploy on Bennett's part, for none of the book reviews he pasted into his scrapbooks mention it.) Foreclosing on an apothecary shop, Geake seizes all its contents. When it rains for weeks (as it did that summer of 1906), rumors grow among the superstitious that in the apothecary's inventory there is a mermaid trapped in a jar; it will only stop raining, they believe, when the imprisoned mermaid is set free. An angry mob, in search of the mermaid, chases Geake out of the low country.

This should not strain credulity, Bennett wrote a trifle disingenuously in his letter. Something similar had, in fact, happened in real life (so, he inferred, it should not be disbelieved). In Charleston in 1853, he wrote (elsewhere he said 1867), blacks had rioted fearing that the heavy rains were triggered by a mermaid trapped by a local apothecary. Bennett then gave a Gullah rendering of the tale, along with the date and the name of the woman who had told it to him.[7] While ostensibly defending his *Treasure*, he was really indulging in a bit of promotion and self-advertising. For he had decided that a collection of folktales such as the mermaid riot would be his next subject.

Soon after his letter appeared in the *Times* the New York *Post* noted it, and one of its writers, in turn, chastised Bennett for his comments in an article called the "The Breaking Point of Credulity." Bennett immediately went on the offensive, asking why only the mermaid episode strained credulity in a book full of other extraordinary things like hidden rooms, secret doors, treasures, and lost maps? Could it be that the public had grown used to these trappings, having encountered them in gothic novels for years? The mermaid riot was something new, he suggested, and maybe that was the reason the public balked. There were many more tales similar to the mermaid's, he noted. The "macabre legends, 'Doctor Ryngo,' 'Old Madame Margot,' 'The Wandering Jew' and 'The Black Constable' . . . are similarly of interest . . . not because they are true in the least degree, but because they are ineffably strange and horrible." [8]

There was no further reply in the press, and Bennett no doubt was happy, having made his subject newsworthy. He had failed to arouse interest in African American music or language, but the public was already commenting on his folktales. He'd have to act quickly to publish them, for the pieces of "fable and myth [were] already far decayed and rapidly passing out of existence. . . . Kicked about from gutter to gutter, straying like an alley cat from squalid court to court," they had disintegrated now to almost nothing; he had had to retrieve them from the "trashcans, gutters and dustbins of the town." For many it was too late; some were so decayed that "only the beginning remained, of others, an end without a beginning. Of others nothing remained but a wandering phrase, a title, a reference." [9]

He had heard tantalizing bits and pieces of them when he first arrived, and slowly he began his investigation of life in the side streets and back allies. He had found entry to the weird world through an odd combination of his own egalitarianism and the paternalism expected of him once he'd married into the local gentry.

"Part of my life [has been] vivified," he explained, "by getting my Negro employees and acquaintances out of courts [from] unjust charges brought against innocent victims of somebody else's rascality." [10] He had intervened when Walter Mayrant of Cromwell Alley and Caesar Grant of James Island were arrested for stealing lumber. Bennett testified that a white man had hired Mayrant and Grant to move the lumber from one place to another, telling them he was the owner; he duped them into stealing for him. [11] This the court would not have believed from Mayrant or Grant but did from the white Bennett, who vouched for them. This intervention, and the fact that the men realized Bennett had "no surreptitious end in view, no wish to ridicule or betray," inspired them to confidence; and suddenly "the hidden doors [like the hidden door in the staircase in *The Treasure of Peyre Gaillard*] were opened to the inner room. Yet even then, my puzzled friend and house guard [Walter Mayrant] said to me, 'Why is that white men are always trying to get the black man's knowledge. . . . Isn't he satisfied to know what the white man knows?'" [12]

If not completely unaffected by prejudice, Bennett was not totally blinded by it. (For a similar non-native's vacillating view on race, there is the case of Francis W. Dawson.) [13] Bennett had listened to the tales for their sheer wonder and strangeness and beauty. Mayrant saw his sincerity, and "from that hour on he and I moved in entire rapport. And through his confident introduction I was able to meet and secure much curious lore from other men and women not in my employ." [14] Most of them were born just before or just after the end of slavery. But he also met former slaves; "the[se] older folk were veritable storehouses of fable, myth, fantasy, and parable, folk wit curiously shrewd and distinguished." [15]

Every now and then, Mayrant, Grant, and their friends came by Legare Street; Bennett slipped out to meet them on the back steps, where they smoked and regaled him with stories of friends, living and dead; they told him tales they had heard from their elders and he kept asking for more and more. "A more curious fellow . . . about the legends, stories, traditions and doings, honorable and memorable . . . I never came across," the narrator of *The Treasure of Peyre Gaillard* says of Jack Gignillatt. [16]

He listened with the same rapture he had as a boy back in Chillicothe listening to Peter Dunn spin tales from the *Arabian Nights;* he heard the superstitious end of things, the silhouettes, so to speak, that certain events, episodes, and persons had cast after them. Now he wanted more—not just the myths but their origins, the real-life events that were so strange that observers had felt compelled to make up stories to make sense of them.

He found help in "Francis Nipson, soldier of Fortune, and sanitary inspector of the city of Charleston [who] knew more of the underside of Charleston life than any other man, white or black." Nipson, Bennett discovered, "was replete with the unrecorded annals of the town. To ride with him through the back streets and purlieus of Charleston was like reading a chapter of Revelation and Rabelais mixed." [17] Nipson was a "health detective" empowered by the local government to search for communicable diseases and subjects for quarantine. [18] He could pass from squalid courts to drawing rooms; every dwelling, stable, or house of prostitution granted him entry.

The Smythes and their connections must have found it odd that Bennett consorted with low-caste blacks and odd men like Nipson, but he kept on. He shared with Nipson the fabulous fragments he had heard from Grant and Mayrant; he pointed out the places stories were supposed to have taken place. Nipson, in turn, culled his memory to see if he could not provide Bennett with the events' more coherent and logical beginnings. It was like solving a cryptogram. Coming in from his rides with Nipson, his evening chats with Grant and Mayrant, and his walks around old cemeteries, Bennett approached his wife, his in-laws, and other whites in Charleston; he asked if they had heard these stories, or if they knew upon what fact, like mold upon damp, these fictions grew. "Stuff and nonsense," they answered dismissively, "such things never occurred." [19] He agreed; he knew no one had caught a mermaid in a jar, but he wanted to find out what had caused folk to believe these things. Was it just due to the ceaseless rain and the seas rising out of the drains in the old city? Or could it be a confusion with the "FeeJee Mermaid" P. T. Barnum had displayed in Charleston in 1843? [20] Like a pearl growing from a grain of sand, so these fantastic stories had arisen from humble beginnings to explain phenomena or events going on around the superstitious of the city. "The . . . shadows projected upon the curtain of years and distorted by misapprehension have become profoundly extravagant," Bennett realized. [21]

He wanted to do justice to the storytellers and their stories, not dissect or explain them away in the light of science or history. So he experimented with form, and with fact and fiction. Explanations would desiccate and deprive the stories of their wonder and mystery. He wanted to keep the rapture and awe and belief of the storytellers attached to them. So working like a jeweler with a gem, he set out to craft the germs of the stories into appropriate settings. He developed a style akin to the new journalism of the 1960s and '70s; as Tom Wolfe and others would tell a true story from the viewpoint of its participants, simulating their affects and beliefs, so Bennett began to cast his collected tales in the vocabularies, moods, and beliefs of those who had told them. It was something he had done with children's stories, telling events from a viewpoint different from his own, trying to capture the ambiance and worldview of the storytellers. In New Orleans about a generation before, George Washington Cable had done somewhat similar things with his tales of Creoles and Cajuns. It had enhanced the exotic reputation of New Orleans, and Bennett wished to do the same for Charleston.

By 1907 he had polished a number of the collected folktales and legends. Fittingly, he decided to first share these stories with Charlestonians. By lecturing to an audience, as he had on Negro spirituals to the Women's Clubs in 1903, he'd both please his public, get some pointers, and maybe trigger memories of those who might come forth with more stories.

He found his opportunity in February 1908 when he was asked to address the Federation of Charleston women's clubs at their annual winter meeting. To make sure it was a true premiere, he only told the subject on which he'd speak; he did not let anyone read it, not even anyone in his family. The title of his talk, the program teased, was "Grotesque Legends of Charleston."

On the nineteenth, he walked up to the St. John's Hotel, on the corner of Meeting and Queen Streets, where the ladies and their male guests gathered in rooms decorated with palms and plush seats. (Robert E. Lee had stayed in the same hotel in the previous century.) The well-dressed, stayed, corseted, hatted, and plumed audience "representative of the most intelligent women of the city," turned their attention to him.[22]

He stepped to the podium. The tales he told included the story of the son of the College of Charleston gatekeeper, who, rejected in his attempt to rise in society, became so melancholy that he earned the reputation, perhaps due to his use of corpses to study anatomy, of being "the Doctor to the Dead." Charleston ladies of Bennett's day still crossed the street to keep the shadow of his house from touching them, although the house itself had burned during the Civil War.[23] He also told the tale of one of Charleston's last obi or conjure men, Jack Domingo.

He lavished the most attention, however, on the story he found most lovely, sad, and haunting. The tale he titled *Madame Margot* was the story of an octoroon milliner who had flourished in Charleston before the Civil War. "Margot," as he called her, had borne a daughter to her white lover; so fair was the daughter that she "passed" for white, as Margot herself, victim to the discoloration of Addison's Disease, turned black and died. The drama of the story was what the superstitious linked together: she sold her soul to the devil, they said, so her daughter could go white as she, herself, went dark to pay the price. In all his stories, his language was evocative, fabulous, and precise.

In "The Black Constable," for instance, he vividly described the street where the conjure man lived:

Mazyck Street . . . sank to the bottom, within a generation and became a dingy domain of dogs, dirt garbage dunghills and stench. . . . The gutter curbing stuck up through the dirt like teeth . . . [and] the mulberry trees . . . turned sallow and withered away; their crooked trunks burst, and what looked too much like their entrails bulged out. . . . He sold a young girl the chemise of a woman who had been happy in love, for twenty-five dollars; it was . . . stained as it had lain long in the ground; even chloride of lime would not bleach it. He was reputed to get such things from the old, old graves on Ghost Island.[24]

He chose words to send a chill up the spines of the ladies. "The audience listened closely. This any speaker knows by the hush in the hall; no syllable of my talk escaped those alert listening ears. But I must have used some syllables which had escaped my own critical disapprobation. I remember two or three which thrilled my audience with revulsion: one of those was the use of the word 'chemise' . . . A shock, not at the time perceived by me, ran through the audience as that dread revelatory word fell like a block of concrete in their midst. . . . What would have happened had I employed the word 'teddy' or 'step in' I cannot surmise; probably swoonings and faint cries of pain . . . and hurried summonings of . . . physicians to revive [the ladies] prone in virtuous consternation."

In was only two decades afterward that he joked about it. "At the time the experience was not amusing; for the sensitive litmus-paper mind of the community turned brilliantly pink with the shock to its moral sensibilities which my . . . [lecture] in Negro legend and folk-lore . . . inflicted."[25]

When he finished, Bennett looked up expectantly. But there was only a ripple of applause. Knowing he was "finer-fibred" than most and prone to an "exquisite sensitiveness," he was often "pained by [things] which to others are of no appreciable force."[26] He wondered if this was the case as he went to greet his audience.

One gentleman . . . pressed forward . . . to say that mine was the most brilliant . . . address he had ever heard . . . in Charleston. I noticed however, with an uneasy sense of something gone wrong somewhere, that . . . none of the women . . . pressed forward to take me by the hand or to compliment . . . me upon the afternoon's address.

I noticed also with a little surprise that the gentleman who so heartily had commended . . . my speech had hardly reached the end of the hall than he was surrounded by a group [of] women in earnest and voluble conversation: and that when . . . I overtook him . . . and said, "So you consider the talk successful?" he gave a sort of startled look over his shoulder, uneasily pushed forward through the crowd . . . and vanished with all speed among the press.[27]

Shrugging to himself, Bennett made his way back to Legare Street; all of his wife's family had been elsewhere that day, so there was no one whose confidence he could seek. He said nothing, and picked up the next day's paper eagerly; the *News and Courier*, and its sister paper the *Evening Post*, always reported on everything he did.

And this was no exception.

The headlines of the afternoon edition were quite large, and in all caps: "BRILLIANT MEETING OF THE CLUB WOMEN." "A remarkable paper read," followed that. "Mr. John Bennett's 'Old and Grotesque Legends of Charleston' a startlingly realistic exposition of Revolting Savage Fancies." That contrasted poorly—to say the least—with "Delightful Music Features."

He read on.

Brilliant and beautiful was the assemblage of Charleston women gathered yesterday afternoon . . . for the . . . ninth annual midwinter literary meeting of the city Federation of Women's Clubs, . . . the beautiful and smartly gowned ladies presenting a picture worthy of . . . a master. Charming and courteous ushers escorted the visitors to the best seats and later presided at the dainty tea . . . where . . . the fair clubwomen sipped fragrant oolong and discussed macaroons, amid flowers and palms.[28]

Then editor Tom Waring, after setting the paradisiacal scene, introduced the serpent into this palmed Eden. Like a cat playing with a mouse, he started in on his victim.

Mr. John Bennett's paper was a piece of bizarre, wonderfully imaginative, forcibly literal and, it must be said, inappropriate literary exposition. That it was a brilliant piece of execution cannot be gainsaid, but it was, to say the least, an unfortunate sample to spread before a public gathering of women, and while the literary quality of it could not fail of high appreciation, the flavor of it was scarcely acceptable. It was rich—not to say reeking—with the distorted and horrible and forbidden fancies of the savage nature still latent in the negro. . . . It was realistic in the extreme and to many it was positively revolting.[29]

Bennett saw it was not just the use of the word "chemise." He was start-ing to see he had combined three taboo ingredients in a fatal witch's brew: he had mixed black "lust" (Madame Margot, partially black, had a daugh-ter) with miscegenation (her lover was white) in front of white women (his audience).

Many of the women knew the story and talked about these things amongst themselves—indeed, his wife's grandmother had mentioned mis-cegenation quite plainly in her diatribe against *Uncle Tom's Cabin*.[30] But for a man, a Yankee, someone not born to Charleston, to mention it in front of them was not acceptable. (President Theodore Roosevelt also expounded on this Charleston hypocrisy.)[31] For this the ladies sought to punish him.

"A fetid atmosphere of demoniacal desire and infernal indulgence per-meated the production, and it was not a pleasant breathing for the audience of refined and sensitive women," wrote editor T. R. Waring. "Mr. Bennett's essay and the stories illustrating it depicted an impossible world of loath-some things, and he set it all forth in wonderfully faithful, and therefore, truly shocking colors."[32]

The paper fell from his hands; the "stunning blow" rendered him unable to speak. His wife was "frightened out of her . . . senses" and burst into tears.[33] Her parents came over, reeling "with the blind staggers," a term he used to describe the victims of the Black Constable's evil magic.[34] How could he have done such a thing, they wanted to know. The *Evening Post* was the voice of the white elite. To revile Bennett was the decree.

As Susan wept and his in-laws paced, and the doors were closed so the servants would not hear, Bennett tried to explain. He had wanted, he kept repeating, to make them happy. But treating blacks with respect, telling their private lives to white ladies, was not allowable. Didn't he see?

He wanted to reply, but his father-in-law perhaps was the one to explain "there could be no striking back, for with the exception of good old Tom Waring, the assailants were women." He might have been able to contradict the editor or write him an explanatory letter, but he could never question a lady.[35] And, as if hiding behind their full skirts, Waring had appended letters from two such anonymous "Charleston ladies." (To have their names appear over the words would not have been fitting.)

One writer bewailed the fact that "the rising young author of such whole-some books as *Master Skylark* and *Barnaby Lee* and of whom South Carolina had been so proud as her adopted son, should forsake the paths of purity and dignity in literature and sink to the sensual level of Elinor Glyn," [36] a reference to the author of the 1907 novel *Three Weeks* that had shocked many with its portrayal of a woman, married to a brute, having an affair with a younger man. When the film was shown in the city, women's clubs attended to decide if it should be censored and chased off the screen.[37] "The *Evening Post*," the outraged Charleston lady concluded, "is to be commended for its criticisms of Mr. Bennett."

Another protester wrote, "Mr. John Bennett came, saw, but this time did not conquer. As Charleston's 'adopted son,' he should have known better than to have compelled . . . ladies to listen to . . . the most bold and vulgar and unnecessarily lewd narrative." She accused him of the ultimate sin. "Mr. Bennett insulted the women who heard him." [38]

Everyone, but for Rabbi Barnett Elzas and Isabel Fraser, wife of a Presbyterian minister, turned against him. He was ridiculed just as Daisy Breaux Simonds, who had tried to advance herself with the black-loving Roosevelt, had been; and he was scorned and excoriated like Lewisohn. In November the paper had castigated him, too, for his portrayal of sex beyond marriage in his novel *The Broken Snare*. Instead of being a "profoundly moving story," as its publisher declared, the *News and Courier* called it

profoundly disgusting . . . reeking with the sweat of the vulgarest human passions. It is of the earth . . . and is saved only from the smell of the bagnio by the fine literary quality of the author's brilliant work. . . . There can be no question as to the extraordinary boldness of the incidents depicted, nor of the cleverness with which the story is told; but the author would not talk about such things to the people he respected. . . . Why should he write about them? [39]

Like Bennett, the paper attacked Lewisohn with almost the same words for using his god-given skills for godless ends and for insulting his audience. The result was that Lewisohn and Bennett both were now taboo; many perhaps remembered how Bennett had been the first to be seen in the street in shirt sleeves. He had kindly been taken in by them, while secretly befriending the Negro, stirring up stories of black lust, and insulting refined white ladies.

"The outcry was really more than a nine-days wonder," Bennett remarked; "it reverberated for years." [40] "The cards of protest" he might have "attributed to hyper-sensitive victorian souls; but the angry criticisms of Waring of the *Evening Post* I could not so easily set aside." [41]

There was panic at 37 Legare. What to do? How to proceed? In one afternoon, he had been toppled from his position, called depraved, demonized, and deprived of his living, for he had planned to publish the legends. "By all means, let us be ignorant," one of the ladies had written of them. "It is not necessary to go to the sewer for information."[42] Ironically, one of these women was Mrs. Octavus Roy Cohen, whose husband in future years would gain fame writing murder mysteries and stereotypical race stories based on black stupidity and rascality. Cohen, a Jew, had the good grace at least to not take blacks seriously or find their behavior anything but amusing.

"The evil influence," Bennett wrote over a decade later, "of that unexpected rebuke, has never been altogether expelled, though I have sought to make light of it."[43] Again and again he was chilled by its bitter memory, as it laid a ghostly hand on his shoulder to stop him from doing certain things.[44] Having accomplished the impossible—finding acceptance in Charleston's innermost social circles—Bennett in February 1908 found himself excoriated, reviled, and despised. It was hard to think that he had recently prophesied in print that his works on local culture would enshrine him.

Instead, he found himself a victim of the same spirit that had heaved bricks over walls at Yankees. And being "finer-fibred" and "exquisitely sensitive," he acted as if he had been hit. Stricken, he plunged into a major depression and drug addiction. The attack on him was so vicious that he would never totally recover or feel the same about Charleston.

CHAPTER 13

# The Prayer of the Brave

IT IS ALMOST IMPOSSIBLE to overestimate the effect the public attack had on Bennett. Try as he might, he could not understand why T. R. Waring had not approached him privately instead of condemning him in print. The event and its aftermath catapulted Bennett into the darkest abyss of his life, far grimmer than any of the depressions he had suffered in Chillicothe. For days he sat stunned on Legare Street, unable to leave.

"Oh," he had written to Susan some years before, "I want to be remembered for a while and not forgotten. . . . It is not fame I care for; I want that men shall love and remember the man that I am for the work he did to please them." [1] He had hoped the folktales would turn the tide of his recent lackluster reputation and earn him respect and admiration in Charleston. But now the reverse was happening. The "treasure" he had laid claim to in *Peyre Gaillard* was trash now, putrid and mortifying.

Any attempt to believe or act differently would just make things more difficult. If he stood his ground and rebuked the paper for what it said (as Ludwig Lewisohn would), he would be accused of acting ungraciously. (Lewisohn would write the *News and Courier*, countering its review of his novel with comments by nationally known critics; and Lancelot Harris, his mentor at the College of Charleston, would also write, trying to soften the decree, but the editor would respond negatively to each. Bennett, by comparison, was not publicly defended by anybody.) [2] Knowing there was no recourse, he gave in. He wrote the editor of the *Evening Post* on February 21st, stating,

In regard to the substance of my lecture before the City Federation of Women's Clubs, I wish to assume absolute . . . responsibility. . . . The ladies of the executive board had never heard of the lecture before its delivery, knew absolutely no more about its substance than did the audience of their invited guests. It is in justice to them, to their discretion, and to their taste [that] I wish to make this absolutely frank statement. . . . Responsibility for any offense unwittingly given to anyone is entirely mine; I wish this to be as generally and widely understood as it is within the power of your circulation to effect. If I have erred in judgement in choice of matter (for any lecture to be delivered in Charleston, to women of refinement or otherwise), I am responsible for the error, not the ladies of the executive committee. Since their good breeding makes it impossible that they take so ungracious a course as to criticize, . . . even by inference, any effort in their behalf, even if that effort be, as it seems, not according to their audience's pleasure, I cannot permit adverse criticism to fall upon their shoulders. I have shoulders of my own. Will you not be so kind, sir, as to give to this communication the prominence in your evening's publication necessary to immediate recognition of my position and theirs in this matter, and very greatly oblige,

JOHN BENNETT.[3]

And Waring did oblige, publishing the groveling letter the same day Bennett presented it. And reading it that night, Bennett might just as well have read his obituary.[4]

He was now as despised as the blacks he had, in his way, tried to champion. "I would with all my heart . . . be her hero of achievement," he wrote of Susan.[5] Disconsolate and chagrined, he sank into a major depression. If he went out on the streets, he was ignored; if he stayed in, his doubts and inability to write preyed on him.

With nothing to occupy his mind, he deteriorated swiftly. By 1909, doctors ordered a complete rest; and as stress mounted, so did his symptoms. He suffered from diphtheria, and his hay fever and allergies, old nemeses, returned. He resorted once more to cocaine and again fell into addiction.[6] In this state, he left Charleston for "the little Charleston of the mountains," the place Charlestonians vacationed in hot weather, Flat Rock, North Carolina.

The Smythes had recently sold Woodburn plantation, where he and Susan had honeymooned, acquiring the North Carolina estate Many Pines instead. Bennett hid himself there as smug Charlestonians enjoyed the measure of grief they doled out to him. To occupy himself, he turned to the land, trying to do something for the Smythes to apologize and please them. (No one seems to have pleaded for him to return to his family.) He tamed the jungle of the woods at Many Pines, planting orchards and gardens. "One of my reasons for . . . undertaking this out-of-door work is the real hope of benefitting my health," he wrote Susan. "For I own very frankly [that] it takes all the strength I have to sustain the . . . physical distress and misery incidental to writing; besides . . . it now takes all the cold courage I have . . . to write at all."[7] Dismayed at his lack of output, Tudor Jenks suggested he, like Henry James, try dictating.[8] Jenks did not understand, for Bennett had not told him the true reasons for his breakdown; bad eyesight and illness, he told Jenks, were the culprits. Bennett even gave up letter writing. He appeared to be intent on punishing himself for having failed and, moreover, for feeling sad about failing.

He stayed at Many Pines for months, numbing his mind with hard work in the gardens. In this manner he broke his cocaine addiction. When he came back to Charleston, he spent time with his children, Jack and Jane, working on the house and doing domestic duties. It was still an uphill battle to do anything else; his correspondence lay unanswered.

Money trickled in from the continued sales of *Barnaby Lee* and *Master Skylark*, which had been adapted dramatically as a play a number of times over the years. In 1903 John Lane Connor had copyrighted a dramatic version; a few years later another writer, Edgar White Burrill, wrote Bennett for permission to adapt it again. Burrill wanted to improve on the Connor version, which, he felt was marred by lack of drama: its indirect action, stilted soliloquies, and a focus shifted from the main character, Nick Attwood.[9] Burrill kept writing; Bennett felt so bad about not answering that he finally granted him the rights in the hopes that Burrill would no longer bother him.

But Burrill was persistent and sent Bennett drafts of the play; Bennett, however, did not read them. "I have shrunk from essaying estimate of the outlined drama you sent me in early January, so weakened in self-reliance and grown so cowardly altogether, as to place no dependence whatever upon my opinions relative to your work, or that of anyone else, inclusive of myself," he explained in March 1909.[10] His outlook was bleak, and he sat nearly paralyzed with the same melancholia or depression that seemed to trap others in his family. In all the pages he recorded for his "possible though improbable autobiography," this era of his life is nearly blank.[11]

The only bright spot was the birth of his third and final child on January 20, 1910. Susan Adger Smythe was named after his wife and bore no name at all from the Bennett side of the family (the only child to do so). It suggests he caved in to the Charleston attitude, a defeated and belated peace offering. "I have produced nothing for four years," he noted the next year, "and am still in the bitter throes of trying." [12] He toyed more with the idea of giving up entirely. "The proposition is open before me to give up the try, and to peddle something commercial."

"Why not, after all," he wondered, "except that youth and its facility are gone; and, forgetting my attention, I should probably pause in the middle of the common-place transaction, to look out of a window and see a windy landscape, a rolled cloud, a shivering tree, and the frightened water under the wind . . . and that doesn't sell pins and needles, threads, clothespins, and eggbeaters." [13] And besides, "being in trade" was looked down upon by the Smythe clan and their peers in the city. But not working lowered him even more in the estimation of the Smythes and made him dependent on his wife's earnings. For it was only due to investments begun by his father-in-law, and carried on by the shrewd and canny Susan Smythe Bennett, that the family's coffers were filled.[14]

"There is [for me] an analogy between confidence and achievement," he wrote Burrill, and achieving nothing, his self-confidence dwindled.[15] He knew he had to do something to get his sense of himself back and get respect from his children, his wife, and her family. He reasoned he might be able to continue writing, if he focused on something less risky than the folktales. The Macmillan publishing company expressed interest in a book on the revolutionary era in South Carolina, the era he had researched and employed in *The Treasure of Peyre Gaillard.* Neighbor had turned against neighbor in these years; and in his fiction, Indigo House had been burned, Gaillard had been hanged, and the treasure buried. Maybe in facts he could avoid offending the sensitive in the city; and in portraying a civil war of sorts (he knew better than to tackle the War between the States, still a sensitive subject in the South) he could find psychological release for his own conflicted emotions. For civil war, and battling himself, tied in with his new view of the city. "I love diatribes against Charleston," he'd write Yates Snowden. "They help me get all such thoughts out of my system; and then . . . move me . . . to love the town, hearing it scandalized by others. . . . There are two natures struggling in me when it comes to Charleston, affection and dislike; what I break with one hand I am ever moved to repair with the other." [16] Still wanting to regain the respect of his neighbors (but also feeling that he had been tried, convicted, and punished too prejudiciously), he said yes to Macmillan.[17]

In researching the period between 1765 and 1785, he read family papers and books and manuscripts in the Library Society; in the process, he found much grandeur and much that was maddening. In many published works, he found "the meanest form of historical lying: the deliberate suppression of matter which does not fit the historian's preconceived statement of his subject."[18] He felt fired to tell the truth and destroy cherished myths simultaneously.

Reading the colonial and revolutionary newspapers at the Library Society, he made notes on other information he stumbled upon.[19] He continued to discover more about slavery—the places of origin of the ships that had brought slaves to Charleston; and one day, he found a notice relating to the Charleston Museum.

This the *News and Courier* reported on pleasantly, noting at the opening of an Audubon and Bachman exhibit in March 1911 that the director "made an announcement of the greatest possible interest, when he stated that at last the date of the founding of the Charleston Museum had been determined."[20] (The director, Paul Rea, was from Massachusetts originally, as was Laura Bragg, whom he brought to town to help him in 1909; she would replace him in 1920.)[21] The Museum was believed to be the oldest in the country, but no one could prove it until "John Bennett, in the course of certain researches in the Charleston Library [Society] chanced on an article in the Charleston Courier describing the actual year of the founding."[22]

It had been founded in 1775, he discovered; he continued to serve the museum as an honorary curator and designed its logo, a drawing of its new building. He must have relished the irony of a castigated Yankee telling locals their woefully unknown history, and it also encouraged him to keep on researching the Revolutionary War, if not actively writing. "I wish that I were near you," Tudor Jenks told him. "What you need is a good dose of don't give a damn."[23]

But he did care, and, having begun his work, he now found it fascinating. It not only provided him a focus, and a reason to get up in the morning, but also gave him the chance to leave Charleston to visit archives and libraries across the country. In the first few years of the next decade, he became a fixture in the Boston libraries; Boston allowed him the chance of spending time with his sister Martha, still teaching English at Dana Hall in nearby Wellesley. In Boston, Bennett befriended the young historian Arthur Schlesinger Sr., then working on his dissertation. Despite Bennett's protests, Schlesinger insisted on calling him Dr. Bennett for his knowledge, scholarship, and integrity; for a man who had not finished high school, it must have been gratifying.[24]

He left Boston in November 1912 for Christmas in Chillicothe; his mother had pneumonia, and he stayed with her and nursed her into the new year instead of returning to his wife and children. "One night she asked, 'Hold me fast in your arms, Jack; it rests me a little.' I raised her and held her in my arms; but even that could not ease her agony. So little, so straight, so light, so pitifully slight and wasted, she lay in my arms all that night until the nurse relieved me. . . . Hour by hour, day after day, we played the losing battle out to the end, postponed again and again by an invincible will to be."[25] When she finally died, in January 1913, Bennett lost another of his moorings.

He stayed in Chillicothe until February and went back to Boston to continue his research on the Partisan War, which is what he called it, keeping away from South Carolina, where his father-in-law was ailing and his wife and children had moved in with the Smythes at 31 Legare Street. It was not until September that he returned to Charleston, having been gone for almost a full year. He continued his research there and elsewhere, punctuating his work with time spent with his children; he took them to Ohio to visit family and to teach them that civilization did exist elsewhere. And he kept on with his studies.

With six long, silent years of scattered research behind him, Bennett sat down to the actual writing of his study in 1915. Again he experimented with form; he did not like dry history, so he planned his work as a narrative focusing on both the great events of the war and the lives of individual participants, a mode of historical writing that did not come into fashion until the mid- and late twentieth century, as exemplified in Bruce Catton's and Shelby Foote's Civil War trilogies.

Bennett also saw his story in three parts. The first era spanned 1765–1771. In it, he'd focus on the up-country vigilante movement of the Regulators, which in South Carolina acted as Whigs and in North Carolina as

Tories. "The Troubles" between the years 1775–1778 would be the second part of his story, centering on the outbreak of the revolution and the struggles between the native Whigs and Tories befor- 'he arrival of the King's armies.[26]

Their arrival would usher in the "The Bloody Years, of 1778–1783," including the invasion and fall of Georgia, then South Carolina, and the attempts on North Carolina. He'd treat the local "risings" and the final and utter catastrophe of the British and the loyalists.[27] This would require "the interminable job of reducing thousands of contradictory notes to a coherent narrative" and "connecting those separate events by the logic of circumstances and time, . . . sweating . . . down by brutal cruel toil . . . each separate incident in proportion of its importance to the rest."[28] With this dogged research, writing, rearranging, and linking of small anecdotes and larger events, he'd draw the "big picture" of history.

For periodic relief, he turned to his first love, drawing. Along with local artist Alice Ravenel Huger Smith, Bennett served as art critic for classes at the Carolina Art Association taught by Susan's nephew Albert Simons, quickly becoming a nationally known architect and one of the preservationists of the city. For the first time, there was a life-drawing class in Charleston, similar to the ones he had taken at the New York Art Students' League.[29] College of Charleston students served as models, but not many artists took advantage of the opportunity. Bennett, following the lead of Laura Bragg at the Charleston Museum, began encouraging a young man named Ned Jennings, an artist with a speech impediment that rendered him inarticulate in talk but eloquent in fabulous drawings. Jennings was the son of the Charleston postmaster, who wanted his son to follow a more traditional path; again and again Bennett went to the elder Jennings to convince him to allow his son an opportunity to pursue his talents, just as he had done for his colleague Rollin Kirby at the New York Art Students' League. Another of Bennett's pupils, Paul Bissell, followed Bennett's advice and later become a professional illustrator in New York City.[30]

Bennett did some of his own work, too, returning to silhouettes occasionally. Instead of drawing with india ink, he preferred to cut them freehand from black japanese paper with a stencil knife. "Cutting gives a certain something to the character of the work which drawing does not possess," he believed. "Perhaps [it is] in part a firm certainty of line and a starker simplicity in composition."[31]

The starkest and most pleasing of these was a series of designs depicting the seasons. Starting with spring in 1911 and adding one for his Christmas card each year, he cut a design for each, finishing with winter's especially dramatic silhouette in 1914. Beneath each he placed a musical fragment of "Charleston street cries of our musical morning peddlers of shrimp and vegetables."[32] These he reproduced in a limited edition the next year to sell at the book store run by Isaac Hammond and at Lanneau's Art Store. Another silhouette, one of a piper, won a design award, appearing on the program of the Academy of Music, the local opera house and theater, for the 1915–16 season. Bennett soon adapted it to his bookplate by joining the piper to the quatrain he had written for Jack Appleton: "We are all but Fellow-Travelers / Along Life's weary way. / If any man can play the pipes, / In God's name, let him play."

There were other small successes in these years. In 1915, the dramatic adaptation of Bennett's *Master Skylark* by Edgar White Burrill appeared in book form from the Century Company with Reginald Birch's familiar drawings.[33] There had been cruder versions, but this one, which followed Bennett's tale most closely, became the most successful of all the adaptations.[34]

With 1916 marking the three hundredth anniversary of Shakespeare's death, its publication was timely. Along with Shakespeare's own works, the play version of *Master Skylark* was staged around the country; productions brought attention to the novel, which was still in print, boosting its sales further and bringing in substantial royalties. It also brought Bennett the opportunity of having an essay he wrote on Shakespeare's genius for good fellowship published in *St. Nicholas.* It pleased him to see his own children, aged thirteen, nine, and six, enjoying the same magazine he had as a boy back in Chillicothe.

He was devoting more and more time to his children, spending much of each summer with his family in Flat Rock; they'd make the adventurous and arduous journey over bad roads in their second-hand Dodge named Betsy.[35] If he could not enjoy success as a writer, he could instead enjoy Jane, Jack, and Susan. "Their anxieties, troubles, griefs, angers and disappointments, magnified by my own affection for them and desire for their welfare, haunt me through the day and walk with me in the gray hours of the sleepless early morning, like troubling ghosts and will not leave me peace," he acknowledged. "Philosophize as I may, I am moved by their emotions, anxious with their anxieties, even more deeply than with my own," to which he said, "I grow a little callous and apathetic; for my way grows short, while theirs lie long before them." [36] And it was at least partly due to his children that he again admitted another agonizing defeat.

While laying out the narrative for his history of the Partisan War, he realized he needed to fill gaps in his research; only in archives in England could he find the information. And without it, and the two extra years it would necessitate, "what I had done was worthless as most American history is . . . or has been . . . and who am I," he thought, "and what are my means, that I should take two years at England at my own expense to an uncertain end?"

"And who should keep my family while I was gone? [Susan would have, no doubt, but this would show him again as a failure and weakling.] Or see how my boy grew up, and keep the friendship of my two girls, as I pleased to do?" [37] It was not just this, however, that convinced him to give up the project. By now he realized he had been tricked again; he had taken a wrong turn, and lost years, just as with his research on black folktales. It was agonizing to admit that again he was coming to grief, so it was better to cloak it in the guise of sacrificing. Only years later did he admit what he realized around 1916. "Perhaps it is as well I never finished, and never shall finish my history of Revolutionary South Carolina," he confessed to Yates Snowden; "sure as the heavens are over us I should have pleased no one, but angered every one, through trying the impossible feat of being just to all the combatants." [38] (From the manuscripts left, it is hard to decipher what he did accomplish; there are notes aplenty and reams of research, but nothing approaching a completed manuscript.)

Another reason he did not want to go overseas was that there was another war brewing. President Woodrow Wilson, whose kin hailed from Chillicothe, was trying to keep America out of the war, and Bennett, like most Americans, supported him. He, like the country itself, looked inward in these years. "My disappointments are not worth detailing, they have not yet kicked the romance out of me," he had written in 1906. "Not sure," he added to it later in 1916. [39]

For escape, and to salvage what he could of his research, he started on a picaresque romance set in a variety of places; but it miscarried, so he blended it with another story, abandoning that, too, for a novel of Revolutionary War–era Charleston. He kept switching plots and scenes: he had a plucky heroine named Margaret (or "Gritty") Cameron, raised poor, growing up dressed as a boy, becoming an heiress suddenly; and he had a hero with amnesia. These he kept moving about in Scotland, Charleston, and the West Indies.[40]

"I am engaged in a region of dreams," he wrote unhappily to his sister Alice as the war fever increased; he was "constructing features of fog; all about me is the cry for real, actual, material, constructive effort, in which if I am to continue at my own profession it is impossible I should lend a hand."[41] He was arguing with himself; for with America's declaring war in 1917, there was a call for volunteers; the naval base north of Charleston brought influxes of people from all over the country. They needed help with housing, entertainment, and other duties. Charleston, accustomed to dozing aloof from issues of the day, waked from her narcissistic slumber to enlist in the fight for democracy.

Susan Smythe Bennett, a born organizer, full of common sense, energy, and a fund of civic pride and duty, sallied forth to serve as chairman of the Red Cross's purchasing committee. It took her out of the house, into many new spheres, and also vicariously reawakened Bennett to the city and its needs. He looked up from his romance on Margaret Cameron. Though "filled with good stuff[,] in the face of red murdering across the sea," it became a thing of peculiar distastefulness suddenly. "For who can play, smiling at Death," he asked himself, "when Death himself, walks abroad?"[42]

The horrors of trench warfare and of young Charleston men dying in France prompted him to put down his pen: he too volunteered. In turning outward and involving himself in the world's day-to-day affairs, he found his way back not just into his own life but also into that of his city's; he was in a way, personifying the theme of a poem he published in these years.

## THE PRAYER OF THE BRAVE

Men grow so great when crisis face
I think we all should pray
Not, "Send us peace, Oh Lord," but, "Send
A crisis every day!"[43]

To help Susan with the Red Cross purchasing committee, Bennett volunteered as the committee's press representative and publicity agent, placing himself in a subservient position, showing his gratitude to her and his need.

He served the same role for the Red Cross committee for civilian relief as well for its supply committee. To help entertain all the servicemen pouring into town, he became vice chairman of the executive committee of the Charleston branch of the War Recreation Service Council and also joined the reserves in the Charleston Light Dragoons. (The Dragoons themselves, including Bennett's artistic protégé Ned Jennings, had been called to the Mexican border in 1916.) Furthermore, he volunteered as assistant director, general chairman, treasurer, and publicity agent for the American Libraries Association's War Libraries Campaign, a national movement that had been started by his old Chillicothe friend Burton Stevenson.

A lot of this work involved writing; he began delivering three-fourths to one and a half columns of prose daily to the *News and Courier* or *Evening Post* to promote the work of his various organizations and committees. Having once chastised him for his inappropriate work, the editor was now accepting his unpaid contributions gladly.

There was a sense of a great change in the air; John Grace, a Catholic populist, would become mayor in 1919, upsetting the conservative regime. His newspaper, the *Charleston American,* criticized the aristocrats (such as those who had chastised Bennett), questioned the war, and broke social taboos; it sent a reporter in to cover the St. Cecilia Ball, the town's highest and most mysterious social rite.

Although he had sided with the entitled elite on many things, Bennett nevertheless broke with them in how many treated the black underclass. He had been troubled by this ever since arriving in Charleston. "Yesterday, while I spaded [the garden]," he wrote his brother back in Chillicothe,

the Jenkins Orphanage band, negro . . . ridiculously small boy band, came down the street, and, seeing our flags, stopped to play before the house. . . . They played one or two banging tunes, such as all poor bands play, and then the leader said, "Boys, take off yo' caps, and play 'Merica' to the flag! . . ." Maybe I'm only an ass, but, truly, the tears went down my cheeks. "My country, 'tis of thee . . . !" The poor devils, young or old, have no country! (They have not even Africa.) They will not even now admit a negro to enlistment, and have been ordered to cease the enlistment of colored men in the United States service here in Carolina unless he has seen previous service. . . . Yet there they stood playing . . . and the flag floated at the top of the house, bright and crisp, and the trees were green with spring, and the wind was keen. . . . And the flag, and the war, and the stir of the great and terrible times and the sight of those poor, pathetic orphaned black boys, playing that hymn, filled me up complete. . . . Susan, who was sewing up stairs, came out to the piazza, and said, "I can't sew; I can't see; my eyes are running over. I think that is the most pathetic sight I have seen in many a year, the rejected, playing 'My country, 'tis of thee, sweet land of liberty; Of thee I sing!' It's too ironical; too pathetic; too tragic!" And I understand, for sufficient reasons, . . . no negroes are to be given a place in the parade of welcome to Gen. Wood, neither as individuals or as members of various organizations. Only such as serve as chauffeurs will move with the city's welcome to the head of our military forces.[44]

With sympathy such as this it is no wonder Bennett, linked in the public mind with the "depravity" of life in the black back alleys, was called upon to canvass African American neighborhoods, when $75,000 was set as the sum in war bonds for Charleston. What he saw going up and down the old streets was astonishing. "It was disheartening and sickening to have to argue and plead with the well-to-do," he wrote Susan when she was away from the city. But the poor were a different story. "'Yes, I will gif; and I am glad to. . . . I gif what I can to my country,' J. Wolper, the Russian Jew cobbler said when we came into his dark little shop, Albert Simons and I; he jumped up smiling and . . . the two men working at their benches both got up and stood smiling. . . . Everyone of them gave a silver dollar," while the wealthy Pringle Smith gave only $2.00.[45] Arthur Manigault, owner of the local newspaper, told Bennett he was broke and gave nothing.[46]

When Bennett went into a shop on King Street, he

was lashed up one side and down the other by Anna Singleton, who keeps a little black restaurant . . . between Tradd and Broad [Streets]. . . . "What chance has my people?" she cried, . . . "living in shacks like this; paying, paying, paying, always paying rent, insurance, high price for black rice and dirty butts what no decent person will eat, only a nigger to the rich who are making the money hand over fist, while we poor people must pay!" "Anna," said I, "there is much in what you say; but I want money for the wounded and the sick! Not the rich or the man." "Whose wounded? What sick?" "American soldiers and sailors; those who are going to fight that we may still have peace and be safe." "They fout befo' I was bo'n; they gwine fout when I is dead. Who the devil cares for a poor nigger, whether she dies or live? . . ." "Anna," said I, "you've a rough tongue, but you know you've a hot heart. So come on; give me a dime for the sick!" "Hyer it is," she said, and laid it on the counter. "I give it to God's cause who died on the cross for me. I give it with a smile; but, mistoh, my heart is bitter. Who ever gave to Anna Singleton?" [47]

The war work also gave Bennett the opportunity to become better acquainted with the other men of his social class who were doing the same work as he. "DuBose Heyward is wisest, best and most ready of all," Bennett wrote his wife in 1919.[48] He liked this younger man and was intrigued by his artistic leanings; an amateurish play he had written had been presented at the South Carolina Society Hall in 1915; one of its actors was Bennett's brother-in-law, Augustine Smythe. Another of Heyward's friends was Bennett's nephew, Sam Gaillard Stoney Jr.; Bennett would often encounter Heyward at Stoney's parents' house, singing to amuse themselves in the evenings.[49]

He began seeking out this slight, polite, stooped young man with big eyes. Heyward was twenty years younger than he was but, like Bennett himself, had known grinding poverty. He had been so poor, in fact, that his widowed mother, Janie Screven Heyward, often had to read her son stories to keep his mind off his hunger. The boy had devoured *Master Skylark* when it first appeared (he would have been eleven) and when asked by a journalist in later years which book he would have most liked to have written, he replied, *Master Skylark*.[50] Heyward, like Bennett, had left school as a teenager to help support his family and, again like Bennett, had been torn between drawing and writing, although he was much less skilled than Bennett in the former field. His first published poem, "Love and Passion," had just appeared in *Snappy Stories* in 1916, but he could not devote himself to writing as much as he'd like, having to support himself and his mother via his insurance business. To help him, Bennett had bought burglary insurance from his firm, Heyward & O'Neill.

They had sailed in the same races at the Yacht Club; in 1918, they corresponded about planting trees.[51] Bennett was eager to help him in any way, moved by the younger man's traumas and illnesses much more serious than his own. As a teen Heyward had contracted polio, which withered his right arm and hand; this not only made him shy and ashamed but kept him from volunteering for active duty in Europe. "He has given Loula [Stoney, Susan Bennett's sister] some pitiful verses, manly but tragic, as you will appreciate remembering his hand, verses in which one unfit by fate sits listening to the tread of marching feet," Bennett wrote his wife in 1917.[52]

To do his part for the war effort, Heyward, too, worked to raise funds for war bonds and "Liberty" loans among the local blacks. Bennett and Heyward grew closer working together, although it evolved that Bennett gave talks in town, Heyward in the country. They witnessed changes in the old patterns of behavior between the races: African Americans wanted to help with the war effort, but whites were slow to allow it; blacks found this insulting and protested. Whites, unused to such reactions, grew nervous and interpreted blacks' dissatisfaction as disloyalty. Bennett was called on immediately.

"It seems I am supposed to know negroes after all. I am called (on the quiet) to attend a meeting at the People's building, with some army and navy people to discuss the negro situation in Charleston, as to the loyalty of the colored folk. Don't mention it," he told his wife wisely.[53] Then a white Charlestonian on the Red Cross committee came across a copy of the *Crisis*, the NAACP's newspaper, and panicked. "He has never even so much as looked at a negro paper before; and has read little negro news, and knows little [about] the negro, except in the famous old Southern way of *knowing all about the negro*, which is three-quarters fudge," Bennett wrote.[54]

There were also problems with the YMCA and Chamber of Commerce. "How can I, a Northerner, tell certain women they do not know how to handle an intelligent capable negro, in 1918?" Bennett asked himself. "I've got to be careful," he knew, remembering the trouble ladies had caused him on the issue a decade before. "I'll use every art I know that's honest, to avoid making a further mess."[55] Things got out of hand quickly; tempers flared in a battle between the white and "colored" Red Cross committees. African Americans wanted to entertain their own troops in the city; the white Red Cross had other ideas.

Bennett went to Spring Street, "where at Dr. Huldah Prioleau's small office we met and talked for an hour and a half, frankly and confidently, each in his own way, to a dozen faithful colored women, of all colors from deep brown to almost white, who have persevered in good work through great discouragement. . . . It puts me in a peculiar situation," Bennett realized, "not member of either YMCA or Chamber of Commerce, [but] used by both [in] pinches."[56] Things were discussed not just in committee rooms but in kitchens; much was being said and listened to and reported on. A certain lady, Bennett reported, "was actually foolish enough to talk about the negro Red Cross surgical dressings work, its place, and the workers in a very injudicious manner in front of her colored house . . . maid!" [57]

There was a strike for better wages for black women on the naval base; the town was full of rumors, and conditions were degenerating quickly. "Mark my words," Bennett told his wife. "Injustice never yet brought good ends. Nor contempt and disdain and harshness." [58]

He was right; violence broke out in the city in 1919. White sailors jostled some blacks on the street in downtown Charleston one evening; a race riot resulted in deaths, vandalism, and beatings. The sailors were ordered back to their base; more rumors of blacks with guns began to circulate in the city.[59] Aristocratic white Charlestonians, who had rebuked Bennett because of his sympathy for local blacks and who had linked him with the "depravity" of their lives, now, without any perceived irony, called on him to serve on an interracial committee. "WE CANNOT GET ALONG WITHOUT EACH OTHER," he had declared in his speeches in black churches to raise money. "Almighty god has put us all here together, to work out our mutual fate." [60]

With his clearheaded and conciliatory manner, and being more empathetic than condescending, he won the respect of many. Dr. Huldah Prioleau of the "Colored Branch" of the American Red Cross recognized Bennett's earnestness; she wrote him that "John Bennett can always come among us, and go out the same gentleman as when he came in. And every negro man and woman will trust him and him ONLY." [61]

For his help in such ticklish situations, Bennett was being welcomed back into the graces of the white elite. Too, World War I had changed things; attitudes were shifting, and the generation of women he had offended was aging. His "sins" were being forgotten and forgiven. The Philo Club, organized for good fellowship, invited him to membership and he accepted quickly. "As for real friends no man needs [them] more than I," he confessed. "The greatness of that need I should not state, lest others think me weak." [62] It was similar to the Chaos Club he had belonged to in 1905; in that club members like Yates Snowden and Gus Pinckney came together to debate various subjects. No one could leave until at least one point was decided upon unanimously. Members of Philo included Walter Wilbur, minister of Grace Episcopal Church; George Croft Williams (who would give Bennett the anecdote for his story "Revival Pon Top Edisto"); [63] Reverend John K. Fraser, whose wife had refused to censure Bennett in 1908; and Rabbi Isaac Marcusson, among other "ministers of almost every denomination . . . with me as the risible exception of the lay villain."[64] This re-welcoming of Bennett reflected the change in his status that had started slowly and continued to grow; from America's entry into the war until the armistice, he kept intensely busy with new friends and volunteer work on various committees. This brought him more and more into the daily orbit of the town, leaving him no time to indulge in his "Scottish melancholy." This was good for him, he knew, but it afforded him little time to write. Overextended and exhausted, he finally complained of feeling like "a delicate machine diverted from its purpose."[65]

"I am far from taking life carelessly or for closing my eyes to affairs," he told Walter Wilbur, "but deeply to partake in them is not for me."[66] Reinvigorated with a greater sense of self and a bit more confidence, he wanted to get back to writing. He resigned from all his committees in 1919 and looked about his third-floor study, considering all the projects on his desk. Looking from his window, he recognized fully the great changes that had come to the city.

For the first time since 1860, American flags were now flying over the crooked rooftops. Bennett's own mother-in-law, Louisa McCord Smythe, local president of the United Daughters of the Confederacy and national president in 1903, had been the first in town to hoist it over her house two doors down the street.[67] Wharves to the east, along the Cooper River, were no longer deserted; servicemen were everywhere; new accents, as well as military tunes and the cash register's ring, were changing the city. "We here are experiencing . . . a revival of repair and rebuilding, particularly of residences, owing to the universal call for quarters from departmental officers," Bennett noted in 1917. The commercial club on Meeting Street was being refitted as a "European hotel called the Timrod, after the local poet, whose bust is in the public park just opposite"; most did not know who Timrod was, Bennett believed.[68]

Indeed, the old was being not just forgotten but discarded. Modernity rose like a devouring beast as centuries-old mansions and tenements were torn down and gas stations sprang up in their stead, with modern offices and stores following. For the Charleston Museum, Bennett saved all the appurtenances of a nineteenth-century apothecary shop associated with the mermaid riot. The proprietor was swept up in the spirit of modernizing.

More and more sun seekers on their way to Florida, stopping off in Charleston, became intrigued with the antique look of the place; the rich began restoring old houses and buying up others. Some houses were gutted and the interiors reassembled in far-away cities. "The City that time forgot," as DuBose Heyward would say in a few years, was now witnessing its own destruction.[69] "Sons, Old Charleston is gone," Bennett lamented from his third-floor study, and "a strange loud, day rolls in."[70]

"Just what I shall do now is uncertain," he wrote Martha, keeping her informed of his reflections. "The thing which charms me most, perhaps, is the collection of legends."[71] Although he had been punished for presenting and preserving them, he had not forgotten them. He had written Martha when he lectured on them to the Philo Club in 1916. (This was a safe group in which to speak; they all were men, and they had even taken up the "sex-question" as an issue at one meeting.)[72] "I shall complete the matter in hand in part to convince myself that my once assured gift is not gone," he told her then.[73] "They are fartherest from reality and so attract me most. Their atmosphere is difficult, but one can only try to rouse ghosts . . . and maybe . . . succeed in recalling the strange, queer, dream-like vision where these things have their being." It would be a way of saving them, too, for "Old Charleston is going with terrible swiftness and these things must get into print or perish utterly."[74]

Writing them down, he knew, would mean "absorption, and deep forgetfulness of the times." But he was willing to do this; he knew it was "the dreamer's fate . . . to depart out of the active life . . . in the hope of living in one's work."[75] Haunted by a decade of loss and disillusionment, he wanted to achieve again. "I should like to leave behind me a book of strange tales of Old Charleston . . . to live a generation or two after me, [and] . . . to prove my right to exist," he wrote Yates Snowden. "I just can't talk about this much; the matter lies too deep at heart."[76]

"Sometimes I greatly hope," he continued in the same vein to Jack Appleton, "sometimes I greatly fear that all my work may be in vain, and I . . . leave behind me nothing of lasting force." But "then I look back on my old friendships and ask . . . can any man [who has] had such friends ever cease trying? . . . Believe me, a vast part of the courage that sustains me . . . arises . . . in remembrance of old friendships, and in thoughts of you and the good lads who made up that rare fellowship so long ago."[77]

So, to honor his past friends and his children succeeding him, he closeted himself in the top floor of 37 Legare Street and took himself out of the "active life" of the city. When his daughter Susan developed scarlet fever, he was literally quarantined from modern Charleston.

What he was doing was a gamble, but he believed in the legends. He sat at his desk trying to conjure up "a tragic exquisite loveliness verging upon fantasy" of the vanished era they came from; he wanted to "convey . . . something . . . of the sense of fantastic beauty the story first gave to me, and especially something of the imaginative loveliness with which popular tradition had invested the past in the south," the time before the war especially.[78] (All who came to Charleston after the fall of the Confederacy were told that the antebellum era had been something of an Eden. Oscar Wilde, visiting in the 1880s, for instance, spoke of the beauty of the moon over the water; you should have seen it before the war, Charlestonians told him, he joked.)[79]

Seeking inspiration, Bennett tried for "the strange loveliness of Fra Angelico and Botticelli," combined with "the grotesquerie of Dürer's Dance of Death" and "the sensuous and unearthly beauty" of pre-Raphaelites like Dante Gabriel Rossetti.[80] In an almost self-induced state of mesmerism, he worked on the legends "Madame Margot" and "Doctor to the Dead" simultaneously. Piece by piece, line by line, he worked to put the stories together, almost like a mosaic. He cut up various versions into narrow strips of paper, one "string" containing a sentence, another a paragraph; he kept changing their order, almost kaleidoscopically, shifting sections, adjectives, and words to summon the tone needed. "She is over the chairs, and over the table, and on the floor, and my typewriter is fair [sic] lousy with Madame Margot."[81] A breath of air or shock of realism would send all his work to nothing. He spun a web of wonder on a gossamer film of words, high above the city. "In an age so glorious, so rich and fine, and so bestarred with splendor that one almost forgets the bottomless abyss into which it plunged at last, there lived a woman in Charleston of whom a very odd story is told," it began.[82]

So intent was he that he did not see the parallels going on around him. He had paid workmen to raise the level of his yard, but he did not realize till they were done that the fill soil they had carted in had come from a cemetery. There were "teeth and bones and coffin-nails and pewter rosettes all over" his garden.[83]

So, too, in his literary one. For upstairs, in a charnel-house atmosphere, it was not just "Madame Margot" and "The Doctor to the Dead" he was raising. Fifteen years before he had disinterred and revived a treasure from the rich earth of the low country in his *Peyre Gaillard*. And now he was doing it again; although he did not know it, it was the Charleston literary renaissance he was beginning.

## CHAPTER 14

# "We Have Waked . . . the Slumbering"

EVER SINCE MOVING TO CHARLESTON, Bennett had worked to encourage both local artistic expression and its appreciation; that had been one of the reasons behind *The Treasure of Peyre Gaillard* and had also prompted him to study folklore, music, and Gullah. By 1906 he had ruminated long enough on the topic to sum up his thoughts on it in a lecture to the Carolina Art Association. He spoke in the Gibbes Art Gallery building on Meeting Street, which had been finished just the year before. His ideas were so novel that the *New York Evening Sun* reported on them. "Mr. Bennett's amiable desire seems to be to establish a distinctively Carolinian, or rather Charlestonian, school of arts and crafts," wrote the journalist.[1] As with his *Treasure*, Bennett was now broadcasting it, for it seems highly unlikely New York could have known of his talk without Bennett himself alerting a reporter and supplying his text.

"I do not care much to talk to amateurs and dilettante admirers [who] . . . pursue the arts as they pursue letters, in a desultory way, for their own amusement," he began. "I prefer to address what I have to say to those, who like myself, make their living by the pursuit of some form of art, their hands executing what their heads plan, earning their bread by their sweat, and often bitter bread, or little of it."[2]

Only artists and craftsmen themselves could launch an arts movement, he knew, and, although he had hopes, he was not blindly optimistic. "Charleston has ever been a generous patron of fine arts; it has inherited refinement," he noted, "but it has never been a center of the production of art; nor am I certain that it has inherited an appreciation of good craftsmanship." In his talk Bennett toyed with the idea of launching a society to help change the city, but he concentrated mostly on advice.

"Mediocrity will not do," he bluntly told his audience. If your work fails to measure up to a national level, "you must make your work the more individual, the more original, the more characteristic of yourself and . . . your ideals." He was not encouraging sheer eccentricity or oddness, however. "If you cannot here, for lack of advantage and lack of training . . . compete . . . with the arts . . . of the North, . . . you must then make your wares distinctively Southern, Carolinian, Charlestonian, local," he said. "Work with materials peculiar to Charleston, Carolina, the low country and the South; stamp it . . . with a certain something, piquant, excellent."

He was referring specifically to products like "stencilled hangings . . . baskets of palmetto fibre and marsh grass," and fanner baskets (of which there was a national dearth), but he also had the craft of writing in mind as well. "In applied art and fine art, as in literature, are you not weary of seasons, in poetry and song, that are not your seasons, flowers . . . [and] birds?" he asked. "Yours are in themselves as good; ay, often better. Strangers come here and rave" over the local scenes, "but who has put them into tangible, purchasable form?" [3]

The answer in 1906 would have been "not many." A local merchant would eventually advertise the sale of sweetgrass baskets, but the attitude Bennett had first remarked upon his arrival was still in evidence years afterward. [4] The Inter-State and West Indian Exposition had ended badly and in debt; some merchants agitated for more trade and promoted the city, but Charleston in many ways was still not welcoming. Nor was there a demand, even among the local population, for local fine arts and crafts.

From early on, the city supported furniture makers, iron workers, and silversmiths, but it also, unsure of its own worth, often looked to the North and to Europe. Nineteenth-century painter and miniaturist Charles Fraser painted imaginary European scenes he had never seen, [5] while novelist William Gilmore Simms, often writing on native themes, had edited an anthology of local writers to promote Charleston, but he complained constantly of lack of support and respect from the city. "In Charleston, a literary man is obnoxious . . . he is decidedly a nuisance & were it not for the outrageous indecency of the thing they would legislate upon him as such," he had written in 1830. [6] Bennett was well aware of the active coterie of writers that had revolved around and included Simms, but many of the antebellum writers, including Susan Bennett's grandmother, Louisa McCord, had expended their creative energies defending the South's politics, policies, and beliefs in slavery instead of writing creatively.

Bennett had discovered their books on the shelves of his father-in-law's library and at the Charleston Library Society. Of all of them, despite his having the least prestigious family tree (something that mattered in Charleston), only the poet Henry Timrod had become well known, even something of a cult figure in the South. He achieved an apotheosis of sorts, being crowned with the title "Poet Laureate of the Confederacy" for dedicating his lyric gifts to his new country. His father, although himself a writer of verse, was looked down upon for being a German immigrant, or so wrote Ludwig Lewisohn, a German immigrant himself; as for the son, Charleston "had every reason to be satisfied with the poet's actual work," Lewisohn believed. "Like all . . . assimilationists he outdid himself in the defense of the institutions and ways that were not his [as did Lewisohn himself]. He gloried in sonorous enough verses . . . and in his war poems called the Yankees 'Huns. . . .' It is a good word. It rhymes with 'guns.'"[7] Timrod celebrated the opening of the first Confederate Congress, the power and beauty of the cotton boll, and Charleston under Yankee siege. His lament for the Confederate dead and his own premature death from tuberculosis soon after the war sealed his transcendence as a martyr of the lost cause; manuscripts said to contain traces of his last hemorrhage were kept like relics in the Library Society.

Tributes to Timrod were more numerous after his death than during his life, and 1898 marked not only Bennett's arrival but also the founding of a committee to literally enshrine Timrod on a pedestal in a park in the city. Simms had already received this honor (also posthumously), to make up, many felt, for how the city had snubbed him while living. Statues were raised to other heroes; a soaring monument to John C. Calhoun, the politician whose ideas lead to secession, had been erected ten years before. But honor was only heaped upon those from the antebellum and war eras; it became the demarcation line that functioned temporally the way the Mason-Dixon Line did geographically. Anything before the war and below the line was of grace and glory; after and above it, everything was ugly. The "cause" was still holy in Charleston: there was a Confederate College to educate daughters of veterans still functioning, and the faces of the Confederate dead shone like daguerreotypes in memory, flashing silver, haloed in glory. At the 1901 May Day ceremony unveiling the bust of Timrod, hundreds gathered to witness the ceremony, which was rife with elegies.

The sixteen-year-old Lewisohn came, dreaming his own ideas of fame, feeling he was in the presence of immortality as the speaker compared Charleston to the great "motherlands of song . . . Greece . . . Italy . . . England. . . . What a comfortable psychical world that was to live in under the blue sky, in the fragrant air."[8]

Bennett witnessed the ceremony, too, and understood what it meant to the city. "Wasn't it just about that time," he asked historian and writer Yates Snowden, that "you printed certain verses of mine under [an] audacious and impertinent heading in the Snoozing Courier? [Snowden had printed Bennett's poem "In a Rose Garden" in the News and Courier under the title, "In a Charleston Rose Garden"]. You were pointed out to me . . . by my wife . . . at the dedication of the monument to Henry Timrod in City Hall Park."[9]

At that moment, other than Bennett, the only other real poet in town was George Herbert Sass, who'd publish a book in a few years (1904) under the pseudonym Barton Grey as if cloaking a youthful indiscretion; they were, indeed, juvenile efforts. Sass, Bennett noted, waxed most eloquent in his tribute to the Confederate dead and Robert E. Lee.[10] As the era retreated, Sass become Master-in-Equity and died soon after his one and only volume appeared. Lewisohn recalled Sass as "a tall, elegant, repressed personality. . . . Himself [like Timrod] of German descent, he . . . married into the inner circles of Charleston aristocracy" and promptly stopped writing.[11] In the next generation, the same thing happened to Beatrice Witte, born in Charleston, the daughter of another German immigrant, C. O. Witte. Wealthier and more cosmopolitan than most of her peers ("half-wits," Charlestonians would sometimes punningly call the children of the Witte girls who married into Charleston society), Beatrice Witte attended Radcliffe and published many stories and poems in national periodicals at the turn of the century. But she apparently renounced writing and gave up a career that some predicted would have been brilliant; she returned to Charleston, married into the aristocratic Ravenel family, and retired into domestic respectability.[12] Bennett married into the Smythe family, and by the time of his 1906 lecture he became inured to the dearth of writers in the city.

There were some books being published: reminiscences of Civil War service and slender volumes of verse, most locally published and some issued by the J. E. Neale Company, a Washington-based publishing house whose authors were often genteel. DuBose Heyward's mother published Wild Roses in 1905, a pallid collection of verse put out by a woman who needed to make money; she also wrote advertisements in verse for the Walker Evans and Cogswell Company. And there was *Magnolia Leaves* by an African American writer, Mary Fordham.

Some novels did appear. Annie Sloan wrote *The Carolinians: An Old Fashioned Love Story of Stirring Times in the Early Colony of Carolina.* Annie Colcock set her romance *Margaret Tudor* at time of the founding of Carolina in St. Augustine; like Henry James, she looked to Europe as a setting for *Her American Daughter.* Attorney Theodore Jervey, later president of the South Carolina Historical Society, used his novel *The Elder Brother* to castigate blacks and radical reconstruction.[13] All were dilettantes. No one, other than Owen Wister and Bennett, whose books appeared in 1906, used the contemporary scene, and none but they garnered national press for their writing; neither were natives of the city. Most insiders, like Mrs. St. Julien Ravenel, whose *Charleston: The Place and the People* was also published in 1906, believed that the arts, or letters at least, had died during the Civil War. She chose the date 1865 to end her history of Charleston.

So, other than Bennett, there was "no one writer, serious abut his writing, to whom it meant a living or the outlet of an irrepressible gift." [14] The only possible exception to this in these years, which was something of a joke, was William (or Billy) Molen, "Charleston's good gray poet." Molen, "with his patriarchal beard when washed, was [as] stately and handsome as Walt Whitman." He had blue eyes, pink cheeks, and was kindly. Like Whitman, "Molen was a writer of extraordinary free verse, extraordinary verse, and extraordinarily free." Sometimes in rhyme, in long lines, he celebrated events like the opening of the new post office, the Battle of Gettysburg, and a local vendor's new flavor of ice cream. His style might have been free, but the poems weren't. "He had his poems printed on small ballad sheets, and peddled them around the offices on Broad Street at 10 cents to a quarter." If his usual buyers were not in, he'd leave one of his broadsheets, returning later to retrieve his fee. "One hardly knows how to classify William Molen," Bennett mused years later, "a herald of free verse . . . or . . . an archaic survivor of the broad-side ballad sheet seller of [the] eighteenth century." Molen died in 1908, the same year Bennett was chastised and ostracized for his folktale lectures. For nearly ten years, as Bennett fell into his depression and ceased publishing, the silence deepened; a hush as profound as that of "the tomb of Pharaoh" fell on the city.[15]

Slowly, either encouraged by Bennett or thinking along the same lines on their own (or both), others began to follow his local-color credo. At first, it was mostly those from "off" (the term Charlestonians used to denote any-one not from Charleston) who recognized and then portrayed the unique-ness of the low country. Painters such as Birge Harrison came to Charleston, his visit prompted by Charles Henry White, a friend of Bennett's from the Art Students' League with whom he was corresponding.[16] Native-born Alice Ravenel Huger Smith sought advice from Harrison as she began experi-menting with her own inward visions; she issued a portfolio of drawings of a local mansion, the Miles Brewton House, in 1914, and soon after illustrated her father's text for a book on Charleston's historic dwelling houses.[17] Dis-tinctly local and idiosyncratic, she nevertheless met the standards, as Bennett said one must, of a national audience, even as national and international events triggered changes in the city and set locals writing.

War in Europe broke out in 1914; many in Charleston looked upon France and England with sympathy. Bennett awoke from his depression to the tune of soldier's marching feet, and that woke others, too. After an ab-sence from print of about fifteen years, Beatrice Witte Ravenel published a poem in the *Atlantic* called "Missing" about a soldier lost in action. After that, she kept on writing. (Bennett published his anti-war poem "The Ac-counting" in *Harper's* on August 20, 1914.) Then the young DuBose Hey-ward, known to recite his mother's confederate odes in Magnolia Cemetery on Confederate Memorial Day, published an elegy for a friend, a young Charlestonian who died in France for his country.[18]

Having been struck dumb by one war, Charleston, ironically, started to find her voice in another. A seaport with a navy base, the city began to fill with officers and enlisted men from all parts of the country; they brought change with them. The advent of modernism was as awkward and unsure as the lame and wounded veterans coming back from overseas.

One such among them was Hervey Allen; a native of Pittsburgh, gassed and wounded in France, he needed braces to walk when he glimpsed Charleston on his way south to pay a visit to an aunt in Florida in 1918. On his way back north, he looked around the quaint, time-trapped place and wondered if it would provide him a quiet place to heal and write; he felt driven to tell of his war experiences in prose and poetry.

He found an apartment and a job and started writing. Being gregarious by nature and wanting to meet other writers, he soon sought them out. (One can imagine him entering a bookstore or the Library Society and inquiring if there were any authors in the city and being told, "There's Mr. Bennett.") Bennett was always cordial meeting others and would have thought it his patriotic duty to help a soldier who had fought for his country. Solitary by choice, he, too, was lonely, remembering his past associates and their writing fraternity at Salt Sulphur Springs. He was intrigued by the picture Allen presented: a brash, unpolished young man who talked openly of becoming a writer and storming Olympus—so different from Bennett's own sideways slide into the profession. Allen was big and gangling, often having to stoop to get through doors, and yet he evoked a desire in others to protect him; sometimes he'd freeze up with shell shock and not be able to speak or move as traumatic memories of the battlefield overcame him. At other times, he belted out poetry and gushed over the beauty of world. His small eye-glasses gave his weak squinting eyes a microscopic intensity. Bennett saw him as "a strange young fellow of great but uncouth powers, a dreamer of aborted beauty [and] a lover of true loveliness." [19] He had accepted a job as a teacher at Porter Military Academy, an all-male high school founded by an Episcopal clergyman at the end of the Civil War. On the campus of old brick buildings and parade grounds on Ashley Avenue (now occupied by the Medical University of South Carolina), Allen employed his "uncouth" powers "teaching little boys dimly to comprehend the Ancient Mariner by hurling furious, Jove-like nodules of chalk at their vague heads." [20] Allen's idiosyncratic ways of teaching were tolerated—even praised; he also taught Bennett's son Jack. "He is having ['The Rime of the Ancient Mariner'] drilled into him at school under a fine teacher, Hervey Allen, writing excellent verse . . . a soldier, wounded in France," Bennett wrote.[21] Allen was shortly thereafter relieved of his job, however, for smoking. He moved onto the public high school; at about the same time Bennett withdrew his son from Porter, sending him off to Phillips Andover Academy.[22]

For Allen, teaching was a way of making a living to support himself to write. Wanting criticism and camaraderie, he began to show up at the Bennetts' house at 37 Legare Street. The older man listened to Allen read from a draft of a work in progress, his war-time autobiography (published eventually as *Toward the Flame*). Allen possessed the "real thing," Bennett saw. At six foot three, Allen towered (not just metaphorically) over the dilettantes in town,[23] and to accommodate his coming and going, Bennett (himself five foot ten) tiptoed up "to unscrew the foot from a chandelier in the hall lest . . . [Allen] damage himself in passing under it." Literary talent, Bennett joked, was now judged by his chandelier.[24]

And so it was: word got out about the strikingly tall, loping new teacher, trying to make a go of it by writing. He seemed to personify the new poetry being published nationally. Charlestonians were used to thinking of poets as feminine, fragile, and weak, like Timrod, or mostly ladies. The Charleston paper would continue printing its literary articles on the women's pages for years. But with the advent of World War I, people saw that poets like Rupert Brooke and others could be warriors and manly; there was a virile, democratic cast to the Chicago poets, who were writing unrhyming lines like Whitman's. The shy but secretly ambitious DuBose Heyward introduced himself to Allen, saying he, too, knew John Bennett and was interested in writing. Both were protégés of sorts of Charleston Museum director Laura Bragg, whose professionalism, missionary zeal, charismatic personality, and fragile beauty attracted many of the bright young men and women in town. She was as bracing as a cool New England breeze in a hot, still Charleston drawing room; she worked deliberately to bring new ideas of culture and professionalism into the city.[25]

Heyward and Allen hit it off. DuBose was four years older and much smaller than Hervey; he had nothing like Allen's confident, braggadocio air, and presented an almost anemic diffidence. He often hid his withered arm from others, just as he hid his true and deep feelings. Without complaint, he, the perfect gentleman, deferred to his widowed mother and sister till she married. He could have fun, display his keen eyes, exhibit a mischievous wit, and be tongue in cheek, but more often he spoke slowly and quietly, spaniel eyes down until they looked up for encouragement. The light in his eyes flickered like a candle in a steady breeze; he was always being struck down with something—the loss of a father, poverty, polio, pleurisy.

In Allen he found a male friend who dared to dream to live from writing; he was tough and did not think it shameful to be literary. "He has great power, great imagination, unusual range, . . . headlong inspirations . . . and a deep fund of great tenderness and susceptibility to loveliness, neither of which he quite admits to . . . the former from dread of he-man's laughter, from which he shrinks, and the latter from a mixed and complex reticence," Bennett wrote of Hervey in these years.[26] Both Allen and Heyward were hungry for life and anxious to achieve despite (or even because of) their infirmities. The more masculine Allen became Heyward's alter ego in a way, something he did not acknowledge in any way until after Heyward's death, and then just tangentially. He hypothesized that it might have been Heyward's paralysis that had attracted him to the crippled street beggar named Sammy Smalls, whom he'd come to immortalize in *Porgy*.[27] Allen's own wounded state provided yet another secret sense of kinship between the two. Heyward was overjoyed when asked to join Allen on his visits to Legare Street. Bennett, already familiar with Heyward through their war work, saw how Heyward had become more outgoing in Allen's company; no longer shyly showing his poems to older women like Bennett's sister-in-law, he was now openly talking about this enthusiasm he shared with Allen. Bennett detected the differences in them, too; Allen had the greater gift and a broader capability, he believed, but Heyward burned with a white-hot intensity. He needed to express himself soon, either due to a crucial developmental point he had reached or because he had been forced, through circumstance, to bank his desire so long and was now like a racehorse at the gate, chomping at the bit to get free.[28]

They were so interesting, and they tempered Bennett's cynicism, doubts, and fears on returning to writing. They made him, the old dog, eager to play and have his day again. They encouraged him by looking up to him. "By sheer chance," he noted, "we three came together as friends and familiars." Heyward and Allen were "driven by the inexorable urge to write"; Bennett, in his self-effacing way, demurred, saying he was only driven to write by necessity.[29] But he too felt some of their enthusiasm and recalled his days with the Cheerful Idiots at Salt Sulphur Springs; perhaps these were the thoughts that prompted him to note that "as my life runs I seem, from time to time, dimly to catch strange glimpses of destiny in my seemingly futile career."[30]

For the next two years, except in the summers (when most people left town to escape the heat), the three men met on Wednesday nights in Bennett's house on Legare Street. They discussed writing, punctuation, choice of words, rhythm, rhyme, and metrics in a process they called "fanging." No social niceties intervened; the sessions were "drastic, unsparing, ruthless [and] stimulating," bracketed with Susan Bennett's supper and midnight sandwiches and coffee.[31] Bennett mostly critiqued their work, but he also showed them his *Madame Margot.* Allen was busy with his war experiences in both prose and poetry; his poem "The Blind Man," about a survivor searching vainly for his family after a battle, was published in 1919 and gained him admirers and fame. Still haunted by bitter memories and war scenes, he often could not sleep and walked the beaches; Bennett teased him with the information that a tortured Edgar Allan Poe had walked the same beaches in the past century. He tempted Allen to write of Poe and use other local themes; Allen would later thank Bennett when he authored a two-volume Poe biography.[32] Bennett also encouraged Heyward, who was having his own difficulties. Having yet to find his voice and themes, Heyward was the least developed and had little to show for his work; as a result, he vacillated from exuberance to despair and often found the "fanging" excruciating.

He had been doing "some rotten sentimental blah stuff about the old South . . . and short stories only half-baked," but Bennett and Allen "put an end to that and drove him into . . . poetry for expression."[33] He'd benefit from it, they were sure, for "there is no better school for prose than . . . poetry; and nothing worse for the prose writer's peace of mind . . . than to become aware of the power of well-employed language, and the difficulty of commanding it."[34] Poetry seemed to be the natural choice in these years. Nearly every Southern writer, from Heyward and Josephine Pinckney to Allen Tate, William Faulkner, and Robert Penn Warren, would be poets first.

Charlestonians and Southerners took to poetry naturally, in their oral traditions of declaiming and fondness for fine-sounding rhythms such as those used by Poe and Sidney Lanier. Besides, fiction seemed the province of social protest in these post-war years. Upton Sinclair was exposing dirty secrets in the meat-packing industry, and Sinclair Lewis was lambasting America with *Babbit* and *Main Street.* In the latter, Charleston would provide the heroine Carol Kennicott a brief respite from Gopher Prairie when she'd come to stay, like Lewis himself, at Daisy Simonds's old house, the Villa Margherita on the battery.

To the natives and visitors, Charleston seemed an oasis of beauty and stability in a new, war-terrorized century. Unlike the Fugitive poets in Tennessee, who would take their name from their flight from the social brahmins and elites, Charlestonians took comfort from the past and did not want to forsake society. The quaint and the old and beautiful appealed to many of them. Besides, they were older than many of those soon to burst forth in Nashville, Richmond, and New Orleans; many were natives, born into old prestigious families, and too comfortable in this ancestor-conscious city to want to flee.

As Heyward worked in poetry and prose, Bennett admonished him to forget what other writers were doing in the slick magazines. He gave Heyward the best advice: listen to your own voice and portray what you know. "Exploit the beauty of your own home. Stamp your handiwork native, characteristic, indigenous to this soil; make it a rare and desirable exotic," was how he had put it in 1906; in 1919 and 1920, he was doing just that with *Madame Margot* and *The Doctor to the Dead* and telling the younger men to do the same thing.[35] Heyward, the native, had not been using Charleston but was employing other locales popular in the marketplace. Ironically, the non-native Bennett was now convincing Heyward of the value and color of the low country.

Hervey Allen, too, helped persuade the locals to what many, afraid perhaps of being provincial, really wanted to believe: that their city was different and worthy of describing. "Hervey . . . agreed," Bennett wrote, "that it is only the rank outsider, the damn-yankee or hill-billy, [who] really sees Old Charleston, and gets the true impression of . . . this queer . . . sometimes drear . . . and perhaps when all is said, dear old town: the real, bonafide Charlestonian has never truly observed [it], but . . . draws in, ready made, . . . some quaint conception of the place, erroneous, though fond, and for the rest of his existence, . . . travels his course, . . . happy and secure, unawake to . . . thrill[s] . . . just around the corner."[36]

What was then happening in Charleston and the rest of the South was startling. The region had been cut off from time and the rest of the country and was suddenly catching up. The disparity between its past separateness and its sudden collision with the twentieth century was fascinating; it would soon fuel much of the genius of Southern writing. Many would go for the new, or describe it at least. Faulkner would show the Snopeses taking the place of the Compsons; others, like the Agrarians, would work to reclaim a world unmarred by the industrialized, dehumanizing forces of the twentieth century. Charlestonians, never a group to intellectualize, would decry the loss of beauty, evoke and mourn the disappearing scene. Herbert Ravenel Sass would uncritically conjure the stereotype of the antebellum South in his novel *Look Back to Glory;* Heyward would compare the golden youth of the 1860s to ripening wheat being mowed down in his own Civil War novel,

*Peter Ashley.* In a poem, he'd dramatize modern machines tearing down old walls and ghosts coming back to retrieve the romantic treasure they had buried.[37] He'd also show upheavals in the class that changed most drastically: he'd concentrate on the black underclass in *Porgy* and *Mamba's Daughters* and on poor mountain whites in *Angel.* The women novelists in town, like Katherine Ball Ripley in *Crowded House* and Josephine Pinckney in *Three o'Clock Dinner,* would show the havoc these changes brought to white, middle-class families in novels of manners and social comedies. Charleston "is beautiful with the past," Amy Lowell would say in 1921; this should provide the artists their atmosphere.[38]

Heyward, with Bennett and Allen to encourage him, and his skills and perceptions sharpened by fanging, began to employ the low country as a setting for his stories. "The Ghost of the *Helen of Troy,*" a story written in 1919, was both Southern and contemporary.[39] With the sudden, fervent ardor of converts, Heyward and Allen planned to collaborate on a volume of poems portraying the history, beauty, and legends of Charleston and the low country. Heyward, with the more lyrical talent, would do the emotive and evocative writing; Allen, with more narrative skills, would capture legends and stories.

They called on Bennett to critique their work, and he did it willingly, so fond was he of these younger men. "The best critic," he believed, "is he who is keenly sensitive to impressions, readily responsive to excellences of many different kinds, graced with perception, contagious in his enthusiasm, rich in ripened personality, and trained thoroughly in self-expression."[40] He had found these qualities in his sister Martha, who he considered the best critic of his own writing; he consulted her about Heyward, too. Recognizing the importance of local color to their work, she recommended that Heyward read Sarah Orne Jewett.[41] "The work, no matter what the agony, must be up to the mark or fail," Bennett had told his Charleston audience in 1906. "When I say that . . . work must be well done I do not mean well done for the capacity or opportunity of the workman." It had to measure up whether one was an amateur or one of the best writers in the city. "Is it pretty well done for me? or for Charleston? or for the South, where opportunity does not stand at the door? is not the question."[42] Works had to compete on their own merits with other works from throughout the United States, regardless of their regional origin.

Heyward was stung by this; he had been lulled into the belief that he was an artist, having seen his 1915 play "An Artistic Triumph," a dull thing, lauded by his city. "I have done DuBose's story—a hard job," Bennett wrote Susan in the summer of 1920, "for while his skeleton idea is good, he has failed, in several important points, to get it across. . . . It is *his* story, truly: but I can see where he has erred in drawing a romantic character. I hope I have helped, and spurred on, not discouraged, the lad!"[43] Bennett told the truth, believing "the blunt truth is kinder and more considerate, more brave than pretty lies and empty flattery . . . if your work be bad to-day then take thought to-morrow to make it better," he advised; "be your own sternest, most unswerving critic, . . . never bending to the right or left."[44]

"I have fanged his work heavily, sheerly because I love the lad," Bennett wrote his wife.[45] She, no doubt, realized that in saying, "I love the lad" he was quoting his own Gaston Carew, who, in *Master Skylark*, said it of Nick as he developed the boy into someone good enough to sing for the Queen. (Heyward's *Porgy*, in play form, would go on to "sing" before the King and Queen of England eventually.)[46] At this time, however, Heyward was not totally grateful; Laura Bragg, for one, believed that he wanted praise only.[47]

Bennett was also worried about Allen. "He . . . says that he *thinks* he has a *publisher already* for the Charleston book. . . . Certainly youth is eager to be on!" he wrote Susan, but "I hope the two will keep their heads! Now is the time they *must*, or they will be betrayed by the pleasant praise of happy-looking circumstance."[48] He contacted them at once: "At this juncture in both your lives, be exacting, not easy, don't rush into print," he told them.[49] It was a lesson he had learned the hard way with *The Treasure of Peyre Gaillard*, giving in too easily to a publisher. Allen, with his budding reputation, had contacts and offers; Heyward was eager and deliriously happy. But they both took the older man's advice and delayed, giving themselves time to finesse their work for a year. As they polished and listened to Bennett's critiques, they saw individual poems of theirs printed in national magazines, of which many in the city had not known before these years.

One who was familiar with them was Laura Bragg, who had subscribed to *Poetry* magazine since 1918.[50] While Bennett and his male protégés were meeting on Wednesdays on Legare Street, she was convening a group of women at Isabel Heyward's house on Sundays on Gibbes Street. (It's interesting to note that both leaders were non-natives.) Her group included Elizabeth Miles (later Horlbeck), Helen von Kolnitz (later Hyer, poet laureate of South Carolina), and the future poet and novelist Josephine Pinck-

ney (who defiantly remained a Pinckney). While the men were exploiting
the local scene, the women were examining more modern poetry and were,
in fact, more abreast of the national trends. Bragg passed on to members of
both groups her copy of *Poetry Magazine.*[51] She introduced DuBose Heyward
to the work of T. S. Eliot; Heyward had, until then, never heard of him.[52]
Bragg's emotional partner, Isabel Heyward, a cousin of DuBose's, acted as
hostess on these evenings and when Bragg invited the Legare Street men to
Gibbes Street. Members of the two groups mixed back and forth occasionally after that, which must have been pleasant, for DuBose Heyward was
rumored to be romantically linked with Josephine Pinckney, who was young,
wealthy, and independently spirited.[53] ("One is always insecure about Josephine's poetry," Bennett wrote in 1921, "if it is Josephine's, and not sprung
from borrowed phosphates."[54] His doubts would continue for years, one
reason being that he believed she had not professed any interest at all in
poetry until Laura Bragg made it social about 1918.)[55]

The interchanges between the two groups were pleasant, but Bennett was
a bit miffed and possibly jealous that Laura Bragg was giving advice on
poetry; unlike Bennett, she had never published any creative writing. (He
also had trouble accepting women like Pinckney and Bragg, of independent
spirit and/or means, who did not defer to men like his equally independent sister, Martha Trimble Bennett, did to him.)[56] Bragg "is rank jealous
of the inner circle of Wednesday nighters," he said of her, "and would give
a pretty [penny] if she could, by offerings of 'adorable flappers' of any sort,
wean DuB[ose] or H[ervey], probably DuB[ose], who seems the readier to
swallow her sweetened words, dear boy, away from 'middle-aged society.'
(Them's her words!)"[57] Despite the petty rivalry, he nevertheless recognized
that she was sincerely interested in helping others. He was over a dozen
years older than she but, like her, was somewhat of a missionary and vision-
ary on what the city of Charleston could be. He was less overtly vocal and
"preachy" than she was and had ten years of "seniority" on her in Charleston. He had been slapped down publicly for his racial beliefs; she worked
differently, opening the museum to blacks, sending exhibits to black schools,
but not actually mixing with blacks on a personal level as unself-consciously
as he. But with their similar goals and beliefs and tendency toward selfless-
ness, they minimized their differences (in public at least) for the benefit of
their protégés. Both grew happy and took credit for the fact that Charleston,
so deficient in writers for generations, was now bustling with many who

took the craft seriously. Like spring, the very air, Bennett felt, seemed to tremble with possibility. "Something like a repressed breath waited for some dynamic force to release it."[58]

For many across the South, the impetus came unwittingly from Baltimore newspaper columnist and social critic Henry Louis Mencken, who derided the South's artistic accomplishments in an essay he called "The Sahara of the Bozart." Published first in 1919, and in expanded form in a book in November 1920, it prompted many injured Southerners to rush into print to contradict him. This was *not* the case in Charleston, however, although Allen and Heyward and Bennett themselves forgot that fact in the coming years. It was not until July of 1921 that Bennett and others in town read the essay;[59] their great leap forward occurred in October 1920, a month before the published book containing Mencken's essay appeared.

It was a Wednesday "evening full of thunder" during one of the "fanging" sessions on Legare Street, the air electric with creative ideas, plans, and future dreams; "all [that was] needed to produce an explosion [was] a spark, an idea." DuBose Heyward provided it. Having recently learned of the Poetry Society of New York, he quietly looked up and said, "Let's start a poetry society here."[60] Instead of two groups, women on Gibbes Street and men on Legare, they could all meet together in a society.

The idea was interesting, and a typical response of Heyward's; he had been doing similar things with friends like Josephine Pinckney for years. With men and women from his social class, he had drawn up rules for the Courting, Wooing and Matrimonial Society, in 1915. When it proved so successful, the male contingent had to institute the Sir Galahad Society; at those meetings poetical dirges were written and mock wakes held when someone "fell from grace" and married.[61]

A poetry society would provide similar social niceties, yet it would also help create an audience and a platform for outreach. No storm of criticism would descend on them, as it had on Bennett in 1908, if their art was made into a civic virtue. Some years earlier, Heyward had even approached the Chamber of Commerce to help float one of his artistic ideas.[62] Heyward was no alienated artist at odds with the world, but someone who naturally took his place among the elite. And he was a good businessman; he believed a society could provide funds, an audience, and a reputation for the city.

He was not the first to think of such things. Bennett had floated the idea of creating a league of artists and artisans in his 1906 lecture to the Carolina

Art Association. "If there were a capable society here . . . it would do much good . . . for the real development of the artistic sense of the community," he said then. But he was cautious, for it "must always be remembered also that while Charleston is a considerable city in rough numbers, its community of refinement is comparatively small and there is nothing to be hoped from the baser portion, or considered, either in association or patronage." He also believed that "the formation of an . . . Association can but in somewhat exploit your labor in advance, and in a small measure expedite transaction[s] between buyer and seller. It cannot work a miracle either in the community nor in you." He knew that good work was often the result of lonely vigils and not of time spent in societies. "The work does not absorb any virtue" from an organization, he argued; "it does not make poor work good."[63]

Bennett expressed his misgivings and argued against Heyward's idea that October evening; Hervey Allen, however, agreed with Heyward immediately. (Amy Lowell, who boosted Allen's career, would soon remark that she thought Allen could be steered into anything by anybody.)[64] The two younger men kept entreating Bennett; he rebuffed them repeatedly. "Sure they're geniuses, and are young, and rebounding in spirits and 'opes of a glorious future; why shouldn't they just do the thing themsel's and not fret the aged at all?" he wondered.[65]

But they badly wanted him. His name, they said, would lend the right impression, an endorsement of sorts from the most literary man in the city, the only one with anything like a national reputation. For his part, Allen could draw on the many contacts he was developing around the country; and Heyward, with his unquestionable background, could contribute his social connections. It would be just another division of labor, similar to the poetry manuscript on which they were collaborating. They would do the work; Bennett could just be a figurehead they could come to for ideas.

Finally Bennett gave in, not for the soundness of the argument but for his "love of the two boys" only.[66] He had reasons to hesitate; there was his family to think of, his volunteer work at the museum, and his own writing. These would have to come first. Heyward and Allen, both single, and neither having to make up for a decade of work lost to outraged Victorian propriety, agreed.[67]

The first move was to recruit the women on Gibbes Street. They were enthusiastic, too; the image of the poet as an outlaw or outside society, fleeing the Brahmins of town, was hardly one in which they believed. With much of the same *noblesse oblige* their class felt toward issues such as race, they believed they could cultivate the town with their poetry.

And indeed, when word got out about such an endeavor, it became news and was written about in the paper. The author of the article, Ellen M. Caroll, a hopeful poet herself, linked the idea of a poetry society with morality. "The language of the poet is truth," she wrote, noting on this day after Christmas 1920 that "our blessed Lord" never told jokes or used oratory, but spoke "pure poetry."

Such social good, however, would not necessarily fill a hall with people; "in a world given over to pelf and money getting, . . . in a State fully abreast with the world in this respect, one must be struck with such an effort, as John Bennett and his associates have made," she wrote, giving Bennett, despite his lack of desire for it, top billing. "They may fail; chances are against them," she thought, "but this has never dampened the ardor of a poet, who, in pursuit of truth, is quite willing to engage with the devil himself." [68]

Bennett did not mind that; he was doing it in *Madame Margot,* a tale wherein the heroine makes a Faustian pact. It was the Charleston elite and their social deities that had him worried. Names for membership were suggested from among their social peers. Since there was no large college or university in town (the College of Charleston and the Citadel both had small faculties and student bodies), they had to seek more supporters; they culled names to canvas from the pages of the Charleston telephone directory.[69] By making it a society with a cut-off number, they could appeal to the exclusive and snobbish nature of the city. And charging dues would enable them to come up with funding.

To make it a legal entity, DuBose Heyward circulated a petition for incorporation on Broad Street, the financial and legal district of Charleston. "So unusual was the idea [of a poetry society, and so soft was DuBose Heyward's speech] that when Heyward solicited signatures to his petition for incorporation, several appended their names thinking that he was organizing a Poultry Raising Society." [70] But he was a Heyward, and if he believed it important, others agreed. All signed up.

The first organizational meeting was held the same month Heyward had his idea, in October 1920, at South Carolina Society Hall; peoples' interests were so piqued that the handsome hall, whose portico extended out over Meeting Street, was nearly filled to capacity (with two hundred or so attending) when the first regular meeting was called to order on January 15 of the new year. Many, no doubt, came to see, if in Carroll's words, Bennett's venture would succeed or fail.

Charleston attorney Frank Frost, who had a distinctive lineage and was also somewhat literary (he had known Owen Wister at Harvard and corresponded with him about *Lady Baltimore*) was elected president. Non-native John Bennett, making sure again that he would only be a figurehead, became vice president. Heyward was elected secretary, and Josephine Pinckney became treasurer. Hervey Allen, Laura Bragg, Beatrice Ravenel, and Herbert Ravenel Sass, a writer for the local paper and son of George Herbert Sass, or "Barton Grey," among others, were elected to the executive committee. From the very beginning, the prime movers, Bennett, Heyward, and Allen, deliberately avoided naming a woman president, "which gives body to the old suspicion of poetry being no modern masculine business."[71] (Tongue-in-cheek, Heyward would later mention in a novel of his how no local man would ever go to a Poetry Society meeting.)[72]

With the speed of the organizing, the mushrooming of details, and Heyward and Allen working full time, some of the work inevitably fell to Bennett, who held no "real" job but was home working on his own writing. (A later Poetry Society official would refer to him as "a man of leisure to do just as he pleases.")[73] Four days before the first January meeting, Bennett, remembering the promises of the younger men, had misgivings. To Laura Bragg he wrote, "Either I must neglect the affairs of the museum or of the Poetry Society, or of my own, or I must resign."[74]

DuBose Heyward stepped in, promising Bennett he would not be bothered after the society got on its feet; but Bennett, with good reason, doubted that. With "no other speaker volunteering for the occasion," Bennett, by default, and with typical grace, found himself heralding the society into existence with a keynote speech the night of the fifteenth.[75] "He read a critique on Poetry in America, quoting several living poets." To inject a note of realism, he warned the audience that not all past poetry was beautiful and not all new poets great.[76]

In February, with payment from membership dues, the Poetry Society was solvent. (Heyward was canny enough to come up with the idea that members had to continue paying dues once they joined and would be assessed for the next year; members could only resign at the annual meeting.)[77] This gave them money to import a speaker; they chose Carl Sandburg, who, with three volumes of poems to his credit, was at the beginning of his career.

He was of the Chicago School of poetry and showed the masculine "side" of poetry. Sandburg performed like a troubadour; he read from his poems, sang, and played the guitar. He spoke on the nature of the "new poetry," which many people in town, bred on Victorian rhymes, found a trifle shocking. He then left to visit his friend Daniel Reed, who was organizing a theater group in Columbia; on the way, Sandburg stopped off at Fort Motte to visit the beginning writer Julia Peterkin, who was sending her short, stark sketches of Negro life to poetry magazines.

Bennett had volunteered to entertain Sandburg and wrote him after he left: "You have been the talk of the town. We have waked up the slumbering, and spurred the quick to broadening views. That we shall all agree with your view of what constitutes poetry [is] too much to ask; but that you persuade even your enemy to be at peace with you . . . is victory." [78]

In March, the executive committee brought in Harriet Monroe to address the society. As editor of one of the best little magazines, known simply as *Poetry*, she was in a natural position to assess the new group and to broadcast its founding across the country. Monroe praised the organization and its work, believing, like others, that "the Society will be of great influence and value in helping to form and direct the taste of creative energy of the new South towards poetry." She hoped others would follow Charleston's lead. "Clubs in every center of the nation [like] this one . . . would create a public alive to poetry, . . . like those Italian Communities in the Renaissance where whole towns were artists and connoisseurs." [79]

Fired with enthusiasm, Bennett and others of the executive committee brought in more speakers to both encourage and calm the members. Jessie Rittenhouse, a popular poet, affiliated with the Poetry Society of America and editor of such volumes as *The Younger American Poets, The Little Book of Modern Poets,* and *The Second Book of Modern Verse,* spoke on "Modern English and Conservative American Poets." Not all poets were casual and strummed a guitar like Carl Sandburg, her audience was comforted to hear. "Needless to say Miss Rittenhouse made many friends for herself and poetry." In thanking the society for its hospitality, she wrote, "My visit . . . was a delight. . . . You have a great opportunity to act as a radiating centre of the appreciation of poetry. . . . Why should not this go on and bring about a poetic revival in the South?" [80]

Even if this was not what they thought from the outset, it now was what many of the movers and shakers in the organization were thinking. They began to formulate a credo and codify their beliefs, articulating many of the ideas that Bennett had expressed back in 1906. In the summer, they'd discover Mencken's "Sahara of the Bozart," and Hervey Allen would fashion a derisive reply.[81] Art had not died in the Civil War, he'd decree; and as the city had been then, Charleston was once again in the lead; instead of leading Southern states into secession, the city was encouraging other states to launch their own poetry societies. Southerners, Allen believed, were wise to sneer at the plebeian works of art, such as *Main Street* from the Midwest and the "Yiddish romances" of New York City.[82] Instead of the writings of immigrant Anzia Yezierska, who wrote of the teeming life of the tenements in New York, he found the ways and works of the South more pleasing. (Yezierska, ironically, would soon champion the exiled Charlestonian, Ludwig Lewisohn.)

In its declaration of intent, the Poetry Society showed its *noblesse oblige* roots and missionary zeal; it announced its aim to be "the assistance of any poet, however obscure, who shows genuine promise, and the winning for his work of such recognition as it deserves." Through its publications and meetings, it would help those with "little or no opportunity of publication for poetry dealing with Southern themes."[83] The organization would thus fulfill those functions Bennett had foreseen for an Arts and Crafts League: it would provide a showcase for exhibiting local workmanship.

To further encourage writers, members put up prizes and prize money for poems in certain categories. Bennett established the Skylark Prize "for the best student poem published in a College Magazine, in the State of South Carolina . . . or written by any student of English Literature in any Academy, College or University of the State"; while Laura Bragg created an award for "the best poem of Local Color, possessing a Universal Appeal," open to Society members only.[84] Out-of-state contributors also volunteered. Caroline Sinker of Philadelphia—a relative of DuBose Heyward who had been helpful in getting him treatment for his polio (he'd dedicate his book *Angel* to her) and who, some said, served as the model for Owen Wister's heroine Eliza LaHeu in *Lady Baltimore*—contributed twenty-five dollars each year for the Southern Prize; even better, Hervey Allen's friend, William van Rensselaer Whitall, a wealthy Pelham, New York, book collector, eagerly contributed an annual prize of $250.[85] Named for Allen's famous antiwar poem, the Blindman Prize was, at the time, apparently the largest cash award for poetry in the country. It garnered the society great attention and raised its status immeasurably.

So did the news that Hervey Allen's first book of poems would appear. *Wampum and Old Gold* was accepted in the Yale Series of Younger Poets.[86] It was quite fitting that many of his poems were read at the spring meeting.

"A poetry society of real importance has succeeded," the executive committee crowed at the end of the year; it had prospered in spite of competition from "the moving picture theater, and other forms of anesthetic enjoyment so popular in America." That it succeeded "proved this city to be possessed of an inherent culture, the discovery of which . . . is at once quite amazing . . . and most heartening," the writers, probably Bennett, crowed.[87] The success *was* dizzying; Allen and Heyward were now receiving their first accolades at the beginning of their careers, and Bennett could put his years of despair behind him now, knowing that he was firmly back in good graces with the city. As a measure of grace and generosity, he worked throughout the summer on the society yearbook, while many other members left the city.

The yearbook would come out in the fall; the first image would be his silhouette of a piper, encouraging fellow poets and lovers of poetry to follow the society's lead. The quatrain beneath the figure's arched feet now took on a new meaning: "We are all but Fellow-Travelers / Along Life's weary way. / If any man can play the pipes, / In God's name, let him play." This was especially appropriate and fitting, for the society had been founded with Bennett's encouragement, tied, at least in part, to an idea he had been thinking about for over a dozen years; and he had given its inaugural speech. Now, in its publication, he was also taking the lead. To meet a rush deadline, he hurriedly created its official seal: "hopelessly Greek, the lettering old Spanish, and the moon turned the wrong way."[88] Carl Sandburg, Maxwell Bodenheim, Amy Lowell, and Edwin Arlington Robinson, among others, contributed good-will wishes, poetry, and congratulations for what they had achieved—which was startling. For, having been founded in October almost on a lark, it had become, by the time of the summer's first heat, a precedent-setting organization getting national attention.

As summer set in, many of the principals scattered. With a recommendation from Bennett, Hervey Allen went off to the artists' colony founded by Mrs. Edward MacDowell in Peterborough, New Hampshire, in her husband's memory (Bennett had met her when she visited Charleston years before).[89]

Heyward, meanwhile, joined the migrating species of Charlestonians who annually took summer leave; he left his business to write in the cool peace of the North Carolina mountains and to join Allen in New England for a brief stay at the colony. "Meeting all those folk should be a good thing for DuB[ose]," Bennett believed.[90]

Bennett also went north for the first time in years; the whole family visited Massachusetts to attend his eldest daughter, Jane's, graduation from Dana Hall High School, where her Aunt Martha taught. Afterward, they all went to New York City, where Bennett met with representatives of the Century Company about the tale he was writing; and later they journeyed to Pelham, New York, to visit William van Renssalaer Whitall, who had put up the money for the Blindman Prize and with whom Bennett had begun corresponding.

Returning to Charleston, Bennett then drove his family up to Many Pines; he returned alone to Charleston to supervise workmen engaged in remodeling 37 Legare Street.

In this sudden oasis of calm after a very tumultuous year, he reflected on the society's success and his own; while in New York, he had met with editors of the Century Company. He had not published a book for fifteen years, but now his *Madame Margot*, the first true product of the city's literary renaissance, was to appear.

Eliza Jane Trimble McClintick Bennett and
John Briscoe Bennett, John Bennett's parents,
in the garden of 76 West Second Street,
Chillicothe, Ohio. ca. 1900. (John Bennett)

"Dumpling" Jack Bennett, around eight years
old. (From the South Carolina Historical
Society [SCHS] Collections)

Bennett family home, 76 West Second Street, Chillicothe, Ohio, July 1900.
Photo by John Bennett. (From the SCHS Collections)

The F.B.S. *(left to right):* Sam Kline, "Jack" Bennett *(seated),* Walter Poland, James Wood, Charles Waddle, and Walter Floyd. The skull belonged to Dr. William Waddle; the crossbones are those of Perry Bowsher. (From the SCHS Collections)

"The Cheerful Idiot." John Bennett *(right)* and unidentified friend in amateur theatricals, ca. 1890s. (From the SCHS Collections)

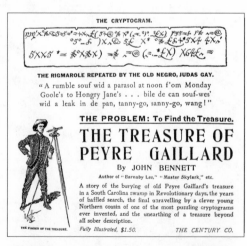

Advertisement for *The Treasure of Peyre Gaillard.* Pictured is Bennett's brother-in-law Augustine Smythe as the hero Jack Gignilliatt. (John Bennett)

Bennett's older sister, Alice Bennett.
(John Bennett)

Bennett's older brother, Henry ("Harry")
Holcomb Bennett. (John Bennett)

John Bennett of Chillicothe, Ohio, ca.
1884–85. (From the SCHS Collections)

Bennett's younger sister, Martha Trimble
Bennett. (John Bennett)

"The Roost." Writing room used by the Bennett brothers, 76 West Second Street, Chillicothe, Ohio. (From the SCHS Collections)

John Bennett's drawing of his desk. (Charleston County Public Library)

John Bennett perfecting his craft, Mackinac Island, September 1898. (Charleston County Public Library)

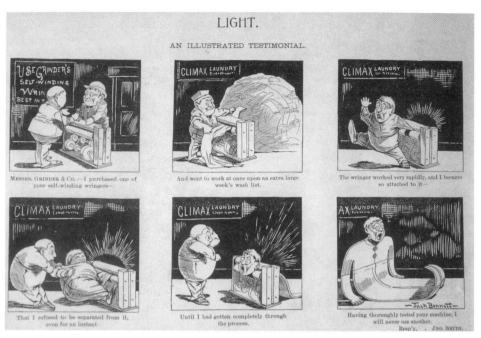

A cartoon from *Light* magazine, by "Jack" Bennett. (John Bennett)

Bennett's pen-and-ink sketch of Tom Egan,
foreman of the *Chillicothe Daily News,* done on the
job, 1884. (From the SCHS Collections)

"A Tiger Tale," verse and drawings by John Bennett, published in *St. Nicholas Magazine*, 1897. (John Bennett)

Bennett's pen-and-ink rendering of Salt Sulphur Springs, 1896. (Collection of author)

Self-portrait, 1898, the year Bennett arrived in Charleston. (From the SCHS Collections)

Susan Smythe, 1901. She sent this photograph to her
prospective in-laws to "introduce" herself.
(From the schs Collections)

John Bennett in New York City, ca. 1900. (John Bennett)

Susan Smythe *(left)* and her older sister, Hannah, ca. 1900.
(From the schs Collections)

Louisa Rebecca McCord Smythe and Augustine Smythe, with two of their grandsons, Bryan H. Wright and John H. Bennett *(sitting)*, son of John Bennett, 1910.
(From the schs Collections)

John Bennett and Susan Smythe Bennett, on the piazza, 37 Legare Street, Charleston, ca. 1914.
(John Bennett)

A portrait of workers at Woodburn plantation by John Bennett, ca. 1905. Jane Hunter *(right)* and her brother Winston ("Dang") Harris in the front. (From the SCHS Collections)

Jane, Jack, and Sue Bennett, with their "Dah" (nanny), Martha Grant, in the Smythe back yard, 31 Legare Street, Charleston, 1914. (John Bennett)

Susan, Jane, "The Kaiser," their archery target, and Jack Bennett, with friend Jenks Robinson, Flat Rock, North Carolina, July 1918. (John Bennett)

John Bennett on the piazza, 37 Legare Street, Charleston, ca. 1920.
(John Bennett)

John Bennett with his son in front of 37 Legare Street, Charleston, ca. 1920.
(John Bennett)

DuBose Heyward *(left)* and Hervey Allen on a boat trip to Kiawah Island, summer 1920. Photograph by Bennett's son, Jack. (From the SCHS Collections)

"Hervey Allen & I," Bennett wrote on the back of this image, "June 11, 1920, West Point Mill wharf." His son Jack snapped the photo before they all left on a boat trip to Kiawah Island. (From the SCHS Collections)

Another self-portrait (from Bennett's 1926 Christmas Card). He titled it "Art and Literature: by one who has somewhat practiced both." (John Bennett)

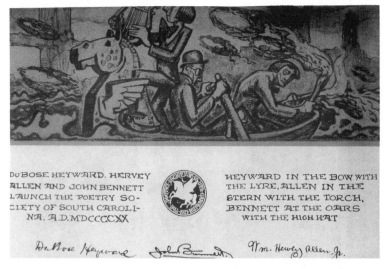

DuBOSE HEYWARD, HERVEY ALLEN AND JOHN BENNETT LAUNCH THE POETRY SOCIETY OF SOUTH CAROLINA, A.D. MDCCCCXX

HEYWARD IN THE BOW WITH THE LYRE, ALLEN IN THE STERN WITH THE TORCH, BENNETT AT THE OARS WITH THE HIGH HAT

Bennett's oddly prophetic spoof on the launching of the Poetry Society of South Carolina. (John Bennett)

John Bennett's only etching, *The House of the Doctor to the Dead.* (Collection of author).

Title page of *The Pigtail of Ah Lee Ben Loo,* designed and executed by John Bennett.

Bennett at his desk in "The Astrologer's Tower," 1938. (From the SCHS Collections)

John and Susan Bennett, "still the most interesting woman I have ever known," 37 Legare Street, late 1940s. (From the SCHS Collections)

John Bennett and Charleston children about to be awarded "diplomas" for summer reading, gardens of the Charleston County Library, 1942. (From the SCHS Collections)

Portrait of John Bennett by Doris Ulmann, 1930, "as I should like
to be known and remembered by all who read my books."
(Charleston County Public Library)

CHAPTER 15

# *"The Golden Age"*

IN BENNETT'S CLUTTERED, THIRD-FLOOR STUDY ("The Astrologer's tower"
is what Heyward and Allen called it), prints, carvings, books, and engravings
in a "grand furor" around him, he put the finishing touches on the tale of
the real-life woman of color who had grown rich through her stylish cre-
ations of dresses and hats for the social elite.[1] From his father-in-law, who
had been the woman's attorney and executor, he found out her name but
never revealed it, knowing that her descendants, "passing" for white, would
be condemned for their African descent.

The details of her having sold her soul to the devil came from associates
of Bennett's friends Caesar Grant and Walter Mayrant. He sought out,
photographed, and overpainted the ruins of the cottage in McBride's Lane,
called "Lilac Lane" in his work. (Now completely obliterated, the lane ran
east from St. Philip Street near the present College of Charleston's Albert
Simons Fine Arts Building [named for Susan's nephew], then south to
George Street.) "The uneasy ghost of Madame Margot, if there be such
things," Bennett later wrote, "should be seen . . . in the shadows of the
parking-space behind the Gloria theatre, in George Street."[2]

Combining legend with truth and fiction with fact, he worked to produce
something "different and difficult."[3] He often despaired of success, feeling
"that to write English is one of the things provided for the gods alone."[4]
But, like a conjurer, Bennett got closer and closer to the fantastic world with
every rewrite—as if polishing something dark to make it mirror-bright. The
time before the Civil War, the fabulous legendary era in which Madame
Margot lived, became in his tale, "a golden age . . . when . . . nothing had
grown old," an era when "the young were younger, the old not so sorry for
everything as they have been since."[5] DuBose Heyward would call up a
similar world a little later in *Porgy*, referring to "the Golden Age . . . when

169

men, not yet old, were boys in an ancient beautiful city that time had for-gotten before it destroyed."[6]

In Margot's world, "the calendar seemed to have paused among the tulips, between the jessamine and June, in that paradise of the year." Charleston, "the languid, lovely, tired old town was then a city brave and gay, with Mediterranean manners and Caribbean ways." "Though Margot was lovely, [her daughter] Gabrielle was lovelier. . . . Margot was like the summer sun, dazzling, opulent, sumptuous; Gabrielle like the young spring moon in her slender loveliness; the lines of her flowed one into the other, like . . . a song." But if Gabrielle were like the moon, there were clouds in front of it; if a song, it was in a minor key. "For, as the rarest beauty remains imperfect without a touch of strangeness . . . there was . . . in Gabrielle's loveliness— a touch of irregularity difficult to define—making her beauty more signifi-cant through being peculiar, more poignant though being strange." Over this Margot worried, knowing "it is a perilous privilege for a girl to possess loveliness rising above her station in life; there is a price always to be paid for it, sorrow the common fee; . . . haggard wisdom reaps in tears what innocence sowed with laughter." To protect her, she kept her daughter im-mured in a garden where "hedge-balked and bewildered, few had seen her twice." Despite that, Margot continually prayed for her safety; for "youth and spring hate convents, and will have life's novitiate. . . . There is a crevice in every hedge, no matter how tall or how thick it may be, and through it, ever, Gabrielle peeps."[7]

"Oh, Mother, feel my heart beating!" she cries one evening. "It beats as if it would burst. Why does my heart beat so? Am I dying?" Or "is it love?" she wonders.

"It is its direst misery," Margot answers bitterly. "God keep you from it. Two parts are pain, two sorrow, and the other two parts are death."

"I don't fear death," Gabrielle answers. "Then why should I fear love?"

"Because it is a lie," crie[s] Margot, beside herself. "I conjure you, by God's sorrow, close your ears against it."[8]

But she is young and beautiful and cannot; a lad, "tall, well-set and slen-der, with a beautiful straight body" finds her in her garden; "silently drinking her loveliness he leaned through the hedge. Among the fire-colored flowers and green, her color was exquisite as the violet sky is, seen through yellow leaves.

"A delicate, throbbing fire came fluttering up through her breast. . . . His eyes met hers; and all her doubts went out in wordless joy.

"She regarded him for an instant—a boy, hot, and hasty, sure of himself, impulsively bold, but abashed . . . her breast heaved and sank; she could not control it. Overwhelmed by the sudden strange rush of emotion, she swayed giddily." [9]

Half a step timidly they approached one another. "You are the god of Love," she said, "else, how could you fly over the hedge? . . ."

"The god of love! *Bien!* Then what shall I have that is godlike?"

"What you will," she said. . . . For the innocent are trustful as doves, helpless as the least creatures, weak as the small birds among the little branches. . . .

"Most of all things on earth I should have a kiss from your mouth." [10]

So their mouths met. . . . His lips . . . burned on hers like a celestial fire. . . . Both shook as love's consuming flame shook through them.

As he to her . . . so she to him; each gave the other life's immaculate gift, the unmeasured, unmeasurable fire of love's first embrace, that passionate anguish of delicate, uncalculated delight, ardent and boundless.

Her fingers stroked his yellow hair; the mere touch thrilled her with unspeakable happiness.

Margot, thunderstruck upon discovering it, begins to pray "[in] the dark and breathless stillness of the night. . . . 'Blessed St. Dominique, lover of souls, preserve my daughter.'"

No answer.

"'Mary, Mother, great in grace, defend and preserve my child. . . .' But all was still. . . . To hearts dismayed there is nothing appallingly still as God." [11]

Then she called for others to help.

There was a queer shuffling sound as of footsteps in the entry. The candles sank to dull blue sparks devoid of radiance; yet instead of darkness there was light. . . . Round and round the room a bewildered host of moths . . . went fluttering. . . . Round and round, like froth-clots on flood-water, swinging around a vortex, whirled slantbat and moth in a dizzy, irregular ring, in the midst of which . . . sat a shriveled . . . mummy-like figure, as thin and fleshless as a skeleton,—an apparition, sinister, white, and wasted as a corpse new risen from the grave. . . .

"Why not try me?" the devil asks. [12]

The next night the lad returns, but the garden is different, the house empty. Gabrielle Lagoux has been taken to a convent school in New Orleans, "lest young love, like death, insist." Years pass. "God made memory cruel, that men might know remorse," the voice of the tale tells us, referring to the young man who pines for her, "but the Devil devised forgetfulness, anodyne of regret." Gabrielle is kept from sorrow at last.

Back in Charleston, Margot starts to change. "Her work was oddly altered: it had more air, less ease; more spell, less charm, more force, and less dexterity. . . . Florid colors and distempered stains were mingled in inharmonious contrast. . . . Her bonnets were like songs in forced falsetto, every line slurred by subtle default." Her clients drifted off, till one day she did not open the shop. "The stuff on the dusty shelves grew faded, discolored, and stained; cobwebs hung from the mouldy walls." She withdrew to her mansion in which "vast cellars boomed and echoed; the chimneys rose like turrets grouped against the darkling sky." [13]

She was lovely still, but in Charleston "piety was troubled by her golden loveliness. More than one sermon from Solomon's Song was inspired by Rita Lagoux; she was known as the woman with a face like a beautiful blasphemy. Time but increased the wildness and singularity of her beauty; it was gossiped about in the market stalls; it was babbled about in the streets."

And when word was received that her daughter had married a white man in New Orleans, "a torpor fell on her loveliness; a dull and leaden look; her beauty grew sullen and lowering as the flame of a fallen fire. . . . As unbleached muslin sallows to dingy isabella, as metal tarnishes from neglect . . . [and] as the spot on bruised fruit turns brown . . . her golden-ruddy cheeks had turned a morbid olive-brown as if a somber fountain were playing in her blood."

Both she and her house deteriorated. "The old enchantment was gone like a necromancer's spell." She ended up in "a dirty hovel in an unkempt alleyway, in the midst of a negro quarter."

One night, the house was bright.

The thunder was terrific; the storm wild without compare. . . . The wind wailed, and sucked down the chimney with a sound like awful weeping.

Dislodged by the tremendous concussions, the cockroaches flew out of the walls: and in the morning, after the storm, the parakeets . . . were all turned gray as ashes.

A gray mist filled the place like a cloud. . . . The walls were covered with green mould. . . . The candles had guttered and . . . gone out; the floor was bespattered with tallow. . . . All the coffers were open, and everything . . . in them was tossed wildly about . . . and trampled underfoot by the neighbor's goat, the print of whose hoof was everywhere.

The coroner found that the woman had died of a visitation of God; but Doe Gou, the tailor, said simply, "Has God feet like a goat?"

The bishop refused to have masses said for the repose of her pitiful soul and they would not allow her to be buried in St. Sebastian's graveyard. . . .

Too black to be buried among the white, too white to lie die with the black, she was buried, in secret, in her own garden, under the magnolia trees.

And that was the end of Madame Margot.[14]

Allen and Heyward had been ecstatic over the fragments Bennett had read to them on Wednesday nights. Allen marveled at Bennett's "acid-bath" of adjectives;[15] Heyward called them "a trained troop" willing to perform magic at the master's bidding.[16] Both, however, suggested changes. "Hervey is going to howl bloody murder when we go over 'Margot' again," Bennett wrote his wife, and "DuBose may be right behind him: my devil won't roar or bellow, my boy refuses to pound on the door of a house which he knows to be utterly empty."[17] He was not going to cave in to other's ideas of how the devil should be portrayed.

Loyal to his own beliefs and to the publisher that had taken his earlier works, Bennett sent his finished manuscript to the Century Company, which, on November 12, 1920 (just as he and Heyward and Allen were founding the Poetry Society), refused it. The editors didn't know what to do with such a strange hybrid. It wasn't a legend, exactly, and wasn't a straightforward story; it was too long for a magazine, too short for book. After their rejection, Bennett sent it to magazines, including the *Atlantic,* but they too passed. While the rejection slips continued to come in, Bennett fretted to his younger friends; Allen, eager to help, wrote to the wealthy book collector Whitall, who was putting up money for the Blindman Prize. Whitall contacted the Century Company, volunteering to subsidize the publication and to guarantee their investment in it so *Margot* could be published.

They were still mulling over this prospect when Bennett went to New York in the summer of 1921, after the first season of the Poetry Society. The city, he wrote Hervey Allen, now seemed as fantastic and unreal as the shimmering mirage he had rendered in *Madame Margot*. "Put yourself in my place," he wrote him, "remembering that within, I am to myself but the same boy out of the middle-western country town, and the world a strange, wide place of metropolitans. [Remember, too] that I shovelled coal and split kindlings, cut the grass with a hand sickle, wore patched breeches . . . and was Johnny to a neighborhood; then, it may be, you will get some thing of the queer feeling that comes over me when I stand in Fifth Avenue." There he talked to booksellers who told him how each year they sold more and more copies of *Master Skylark* and also sold numerous copies of *Barnaby Lee*. "It's all very strange, and sometimes quite unreal," he told Allen, "indeed, the stuff . . . dreams are made of." [18]

I have been over the hills. . . . All runs on . . . more unreal from year to year; and the experiences of life strangest of all; sometimes terribly bitter, and sometimes blessedly sweet; but always dreamlike and strange. . . .

This is why . . . I pinched myself a dozen times to reassure [myself] . . . that I was awake and not asleep, as I sat there in van R. Whitall's library . . . realizing that he, strangely enough, had been according me a minor place of the men collected there. . . . We lunched at the Hotel Belmont with [George] Abbott and [Lyman] Sturgis, of the Century Company . . . and . . . dived under the roaring city and emerged at the *Evening Post*, to meet a very clever and cordial young fellow, Christopher Morley, and his confrere, William Rose Benét . . . and hear them speak of work that I had done in a most charming way! [Charmed by Bennett and his role in the Poetry Society, they invited him to become a regular contributor to the Literary Review of the *New York Evening Post*, where they'd publish every review and occasional piece he'd send them.] . . . "Is it I?" I said, and wondered at the oddness of it: that I should have done something that they remembered with pleasure, and that I should be there, in New York, at all, with a new work in hand . . . uncertain of its welcome, of the critics' ultimate verdict. So strange, and so dreamlike the whole situation that . . . Arabia hardly matched it. . . . If this legend should be granted anything of success it may obliterate in part the recollection of long, un-successful years, which haunt me like gray devils. . . .

Even at Whitall's house I awoke from uneasy slumber, crying like a child, a most unmanly thing; but . . . I assure you, however, that it was not for myself I wept, but for old grief shared with others . . . long ago.

If 'Margot' shall be put across, and finds appreciation, genuine and not fictitious . . . it should go far to cure this unmanly terror of the night-time which has for some years bedeviled me.[19]

The unreality and the beauty that he had tried to incorporate in *Madame Margot* and had glimpsed in New York City continued to be part of the book's life. After Bennett returned to Charleston and drove his family to North Carolina, he returned to Charleston—to supervise the workmen doing major remodeling on the house at 37 Legare.

Here, he finally received word from the Century Company. They agreed to Whitall's projected deal; papers were signed on July 12, 1921, and a few months later the book appeared, the first truly Charleston book produced by one of the founders of the Poetry Society. The first copy in Charleston of Hervey Allen's *Wampum and Old Gold*, a collection of earlier, non—South Carolina writings, was in Laura Bragg's hands on the last day of August 1921 (DuBose Heyward's birthday), "apparently a complimentary copy of which she [was] very proud." Bennett was called upon to read aloud from it; "make a red letter on the calendar to mark the event," he directed everyone. He called the book "a charming little volume. I hope *Margot* will be as presentable."[20]

When he unwrapped his own author's copy of his book two months later, however, he was horrified. It was as if, like Margot herself, he had made a pact with the devil in the guise of the Century Company. The firm's advertisers and designers, obviously not knowing what they had, praised it faintly with left-handed compliments, castigating it as "an anachronism" in their own advertisements; horrifyingly to Bennett, they had mismatched the subtitle in various places in the book. On the title page, Bennett called it "A Grotesque Legend of Old Charleston"; the publishers, apparently scared of that, made it "A Romance of Old Charleston."

Local reviewer Lancelot Harris noted this but countered that, in fact, the book was better for being anachronistic; he held up Evelyn Scott's *The Wave*, championed by Sinclair Lewis, as an example of modern literature; he quoted her lines on dead chickens hung upside down and compared them to Gabrielle's secret garden sarabandes. Compared to Scott, Harris claimed that Bennett was "admirably audacious."[21]

Despite the mistake on its cover, reviewers realized nevertheless what the book was. It "should be laid up in the archives of our literature to remind future generations that America's past has been rich with color and beauty," wrote one early critic who gushed, "it is quivering with sensual loveliness," which is exactly what had outraged his 1908 Charleston audience.[22] *Margot* sold well in Charleston and South Carolina; two-thirds of the first printing sold fast, and bookstores had trouble keeping it in stock. But others still balked.

When a lady dropped into Isaac Hammond's book store on Broad Street, "asking for something to read, [a] clerk offered her *Madame Margot.* Would not have it in the house, says she," Bennett wrote in a letter, "purpling lovely, 'It is a nasty book.'"[23] She had apparently taken too literally the adolescent kisses, the heaving of a young girl's breast; to Bennett it was magic that he, an aging author, could still summon up youth's passion and lyricism. But the reaction of other local critics angered him.

Beatrice Ravenel, in the *Columbia State,* noted that it could not have been written by a Southern gentleman; and even DuBose Heyward agreed, saying, "that none but a Northerner would elect to treat such a theme such a way, if at all."[24] Charlestonian Arthur J. Stoney complained Bennett had found romance in blacks, and was thrilled with rot and degradation.[25] And even Edwin Arlington Robinson noted cryptically that, though "beautifully written, . . . we . . . are surprised it could have been written in the south or anywhere else."[26]

Bennett found a more sympathetic reader in Hervey Allen, who undoubtedly had been told of the folktale's initial negative reception. "Let us be frank in saying," Allen wrote in the local paper, "that there was this [coarse] element in the legend as it first existed; perhaps for that very reason a native Southerner would not have chosen it . . . but this has been [so] delicately and wisely handled that it . . . shows that its author understood . . . what . . . convention and a wise prejudice demands."[27] Bennett believed that it was the fact that a white man could be in love with a woman with "one drop" of Negro blood in her that angered and upset everyone. They focused on and balked at that, forgetting that it was a fable (one in which even the devil appears). Racism was still raising its head—and Bennett was still serving as a lightning rod for it. (It would "get" DuBose Heyward, too: *Brass Ankle,* his play on miscegenation, would fail dismally on Broadway.) Like Simms, Bennett was being castigated by many in the state and city. "Being literary for a living in South Carolina takes recklessness of courage," he wrote.[28]

His salvation on this issue came from those outside Charleston. His pre-

vious mentor, Charles Graham Dunlap, who had once facetiously warned
him that if he did not watch out he'd write good English, now wrote to say
that he had done just that. Then a stunning national review by Lawrence
Mason appeared in the *New York Evening Post.* "This little volume must be
credited with accomplishing at least three most interesting and unusual
things," he argued. "In the first place, the author has given us a genuine
American myth. . . . Secondly, Mr. Bennett['s] idyll of first love . . . challenges comparison with the few choicest in English this side of Shakespeare,
[and] thirdly, Mr. Bennett has given us a true jewel of English prose in the
'ornate' or 'impassioned' mode of the famous 'prose poems.'"[29]

*Madame Margot* is, in fact, an unusual piece of writing. It is not standard
fiction but something mildly and beautifully hallucinogenic, touched with
magic and mystery. One must take it like a liqueur, in small dizzying sips.
"As a technical piece of English, *Madame Margot* is perhaps the best piece of
purely literary work . . . I have ever done," Bennett wrote.[30]

A few years after it appeared, *Madame Margot* was translated "for the beauty
of its descriptions, and its marvelous use of English to attest the facility of
Esperanto as a universally pliant language."[31] The firm that had sponsored
its translation foundered, however, and the Esperanto version was never
published.

The story also caught the eye of Mignon Ziegfeld, brother of Florenz
Ziegfeld, famous for his Follies on Broadway; he wanted to adapt it in some
way.[32] Bennett was also courted by those who considered dramatic and film
adaptations. (Albert Greaser wrote a scenario in 1922, and Max Wald, of the
Chicago School of Music, wanted to turn it into an opera in 1946.) Desiring
commercial success, they sought his permission to change the miscegenation
theme of the story. But Bennett refused them all, not allowing the story to
be whitewashed.

*Margot* brought him the riches of critical success; it revived his literary
fortunes. That was enough. He pictured a collection of his folktales appearing in small, separate matching volumes in "The Bat Series" (the paper label
for *Margot* does say that), "bats being connected with eerie twilight and ill-
omened hollow night."[33]

The next folktale would be *The Strange Story of the Doctor to the Dead,* a story
which Bennett, in a way, was now living; for as the doctor saved the dead,
so Bennett, in his writing and his work with the Poetry Society, was now
reviving the dead literary traditions of the city. He envisioned the *Doctor* as

"a charming, *different* tale, to be read . . . in warm weather for the cooling of the blood. But what with building me a house all summer, and having a daughter come out in Society this winter, I have not gone far," he wrote in the fall of 1921.[34] He tried once again to lose himself in his work, but this was becoming difficult, for he was now spending more and more time doing work for the Poetry Society.

## CHAPTER 16

# *"Your Affections Have Betrayed You"*

To BENNETT, DuBose Heyward and Hervey Allen *were* the Poetry Society, and in the summer of 1921 he watched their progress eagerly.

I have a hasty note from DuBose, rushing off to New Hampshire [to join Allen at the MacDowell Colony, he wrote Susan]. I hope [Edwin Arlington] Robinson and [Padraic] Colum will give them both the stiffest sort of criticisms; they must be . . . careful . . . what they print or offer: reputation's to be made. DuB[ose] seems to depend on me and my work with Hervey, in Flat Rock, in September for *"the final whipping into shape"* of the Poetry Society Bulletin.[1]

But before he could make it up to North Carolina, Bennett saw Heyward in Charleston.

DuBose came to see me, last night, and we had a large, very large and uproarious talk for two hours. He is certainly full of Peterborough, but says, too, that he has actually done what he never had thought could be done—worked himself to a pass over poesy such as leaves him glad to lay such acute mental labor aside for awhile and get back at common . . . business. . . . He and Hervey seem to have burglarized American letters and come home with a sack full of silver-plate, lifted from everybody they met. . . . He says he and H[ervey] have determined to show the poems . . . for the new book to no one in Charleston but me. . . . This . . . [is] a lovely compliment though . . . it carries considerable responsibility. . . . Altogether the two young scalawags put it across tremendously, and were urged to return to Peterborough, as . . . gentry. . . . A more cordial and heart-warming treatment they could not have had, everywhere they went. The dinner at Amy Lowell's was "wonderful." DuBose fair rippled and bubbled: and Hervey, I fancy, will sizz like a rocket when next we meet! They were tremendously encouraged about their book by everyone, including Robinson, Benét and Colum, not to mention [Maxwell] Bodenheim.[2]

There were others who also wanted Bennett's encouragement. "Ned Jennings has asked me to come round to his room, this evening, to see some of his latest sketches," he wrote his Susan.[3] Bennett put in a good word for the young Jennings with his parents, and helped convince them it would be beneficial for Ned to go to Carnegie-Mellon. He wrote a friend there to look out for him, and Harvey Gaul wrote back, "If he's a friend of yours that's Open Sesame."[4] Then Heyward re-contacted Bennett and told him "he is quite earnest that I shall go over the MS. in Hervey's hands most thoroughly. . . . 'When do I rest, young fellow?' interrogates yours curiously; 'Oh, that's quite immaterial, my good friend!' says he and flees hastily up King Street."[5] All three, Heyward, Allen, and Bennett, soon met together in Flat Rock to work on the *Year Book*. They returned to Charleston by October 24, the first meeting of the new season.

Frank Frost, perhaps realizing how much work the suddenly successful society demanded, resigned and was replaced by Thomas R. Waring. Since so many people were suddenly writing and seeking criticism; it became necessary to submit poems in advance instead of just reading them in the general meetings. The poems would be discussed at working group meetings, and only those deserving of special attention would be read aloud in open forum events, coming after the main speakers.[6]

Padraic Colum was the speaker for the November meeting, speaking on "Irish Poets and Poetry"; he also told stories for children at the Charleston Museum. Before coming to Charleston the Irish poet and folklorist had been given a fresh animal skin. Staying at the Bennetts, he had forgotten about it until his suitcase began to smell; Bennett conveyed the rotting skin to the garden where he buried it. (When they planted a holly tree for Amy Lowell over the spot, it flourished.)[7]

Therese Lindsay from Texas came next to see how the society worked and, indeed, to follow its lead. In December Henry Bellaman, a teacher at Converse College, addressed the society on music and poetry. (His poems would soon appear in book form, and he would teach at Julliard eventually. His greatest contribution to South Carolina literature, however, would come from his encouragement of Julia Peterkin, who came to him for music lessons; sensing she had so much to say, he pushed her into writing.[8] (His novel *King's Row* would eventually serve as a dramatic vehicle for Ronald Reagan, earning him the only Academy Award nomination of his acting career and supplying him with a line [ "Where's the rest of me?" ] that would become the title for his autobiography.) [9]

In January another tangential figure addressed the Poetry Society. Lancelot Harris, of the English Department of the College of Charleston, had earlier inspired Ludwig Lewisohn, whose brilliant mind Harris admired (but whose Semitic roots and looks the aristocratic Virginian disdained). Lewisohn skewered him tenderly in his 1922 best seller *Upstream,* which shined a light on the city. [10]

If this was not enough for Charleston's sudden literary fame, DuBose Heyward and Hervey Allen made quite a stir at the February meeting by reading from their poetry, which, they announced, would be published in book form the next fall. Then in March Charles Wharton Stork, who had published many Charlestonians in his *Contemporary Verse* magazine, occupied the podium. Heyward's poem "Gamesters All" had recently won *Contemporary Verse's* award for best poem, and Stork had many good things to say about the city. [11]

The next month the imagist poet Amy Lowell came from Boston, creating a sensation by smoking cigars and staying in a hotel instead of accepting the invitation to stay with Josephine Pinckney and her mother at their elegant mansion on lower King Street. (Lowell, incidentally, had written of an ancestor of Josephine's even before their meeting.) Ignorant of the fact that most Charlestonians ate their main meal at 2:30 or 3:00 P.M., Lowell was vexed when no one invited her to dinner in the evening. She did not endear herself to others when she found the colors of a local garden garish and unsettling. [12] In her official capacity as judge, however, she chose the first Blindman Prize and read the poem "Variations on a Theme," by Grace Hazard Conkling, aloud; the society published it separately.

Bennett was no great admirer of hers, thinking her a bad influence on Hervey Allen. "Allen and Heyward are worn out with public and private entertainment of Miss Amy Lowell," he wrote a friend. "She is a most interesting, but most exacting person. She leaves for Boston, Saturday April 1st. They then may catch their breath. Allen looks a trifle haggard with it." [13]

The final meeting in May was taken up with the reading of submitted poems and other society business. It again became Bennett's, Heyward's, and Allen's task to edit the yearbook, which would appear in the fall with poems contributed by Ford Madox Ford, Amy Lowell, William Alexander Percy, and Elinor Wylie. It would also record the literary accomplishments of the members of the society, and in a section edited by Bennett named (by Hervey Allen) "Comment, Criticism, and Review" he'd boost others' works and organizations. Among other things, he'd record the fact that a "number of our members . . . have been doing reviews for the 'State' books page . . . every Sunday."[14] He'd not mention the fact that he was doing a lot of it.

"I will not praise poor books to please a publisher," he noted firmly, "though I might strain a point for an unfortunate author and at least be charitable."[15] One day years later, "Harriette [Kershaw] Leiding, that clever, witty, kindly, charming, and eccentric woman, met me in King Street . . . with the exclamation, 'John Bennett, you are the finest specimen of dena-tured hornet in town.' 'Now, Harriette,' [he] expostulated, . . . 'Why that?' 'You're the only book-reviewer I know who can sharply criticize a faulty book and leave the victim grateful.'"[16]

Aside from contributing criticism to the *State* in these years, he was also contributing poetry, a suddenly resumed and resurrected habit. He presented his work under the name Alexander Findlay McClintock, "who dwelt in Jockey's Glen, North Carolina, a place quite off the map." His "poems . . . have a really haunting and Scottish melancholy about them," he noted anonymously, tongue-in-cheek, in the *Year Book*.[17]

He donated them "for the cause" and for another reason, too: "there is much to be said for pseudonymous writing . . . [for] it is a way . . . to get off [one's] . . . chest surreptitiously the things which irk the spirit. Things to which one does not care frankly to give tongue in his own charac-ter."[18] McClintock's poems are darker than the poems of John Bennett (though some were really poems he had written over twenty years before while still a young pessimist in Ohio). "Terror Was My Jest-Book" is a fit-ting example:

> Awhile ago I was afraid of nothing on the wide green heath . . .
> I rose unterrified to meet the day:
> I sank unterrified to sleep;
> Terror was my jest-book,
> Horror was my horn-book;
> I made a criss-cross row of surly dread
> To pass the hours away!

But since you lied to me
I am afraid of everything . . .
Of beauty most of all.

Over the years, he'd tease the public about this phantom poet, writing letters from and about him to the *State* and other papers, but no one would rise to the bait; the deception was to be noticed or commented on by no one.

Much of this was fun, and he enjoyed working for the reputation of the city and the Poetry Society but mostly for Heyward and Allen. "I long that you two . . . run a clear course through your day," he wrote them; "I am mentally running with you, all my twisted incomplete road over again, seeing clearly my own mistakes and just too clearly all the faults, wishing that you shall successfully avoid them." [19] It was as if he were back with the Cheerful Idiots at Salt Sulphur Springs, when he joined the two in Peterborough, New Hampshire, to work at the MacDowell Colony; this feat allowed them all to be included in the *Peterborough Anthology*.[20]

He did not go to work on his own projects (although one evening he did give a reading of his legends to the colonists; afterward, a Frenchman spoke enviously of Bennett's mastery of English, unaware it had been Gullah he was speaking).[21] His real reason for going was to help Allen and Heyward with the final edit of their poetry manuscript, "the ideas they possessed as to the dexterous usage of punctuation being uncommonly hazy." [22] Otherwise, he wrote Susan from the colony, "I am not certain what this odd experience may have for me. At least a closer acquaintance with the two lads—and that's always good and gladly met." To advance their cause, he'd try "to make as pleasant an impression as I can upon as many as possible whom I may meet—and maybe the yeast may work." [23] Some there he avoided, however, like Elinor Wylie, "a psycho-neurotic, a genius, a freak." And then there was Edwin Arlington Robinson: "He is quiet, pleasant, withdrawn—one sees his negation in his face, and . . . in his very manner, without enthusiasm . . . his great strength negation, not affirmation." Bennett had breakfasted with him and others; "the entire table decoration . . . of amazing large and handsome potsful of dead-white Indianpipe, or corpseplant, large and taller and more striking than any I have ever seen. There was something . . . queer and unusual about it[;] . . . it had a macabre touch, as I looked across the table at Robinson, with his philosophy of negation, and at the Frenchman, Bois, the psychoanalist [sic], at my side, and at DuBose, with all his enthusiasm and young hopes—for he is young, despite his 36th birthday, yesterday." [24]

Bennett was also disturbed by the whispering going on about Hervey Allen's latest work, *The Bride of Huitzal*. "It did him absolutely no good, and really some harm. . . . *It is to be lived down*—buried under better work. It has so reacted on people that DuBose has actually been warned [not] to print a collaboration with H[ervey]. . . . I have . . . just seen part of DuBose's output, some clear-cut, some promising, but all . . . needing time and the finish of mature consideration, none . . . with the entire . . . brief power found in the 3 or 4 mountain poems. Fortunately, he seems warned against hasty publication and will hold and revise." [25] Heyward, he noted, was also finding time to socialize with Dorothy Kuhns, a young student of George Pierce Baker's, soon to have her Harvard Prize–winning play *Nancy Ann* produced on Broadway. Heyward was also interested in writing scenarios for films and in play-writing; in 1915 he had written a short play for a local audience and would do so again in a few months. In 1923, at the behest of Miss Bragg, he would do a skit on the founding of the Charleston Museum, in which he'd play his ancestor and Josephine Pinckney would play hers, to celebrate the 150th anniversary of the Museum's founding. [26] It was rumored in this era that Pinckney had spurned Heyward's romantic intentions—if so, that would have given him more reason to be receptive to the young woman at the colony, and it seemed natural for them to spend time together; they were similar enough looking to be able to pass themselves off as brother and sister. [27]

"DuBose has . . . a pet interest in . . . a young girl, slight, bobbed dark hair, attractive face and vivacious—Dorothy Kuhns (of Canton, Ohio, *and Porto Rico*—the latter, she says, goes fine for introduction, eliminating chance impressions of 'Main Street' origins suggested by the former, her birthplace)." [28] They went on moonlit walks, and in a few days Bennett was telling Susan that "Hervey seems to think DuBose and Dorothy Kuhns are very dangerously and fatally involved in mutual regard." [29] In two years they would marry and eventually ask Mrs. MacDowell to serve as godparent of their daughter, Jenifer. Bennett, however, was now serving in the same capacity for Heyward's literary firstborn.

*Carolina Chansons: Legends of the Lowcountry* appeared in the fall of 1922, another proof now of the success of the Southern literary renaissance; fittingly, it carried the dedication, "To John Bennett." Bennett also lent the two poets money to help finance their purchase of the hundreds of copies they bought to market in the Carolinas in a special signed edition.[30]

"About half [that] I put in the book fell from your lips," Allen wrote him gratefully. "Sitting by your fireside and toasting my plagiaristic shins has been a delightful experience."[31] It had been for Bennett, as well, and he eagerly looked forward to more of their fanging sessions once summer passed and they all returned to Charleston. But those literary evenings were now coming less and less often. "Allen is a busy schoolteacher, exhausted by night, and employed daily throughout the year," Bennett wrote an acquaintance.

> Sunday is his day of rest, if it admits of rest. Heyward, throughout the week, is as occupied with business as is Allen. We see each other . . . seldom. . . . Allen has not taken a meal under my roof for three weeks, and has been [here] . . . but for a few moments, those scarce as Angel's visits, in passing to and fro from his school sessions, though he lives just across the street. Heyward has not been in my house in that time; nor have I seen [him] during three weeks but twice, once at a business meeting at his residence, once a moment at his office. I saw them both, last night . . . briefly at a meeting of the Poetry Society.[32]

To another, however, Bennett wrote more candidly: "I do not believe either Allen or Heyward set as much store by my criticisms and opinions as they did two years ago," he told William van Rensselaer Whitall. "I am admittedly unmodern . . . [and] . . . feel that I am . . . a . . . discredited authority upon the quality of success and the method of obtaining it. . . . The young want success Now."[33]

Both DuBose Heyward and Hervey Allen were now tasting success, and Bennett did not begrudge them this in the least. He did feel a bit abandoned, however, and missed their company. What hurt more was the disparity between their words and actions—in regard to the Poetry Society. Both, from the very beginning, had promised to shoulder the organization's work, but as their careers took off, they did, too. They were relatively young, starting their careers; Bennett's own, after a hiatus, was reviving.

Ever the businessman, Heyward printed up brochures and marketed himself as a lecturer on Southern poetry and toured, reading from his own works, for a fee. (One cannot fault him for trying to get money to be able to marry and spend all his time writing, but at least one of his friends believed he had planned this from the start. It was to make such valuable contacts, Laura Bragg once said, that Heyward became corresponding secretary. Once he got what he wanted, she believed, he stopped working for the society.)[34]

Although the organization had been founded at his insistence, in 1922 Heyward resigned as secretary and begged off from any office at all. Cajoled and gently berated, he reluctantly accepted the role of second vice president, an office created especially for him. He still ranked behind "first" vice president John Bennett. This defection hurt. "Yet, shaken as I am," Bennett confessed, "I still believe in the kind, the gentle, the fine and human things that I have shrunk from advocating stoutly in season and out."[35] Although hurt, he still wished Heyward and Allen the best. "I hope . . . all good things . . . for Hervey and DuBose," he'd tell his family, noting all had "things to still be grateful for. I have thought that every time I looked at DuBose's crippled hands and frail body. How better I am . . . than he: and how much better we are, everyone, in so many great ways than that boy."[36] Bennett would similarly try to help Rex Fuller, an officer of the Poetry Society, publish a novel, despite the fact that he had been careless with the organization's money.[37]

With Allen also working less, Josephine Pinckney constantly traveling, and Bennett so identified with and cognizant of all the affairs of the society, he found himself saddled with more responsibility. He assumed many of Heyward's duties, seeing to correspondence and public relations regarding the annual poetry prizes offered by the society. Submissions to the Blindman Prize brought in hundreds of manuscripts from around the world, the mail bag tipping the scale at seventeen pounds one year; as if measuring the exact burden placed on him, Bennett apparently weighed it. The award's prestige grew so great that in 1925 the winner was announced on the radio in a live national broadcast, and in 1926 a book contract was awarded to the winning poem, "The City."[38] Bennett also critiqued poems for local writers and served as a judge on several prize panels as well as on the program and editorial committees; he wrote much of the yearbooks, contributing silhouettes and poetry, shepherding the annuals through publication, and personally subsidizing their printing. He also used his tact and acumen in solving two ticklish situations that could have lead to the decimation or demise of the society in its beginning years.

When the mixed-race poet Jean Toomer joined the rolls as an out-of-state member, no one realized his color, but the publication of his work *Cane*, and the national attention it brought him, made the board nervous. (Bennett, of all the members, was the only one to note the biographical connection in *Cane*.) Some panicked, wondering if Toomer would try to use his membership to "prove" something. (It is a sign of their racism, perhaps, that they could not believe that Toomer had joined to support Southern letters but might want to use their prestige for something.) Although he was by all appearances white, Toomer proclaimed his black heritage; and as Bennett knew from his 1908 experience with the Ladies Clubs, and from some Charlestonians' reactions to *Madame Margot*, many would object to someone with "one drop" of black blood being associated with them. What if Toomer crowed to the world that he was a member of this South Carolina society? People would resign and someone would be blamed, probably not Heyward, for he was one of the locals and not really working with the society. Bennett feared he would be fingered again.

Not knowing what to do to solve this tempest in a teapot, Bennett acted, and although later writers, such as Heyward's first biographer Frank Durham, chastise him somewhat for it, he nevertheless found the solution that saved the society and was the least offensive to Toomer.[39] Toomer was listed as an out-of-state member in the 1923 yearbook, but Bennett, in a sin of omission, merely neglected to mention the fact that this member of the society had written a book. (Toomer probably was not invoiced in the coming year; his name no longer appears on the membership rolls.) No one noticed, just as no one paid any attention to Alexander Findlay McClintock, also listed in 1923 as an out-of-town member of the society.

Bennett used his diplomacy again that same year when John Crowe Ransom won the Southern Prize for his poem "Armageddon." (Two non–South Carolina judges, one from Texas and the other from Louisiana, along with Henry Bellaman, awarded it.) Bennett knew that if the winning work was printed in the yearbook, sensitive Charleston souls would react violently to Ransom's themes and perhaps withdraw from membership. The poem, about Christ and the Anti-Christ meeting and drinking together (with Christ diluting the wine with water!), was published separately. The "limited edition for members, critics, and lovers of verse," also contained honorary-mention poems by William Alexander Percy and Donald Davidson. Once selling for pennies in Charleston bookstores, it has now become the "item of unusual interest to collectors" Bennett guessed it would be.[40] (It's interesting to note that, unlike Toomer, neither Ransom, Davidson, nor Percy, supported the society with their memberships or money.)

In this same season of 1922–23, the Charleston Museum issued an essay Bennett had written about the apothecary shop he had saved for its collections, but the museum gutted it by dropping all his footnotes and making it not so much a scholarly contribution to knowledge as an interesting story.[41]

He also contributed thousands of words of criticism a week to the *State* and found his national audience in William Rose Benét and Christopher Morley's *New York Post Literary Review* more satisfying. He reviewed books, contributed essays and promoted the work of Heyward, Allen, and the Poetry Society at every opportunity. He also praised unstintingly the works of other South Carolina writers such as Ambrose Gonzales, who was now issuing books on Gullah, and he "puffed" poet Archibald Rutledge, too.

In this way, he served as the unofficial head of the Charleston literary "Chamber of Commerce"; Sidney Rittenberg, the Chamber of Commerce's public relations man, thanked him, and the Lions Club wrote to ask him for more help promoting "Charleston to Charlestonians and the world at large."[42] This Bennett found distasteful; "I am trying to sell Charleston to the world, myself, but I don't care for it, put just that way," he replied.[43] Doing so much for others, he found little time for his manuscript of *Doctor to the Dead*, which was buried on his desk.

"As I start to work," he confessed to Whitall, "I hear that subtle, slinking voice. . . . 'Come, fool, why begin? You'll never finish. . . . Just around the corner waits another interruption. . . . Your affections have betrayed you; . . . success should be formed of sterner, stonier stuff, you [should] never care a damn what happens, except and only to yourself.' "[44]

But he was not that way; he sacrificed for others (but made sure that they knew about it, nevertheless. He had an eye on the future, hoping that someone would eventually read all the notes he left on the subject, and portray him admirably). Yet he sincerely "loved the lads," and for them he labored to keep the Poetry Society going. They would look like fools, he felt, if it collapsed. (And he also felt that he might become a convenient scapegoat for its failing.)

So he kept on and kept a sense of humor about it, too, relishing a major irony: despite his acclaim and position, he knew he was not a true poet. In fact, just as he had started to help Allen and Heyward with theirs, he had abandoned poetry altogether. "I scarcely read any real poetry," he had told a friend in 1919, "because [in] poetry . . . emotion rises too swiftly and such sharp emotion shakes the nerve[s] . . . and saps the base of things. One cannot feel so much, nor dare not, if [he] means to do actual work."[45]

This, of course, no one believed; Heyward and Allen thought him keenly interested in the subject, and Josephine Pinckney sought his help in 1923. He replied, saying he could only help with the Gullah in her dialect poem "Lonesome Grabeya'ad." "Of classic prosodic rules, spondees, trochees, pentameter or what not I am ignorant absolutely," he told her, quite an admission for the vice president of a nationally renowned poetry society.[46] (This had not stopped Bennett from helping "the lads," and it points to the distance he kept between himself and Josephine Pinckney.)[47] He, no doubt, was skeptical when, in January 1923, she accompanied Heyward and Allen to New York to represent the South Carolina Poetry Society at the Poetry Society of America. She had been publishing some; Allen and Heyward needed to move in these circles professionally. DuBose Heyward even stepped up to the dais as "spokesman for the South."[48]

Bennett did not participate and could not have, even if he had wanted to: in the fall of 1922 his sister Alice grew ill, and he went to Ohio to nurse her for weeks. She died in January; perhaps there was something of himself in his defense of her when he wrote, "She [was] content in giving others comfort and peace, and in her last days and in the face of death displayed a cheerful fortitude as noble as it was unexpected." It served as "a rebuke to those who had doubted her strengths of character and the power of spirit over the misery of [her] disintegrating life."[49]

When he returned to Charleston there was much to do. With natives Alice Ravenel Huger Smith, Elizabeth O'Neill Verner, and non-native Alfred Hutty, who spent part of each year in the city, etching and serving as director of the winter art school at the Gibbes Art Gallery, Bennett organized the Charleston Etchers' Club. Other founders included Gabriella Clement, Ellen Hale, Mrs. Alexander Mikell, Mrs. Arthur Rhett, and Leila Waring. "The office of scribe," Bennett noted, "seems to have fallen on me."[50] Smith was moderator, and the professionals Verner and Hutty purchased a press and installed it in the museum where "acceptable" students and visiting artists could use it for a small fee. Members also helped in the free art classes for children at the Charleston Museum. According to the bylaws of the club, each member had to produce an etching; so Bennett produced his only one, a view similar to the drawing he had done on Indigo House for *The Treasure of Peyre Gaillard.* He fashioned a dramatic rendering of the tall, foreboding house of *The Doctor to the Dead,* based on his research of the building burned in the Charleston fire of 1861. It was done "on a summer's afternoon, with a sail maker's needle, a bottle of aquafortis, a goose wing, a friendly back porch, plus advice from six, and with a youngster reading poetry aloud, while acrid acid gnawed." [51]

He now had an image to serve as frontispiece for the story, but the manuscript itself still languished. One reason for that was that in 1923, at the age of twenty-one, Jane McClintock Bennett, his oldest child, announced her engagement to be married. Her fiancé was Forrest H. Wells, stationed at the naval base in Charleston. (One of his earlier duties had been to keep sailors away from the prostitutes in Cabbage Row, soon to be memorialized as "Catfish Row" by DuBose Heyward in *Porgy.*) Bennett had befriended various "noble young gentlemen then," serving them hot cocoa at midnight at 37 Legare. [52]

As Jane and Forrest were finalizing their wedding plans, Wells was transferred to the Philippines; it was there then that the young couple decided they would be married. So Bennett (for the first and last time in his life) planned to leave the country. At the end of the 1922–23 Poetry Society season, Bennett, Susan, and Jane took a train to the west coast; they boarded ship in Vancouver, British Columbia, reaching Japan in early September. There they were met by Susan Bennett's brother, the missionary Cheves Smythe. With Smythe they toured Shanghai, and in October were in the Philippines.

Earthquakes rocked the island that morning, but the ceremony proceeded smoothly. On the afternoon of November 1, 1923, wearing the dress her grandmother Eliza Jane had worn in 1848 in Chillicothe, Jane McClintock Bennett married Ensign Forest Hampton Wells. The newlyweds went off to honeymoon while her parents stayed for awhile in the Philippines. Bennett addressed the Manila rotary club, and he and Susan traveled back to Japan, where he spoke to the Japanese Young Men's English Club in Nagoya. For Alice Smith, he searched out and purchased engraver's knives, chisels, and inks to help her work with wood blocks. [53] With his white hair, polite manner and dignified bearing, Bennett was noticed; he was catered and bowed to in temples, china shops, and on the streets. Many assumed him to be a clergyman, scholar, or dignitary; that, along with Cheves Smythe's connections, afforded the Bennetts special treatment. "We were set aside and got entree to private homes such as the common traveller never sees," he told a friend.

"At the Middle Kingdom palaces we so impressed someone . . . that separating us dexterously from the two [or] three Japanese visitors, . . . he slipped us behind barriers, into all apartments, through all closed corridors, across all forbidden floors, into sanctum sanctorum, where the floors whistled like nightingales."[54] After that, he "went out like a reckless ass on a . . . black and starless night in a stray sampan . . . on bubbling waters of the Whang-Poo, with my wife and a box of jewels, and came ashore alive through the ignorance of the boatman."

Later back in the Philippines he wrote, "I had every hair upon my head and flesh creep . . . as we listened to the wild air played on trombones and flageolets behind a little funeral cortege through the . . . streets of a Tagalog town. I can smell the blue smoke beneath the papayas still and see the red bonfires behind the bamboo fences . . . and the little yellow coffin going up and down on the shoulders of the bearers, with its tawdry canopy of colored tissue papers and tinsel, and the old bell tolling harshly . . . from the tower of the Spanish church whose top was against the stars as we came down through the twilight."[55] In Manila, he found an old friend—his own Nicholas Attwood in the position of honor in the window of a book shop; the Century Company had issued a large holiday edition the year before with color illustrations by Henry Pitz.

"I came home much the man I left, with a wider outlook, and more knowledge, and a daughter left behind me in the East; I think my travel made no impact on my soul; it only interrupted the course of life for me, and made me less sympathetic with our so-called modern civilization and haste to accomplish half-unworthy ends. . . . [The trip] made me like the Japanese, look hopelessly on China . . . and despise the example white men set before ancient civilizations . . . and [made me] seriously question my own."

"I liked the slowness and the patient skill of the East, and the age-enduring crafts that [they] were making . . . when we were still painting our legs blue in the forests of Britain," he wrote.[56] While still abroad, however, he scribbled on a scrap of paper: "I am supposed to be resting; I assure you I am not; but, on the contrary, am pursuing a varied course of tumult through Japan, China and the Philippines, humming somewhat wistful[ly], as I go . . . 'Home Sweet Home.'"[57] He longed to be back in his study, writing. "Too many of the old and apparently settled layers of he brain get strangely turned upside down in travelling," he'd acknowledge in *Buckhorn Johnny*.[58]

Having left Japan on the first day of 1924, they arrived in Honolulu on January 8 and in San Francisco on the fifteenth, their ship carrying refugees from the recent Japanese earthquake and, apparently, some afflicted with smallpox. Off board, they escaped further misadventures. Swinging south, Bennett addressed an association of librarians in Los Angeles and visited the writer Charles Lummis, whom he had known back in Chillicothe. When Bennett walked into the room, Lummis "looked up from his long table in the twilight. 'By God!' he said, 'It's Jack Bennett!' threw both arms around me, in the fashion of the Spanish among whom he had lived . . . and saluted me on both cheeks. And when we left California, . . . 'I'll never see you again,' he said, 'But I never have forgotten a friend. . . . *Vaya con Dios, amigo!*'"[59]

Finally (after visiting the Grand Canyon), he gratefully returned to Charleston in February 1924, having been absent for about six months. In Shanghai, he had been notified of the marriage of DuBose Heyward to Dorothy Kuhns, in New York City. "DuBose Heyward's wife, after nine days wonder, and consternation over his wedding any but a certified Carolinienne . . . has quite won the hearts of the Charleston folk," Bennett announced, "though it is reported that Josephine Pinckney is put out."[60]

Dorothy Heyward and Pinckney eventually became great friends, Dorothy apparently evoking many of the same emotions in others as her husband did. She was so fragile, Laura Bragg said, that one wanted to reach out and hold her. She spoke with a slight lisp, and she and DuBose together, Emily Clark noted, looked like Hansel and Gretel lost in their own forest.[61] Dorothy was at ease in Charleston society. Her mother having died when she was young, she was raised by a variety of aunts who demanded much of her; many of them she lampooned gently in her plays that would open and close quickly on Broadway. As a member of the Daughters of the American Revolution, she was quite used to closed and high societies, and for awhile attended social functions in Puerto Rico, where her uncle was a diplomat. Theirs was a marriage of true minds; she and DuBose would write plays together, with only their collaborations succeeding. The one play DuBose wrote without her (*Brass Ankle*) failed on Broadway, as did those she wrote alone.[62] She co-wrote a play with Howard Rigsby called *New Georgia*, which opened under the title *South Pacific* (no connection to the later famous musical); had a play on Broadway for a few weeks based on Denmark Vesey (Heyward had written part of it before his death); and lost the approval of Rumer Godden on a dramatization of her novel, *A Candle for St. Jude*, a story of ballet dancers. Her daughter, Jenifer, would dance with the Ballets Russes de Monte Carlo briefly.

Bennett looked upon these "youngsters" approvingly; he called them his "two glorious golden waifs of genius" and vowed he would be fascinated by them for years.[63] But just as he was settling down to a routine, he heard on April 30, 1924, of the sudden death of his brother Henry, who was only two years older. He went immediately to Chillicothe and lingered there with his sister Martha, who had returned home after retiring from teaching at Dana Hall. She, the youngest, was now fifty-seven; Bennett was fifty-nine. They consoled each other, as she settled herself into the old family homestead; with most of his family gone now, his daughter in the East, Bennett was more and more aware of the passing of time and the breaking of links.

In May another change came. Under very strange circumstances, Hervey Allen fled, indeed had been forced to flee, the city. It was quite odd; there had been no warning. One day he was happy, the next he disappeared. No one knew for sure what was going on, although there were hushed whisperings about it in Charleston for the next fifty years.[64]

At first many wondered if Hervey's sudden departure might have been brought about by his troublesome Aunt May, who had been living with him in an apartment on Savage Street. Since it was summer and Heyward was away in the North Carolina mountains, some hypothesized that May had put it into Allen's ear that he, too, might be better off forsaking small Charleston for a larger city and greener fields.[65]

But that did not seem to be the real reason for his flight, many of his friends discovered. In some circles it was whispered that Allen had molested several male students at the High School of Charleston where he taught, was confronted, and was forced by threats to get out of town immediately. That was the story that Josephine Pinckney heard. She contacted Heyward to find out what he knew; amazed and distressed, Heyward had to confess that Allen had told him nothing.[66] Some boys, later as grown men, said they remembered Allen fondling them.[67] Laura Bragg, who often lent her country retreat Snug Harbor for Allen to take boys camping, said that was not true; it was just the parents' reaction to Allen speaking to the boys too frankly of sex, which no doubt Bennett, with the experience of his lecture in 1908, was prone to believe.[68]

Josephine Pinckney wrote to Amy Lowell, a dedicated friend of Allen's, to get to the bottom of things. She told Lowell the details Allen had told her. He said several children in his neighborhood had asked him to come up with some sort of ritual, perhaps a secret swearing-in ceremony. Allen told them a mildly "dirty" story about himself, he said; one boy told his father something else instead, and the man went to the trustees of the high school. They called Allen in immediately to face the boy and the charges.

The boy would not back down; and Allen, being "shell shocked" (in the language of the day), apparently froze and could not reply. His glasses glinted, his big body froze, he opened his mouth, but he could not speak. He later said the boy had not been malicious; he did not understand why he said what he did. The father threatened legal action if Allen did not leave and if he ever showed his face again. So, in town one day, he was gone the next.[69] For all intents and purposes, Allen took the threat seriously, never publicly appearing in Charleston again. (He did "sneak" back to town later, meeting with publishers John Farrar and Stanley Rinehart and their wives, along with DuBose Heyward and Josephine Pinckney.)[70] Some years after that, with very little warning, Allen stopped by Bennett's house in his car on his way to Miami.[71] But again, with no warning, there was no publicity.

In the summer of 1924, Amy Lowell wrote Josephine Pinckney that she had heard this same version of events from Allen. Pinckney called him "a dear lamb" but then washed her hands of him, while Lowell herself wondered if it might be a case of "arrested development."[72]

It's hard to know what John Bennett believed, especially since he had encouraged his son's friendship with Allen so willingly. (Bennett and his son had gone camping on the uninhabited Kiawah Island with Allen.) He obviously knew some of the rumors circulating; for when the apparently gay writer Harry Hervey visited Charleston, and a *News and Courier* reporter noted that Harry Hervey and Hervey Allen were in town together, Bennett rushed into action:

[My] immediate inquiry scotched the . . . [story]; Harry's travelling companion was one HENRY ALLEN, of New York; the entry [in the hotel registry] was scrawled, and the reporter leaped recklessly to a conclusion, not particularly welcome to H[ervey] Allen's friends, for H. does not train with Harry's crowd, and moreover, is in Bermuda [beyond U.S. law, incidentally], nor would he ever come to this town, without our long-since acknowledgement of it. . . .

The undesirability of his being announced as travelling companion of Harry Hervey was such that I immediately investigated at the hotel, while Susan called up Jo Pinckney. . . . She certified Harry Hervey and Henry Allen, whom she had seen. In consequence of which I have writ an able article for the *Courier*, which I hope may be printed tomorrow, correcting the error: Hervey is of course with Anne [a student of his whom he married], who is expecting her child within a month or two.[73]

A bit earlier, Bennett had punned on Harry Hervey's sexuality, saying the latter divided the world into "Es-Sex, Wes-Sex, and Middle-Sex" and had a male companion, Carlton Hildreth of Savannah, who had "gone upon the stage in New York, playing juvenile parts."[74]

Bennett spoke of Hervey Allen only with praise in the coming years (and passed on derogatory comments on Harry Hervey). As a lingering memento, as if to objectify the hole Allen left, Bennett kept in a drawer the crystal foot he had removed from the light fixture in the entry; writing still would be measured, it seemed, by the chandelier.[75]

On May 24, 1924, Allen, gone for good, wrote to Susan Bennett sadly, "*la renaissance de sud est fini[e], je pense.*"[76] Bennett was sad over it all, too, but almost immediately his grief turned to anger and fear. For with Allen out of the picture and Heyward married and working on a literary project in North Carolina, who would carry on the affairs of the Poetry Society? "Do I, as the last of the three pioneers, and a reluctant one at that, remain to hold the bag for the decay of a fine gesture?" he asked his wife.[77] It was a mixed metaphor, he conceded, but he was just as addled and confused. For he might have to carry on the affairs of the Poetry Society single-handedly.

## CHAPTER 17

# *Porgy vs. Buckhorn Johnny*

IN THE HAPPIER, GIDDY ERA of the Poetry Society's founding, Bennett had come upon a drawing of three men in a pegasus-bowed ship; he clipped and embellished it, labeling it as the launching of the ship of the Poetry Society. The young, long-haired man in the bow with the lyre he dubbed Heyward; he called Allen the somber, hunched fellow in the back with a torch, while the older gentleman with spectacles and "high hat" in the center was himself; this is the only figure rowing, while the other two pose grandly.[1]

He attached the seal of the Poetry Society to it in jest; but now, at the first meeting of the 1924–25 season, the joke had become prophetic. With no prior warning, Thomas Waring (who had decried Bennett's behavior in 1908) resigned as president. (One wonders if it was a very conservative man's objection to an organization linked to Hervey Allen.)

"Tom's monologue was . . . amusingly clever and witty," Bennett wrote his family.

He was at his best, stepping out adroitly from under the duties and responsibilities of office, handing it over, apparently to DuBose, who established the Society. But [wait] a moment, my dears. Yesterday I received a letter of anguish and consternation from DuBose: "Calamity!" he cried, and faints along his pages: "What is to be done. I cannot come to Charleston until December; all my plans are laid to work, here in the mountains, until then; and during the remainder of the winter, as you know, I have planned, and engaged to be much out of town, on my lectures. Leap in, old friend, time-tried and faithful! Call a meeting of the executive committee, and make all arrangements to care for the meeting and affairs of the year without us. Being Vice-President, you are actually president pro-tem, while I am out of the city; and must take charge of the Society's affairs."

There is, I believe, a skilled maneuver known among the adroit, as "passing the buck"; known also . . . as "ducking out."

It looks to me . . . that someone has very successfully passed the buck. It looks to me as if DuBose and Hervey have left a foundling on my steps![2]

With two of the founding three gone, Bennett, an "honorary vice president," now was the only one left of the original three to steer.

Continuing his earlier metaphor, John Bennett wrote Heyward sarcastically, "Well, old chap, hearing a sharp ring at the bell, I went to the door, curious to see who, at that desolate time of the night, had rung; and there, on the steps was a foundling whose parents had deserted it! On the side of the basket was writ, in a fine, cramp[ed] hand, the cabalistic letters: P[oetry] S[ociety of] S[outh] C[arolina]."[3]

"God, it's great to be free," DuBose had written Bennett earlier. "Of course, that refers to drudging confines of insurance solicitation and underwriting," Bennett had explained to his family. "Dear lad, does he think that any one . . . is free to do what he will?" he asked.[4] Apparently so, Bennett was now discovering as he found himself in charge of an organization that "has been to me a source of constant uncertainty and anxious, responsible uneasiness since its inception." He reiterated to Susan that "all that I did was for the sake and companionship of the two dreaming boys."[5] "I am simply getting the boat ashore that we may decently end the year," he added. "End it decently . . . we must. Then, the deluge, or the trickle."[6]

What made it even more difficult for him was the fact that he had just contracted with Doubleday, Page and Company to tell the long-deferred story of his father's early life; he had given it up nearly thirty years before for *Barnaby Lee.* In the same letter in which he had told his family of Tom Waring's resignation, he wrote of Miss Mary Massee, Doubleday's representative, coming to his door in a yellow cab, "to see if by any chance the pen of genius might be secured to do for them . . . a book which in nature and method might be what SKYLARK and B. LEE have been for some years, classic, certified, standard historical, romantic reading for the young."[7]

This put him in a quandary, for when the Century Company the year before had asked him for a novel, he had sent them a full synopsis of *Buckhorn Johnny* but had heard nothing back. Still he felt duty bound to them; so he wrote the editors to tell them that *Buckhorn* was too realistic and frank and unhappy for something like *St. Nicholas.* If he could get free from them, he told Massee, he'd work with her. They spent the whole day talking, and she departed that afternoon for New York; "with her went my verbal agreement, to be further confirmed by unlimited contract." [8] To get *Buckhorn Johnny* finished and into print, he was willing to defer even *The Doctor to the Dead*. But now the abandoned Poetry Society, like a spoilt child, was demanding all his attention, derailing even *Buckhorn Johnny*.

"They all say I am too good-natured," he wrote angrily to his family and friends, noting that "they all take advantage of [me], at the same time." He was concerned that

if the Poetry Society of South Carolina, proud thing, caves in, having been a beacon of new birth across our dear Southland, and hailed and proclaimed, as head . . . of this renaissance in this desert of the Bozarts, what shall save us from the just jibes of Henry Mencken and the brass band? What becomes of our good DuBose, who, stoutly on the foundations of the fine Poetry Society of South Carolina, goes forth to speak [in lecture tours around the country] of the strength of the new awakening in our land? [9]

So from the summer of 1924, on into the new season and 1925's beginning, he worked for the South's and his city's reputation and for DuBose Heyward. "I wonder how long the Poetry Society would run itself if I just stepped out?" he asked himself. "It might abash my conceit by running fine. If I thought it would, I'd quit next week. . . . But I'd hate to hear them hoot at Charleston's vain endeavor to rise from ruin." [10] By taking up the duties that were rightfully Heyward's, Bennett furthered Heyward's career, which was at a crucial point. For Heyward was moving away from poetry and proving a theory he'd later develop in his novel *Peter Ashley*. In his notes for it, he'd equate youth with poetry and love and maturity with prose and marriage; age would bring philosophy and regrets. [11] Now married and mature, he was forsaking poetry and wrote Bennett he was "hell-bent on the negro novel," writing about a character he had seen on the streets of Charleston—a beggar named Sammy Smalls. He changed his name to Porgo (and then Porgy), taken from one of his mother's Gullah stories she told in Charleston during tourist season. [12]

Hervey Allen, discovering Heyward's subject, "was quite disturbed, thinking DuBose falling into the error of writing from the undiluted, unchanged point-of-view of the defensive Southerner." [13] Allen asked Bennett to caution Heyward, but Bennett let him take his own course, hoping Heyward would do blacks justice, something that was not happening politically. For in the November 1924 general election, many African Americans had gone to the polls to cast their vote for Calvin Coolidge but found they could not, there being no supply of Republican ballots on hand. "This may be necessary, lest white men be flooded out by a negro vote," Bennett prevaricated, "but I get weary of living in a land where the first principle of freedom and personal liberty must need be thrown aside and law broken by constant trickery to preserve the better rule. I cannot solve the problem of the South. But the situation irks." [14]

So did the situation with the Poetry Society, but Bennett tended to it so Heyward could stay undisturbed in the mountains and write of low-country blacks. He was giving Heyward more than the opportunity to write, however, for in many ways he had planted the seed, having shown Heyward that blacks could be fitting subjects for serious art. As the older man had earlier done with Margot, Heyward now plucked a real-life character out of Charleston's streets, changed his name, and used the bare outlines of his life to tell a more dramatic story.

Unlike Margot, most people in town knew Goat Sammy by sight and had seen an article in the *News and Courier* about him, trying to flee the police in his goat-pulled cart. The man was crippled, either from birth or an accident soon after, begged for a living, and made his rounds in an upside-down soap box pulled by a goat (goat carts had for a generation been a favored mode of transportation for children around the city). Heyward, linked to Smalls by a common crippled condition and imagining him fleeing in his cart, had been moved by a scene that others might have viewed as comic; to him it was as tragic as someone trying to escape Fate.

He had begun writing a first draft in July 1924 at the MacDowell Colony, just after Allen fled Charleston. The colonists there advised him to abandon such a sad project, but Bennett, by shouldering Heyward's work in Charleston, let him pursue *Porgy.* Heyward worked on his novel, Bennett did not. *Porgy* prospered at the expense of *Buckhorn Johnny.*

Although Bennett deferred writing about his father's life, he was, nevertheless, living it; for just as his father John Briscoe Bennett had needed to prove his honesty and clear his name by paying creditors instead of taking care of his own family, so Bennett himself, at the expense of his own work, blindly worked for Heyward, for Charleston, and the Poetry Society. He knew what he was doing; while grumbling about it, he nevertheless promised Heyward to do everything he could for Porgy and his career.

Popular report . . . says that . . . this book will shock Charleston: I have no doubt there will be some . . . fictitious, conventional shock, such as cities like to think to be proper at anything off the beaten track . . . but DuBose may truly have produced a work which will make Charleston sit up. . . .

What old Charleston's select will do when their own beloved Poet produces a . . . much advanced novel on Negro life, remains to be seen: it promises a winter amusement. I hope it will be a *real* book, and a contribution to the subject.[15]

Even though he had not read it, Bennett nevertheless worked for its success. Knowing that John Farrar, editor of the literary magazine the *Bookman* and scout for the Doran Publishing Company, was coming to town to address the Poetry Society, Bennett set his sights on him. On December 5, he put on a purple ribbon with the seal of the Poetry Society to identify himself and went to the train station to pick up Farrar and take him to Josephine and Camilla Pinckney's mansion;[16] due in at 5:00 P.M., Farrar had hopped an earlier train, arrived at 4:00, and taken a cab to the Pinckney's. While looking for him on the platform, Bennett was paged; he had an urgent phone call from Josephine Pinckney asking him

to hustle down town, get [Susan], . . . come right round to the rescue, and have a cup of tea, she having been caught wholly unprepared, 'hair down, and everything,' by Farrar's quite unexpected arrival, which we did, and found F. somewhat overwhelmed by the general pomp of the Pinckney mansion, he being quite a simple Vermont New Yorker. After privately reassuring him that his preferred familiar chat would better please our membership than an old-line academic speech, provided . . . he filled it with real meat of criticism, we went home to purple. Being purpled, we gathered again at the [South] Carolina [Society] Hall, where a most successful event was engineered, everyone entertained, informed, and pleased. . . .

A little chat afterward, while the loud hum of the informal reception went up among the oil paintings.[17]

Bennett and Susan went home at 11:00 and were met by Joan Williman, assistant secretary of the Poetry Society; they put their notes together and "in old news paper style," dashed out an article on the evening and took it to the *News and Courier* for printing.[18] Bennett was kind in the paper; Josephine Pinckney personally thought Farrar's lecture dull.[19]

Wanting to talk business, Farrar came to Legare Street at 11:00 A.M. the next morning (Saturday), and Bennett invited him to stay for lunch. While eating, Farrar mentioned that Doran had been doing too many English novels, and wanted to publish "American stuff of superior and authentic quality."[20] He lured Bennett on by saying he was interested in folklore, but Bennett held aloof, despite having the *Doctor to the Dead* manuscript in the works. Instead, he deftly steered the conversation to Heyward. He whetted Farrar's literary appetite while his wife appealed to his gastronomical one, feeding him mackerel, grapefruit, a lettuce and nut salad, potatoes, brussels sprouts, and Farrar's first taste of sweet potato pone.[21] By the time lunch was over, Farrar was begging for first refusal of Heyward's manuscript. As soon as he left, Bennett sat down and wrote Heyward excitedly, "Farrar seems anxious, genuinely, not politely, to have a look-in at PORGY, and asks me to say quite earnestly to you, that they would push the book in every way and not spare the advertising." He concluded his letter prophetically: "Roses strew your path, and Meeting Street shall be spent with nigger-head daises, symbolical of PORGY. . . . Come on; your welcome awaits."[22]

Heyward, manuscript in hand, returned to Charleston with Dorothy for Christmas; Bennett now had the chance to read the novel and saw right off how promising it was (the best one Heyward would ever produce), one that would become the most well-known work of the Charleston literary renaissance. As such, Bennett's role in its life is worth noting: first he helped Heyward find himself as a writer and then define his subject matter, encouraging him to write of Charleston honestly. He then found *Porgy* a publisher and edited the manuscript, correcting the native's use of Gullah; he also "threw in a deuce of a lot of old-fashioned punctuation"[23] and corrected "his vivid and interesting spelling."

There is some uncommon work in it; I believe it better work than DuBose himself quite knows: it reminds me of a genre painting by Teniers, of a low interior: it is astonishingly fresh and vivid, unmistakably new material, and has admirable qualities, and some dramatic description, particularly of a storm, quite the most vivid and impressive analysis I have read since *Nigger of the Narcissus*, though DuBose has manipulated his storm to fit his book quite autocratically. I have warned him against permitting any of the present-day wood-cut illustrators to picture it. . . . I do not know when it will be out; probably for the Fall. I wonder, too, what will be Charleston's polite reaction to a Charleston book devoted to low life among the negroes: one anticipates a breeze of one sort or another; I can hear certain [people] saying, "And is that all he finds in Charleston to write about? Well!" But if he can do other books as genuine, as graphic and as fresh as PORGY, he can establish a field for himself: it is unmistakably a new thing, not like any other negro book that has, as yet, been printed.[24]

Aside from giving one of the earliest and most astute critiques of *Porgy*, Bennett also kept track of its eponymous hero. Many came to believe that Sammy Smalls disappeared from the streets as soon as Heyward's book appeared. There were searches for him and attempts to discover what happened to him over the years, and Dorothy Heyward would try to establish a trust fund for his family in the 1950s. One Charleston writer cryptically inferred that what happened to Sammy Smalls was too sad to tell, while most others said he died in 1924.[25] Herschel Brickell, in the *Baltimore Sun*, made allusions to Pirandello and his famous masterpiece, saying, "I think [he'd] . . . agree that Samuel Smalls was no more than a character in search of an author and once he had made sure of his immortality as Porgy, . . . drove off into the fourth dimension."[26] Many, including Dorothy Heyward, would come to believe Smalls did die just as the book was published; Bennett let the fiction live, even when he found Smalls, fat and prosperous, the proprietor of a small illegal bar on King Street the following year.[27]

Ironically, as the most famous artistic product of the Charleston literary renaissance was being born, the movement's most visible icon, the Poetry Society of South Carolina, was in danger of failing. "The whole house of cards . . . may fall about my ears," Bennett warned Susan, who was angry at her husband for allowing it to continue. She told him this in no uncertain terms, calling him foolish. "I have since the beginning known clearly the error of permitting my name . . . to have been used as one of the prosperers, charter members, and titular officers of an organization dangerous[ly] factitious," he assured her, explaining once again that "it was [for] Hervey's sake and DuBose's alone that I joined the organization of the Poetry Society. If my love and hope to promote the fortunes of the two young fellows have involved me deeper than is right, at least be just enough not to 'fight' me, nor scold a foolish and kind-hearted man. Fight anyone else you will; but don't 'fight' me for being what I am, and always have been: one who honestly tries to lend a hand to those who pass his turning path; and who has often, as now, paid the price of termless generosity."[28]

Susan did not like these things; she had been born into a world that knew her worth and what she had to do. The idea of sacrificing oneself to absent friends who were not thankful rankled her common sense and was not part of her emotional vocabulary. But ever pragmatic and devoted to her husband, she went "shopping," a little later on, for a new president for the Poetry Society to take the pressure off her husband. She'd offer it to Harrison Randolph, president of the College of Charleston; Alfred Huger of the Society for the Preservation of Spirituals; Gordon Miller, a former officer of the society; her nephew and preservation architect Albert Simons; and solicitor Arthur Stoney (who would agree to serve as vice president), but all eluded her grasp that year.[29]

Bennett toiled on; always having seen himself as giving, he may have derived some kind of martyr's reward for it. As the new year came in, he carried on valiantly, appealing to his wife's civic pride and no doubt her memory; he reminded her of how he had been attacked by the city in 1908 and how that had affected her, her parents, and the Smythe family. "If the society shuts its door, it will come down . . . to our no little discredit," he told her; "for the sake of the town where I have cast my lost, *I would not have it laughed at. . . . It is not my town,* and often tells me so. But . . . I do not want her to provide a jest for Henry Mencken. . . . I know as well as you I am giving far too much: my friends betrayed me to it."[30]

So he did it all, despairing of ever getting back to his desk. The Blindman Prize had to be seen to. Speakers such as Margaret Widdemer, writer Richard Burton, and poet James Stephen all addressed the society that year, while Bennett stage-managed most of the events, provided talks and reports, and continually praised the works of both Heyward and Allen, comparing them both favorably to the deceased poet Henry Timrod.[31] (The town of Camden, he noted, had two literary clubs, one named for Heyward and one for Timrod.[32] As for Allen, he wrote that "Henry Timrod could not endure the sights of a battlefield; Allen, no whit less sensitive, and a greater man, endured, and came back . . . his faith cut to the core.")[33]

And as an example of how Bennett's own status had changed by this time, he, who had come to town to see the monument of Henry Timrod dedicated, was now being called upon to help the city with others; he helped with the wording on the Charles Fort Monument at Parris Island, and as part of the Charleston Arts Commission also helped memorialize the submarine *Hunley* at the monument on South Battery at the foot of Meeting Street, "where the dolphins [designs on the monument] sport."[34]

At this same time, Bennett wrote Heyward a "most intimate and private

letter concerning the Poetry Society and [his] opinion" of it and was galled
when DuBose handed it over, without permission, to his cousin Isabel Heyward, a hostess for the society; she, at least, burned it "and promptly told
me he had sent it, honest person."[35] Then he met with Laura Bragg to seek
her help with the Poetry Society.[36] "I do not love to be angry or violent," he
told his family, "I am, by nature . . . truly patient, and not ungentle; these
things upset me greatly, and put me utterly out of key."[37] As usual, his health
gave out in time of crisis, but it was not psychosomatic. He had been having
flashes of pain since January and in April was diagnosed, finally, with appendicitis. An operation ensued. But still the final meeting of the Poetry Society
loomed; Joan Williman came to the hospital to take dictation from him. At
night, seeking relief, he spoofed his predicament in a tongue-in-cheek sum-
mation of his own career by producing "an absurd imitation of a publisher's
circular . . . 'The Appendix to John Bennett's Work Is Just Out'" for his
doctors, Wilson and Cathcart.[38] Yates Snowden later published the humorous pastiche; so sly and subtly funny are its contents that some librarians
have cataloged it as a true appendix to his work instead of as a humorous
dissection of an appendicitis.[39]

Joking aside, Bennett, according to the News and Courier, was "rather pale
and shaking" as he chaired the May meeting of the Poetry Society.[40] "I ran
the whole thing; I made all the committee and official reports, . . . wrote all
the pabulum, [the] resolution of respect for Amy [Lowell, who had died a
few months earlier], and did part of the reading of poems. We slipped over
our amendment to the Constitution [to elect new officers at the beginning
of summer so they, and not he, could do all the work] and our new executive
slate; and accepted DuBose Heyward's presidential resignation."[41] Despite
his "ducking out," Bennett praised Heyward lavishly, and a resolution was
passed accepting Heyward's resignation with regret and praising him for
his contributions. Finally, Thomas R. Waring (whose own resignation had
propelled Bennett into the role of leader) rose to thank Bennett. Waring
"moved a rising vote of thanks which was responded to unanimously and
with enthusiastic applause."[42] He would call Bennett the "Grand Old Man
of the Poetry Society" within a year.[43]

Bennett smiled; white-haired and dignified, he came to the podium and
adjourned the meeting; he attended to the tying up of loose ends. On June 8,
1925, he wrote a letter to the board, summarizing his history with the Poetry
Society, noting for the record that he had agreed to stand for election in

1920 to lend his name only, but "by chance, mischance and emergency," more and more duties had fallen his way until he was now at the point where he could "not carry on without neglect of my own profession." The last year had been especially difficult. Heyward had been out of town; although president, he had not appointed anyone else to act in his stead. The president's work and that of the secretary, Henrietta Kollock, out due to illness, had fallen to him; he brought the society back from near financial ruin, which had happened during his Oriental trip, but now his health had suffered and his doctors ordered rest. "We have touched distinction," he told the board. Promising to see the *Year Book* through printing, as he did each year, he tendered his own resignation. To avoid their excuses and appeals, he immediately left the city.[44]

"God! it is great to be free!" Heyward had written him the summer before as he slipped away from Charleston and the Poetry Society to work on *Porgy*.[45] Now Bennett could say the same thing about *Buckhorn Johnny*.

CHAPTER 18

# "Changed by the Years"

DRIVING OUT OF CHARLESTON, Bennett went to Shephardstown, West Virginia, his father's birthplace, to gather material for the novel to be written in his memory. There he delighted in finding distant relatives, old homesites, and even family possessions. Wanting to see the places his father knew as a boy, he researched and looked at pictures, an essential part of creating "that inward vision by which I give the sense of actual things to the flimsy dream."[1] After finding what he could in West Virginia, he drove to Chillicothe to do research there and spend time with Martha. Visiting there the spring before at Harry's funeral, he had taken a small car and a "stout boy" to Lawrence County on the Ohio River where they had "dived back into the departed days, and hills back of Hanging Rock and tramped all over . . . Buckhorn Furnace, where about 1835 Father was a store-boy."

The visit had been bittersweet. "I gathered wild flowers in the mouth of the old stack, thrust among the sycamores . . . and found the grapevines cascading . . . wild over trees. . . . [I] dreamed a bit, visioned a bit . . . and rebuilt in fancy the vanished . . . wild, hard, stirring life, near a century ago."[2]

With these gathered visions, he returned to Charleston and spent the next year and half up in his "Astrologer's Tower" writing almost two hundred and seventy-five thousand words, "material merely preliminary to beginning . . . drab data from which Imagination is supposed to construct its ivory tower."[3] If not actually constructing the plot, he was fashioning the world of *Buckhorn Johnny*. It was to be different from his other children's books. Although both had been touched with sadness and melancholy, they nevertheless had been romances. *Buckhorn* would be more realistic, containing "some satire and much humor; some tragedy . . . and constant basic truths."[4]

Unlike *Barnaby Lee*, he did not have to struggle with plot; he knew the events of his father's life, but the work still progressed slowly, since characters "cannot be made of wind."[5] Instead he gathered them gesture by gesture,

206

whim by whim. Names, in particular, troubled him. "I am peculiar about names," he conceded,

select them as one will, by shrewdness or wit, they must . . . seem inevitably right or go into the discard. . . . So I am compelled, time and again, to select new names for characters which fit and convince ME of their aptness and authenticity. I cannot just take extraordinary or amusing names, as Dickens did . . . and draw characters to fit . . . [and] I cannot persuade myself to play . . . puppets.[6]

He also had trouble focusing, distinguishing background from foreground, as he had with *Barnaby Lee*, published more than twenty years before. It was not trouble with individual scenes, but one did not lead to another. They did not speed or progress; he kept losing his way on tangents, writing of real, but renamed, people and events but not adding to the drama of the story.

He still had only a verbal agreement with Doubleday, Page and Company. So when a representative of Longmans, Green and Company came to this now literarily lucrative town, looking for publishable manuscripts, Bennett approached her with his idea for *Buckhorn Johnny*. The scout passed on that, extracting instead a deal for another work, one for children featuring his silhouettes. This meant derailing *Buckhorn* yet again, but Bennett was willing, for this was another dream he had hoped to achieve. As far back as the appearance of *Skylark*, he had hoped the Century Company would republish his whimsical tales, poems, and silhouette stories from *St. Nicholas.* Mary Mapes Dodge had expressed an interest, but all vanished with her death. He periodically tried to float the idea; there were nibbles, but never any bites.[7] "The world has failed to get out of me all the quaint conceit . . . and . . . comical outlook [possible]," he had noted in 1918, finding it a shame, "for often when I have not amused myself, I find I have amused the world."[8] Now he was over sixty, and if any of his art work was to survive, it would be his silhouettes. He wanted to follow in Paul Konewka's shoes—the best silhouettist ever, in Bennett's opinion.[9] This would also give him a rest from the troubles with *Buckhorn Johnny*.

Since they were previously published, Bennett did not have to invent anything. He could exhume or fix them up a bit and pass them on verbatim, but in these days before offset presses, he had to redo all his old cuttings. And as he had originally, he refused to use india ink, insisting instead on cutting them freehand.

He used Japanese paper and a stencil knife, mounting the pieces on white art board; he was so adept that the large sheets from which the design had been cut could be mounted as the silhouette's reverse. This intrigued his nephews and neighborhood children, who watched the process.

To all others (especially adults), Bennett denied entry. Children, however, were always welcome in his work room, "and there wandering boys [were] frequently found, on dark days, curled comfortably in a sofa corner, deep in some juvenile classic." There were "old Kentucky rifles on the wall, strange weapons from foreign parts, swords from Japan, poniards from France, bowie knifes from the southwest . . . and frequently an unanticipated handful of sugar biscuit to allay the pangs of uninterrupted literature." [10]

While the children lingered, he used them to test his theories. His editors at Longmans Green thought his 1890s tales and language "above the heads of the young" of the 1920s; Bennett agreed but saw no problem in that, knowing "that youth enjoys much it does not understand or comprehend." [11] So he tried his stories on the visiting children; his nephews said they didn't know all that what was going on, but they loved the sound of the big words and nonsense.

"Adult readers get the meaning in full; but the boys and girls, growing slowly, will gather more and more the real purport of the high sounding paragraphs." For within the tales, "language is used simply to mask . . . with pompous thunder a small . . . ridiculous meaning." He read the tales aloud and his nephews laughed. "Why not tell them it is I who is foolish?" he wondered to himself, and "not the shadow folk in the tales." [12]

The shadow folk appeared magically with his stencil knife; when his eyes and fingers ached, he switched to something else. This shifting from project to project reminded him of his "old newspaper-man's habit of turning indifferently but with immediate interest from one topic to another." "I write a page of ideas for *Buckhorn Johnny*, file it; write a page or two of Ballad hunting and mountain music [magazine articles he was working on], or six pages of humorous spoof [for his work in progress], or a paragraph . . . for the ripening raw spots in *The Doctor to the Dead*. If this seems to indicate a mind still active, still nimble, still relatively free from arteriosclerosis [then] hooray!" [13]

There were many other reasons to be happy. In 1927, his daughter Jane Wells and her husband, Forrest, were transferred back to the United States and safely ensconced in DuBose Heyward's old house on Church Street, the setting of his novel *Mamba's Daughters*.[14] There were others in town as well; as the city became more and more of an artist's colony, Bennett was in great demand. All around him were native writers, those visiting and others who had moved to the city, one of them being World War I veteran and cousin of Lawrence of Arabia, Peter Gething.

Before the war, a writer of some success, he found himself at war's close, so shaken as to be literally unable to compel his mind to write . . . his body, his mind, and his old ideas all having received most rough treatment while in France; his father, his elder and younger brother, and himself were in service: they buried one brother [whose body Gething had removed from where he was snagged in barbed wire];[15] his father is professor of Tactics in the great English Military or War College; and Maj. Peter was gassed horribly and shot through a number of times, leaving him with one arm disabled permanently, though marvelously cobbled [together] . . . by French surgeons. He is located here, traveller for an auto-truck company, his wife . . . kin to Mrs. Elliott [White] Springs of Fort Mill. (Lieutenant Elliott Springs made quite a reputation as a writer of wartime short stories in *McClure's*), and as a member of the Poetry Society is trying desperately to persuade his palsied fancy to come back, and enable him . . . to make a living by his writing, as he did before the war. . . . For these reasons, though I have systemically declined such work, I did not refuse Major Gething; and hope what I said to him of his verse may help and not hinder, his hope.[16]

His full name was Terence Arthur Peter Neville Gething; "he talks like a profligate radical, swears like a dirty stevedore, and weeps genuine tears when his wife reads . . . *Mars Chan* aloud. Yet he has done a queer sensitive story, in which the ghostly figure of Christ is the companion of the widowed mother whose one boy has gone down to be drowned."[17]

An even more exotic transplant to the city was a group of Chinese men attending the Citadel and taken up by Laura Bragg; she brought them over to Bennett when they needed counseling over homesickness and troubles in the family.[18] Bennett also continued to encourage locals, such as the Porter School teacher (taking Hervey Allen's place as Porter poet, Bennett joked) Granville Paul Smith, originally from Texas. Bennett introduced Gething and Smith and hoped Gething would "spurt Paul to increased productiveness; his quality rises steadily, an odd, strange, ironic strain."[19]

And there were others now wintering in the city: novelist Tristam Tupper, called away from town to Hollywood to adapt his stories to the movies, and Harry Hervey, living here for a number of seasons with his mother and companion (Gething disliked him: "a bland smeary fellow with a nasty bend in his make up").[20] Wilbur Daniel Steele, the country's most honored short-story writer, who won more O. Henry Awards than any other artist, was also around. He and his wife

had heard from many friends so many pleasant things of Charleston, that . . . they took a house . . . to spend the winter here, with [their] two small boys. . . . They have many letters of introduction; we were the first to call. . . . Friday evening, sauntering in the moonlight, Steele found himself staring at the GATE OF SWORDS, across from our [house], so 'just dropped in' for a chatter, and happily, also in dropped Peter Gething, and we think both found it entertaining.[21]

The Steeles invited John and Susan Bennett over for

dinner, *en famille,* their two small boys most amusing, the dinner good, and both Steeles pleasant, talkable folk. Steele surprised me by telling Susan that, in spite of his output, he is a slow workman, and that he has never done what might be called "a successful book. . . ." After supper, Janet Gething was gathered in, and they four played Bridge, while I read and gave a name to the last short story Steele had written, and was unable to entitle: I called it "Never Anything which Withered," which he protests shall be its name.[22]

The story appeared in the June 1928 *Harper's Magazine* as "Never Anything That Fades. . . ." Peter Gething had a story in the same issue as well, "Eggs-A-Cook!" about the Gallipoli campaign; and Granville Paul Smith's poem "Career" also was present.[23] Charleston could feel proud that three of its writers appeared in one issue, but tribute was truly due to the one man who had helped them all, John Bennett.

In these years Bennett ran into other visitors; he encountered Joseph Hergesheimer at a Society for the Preservation of Spirituals concert[24] and noted in the 1928 Poetry Society *Year Book* that writers Edna Ferber, Winston Churchill, John Maroso (originally from Charleston, back on a visit), Ring Lardner, Percy MacKaye, Lawrence Stallings, Marie Conway Oemler, Henry Seidel Canby, Julia Peterkin, Samuel Scoville, Edison Marshall, as well as illustrator Charles Livingston Bull had been visiting.[25] In March 1927, in etcher Alfred Hutty's "cozy, picturesque 17th-century [sic] chop-house and tap-room kitchen," he met "Booth Tarkington, whom I knew slightly in Michigan at Mackinac, thirty years ago." Others present included the local writer Hobo (Herbert) Sass, big-game hunter Will Bogart, and H. F. Church, a Northern businessman.

The table with flowers and red candles, and in the firelight, was charming . . . the talk devious and excellent. . . . Tarkington, who has aged most uncomfortably, with faded sight, slightly aided by a thick monocular glass, peered to and fro through the candleshine . . . his hands so shaking that he knocked out the light of his own cigarette . . . [but he] remained animatedly chatting and questioning us all, of ghosts, apparitions, history and folklore, until long past his accustomed hour for retiring. . . . We did not speak once of books. . . . As he evidently did not know me, nor recall even a moment of our previous acquaintance, I let it go until we parted; when I asked him when last he had visited Mackinac Island, or recited "Danny Deaver" in the starlight on Arch Rock to a circlet of thrilled young girls. 'Why, we did! Sure enough!' he said looking closely at me and recalled the occasion clearly, much surprised that we should at so long a time, meet again. So home, at midnight.[26]

Certainly Bennett knew that, with such phrasing, he was copying the London diarist Samuel Pepys; perhaps he had an inkling how valuable his own papers would be in allowing future readers a peep at life in Charleston in his years. He saved many of his outgoing letters in carbon and took notes during the week to remind him of activities in town he could write of in his "Sunday Budgets"—often four to eight single-spaced, legal-sized sheets he sent to family members all over the country.[27] Sometimes he spent more time on these letters than his literary productions, but he kept on track with his silhouettes and story book, responding to the anxious queries of his editor Bertha Gunterman.

In September 1928 his new book appeared under the title, *The Pigtail of Ah Lee Ben Loo; with Seventeen Other Laughable Tales and 200 Comical Silhouettes.* The title story tells in verse the tale of a Chinese man who cuts his hair to win his love, and in prose there is "The Astonishing Story of the Caliph's Clock." The characters bursting out of the pages in active silhouettes include giants, knights, scullions, kings, lovers, dairymaids, barbers, knaves, and fools. A coffee grinder swallowed by a feline explains "How Cats Came to Purr," reprinted again and again over the years in numerous cat anthologies.[28] In "The Land of the Impossible," a spoof equating politicians and thieves, language is strained to the utmost and miracles occur. The action is as irrepressible as the drawings.

"This book is a wow," one bookseller wrote the publishers.[29] Others agreed. The Junior League endorsed it, and it was nominated for the Newberry Medal for best children's book of the year. Although *The Trumpeter of Krakow* won the prize, the *New York Herald Tribune* called the book "delightful," and William Rose Benét proclaimed Bennett "one of the finest silhouette artists in the country."[30] "In sheer creative fantasy, variety of grotesque characterization [and] exuberance of spirit," he felt he had matched his idol Paul Konewka, "The Prince of Silhouettists."[31]

He had designed writing paper for children in the past, but that was nothing compared to the craze engendered by the silhouettes.[32] As *Pigtail* went through at least three editions and the original silhouettes went on national tours through galleries, bookstores, and libraries, they were pirated again and again and were adapted, with his permission, as designs for decorative ironwork for a new suburb being designed in New Jersey.[33] Longmans Green commissioned him to design silhouette book jackets for four books they published,[34] just as he had created other silhouettes to decorate volumes of the South Carolina Gullah writer Ambrose Gonzales.[35] Yet it was the fact that a new generation of children was being introduced to the same works that their parents had enjoyed was what thrilled him most. "I do not think that many writers, at 63 years, completed a volume begun at 26, and found no difference in the crooked grin of nonsense."[36] He was at the crest of his career and was soon inducted in the Phi Beta Kappa, a nice accomplishment for a high-school dropout.

The successes of his protégés and friends also brought him pride and a sense of accomplishment.[37] Ned Jennings, the artist he had taught, also designed and published a book jacket for a New York publishing house,[38] and Josephine Pinckney, of whom he was still wary, had published a book of poetry. He attributed that to the intervention of Hervey Allen and laughed unkindly, speculating what her mother's reaction would be when they discovered the dust jacket of her volume carried an advertisement for the African American poet Countee Cullen.[39]

Hervey Allen was also prospering; although yet to gain the fame that would come his way with his history-making best seller, *Anthony Adverse*, his latest book of poems, *Earth Moods*, much of which had been written in Charleston, was hailed by the critics. And his biography of Edgar Allan Poe, *Israfel*, had won him both fame and money.

The era was good to DuBose Heyward, too. He had followed up his best seller *Porgy* with *Angel*, a novel of rustic life in the North Carolina mountains, which Bennett did not especially like.[40] With his wife Dorothy's prompting, he was working on a dramatization of *Porgy*. The Theatre Guild would present it on Broadway.

Busy in New York in the summer of 1927, Heyward sent scenic designer Cleon Throckmorton to Charleston with a note to Bennett asking him, please, to "show him the stuff."[41] "DuBose knew that I was well acquainted with all the purlieus of the old town . . . and requested that I show Mr. Throckmorton the localities referred to in that book."[42] They went "from 'Catfish Row' (in fact, Cabbage Row, in Church Street, renamed by DuBose for better fitting his tale), to the sea islands." They combed "every dingy . . . perfumed, colorful court south of Broad and east of Church [Streets]." He did many sketches and so the "main stage setting was an extraordinarily faithful reproduction of the court-yard view of 'Catfish Row' as he and I viewed and photographed it."[43]

Director Rouben Mamoulian came next, and

Susan immediately popped him, a most courteous, intelligent man, into the car, and drove him down to the back stretches and beach of Folly Island, where he soon saw all the palmetto jungle, scrub-oak, myrtle and Spanish bayonet thickets he needed; fiddler-crabs and sand-pipers . . . delighted him. . . . He . . . returned to this house after tea for the evening; we showed him photographs from my collection of negro types and scenes. . . . After lunch [the next day], Mamoulian returned to us again, whereupon, finding that his morning guides [William Watts Ball and Tom Waring] had failed to find the odor and grip of our colored democracy in its lairiest lairs, Mammy and Mamoulian and I sallied out in the Dodge and navigated the most picturesque and disreputable sections of the city, the courts off Elliot Street, E. Tradd, Queen Street, and Bedon's Alley, where we found . . . boys gambling under the fig-trees, negro men loafing in indescribable purlieus, and women in costumes that soothed his soul, then through festive Archdale, Short, Magazine, Mazyck [now Logan], Franklin and contiguous streets, closing at Jenkins' orphanage, where by a few "well-chosen words" we arranged for a private hearing of one of the famous orphanage brass bands, of small boys, of every color, and . . . ages from 8 to 16; and so having kept him to supper, we all went to the Orphanage at 8:30, and the band-boys played for us, and with several girls and women, sang several spirituals also. . . . Mamoulian was so charmed with the melodious discordance of the band . . . that he was inspired by a desire to hire one of the Orphanage's travelling bands for use during the production of *Porgy* . . . but consulting with [Reverend Daniel] Jenkins himself, who returned to town during the evening, found the cost . . . prohibitive. . . .

The play opens Oct. 3rd; and Mamoulian has his hands FULL; forty negroes, cast and supers, to coach, correct and perfect, and he a foreigner. . . .

He was astonished at the extreme reluctance of pale-colored negroes to associate, even on the stage, with those darker then they themselves; and at their arrogance when successful. . . .

DuBose's friends here have certainly done everything possible to assist the production of his play. . . . I hope it will prove a real hit, and help DuB[ose] to independence.[44]

Next a special-delivery letter came from DuBose Heyward within a few weeks, "begging assistance in securing a Jenkins Orphanage Band for appearance in the dramatization of *Porgy* . . . a five weeks' engagement. . . . I simply could not take it on; but Susannah did not cry! She bustled about swiftly, and saw . . . Henry Williams and Robt. Duryea, the former of the family which in the past has stood by Jenkins in every time of stress, and the latter an Orphanage trustee. . . . Since they could not assist . . . next morning I called at the Orphanage, got addresses and information" of one of the bands which was then already fund-raising in New York. "Fancy a Jenkins Pickaninny Band snorting harmonics on the stage! with their small ebony automaton leading with a baton!"[45]

All in the city listened anxiously for the verdict over the play, its opening having been moved back a week; on October 9 Bennett was telling his family, "*Porgy* opens tomorrow night. Sam Stoney [who had gone to New York to help with the Gullah] says Throckmorton has done one good scenic design." Stoney also passed on the story of Mamoulian's failure to persuade "the colored multicolored cast to sing the local song used in the book and called for in the play, 'It's hard to be a nigger.' They just simply wouldn't sing it." The play was not popular for the first few weeks, and Bennett was still praying for its success on the sixteenth; he noted too that another Charlestonian had a play on Broadway, "now arousing angry comment in New York for indecency. . . . One [Daniel] Rubin, . . . who is here, avers that the indecency was introduced by the management, not by himself."[46] The same charge would be leveled against Harry Hervey, whose play *Congai,* based on the novel of the same name that he had written in Charleston, would open the next year.

"I'm soft, there is no doubt," Bennett confessed to Yates Snowden in 1927.[47] Unable to be as cold-blooded as he had vowed to be regarding the Poetry Society, he continually relented. Serving on various committees, he also helped with the *Year Book,* often filling in for the titular editor Josephine Pinckney while she was away traveling in Europe. For the 1928 volume he "did the foreword, most of the illustrations (at second-hand) from my own book [*The Pigtail of Ah Lee Ben Loo*], the exhaustive reports of member activities . . . [in which, each year, he listed all the literary activities of members and all the visits to town by literati] as well as the format and make-up of the whole."[48] Many of the Poetry Society members were publishing, but with Allen and Heyward out of town and Bennett technically removed, it was a changed organization. Though it still received national attention, it was being eclipsed by others outside the city.

The society no longer gave out the Blindman Prize; Bennett felt that only the final prize poem, "The City" by Ruth Manning Sanders, had been deserving (she dedicated it to Virginia Woolf). Bennett requested that Heyward, going off to New York, find a publisher for it, which he did; Bennett helped punctuate it before its publication, and it carried the designation "Blindman Prize Winner" proudly on its gold dust jacket.[49]

Other donors such as Laura Bragg, being poorly paid and unskilled with managing money, stopped their contributions. Bennett, however, continued to sponsor the Skylark Prize, awarded to the best poem by a college student; he also continued to serve as critic at the poetry writing meetings. "This constant critical analysis and disciplinary comment is unavoidably detrimental to my own work," he began to realize; "I have seriously developed the critical side of my mind at . . . expense of the creative side, adding greatly to . . . the reverse which chills bright imagination with the galloping of time."[50]

Indeed, as the years sped by, he had a harder and harder time with *Buckhorn Johnny.* Scenes he had, dozens of them, but no compelling narrative, and the story began to sink under the weight of its trappings. He took consolation outside his work room: his first grandchild, Anne, was born to Jane and

Forrest on March 5, 1929. But Walter Mayrant, who had helped him with the origins of *Madame Margot* and *The Doctor to the Dead*, on which he was also still working, died the same year.

He looked for other bright spots, but on May 12, 1929, he was dumbstruck. "No matter where we . . . turned, or what we talked of, behind [it] was . . . Ned Jennings's suicide, Wednesday night in his studio down Broad Street."[51] As he composed his Sunday "budget," he remembered the young artist he and Laura Bragg had tried to prosper; Bennett had given him art lessons at the Carolina Art Association and had taken a shine to Ned (Edward Ireland Renwick) Jennings. Bennett had fought for Ned, encouraged him to pursue his art, and had vouched for him and his skill to his doubting father and family.

"Ned had genius, narrow if you will, though I think differently: its constricting limit was his mortal handicap of being unable to speak clearly with his cleft palate, a defect no surgery or time could ever repair to give him speech like other men. . . . This was more than he could stand: [he] had closed in upon himself a queer emotional defense, and outlet, in his macabre dances."[52] These he had acted out in drawing rooms and outdoor settings for the social elite and the artists in the city; Bennett had first praised, then criticized them.[53]

A friend, who had for some time, made his home with him, had latterly been drawn away by his own hopes, to house with Wilbur [Daniel] Steele. Thus seemingly deserted by his last most intimate companion, Ned seemed bewildered and disturbed, wavering between new resolutions and new gatherings of hope and plans. . . . On Wednesday night . . . his conduct was irregular and extraordinary, wild, nervous and disturbed, pacing around the room, or going out to the little landing to stare . . . at the stars, as if groping, truly, out into that eternal void into which he evidently even then was quite determined he should go within an hour. . . . Next morning . . . he was found there [in his studio], . . . still sitting in his chair, a Bible opened in his lap, a dry and empty champagne bottle . . . upon the table . . . a revolver brought from home dropped from his hand [in] a strange characteristic gesture of dramatic, stage-like artifice. . . . I was fond of the boy, and bowed with his pathetic figure desperately struggling on; and . . . seeking forgetfulness and distraction from the nearing end.[54]

Bennett had tried to encourage Jennings and had watched the young, handsome man, apparently gay, lavishing more and more time on weird drawings of strange creatures and phallic designs, "as he took himself from our quiet, although sympathetic ring, into the swift and cocktail-drinking set of younger people trying to be mature, and middle-aged men and women trying vainly to remain young; but he was not a drinking man, nor ever was; although he always drank a cocktail or more to stir his fancy for his dances, which were strange things." [55]

Drinking was now the rage in Charleston, much changed from the town whose folk disapproved of parties with wine, as Bennett had been told in the 1890s. In 1925, for instance, a visiting Frenchman was outdrunk by Charlestonians, and he claimed that he had consumed more alcohol in Charleston in a few days than he had back home in a year; [56] and Schuyler Parsons, a much-traveled New York City clubman, member of the old Knickerbocker social elite, claimed to have first encountered cocktail parties in Charleston in the early 1920s. He said, in fact, that such parties had originated in that city.

Charleston people had a perfectly good reason for developing this form of entertainment because their colored help left after 'dinner,' usually served at two to three in the afternoon, and so evening entertaining was limited to the number for whom the hostess cared to provide by herself. She could put out a ham or a turkey, some salad, and sandwiches, with a large punch bowl, and have the town [in], with little preparatory work. They did not serve cocktails as we know them, but a punch made from corn liquor well disguised with fruit juices, usually in a carved out block of ice.[57]

There was much drinking and partying in Charleston in the 1920s. Jennings, having given up making small historical dioramas for the museum for morbid and macabre masks that ultimately were more revealing of his feelings, threw himself into this frenzy. Leaving the representational and didactic for the obscure and obscene, he became the city's most visible symbol of the Jazz Age, which flowered most fully, perhaps, in the dance named for the city. Both the decade and Jennings died dramatically, for soon after his May suicide came the October stock-market crash. "An age so glorious, so rich and fine, and so bestarred with splendor that one almost forgets the bottomless abyss into which it plunged at last" is how John Bennett termed it, prophetically writing the era's epitaph years before in *Madame Margot.*

Saddened with the loss of Jennings and his innocence, Bennett could not work for weeks; he turned in despair once more to his tale of lost youth,

*Buckhorn Johnny.* "It ripens with enormous slowness, like a pumpkin," he reported gloomily,[58] wondering "if I shan't be still writing that fine tale [in
Hell] on sheets of asbestos with a red hot pen."[59]

He sent it off to his sister Martha when he could do no more. "So much
turbid water, of which she knows nothing, has run under the bridge since
she and I parted," he reflected, wondering if she would like it; he mused that
it "would . . . be strange were I still the man who wrote *Master Skylark,* the
romantic idyll of a boy's love for his mother, . . . [and] not [be] changed by
the years."[60] Strange indeed, if not impossible, for he was soon to turn sixty-
five, and a chastened new era was dawning.

PART THREE

# *Fall*

## CHAPTER 19

# "The Real John Bennett"

As he waited for Martha to share with him her critical opinion of *Buckhorn Johnny*, Bennett sat nervously in his Astrologer's Tower, surveying the steeples and alleys of his adopted city as well as the peaks and valleys of his own career. Musing, he worked on a long-term project, amassing and compiling scrapbook after scrapbook of clippings and newspaper appearances of his poems and stories. Doing this a few years previously, he had come across an article saying he was dead. He was so alarmed that he decided to start an autobiography, something which he believed to be "a selective, analytic and interpretive, . . . [but] not a creative art." He felt "an attractive sinner is an easier subject . . . than a dull saint." Selecting and analyzing, he wrote down various versions of childhood experiences and events, but then he confessed that "having lived too long to die young, [and] thus knowing myself to be . . . unloved by the gods, I have . . . forbore to dream dreams of myself." He typed on for a page or so more, then pulled the sheet out of the machine, dismayingly penciling at the bottom of the page, "Oh, I guess it will be wiser not to write at all." [1]

Although ostensibly rejecting the project, he kept jotting down comments and memories and annotating his scrapbooks; if he didn't author a book on himself, someone else might. There was hope and vanity in this, of course; some did float the project to him over the years, but he despaired of all who mentioned it. [2] Requests for information about him kept coming in from students and readers and journalists around the country; "it makes one feel very queer . . . to receive such well-meant and really earnest adulation," he said reading over a short sketch of his life by Janie Smith, children's librarian at the Charleston County Free Library. [3] Yet he knew his "strange adventures of an Ohio Yankee at the ancient brain of Secessia" would be interesting to many. [4]

Like Ramses building his pyramid in the nonsense poem "Ben Ali the

Egyptian" (in *The Pigtail of Ah Lee Ben Loo*), Bennett kept compiling information on his life for the times after him (being a curator at the South Carolina
Historical Society, perhaps he already knew his papers would be donated
there eventually). By noting his thoughts on various events and compiling
clippings, he'd have some control over his legacy. Already there were mis-
statements (such as the one about his death) circulating; they grew as did
the honors and laurels that came to him: he was called the dean of South
Carolina writers by 1930 ("It's funny being a dean," he responded laconi-
cally).[5] With the success of Heyward and Allen and the slow decline of the
Poetry Society, the era of the 1920s was already assuming a fabulous aura;
journalists were now demanding to be shown where they had made literary
history.

"I felt I was treading on holy ground," one Birmingham, Alabama, journalist gushed rhapsodically as Bennett, "with beautiful courtesy and gra-
ciousness, pointed out the room where he and Heyward and Allen used to
meet." He had to admit that it was not the same mantel they had leaned on;
it had been replaced during the remodeling, but the journalist was nevertheless impressed.[6]

"In order to see and know Charleston from the inside," another newspaper writer declared, "one must know John Bennett, author, antiquarian,
historian and the grandest walking encyclopedia of folklore, Negro and
White, that has ever lived South of the Mason-Dixon Line."[7]

It certainly was flattering, as was a 1931 article written by George
Wauchope of the University of South Carolina. Wauchope included Bennett in his list of top five writers in the state (along with Heyward, Julia
Peterkin, Archibald Rutledge, and Herbert Ravenel Sass). "To Bennett,
more than any other" he attributed "the honor of initiating the literary
movement in South Carolina since 1900." Comparing the era to the medieval
period and Bennett to the Irish monks, Wauchope wrote, "In that dark and
discouraging hour, he almost single-handedly kept literature alive, and by
his example showed the wealth of material that lay untouched in Charleston
and in the coastal country."[8] The only jarring note was the elegiac tone in
which he was lauded. Wauchope and others were referring to him as if he
were dead or at least retired. Bennett felt he still had contributions to make,
and now that he had heard back from Martha, who liked what she had read
of their father's life, he redoubled his efforts on *Buckhorn Johnny*.

He also worked on his *Doctor to the Dead* manuscript; many more were doing similar work. Although he had nearly been driven out of town and deprived of his profession for insisting on working on blacks, now nearly all Charlestonians who called themselves writers were focusing on "our Negroes, their lives and their folklore."[9]

DuBose Heyward had gone from modest acclaim for his poetry to outright fame with his *Porgy*. The play version had gone to Broadway; an operatic version would soon bring George Gershwin to the city. In 1929 he published another novel: *Mamba's Daughters* was the story of two intertwined Charleston families, one white, one black, and many white locals were displeased.[10] In dramatic form, Heyward and his wife Dorothy would nearly eliminate all the white characters and focus on the black family almost exclusively, launching Ethel Waters as a major dramatic actress. Heyward's stark tragedy of miscegenation, *Brass Ankle*, however, would fail on Broadway. He'd write a lovely but pale elegy to the Civil War, *Peter Ashley*, and do another pallid, shallow novel, *Lost Morning* (based on Alfred Hutty, his businesswoman wife, and an affair rumored between the artist and a younger woman).[11] His final book would take up black folk life in the Virgin Islands, *Star Spangled Virgin*.

Outstripping Heyward in fame in these years was fellow South Carolinian Julia Peterkin, who had gone from stark gothic tales of blacks, assembled in her collection *Green Thursday*, to the novels *Black April* and her Pulitzer Prize–winning *Scarlet Sister Mary* and then *Bright Skin*. Bennett did not know her but felt a kinship with her partly because she now lived on Lang Syne Plantation, once the property of his wife's grandmother Louisa McCord, and because she, too, had been strongly attacked for her empathy with blacks. When she joined the Poetry Society as a nonresident member in 1925, Bennett wrote her; "it was not one of those 'common' letters the two boys [Allen and Heyward] used to shout over during the evil days of the organization of the Po. Socy" but a sincere tribute to her talent.[12] When they met, he found her "An odd-faced woman, medium high; Mother thought her face like a mask, rather curious carved, meaning something not sure at the glance: I but noted a mouth and a complexion and a coiffure of odd-colored hair: a different voice, and an affable way. I should indeed like to see more of this lady; her work has curious power, unpleasantly true."[13] He sent her his copies of her books for autographing. "She is certainly more consistently veritable than DuB—— H-y——d. Yes?"[14] he asked his family. And when she confessed to being troubled at the reaction of South Carolina writers to her works (Yates Snowden left the room when her name was mentioned, and Reed Smith of the University of South Carolina withdrew his request for her to speak to his classes), Bennett sent her an article about his treatment by the Charleston ladies in 1908.[15] He also praised Peterkin for working with photographer Doris Ulmann to document African American life in *Roll, Jordan, Roll*, something he had tried to do with his "little old Hawk-eye box camera" thirty years before. Ulman, he noted, "travels in a gilt-edged great car, with cameras and chauffeur, and dwells at 1000 Park Avenue, N.Y."[16] The photographs she took of Bennett were, he believed, "superior portraits . . . myself as I should like to be known and remembered by all who read my books"; the less successful ones "looked for the most part perhaps what I appeared, a tired, mild quizzical old man sitting awkwardly about in deep twilight."[17]

Archibald Rutledge, also selected by Wauchope, wrote mostly nature stories but also issued books about blacks on the old plantation; Bennett's opinion of him was mixed.[18] Herbert Ravenel Sass's novels and nature stories relied to a lesser extent on black characters, but his November 1956 article in the *Atlantic*, equating Mixed Schools and Mixed Blood, would give him the greatest attention of his career, and raise him to the status of hero to staunch segregationists.[19] "As the pioneer in the discovery of the Negro as [a non sentimental] subject for Southern literature . . . and as the one who for the first time in the annals of Charleston caused . . . women to appear interested in bold and vulgar language I claim this slight distinction," Bennett wrote. "I rushed in where angels feared to tread, and was promptly burned at the prudent stake of outraged propriety."[20]

Thanks in part to his trail-blazing, the field was coming into respectability. In fact, "Just at present, what would Southern Literature be without the Negro?" was his sagacious question in 1930.[21] The apotheosis of attitudinal shift appeared in 1931 when Macmillan published *The Carolina Low-Country*, the closest thing, perhaps, since Simms's attempt in the 1840s, to a Charleston anthology. The book owed its origins to a fundraising attempt by the Society for the Preservation of Spirituals, an organization in which descendants of the white plantation gentry, fearing the demise of the Negro spiritual, dressed up in antebellum finery and sang in Gullah, in segregated halls, the "darkey songs" of memory.[22] They wanted to raise money to take care of those blacks of the old school who were devastated by the Depression.

The book quickly outgrew its origins, a work meant to draw attention to spirituals, a black art form; it soon included not just "the songs themselves . . . [but essays on] the black people who sing them," and the authors' attitudes "towards the region . . . its natural aspects, its history, triumphs, defeats, despairs and recoveries, and its tremendous hold upon the hearts, lives and thoughts of those to whom it is home."[23] That a book on spirituals could evolve into a tribute to the antebellum, white, aristocratic way of life entirely by white authors is quite telling. (There was no excuse, other than established prejudice, for the sixteen white artists and authors not to mention the triumphs of Edwin Augustus Harleston, a portrait painter, the critic and historian Benjamin Brawley, and Charleston-born scientist Charles Just. Addison Hibbard had acted differently by including Brawley in his *Stories of the South*, published the same year.)

That John Bennett did not contribute to it, though he had been requested to, is also interesting.[24] (He had reported on one black South Carolina poet in a Poetry Society *Year Book*, the conflict over Jean Toomer notwithstanding.)[25] The reason he gave for not participating (even though his name was included in the initial prospectus) was that he felt it should be the work of natives only.[26] Dorothy Heyward did not contribute, and no contributions were sought from Alfred Hutty, the most famous artist in town. Even though Bennett did not contribute text, he nevertheless worked on the project, unacknowledged, by punctuating and editing the articles and reviewing, at his request, DuBose Heyward's contribution to the volume.[27]

The book that was produced was exceedingly handsome, a landmark in beautiful book design in these years and a feat John Bennett, as an old newspaper man, designer, artist, and craftsman, appreciated. Having done his duty in these fields and having grown more and more disenchanted with the contemporary state of books, their odd typefaces and bindings, and especially the illustrations of mass merchandising (he deplored the woodcuts by Theodore Nadjean in the novel *Porgy*), he wrote a letter in September 1930 to the *Saturday Review of Literature* "against the eccentricities and perversions of modern illustration and typography."[28] It struck a responsive chord; Hal Marchbanks of Marchbanks Press reprinted the letter verbatim. In pamphlet form it was mailed to all the publishers and publishing houses in the country and even used in university courses on typography. He called it, aptly enough, "A Protest of an Old Timer."[29]

Heartened by this small success, he went on to register another protest by *not* writing. Needing funds to offset money lost in the 1929 crash, and finding that the *Columbia State* still refused to pay for his contributions to their literary page (as they refused to pay for the poems of Alexander Findlay McClintock), he stopped both their contributions. (A little while later, he'd have his alter ego write the paper—on April Fool's Day—to say that the rumor that McClintock and Bennett were the same person was not true and that he, McClintock, just wanted to be left alone in peace.)[30]

Others closer to home still expected his work and time for free, however; in 1930, he was again "the bearded goat who finds the orphan left at his door imputed to his parentage; in other words Comment, Criticism, and Review for the Year Book of the abandoned Poetry Society of sc has again fallen my lot to prepare."[31] He completed the task and then promptly submitted a letter of resignation to the Poetry Society. (So did Alexander Findlay McClintock.) But "then, confound it, they elected me an honorary member for life, as if they thought so to entice me to attend . . . Free!"[32] It was funny and he liked a good laugh, but "I have grown old," he saw, "and I can sit in a chair at home and reflect upon my own as amusing and various past with quite as much pleasure."[33]

He stayed in more and more. The Depression was settling in; people lost money. Banks closed and cash flow stopped. The government of the city itself became bankrupt, issuing script instead of money to its employees. "We dropped a cool $40,000," Bennett noted;[34] book royalties fell by 66 percent.[35] One day, as he came upon Josephine Pinckney, she smiled ruefully, showing him "her year's royalty report . . . with a sardonic laugh. 'Behold,' said she, exhibiting her check, 'the rewards of genius and verse!' One dollar."[36] She, however, had a private income. Bennett himself had nothing. For years his wife Susan had been providing the larger share of income to the family. Bennett apparently found this worrying and noted in 1942, at least to himself, that "since coming to South Carolina, I have brought the family bank account $63,019.66. Of this $18,000 was lost in the depression, and $12,000 I gave to my children."[37] To prove himself worthwhile and to keep the family functioning, Bennett settled down to work. Articles on music in the North Carolina mountains and ballad hunting did not sell, but "Don Adumbras and the Dragon," a three-month installment with silhouettes for *St. Nicholas Magazine,* did.[38] In addition, he manufactured a Charleston edition of *Madame Margot* (bound by a firm in Chillicothe), reissuing the rare little volume himself. To the unbound sheets bought from the Century Company he appended an essay he had written on *Madame Margot* for the *Saturday Review of Literature.* He typed the word "Legend" on a sheet and pasted it crudely over the Century Company's "Romance" on the front board of many of these copies. Some appendixes he signed; others he marked with a cartouche or Chinese character. An apt merchandiser, he added, "THE NEXT VOLUME OF THIS SERIES WILL BE THE STRANGE STORY OF THE DOCTOR TO THE DEAD." For the final endsheet, flyleaf and paste-down, he used paper from the estate of the nineteenth-century Charleston miniaturist, Charles Fraser, its laid and chain lines evident. He stamped "Charleston 1933" on the title page and a copyright 1933 on its reverse.[39] With that, and with cutting of silhouette portraits of Hervey Allen to paste in copies of *Earth Moods* provided by Columbia bookseller J. T. Gittman, Bennett managed to get cash flowing again.[40]

Such overwork led him to "crack up . . . badly" by Thanksgiving 1932, following "three foolish years of extravagant effort to write two books and innumerable magazine articles."[41] His physicians ordered rest, gentle exercise, and no more writing, so yet again he put down *The Doctor to the Dead* and even *Buckhorn Johnny.* Staying in more often, he looked back over the past, jotting down fragments of his philosophy.[42] "I always . . . felt certain that somehow life was good," he acknowledged,

if only I [could] get it straightened out somehow. . . . I hated the things which happened to me; and . . . heartily . . . wished that I were . . . just peacefully dead and asleep under the green earth-smelling sod. . . .

Yet I was conscious all the time that . . . there might be . . . something in it somewhere, after all. . . . No power great enough to conceive and set in motion so strange and tremendous a thing as this stellar universe, and to operate it and control its awful motions, would stoop to play so cheap [and] so dirty smutty a trick . . . upon helpless beings."[43]

That led to a belief in God, despite the fact that he had "never been able to silence those . . . honest questioning doubts and disbeliefs; and [had] long since given over any effort to accept any theological structure known to mankind." He always linked thoughts of God to another theme. On the same page he wrote, "Of friendship I can speak not . . . facil[ely] . . . but as one having the authority of possession. I have had friends and by . . . grace . . . have somehow kept them, and still, I rejoice to say, [am] keeping them."[44] "I begin to believe," he elaborated later, "that true affection is the best thing the world has to offer us," giving thanks for "the friendship and affection of my children, [and] the comrades of my wife and me [sic]; the responsibility is heavy, the reward great."[45]

It was for friends and family that he kept going. If physicians told him not to write books, he nevertheless refused to abandon letter writing. Week after week, since the late 1910s, he had cranked out his "Sunday Budgets" while his wife and children were in church (or "Synagogue," he often called it); he filled the pages with news, gossip, philosophy, unusual events and memories, sending carbons all over the globe "for greens," by which he meant his attempt "to keep remembrance fresh and love unwithered."[46]

These missives often turned out to be paths of self-discovery; writing one to his family later, he'd tell them,

> Once I thought my part in the great cast of living was to play a minor "Touchstone," and entertain folk by jesting wisdom as in my child's tale, "Hans, the Otherwise," a very small role, but after . . . Shakespearean design. I have come to the conclusion that I am not a "Touchstone," but merely a version of "the melancholy Jacques," the gentle cynic who pulls out his watch and sees the world wag, and can do little about it but make sardonic remarks.[47]

He rarely made these remarks at the expense of others, so his circle of correspondents grew in these years; fans, children, and friends wrote him constantly. The unanswered stockpile of mail grew, taking up, at one point, "three tables, two boxes and a shelf" in his study.[48]

Looking them over, "a desperate sort of apathy seizes me," he wrote. "What is the use of the effort?" he'd wonder, but then rally, "I'll be damned if I give over the effort to reply to . . . my friends, the unforgetting hearts, the rememberers of days and years, . . . and comrades of the vicissitudes of my roadway to the End," he decided. "I'll be damned if I forget them or permit them to believe me forgetful of their long-unchanged affection."[49] So he kept on writing, telling one correspondent, "If I had been able to write all the letters I have thought to . . . , your house would be choked . . . with them; the drifts . . . would rise to the window-sills, and obstruct the doors; you would cry for shovels."[50]

He also sent countless Christmas cards each year, bearing an original silhouette design,[51] each further embellished with his ornate calligraphy, which many thought mechanically done, so exact and handsome was his script. "Let me assure you," he wrote to correct that impression, "I do all my printing with my own good pen, or pencil." He developed this skill due to his experience in Chillicothe, when he "found [newspaper] compositors invariably mis-spelled every proper name . . . in one's hurried written manuscript. I therefore began printing every proper, and some improper, names." [52]

And it was not just the beauty of his hand that charmed his correspondents. "The real John Bennett is in his letters," wrote a friend he had made through the mail: Columbia, South Carolina, bookseller J. T. Gittman, who kept police dogs and put up a misanthropic facade, Bennett guessed, to mask a nature too deeply and too often hurt by caring. Recognizing a confrere in Bennett, Gittman wrote him, "YOU are too kindly—too kind—too polite, too whimsically affectionate. I do resent the fact that they [Bennett's letters] may not at all be appreciated." [53]

Gittman advised him to not be so generous, but Bennett could not stop. In these years, others reaped the benefit of his largesse. For again there arose a group of writers in Charleston who clamored for his help and appealed to him for attention.

CHAPTER 20

# "A Life . . . Not a Career"

THE LITERARY CIRCLES IN CHARLESTON were different in the 1930s. Du-
Bose Heyward had left for New York, Hervey Allen was married and living
in Bermuda, and the Poetry Society ceased publishing yearbooks after the
1931–32 season. There were still some left, however, who were serious about
writing. A trinity consisting of naturalist author Alexander Sprunt, Herbert
Ravenel Sass (called Hobo for his peripatetic wanderings and his precarious
hobbling together of funds for his family), and Englishman Peter Gething
met together for mutual support and asked John Bennett to join them. Instead of fanging Heyward and Allen in his own house on Wednesdays, he
met these younger men on Mondays in 1931 and '32 at Herbert Ravenel Sass's
"eyrie" a short distance away at 23 Legare Street;[1] he went down the alley
through iron gates and up to "Herbert's study to discuss how the labors of
men may prosper and . . . persist in trying to do creative writing." In this
"Circle of Four," Bennett found himself cast as "a sort of Ancient Mariner,
who from time to time, stops one of [the] three, and tells them [sic]
some . . . things they can, should, and of course must do better."[2] In the
winter of 1932, DuBose Heyward returned to Charleston to do research
for his novel *Peter Ashley* (earlier called *They Never Come Back*), and he, too,
joined the fraternity.[3] "These lads appear to think that in someway I can
help their stories crystallize," Bennett wrote.[4] Gething wanted help with his
pieces for magazines; Alex Sprunt needed help to put the "sting" in his
nature stories;[5] and Herbert Sass, like Heyward, was working on a novel
about Civil War Charleston.

"Such agonies of composition were seldom witnessed," Bennett commented after a series of Mondays when Sass had trouble with his work on
*Look Back to Glory.* (Sass and Heyward would contribute a chapter each from
their novels to a small volume titled *Fort Sumter*, about its attack and siege.)
"I at one time had high hopes that the novel would be extraordinarily good,"

Bennett wrote, "then Herbert lost his way, and bogged down"; he had not "the slightest idea of how the damaged tale was to end, or what to do with the excellent characters he had created." [6]

Bennett despaired of him ever finishing it, but, as he had with Heyward and Allen, he kept encouraging him. "Herbert finally vanquished DuPont's ironclad armada in a pretty fair battle scene," he reported happily in March 1931, "but does not know what comes next, and WE refuse to tell him." [7] A year later they put their heads together and "straightened out the difficulty in plotting." [8] Another year passed before he wrote, "Herbert struggles forward at last . . . having made up his mind, and will pull the thing off successfully." [9]

It was a story nearly as epic as the one the author was telling. When the novel finally appeared in 1933, Bobbs Merrill, the publishers, dubbed Bennett its "literary godfather." [10] Sass wrote him gratefully, "Your commentary is the most helpful thing that has happened to me since I tackled the book, and it will remain in my drawer by my elbow for constant reference and study." [11] Indeed, it is the best piece of writing of his career, and Sass knew it. "We fought, bled, and all but died together, and but for your care, how different my book would have been." [12]

Bennett was amused. "I expect," he commented soon afterward, "every Monday for some time now, to hear H. Sass expand romantically on how we whupped the whey out of the Damned Yankees. . . . Altogether I ought to be getting to be a hell-raising Confederate by now. And yet I aren't. What is it in my nasty disposition [that] makes me so unreasonable and stubbornt [sic]? Perhaps," he mused, "it is horse sense." [13]

As if the fertile earth of the low country nurtured creation, writers continued to come to Charleston despite the Depression, and Bennett met many of them in the company of these younger men. He joined Sass and Sprunt down on Edisto Island one weekend with visiting writers Edison Marshall and Francis Griswold; Marshall would write many adventure yarns using the low country as a setting, such as *The Gentleman* and *Castle in the Swamp*, the latter's lush descriptions owing something perhaps to Bennett's *The Treasure of Peyre Gaillard*. Griswold would soon produce *The Tides of Malvern* and, later, *Sea Island Lady*, with a character in it very much like Herbert Sass. But this weekend they held their peace; all they did was watch "the tide go in and out, talking mutual shop in a state of otherwise gloriously unkempt idleness." [14] (When *Sea Island Lady* did appear, Bennett called it "a depressing book, though very well done, discouragingly well-done. I can do nothing like that.")[15]

The company of these younger men was sweet to Bennett, and he looked forward to more of the meetings that "promised pleasure, but petered out, somehow for reasons obscure and psychological."[16] Later, he thought that the "trouble with that group was the thing they wanted most was for *me* . . . to suggest how they might mend unsatisfactory work . . . to assure a sale, and . . . how could I, or any man, do that? The rest was wrangling with obdurate stubbornness. . . . [They] asked advice and never took it, or could not, which secures originality, but baffles advice."[17]

But sales were important in a shrinking market. The demand for Sass's nature and blood and thunder adventure stories was drying up; and for the first time in his life he was getting rejection slips, sending him down to Edisto in a funk. Similarly, Alfred Hutty's etching plates were literally rusting.[18] Alex Sprunt started working more for the Charleston Museum and considered becoming a guide in the Grand Tetons.[19] Peter Gething lectured at the army base at Fort Moultrie on war theory;[20] and his wife Janet begged him "to take a job, instead of killing himself trying to be a writer."[21] Of all the local writers, the only one finding true success in this era was local newspaper editor William Watts Ball's son-in-law, Clements Ripley, who had met and married Katharine Ball when he was stationed in Columbia, South Carolina, during World War I. He managed to sell a work of his to the movies for $8,000 and was soon lured off to Hollywood to write scripts for $300 a week.[22] It seemed, too, that Heyward might be able to make money collaborating with composer George Gershwin, who came to town to work on the score of an opera he was basing on Heyward's *Porgy*. Bennett heard from a Smythe family member "that the Sperritual [sic] singers met at Jimmy Hagood's, and were most agreeably met by G. Gershwin, who contrary to . . . suspicions, was simple, unpretentious, attractive and intensely interesting; they sang for him; and he played over an hour for them, on the piano, portions from his score for 'PORGY,' which . . . were most interesting, some quite delightful, rhythms, particularly."[23]

Just before the opening of *Porgy and Bess*, Bennett wrote, "I hope every success, the greater the better, and reflect on ancient criticism of DuB[ose]'s prose with quiet pleasure in this most astonishing and happy upshot. His story is a genuine romance."[24] Although it was later acclaimed world-wide, the first production was not a financial success, however, and both Heyward and Gershwin lost their investments.

Also delighting Bennett in these years was his family. His daughter Jane gave birth to his second grandchild in 1933. Another girl, she was named Martha for Bennett's sister (and called Peggy, for Bennett's grandmother); she would take on the Bennett family talent and become an author of children's and adult books herself. His other daughter, Susan, went from the College of Charleston to Stanford to Columbia University. His son John finished Phillips Andover Academy, graduated from Yale and then Sheffield Forestry School; he'd work for the government and would soon report for duty in Hell Hole Swamp in nearby Berkeley County, where many outrageous things were occurring in these years: "Sabb Cumbee, King of Hell Hole Swamp" and his son were shot in an ambush by a member of his family, the son dying and Cumbee surviving, Bennett told his far-flung family in one of his weekly letters;[25] a few months later, in broad daylight, a gunman would shoot state senator Rembert Dennis in the streets of Moncks Corner, the county seat. Zane Grey "could do a wonderful novel and call it 'Hell Hole,'" Bennett commented, trying to interest someone in the subject, little realizing that his own son would soon take him up on it.[26]

In 1934 rumors reached Bennett that he was up for an honorary doctorate from the University of South Carolina, an idea he discussed with his bookseller friend from Columbia, J. T. Gittman. "I don't know exactly what I have done to call for this distinction," he wrote a bit disingenuously. "They say I have not many rivals, today, as a popular writer for children. . . . It may be that I pushed a number of young aspirants to luck . . . as with Heyward and Allen." Just as important, he felt, was his striving to "prevent hope in the hopeless; to curb a dangerous tendency to futile struggles on the part of a good many." Not all had been smooth sailing. "I tried to write South Carolina history; studied Negro music and superstition; and got nowhere profitably with either. An appreciative public allowed two of my books [*Madame Margot* and *The Treasure of Peyre Gaillard*] to go out of print." Summing it up he said, "I have had a life, but not a career."[27]

"All who attempt to write meet and have this question to settle," he knew, and others did it differently than he.[28] Sass found a solution by keeping his family on Folly Beach while he wrote in the city, going down to join them in the evenings.[29] DuBose Heyward also used his house on Folly Beach "to escape interruptions"; he told Bennett "he asked Sherwood Anderson how he got time to write. Anderson said, 'I looked all over the United States for a town in which I knew no one, and where no one knew me; picked Browns-ville, Texas; went there, answered no letters; nobody had my address; went nowhere: was free from interruption and wrote a book in six months.' 'That,' said DuBose, 'is the way it is done.' 'Son,' said I, 'You are growing up.'"[30]

Others were not able to solve the problem so happily. Poet and novelist Frances Frost had married Samuel Gaillard Stoney but could not make a success of it. "Her ambition was greater than her affection," Bennett said; "a personal desire for accomplishment wiped out her sense of responsibility," and she left Stoney, who had to go to Florida to establish residency and get a divorce.[31] At her wedding, Frost had hurled her bouquet at Josephine Pinckney ("I didn't mean to hit you so hard," she later apologized, "I'm blind as a bat without my specs.")[32] Pinckney had refused to catch it, and she now avoided matrimony. "I have a foot on sea and on shore," she mused. "Tags of my victorian upbringing make me believe in responsibility, chil-dren, etc. [but] my writing keeps me from being free. Yet my occasional flings in Europe make me aware how fascinating it all is."[33]

Bennett was caught in the middle; he wrote at home and for years had let friends, his family, and the Poetry Society interrupt him. Even though his professional life had suffered, what career he had managed to have was capped happily in June of 1934 when he was awarded an honorary degree from the University of South Carolina. "George Wauchope assured me, on my asking, that the award was as much for thirty five years' inspirational influence as for actual product," he wrote his family; "that, perhaps, I may believe to be just: I have helped no few, and corrected many."[34]

But there were his accomplishments, too: besides being acknowledged as an expert in local history and having been instigator of a literary movement that had produced many of the best-known writers of the day, his own works were still well-known, still garnering praise, and, more than a genera-tion after their appearance, still selling. *Master Skylark* had gone through thirty editions, appearing in Canada, England, Australia, Poland, and Germany; having been christened "Mr. Skylark" upon arriving in Charleston thirty years later, Katherine Anthony, acclaimed biographer of Catherine the Great and other historical personages, called him that in an article in the *Yale Re-view*. She cloaked the identities of other Charlestonians with clever names; "Mr. Skylark" revealed him immediately.[35] Recommended by the American

Library Association and the Federal Bureau of Education, *Skylark* was judged by the *Bookman* to be in the company of *David Copperfield, Tom Sawyer, Huckleberry Finn, Treasure Island,* and other classics for the young.[36] *Redbook* magazine would name it as one of the "one hundred best books of all time."[37] Dramatized at least half a dozen times, it had been performed by amateurs, professionals and even marionettes; it aired as a radio show—and a few years after his honorary degree, following decades of dickering, the film rights were finally sold, partially through the help of George C. Tyler, from Chillicothe.[38]

The son of a newspaper editor in Bennett's home town, Tyler had become a famous and successful theatrical producer and had published his autobiography.[39] Tyler helped Bennett get $16,000 for the sale, a great amount to help the family pull out from the Depression. Bennett was invited to come to Hollywood to help supervise the screen adaptation, but, unlike Heyward, who had spent some time in Hollywood screen writing, he declined—partly due to the remonstrances of Clements Ripley who told him, "the work is irritating beyond measure, and dislocating to the brain."[40] He nevertheless followed the project eagerly, reporting on the film's progress to his friends and family. Sol Lesser of Principal Productions went to England, he told them, to shoot the early scenes. "He returned to America with an English 'Gaston Carew' . . . but he had no small girl to play [Cecily]; and waited too long to find one. . . . Meantime his boy [a child actor with the stage name Bobby Breen] had come into adolescence . . . [and] his lovely voice broke badly. . . . That was anticipated, and had been provided against by recording every vocalization. . . . *But* as the boy developed, his appearance altered fatally, and his racial [i.e., Jewish] characteristics became too strongly marked for playing the part of an English lad fair haired, blue eyed and Anglo Saxon."[41]

Later Bennett learned a bit more about the project and wrote Susan that Lesser, after spending much, "found that the result was bum, and blame[d] it on Bobby's growing up. Po' little ol' Jew! Too bad! I am perfectly apathetic about it. . . . Lesser will probably sell . . . his right to the story to some producer with a promising boy, one of these days."[42] But it never came to pass, and the film languished.

A similar fate, ironically, had also befallen *Barnaby Lee* back in the era of the silent films, by the Edison Company. It bought the rights but never distributed it.[43] The novel was still available, however, having sold over eighty thousand copies in four countries. *The Pigtail of Ah Lee Ben Loo* had gone through several editions despite the depression.[44] And Bennett, alone of the South Carolina writers, could point out quotes from his works in *Bartlett's Familiar Quotations,* including stanzas from "In a Rose Garden," his "piper" poem and personal motto, as well as lines from *Madame Margot.*[45] The only other to be awarded similar prestige would be Hervey Allen.[46] "It must be . . . wonderful to be the wife of a genius!" Bennett heard one fan gush to his wife Susan admiringly. But "a genius is just as hard to get along with as any other damned fool," she replied.[47]

Now in her prime, she had outgrown her young girl's adulation of and infatuation with him; she still loved him tenderly, but, as with his continuing support of the Poetry Society, Susan could not agree with some of the unprofitable and quixotic things he did. Others thought Suso, as she was called now, was responsible for driving a wedge between him and others.

But this was a façade. She was willing to be characterized as cool and unfriendly to protect her husband from those who would take his time and energy; this allowed him to be regarded by all as delightful and charming. Eola Willis, a local theatrical historian, "a social nuisance,"[48] and "one of Charles Dickens' characters who arrived too late be included in that gentleman's humorous and satiric character-sketches" believed Suso to be jealous of her relationship with her husband.[49] "I suppose it is a weakness; but I indulge many fools," Bennett confessed, grateful that Susan had helped him elude the woman's thorny grasp.[50] He had never given up his awe at Susan's trusting and committing herself to him; he respected her opinions highly.

So much so, in fact, that he printed her words about genius and fools on a card and kept it on his dressing table, "where it should catch my eye whenever I adjusted collar or tie, or used comb or brush to dress my whitening hair." This, he believed, would keep him from soaring into "realms of unwarranted conceit."[51] He agreed with her reasoning, noting at another point that "the surest proof that I am not truly possessed of genius is the fact that I have never been able to forget or decline my common responsibilities."[52]

Although praise and pandering from adults often made him cringe, he was carried away with delight when he heard little children cry, "Skylark, Skylark!" at him from the tops of trees on Orange Street.[53] Their comments brought tears to his eyes; they made him feel happy and complete. "I can get on with children, my mental equals, he admitted, [for they are not] so stodged up with events and inessentials as their elders."[54] Furthermore, "I hold that in spite of earth and its troubles if a man but regard the world as a child does . . . unsophisticated, unprejudiced, ready to accept each bright beauty for what it seems, he can find both wonder and charm to sustain him." For that reason, "I was ever a lover a children. And shall ever be."[55]

With this love of children to guide him, a silhouette of his wife inked into the wall, and a stuffed dog with the notation "every dog shall have his day" in front of him in his study, Bennett, after his doctor-enforced rest, went back to working on his "beloved white elephant," *Buckhorn Johnny*.[56] But it was tough going. "It is not possible to compel the mind to write spontaneous beauty or to produce winged words and phrases . . . after one has passed beyond a certain, or uncertain, age."[57] *Johnny* kept going off in all directions, like unimpeded memory; he seemed to be building more a portrait of the world and events his father had lived in than focusing in on a dramatic, plot-propelled story. "I keep making notes and writing paragraphs, passages and particulars . . . and file them in mental pigeonholes in my mind, and in manila folders on my table."[58]

More and more, he was leaving it for *The Doctor to the Dead*, just a shred of a folk legend, depending not too much on plot but needing a moody, dark atmosphere. This he wanted to finish and did. In December 1936, at the age of seventy-one, after an operation in which he "got his insides worked over," he announced with great relief and triumph that, after working on it off and on for more than fifteen years, the *Doctor* was finished.[59]

Before anyone else could see it, he sent the manuscript to Martha, still his best critic. She prized it, but when she readied to return it she realized to her horror, that it, the only finished copy of the work, had somehow disappeared. She panicked and shed tears. To console her, Bennett assured her it was all right, he had other nearly done copies; it was no great loss.

But he had spared her his true feelings; for on a stray sheet of paper he confessed that "written like a poem, line upon line, every word weighed and charged with significance, its ghost haunts me."[60] And in his copy of the Charleston edition of *Madame Margot* he used a rubber stamp on the book's rear flyleaf to note that, "the completed manuscript of the Doctor to the Dead was by unfortunate accident destroyed."[61] Nearly twenty years of work was lost; persistent though he was, he sat down to rewrite it in anguish.

But he was too tired and too beleaguered to face it. He turned instead to smaller tasks easier to complete. After some research, he wrote up the history

of the bells taken out of Charleston's church steeples for melting into cannon for the Confederate cause, and in the case of St. Michael's Episcopal
Church, for safekeeping. In his series of newspaper articles, he demolished
many of the myths that had grown up about the subject, saying in one of
his articles that "one of the strangest things about Charleston is that a city,
so proud of its history, should have forgotten so much of it." [62] He also
helped his Chillicothe friend, Dard Hunter, the world's authority on paper,
on a book he was preparing; for him, Bennett turned up the earliest manu-
facture of paper in South Carolina. "Your John Bennett . . . helped me with
all the South Carolina history," he said to a news reporter when he visited
the city. [63]

This success in illuminating dark spots of previously unexplored history
stirred and encouraged him to turn to other smaller projects, for "to leave
unfinished work undertaken cuts the desire to complete anything for me." [64]
He returned to his vast piles of research notes in his third-floor study and
took up his work on blacks first; he decided to weigh in and settle once and
for all the debate on the origin of the word Gullah. Some claimed the name
for the dialect came from Angola; Bennett was convinced that it derived
from the Gora tribe instead.

Sitting in the Charleston Library Society before the First World War, he
had gone though the colonial newspapers; and with the knowledge gained
from that, with his lists of slave ships, stating where they had come from,
he broadened his study to become an "An Inquiry into the . . . African Slave
Trade from South Carolina's Point of View"; for the first time, "the peculiar
circumstances surrounding the trade, which governed the kind and quantity
and sources of the negroes imported in South Carolina would be revealed." [65]

But again, as a trailblazer, he had trouble interesting others in his findings;
generations later, such statistical breakdowns would bring on a new wave of
scholarship. "God alone knows why I ever undertook this austere labor," he
commented to himself. [66] But he was "sick of lies, half truths, and air set
forth as history and immortal truth. I hope to set one facet in the history of
South Carolina straight if I never accomplish another formal thing on this
queer earth of ours," he said, but no one was interested in old things about
slaves and African beginnings; [67] people were happy and smug in their de-
luded beliefs. He argued and argued but no one, not even his wife—as
"withdrawn from zeal as a public charity"—believed him. This chilled him;
once more, in the circling of time, he saw again that perhaps the people of

Charleston would again turn on him. He gave up his task, hoping to achieve "a cool disinclination to care at all about the whole damn subject."[68]

Just before he gave up, however, he heard from someone who had helped launch his interest in African American topics almost forty years before. Jane Hunter, a Smythe family servant who had worked on Woodburn plantation and whose singing had helped spark his interest in black music, was now writing her autobiography, detailing her life in Pendleton, Charleston, and then as founder of the Phillis Wheatley Association; she turned to Bennett to read over her manuscript.

There was much to catch her up on since he had seen her last. His eldest daughter, Jane, and her husband were living with their children in Smithfield, Virginia, he told her; his son Jack was now thirty-two and engaged to Leonora Broughton Stack; and daughter Sue had come back to Charleston after her schooling and was living at home, pursuing instrumental and vocal music; she'd eventually work as secretary for General Summerall, head of the Citadel.

"Mrs. Bennett and I are both white-haired now, but well, and busy, she about many affairs; . . . she makes our house the center of social interest to a group of more than commonly intelligent young people, friends of ours and our youngest daughter. I am steadily employed in writing history and . . . fiction, juvenile stories and . . . the sources, character and . . . origins of our first Negroes in Carolina."[69]

That sounded like a lot, but he was slowing down, and he knew it. Yet "they call me curiously young," he saw gratefully, believing that if "I am so it is because I have kept my sympathy."[70] And he had kept his friends, one of whom had returned to Charleston. "DuBose says that he does not dare to live in New York," Bennett had reported as early as a dozen years before; "the familiarity and intimate association with the Porgy [acting] troupe, in which there seems there was much lava-lava, makes residence there without complications along the color-line there a problem."[71] He moved back to Charleston in the late 1930s, buying the inevitable local symbol of success, a mansion across from the public gardens along the Battery.

Heyward was now interested in playwriting; with Rockefeller Foundation funding, he was to function as playwright in residence at the recently reconstructed Dock Street Theatre, a WPA-funded theatre built to resemble an eighteenth-century playhouse, on the site of one of the earliest theaters in the colonies. In it, he would revive and adapt the procedure for poetry criticism that he and Bennett and Allen had hammered out for the Poetry Society. Bennett had earlier seen the shift going on in Southern writing, noting by 1930 that "poetry has been metamorphosed to prose, and prose to drama, in this section of the Southern literary renaissance."[72]

Bennett was also involved in the Dock Street Theatre project, having served on the mayor's committee on locating and reconstructing the theater within the walls of the old Planters Hotel; his picture had appeared in the opening-night coverage of the *New York Times* and *Life Magazine*, as the national press continued to interest itself in the cultural activities of the city.[73] Because of the fame of the Poetry Society and its related cultural accomplishments, more and more people were coming—the wealthy, the artistic, and visitors in search of the beauty of the low country. (Even the characters in the syndicated cartoon strip "Washtubs" would be seen passing by the landmarks on Church Street.) A climax to this movement came in February of 1940, when Bennett and his wife were invited "to a dinner given by Wendell Willkie, of New York, to the alleged . . . colony of literary and demiliterary folk of this community."[74] Not yet a presidential candidate, Willkie was known for his wealth, occasional magazine articles, and book reviews. He came to town several times a year, being an owner of the local electric utility. Visiting, he corralled William Watts Ball, editor of the *News and Courier*, to give a dinner to meet the literati.

Ball himself was a member of the literary group, being the author of the book *The State That Forgot: South Carolina's Surrender to Democracy*, and as husband to one of the Witte sisters he was connected to Beatrice Witte Ravenel. His daughter was the author of two memoirs, *Sand in My Shoes*, about raising peaches in North Carolina, and *Sand Dollars*, detailing the Depression in Charleston, as well as *Crowded House*, a novel of a new generation growing up in Charleston. Her husband Clements had recently co-written the screenplay *Jezebel*, for which Bette Davis had won an academy award; this antebellum-era film cashed in on the interest spun off by *Gone with the Wind*, and the novel *Reap the Wild Wind* of the same era, would be partially filmed in the city in a year or two. Ball invited nearly everybody.

"Herbert Sass could not come, being detained by a death in his wife's island family circle. But the rest of us were present, barring Beatrice Witte Ravenel, who it is said never leaves her very invalid husband long enough for the clock to tick. The guests besides myself and S[usan] S[mythe]

B[ennett] were Irita van Doren, of NY, sister to Carl van D[oren] and Lambert Davis, also of NY, Glenn Allan, of Summerville [whose "Boysi" stories became immensely popular in national magazines and which provided a playwriting idea for Dorothy Heyward]; Jo[sephine] Pinckney, Mr. and Mrs. Archibald Rutledge of Hampton Plantation; DuBose and Dorothy Heyward; Clem and Katti [Katherine Ball] Ripley, S[amuel] G[aillard] Stoney [and Julia Peterkin]. . . . I was sorry that the social ring could not include [Granville] Paul Smith; but it never has done so."[75]

Before the dinner and after, many began to wonder what really had drawn Willkie to the city. He was a frequent visitor and, though married, was being romantically linked by public gossip to Josephine Pinckney; Beatrice Ravenel's daughter would report in two years, "A story has been buzzing around that Wendell Willkie was going to divorce his wife and marry Josephine Pinckney . . . but we hear that it is absolutely false."[76]

"Gossip in Charleston is like dredging for shrimp," Bennett agreed; "strange things are fetched up from the deep."[77] He found Willkie "a brusquely cordial, able-looking, pleasantly intelligent gentleman, more like an upcountryman, than a lowcountry type."[78] Like many in the low country fed up with FDR's liberal politics, Bennett would desert the Democratic party to vote for Willkie when he ran for president; to save face, the locals would call themselves "Jeffersonian Democrats," in support of Republican Willkie.

Regarding the rumors of Willkie and Pinckney, it's interesting to note that Irita van Doren, also romantically linked with Willkie, was also at that meal, and that Willkie would soon note a line in a novel of Josephine Pinckney's, a line about two women, angry at the same man, who "had never given himself wholly to either woman, and they had rewarded his half-measures— sensible women—by taking their wares to other markets."[79] "Nobody but a Feminist, a Southern Lady, and a Pinckney could have written it," he telegraphed her, hoping that it would be expunged from all future editions.[80]

Willkie [sat] at one end of the long table, W. W. Ball at the other; Jo Pinckney and Mrs. Peterkin flanking Willkie, Archie Rutledge and I next opposite; DuBose at my left, and Mrs. Rutledge just beyond. . . . Mother was down at the W. W. B[all] end, and I could hear her sweet voice occasionally raised amid laughter and retort, while Sam S[toney] kept things moving along his battle front. I found Jo P[inckney] unexpectedly congenial, she having at last graduated . . . from the . . .

haughty ranks of amateur authorship and politesse into the professional grind of rehashing a book [her first novel *Hilton Head*, in which she'd include the line to so amuse Willkie ] to meet a publisher's liking. . . . So we chattered of revisions and perplexities; and I really believe Jo was refreshed and relieved to find that an old-stager like me finds it ever necessary to write, re-write, shift, change, amend, delete, ripen, omit, restore, doubt, fear and at last decide that one has done his darn-dest . . . and the rest must be on the lap of the gods, and the publisher. . . . DuBose asked if he might turn the tables on me—I introduced him and "Porgy" to John Farrar—and write Farrar that I have a book [his revised and rewritten *Doctor to the Dead*] on its last quarter mile, and advise F. to take that fact into active considera-tion. Whereat we both grinned; and I said, "To it!"

Dorothy Heyward is doing a play, local theme, on the Denmark Vesey Gullah Jack insurrection, 1822, and wants to come up to quiz me upon the character of the negro tribes involved in that thwarted insurrection. [Heyward had helped her, too; it would not be produced until 1948 and only ran a few disappointing weeks.] If I can but put my hands upon my material I can oblige her . . . having been the only one foolish enough to attempt such study seriously.

Archie R[utledge] and his wife were rather singularly out of it; . . . S[usan] S[mythe] B[ennett] seeing their isolation, broke in, settled herself with them; and a few moments later, seeing the situation, [Clements] Ripley and I pulled up chairs and joined. I found, luckily, a bond of interest in Rutledge's avid interest in the mound-builder works and . . . knowing . . . my old friend Warren Moorehead, . . . he talked of Flint Ridge, Ohio, and I of the Hopewell Mound, and he was inter-ested to know I had illustrated Moorehead's book, "Primitive Man in Ohio. . . ." I think the man is hurt deeply; he has been resident on the old plantation at Hamp-ton now for several years; but, Friday night was the first time he has ever been remembered by invitation to a Charleston affair. [Bennett seemed to be forgetting his often strong criticism of Rutledge for his unlikely nature stories and feeble poetry.] "People are introduced to me as a writer; and know nothing that I have written," he said to S[usan] S[mythe] B[ennett]. I happily recalled his stories . . . and remembered them clearly, as well as his early amateurish pseudonym of "Ilex" over which I first saw his poetry forty years ago. And Mother capped the climax by telling that one of the first books we had given Jack [their son] was "Tom and I on the Old Plantation" and "Old Plantation Days. . . ." He urged me to come out to Hampton to see him. He added that he sees very few Charlestonians but many . . . people from the North, who come to see the old place during the winter sea-son. . . . It is agreeable, now and then, to hear someone speak a good word for the

Yankees, now that we are all ostentatiously Southern again with [the excitement over *Gone with the*] *Wind.*[81]

Indeed, the city, like the rest of the country, had been in a frenzy over the book and film. George Cukor had been in town staging auditions at the Fort Sumter Hotel;[82] and Alicia Rhett of Charleston had been cast as India Wilkes. The film opened in Charleston the same month as the Ball/Willkie dinner party.

Ironically, there were now more Yankees in Charleston than there had been immediately after the Civil War. Clare Boothe Luce and her husband Henry would buy the old Henry Laurens estate of Mepkin and use it for a retreat. Benjamin Kittredge had earlier bought Dean Hall and turned it into Cypress Gardens (and he, like many in these years, tried his hand at novel writing, producing *Crowded Solitude*). Solomon Guggenheim bought Daniel's Island and often stayed at 9 East Bay Street. Nelson Doubleday would bring friends down for hunting at his estate in nearby Yemasee, offering a retreat to some of his writers, including Somerset Maugham, who would visit the city in the early 1940s and write *The Razor's Edge* in the low country.[83]

Expatriates Gertrude Stein and Ludwig Lewisohn had come, too, at the behest of the Poetry Society; Stein was ridiculed,[84] but the city had welcomed its prodigal son Lewisohn back a bit more warmly, especially after he complimented the city, saying it had "surrendered to the vulgarity and glare of modern civilization less than any other American city." Lewisohn further pleased Charlestonians by making fun of obscure writers, like Stein herself, for abandoning the old-fashioned novel. On the same day of Lewisohn's lecture, the Gibbes Art Gallery opened a show featuring Solomon Guggenheim's collection of non-objective art, as abstract art was called then, and Lewisohn said, "The reason why people paint non-objective pictures is because they don't know anything about anybody anymore."[85] Charleston was treated to the first Guggenheim show in the country, but it was not impressed; Bennett was polite over it only out of respect for local gallery director Robert Whitelaw.[86]

He and others at the dinner party for Willkie were more comfortable with the old-fashioned novel and the representational artwork of Elizabeth O'Neill Verner, Alice Smith, and Alfred Hutty. They ruled in the insular, peninsular city and were in control here, but the world of the Charleston literary renaissance was ending, and here Bennett witnessed a last gathering

of many present at its beginnings. For within six months, DuBose Heyward would die suddenly and unexpectedly of a coronary thrombosis in the
North Carolina mountains. It was a shock to the city, and an end to the era
that had produced the Poetry Society and *Porgy*.

Bennett sadly attended the fifty-five-year-old man's funeral. "DuBose was
buried on a sun shiny day under the green trees of St. Philip's west yard,
with Merritt Williams, rector, conducting the funeral service," he wrote of
the late June ceremony. "Harriet Simons was with the family group; Sam
[Gaillard Stoney], Louisa [Stoney], Mother and I stood together in a pleasant spot of shade. . . . Mr. Williams read a poem of DuBose's written when
first success acclaimed his verse, a poet's epitaph. Dorothy . . . is just a wisp
of a body, gray and wasted, frailer than I have ever seen her: how she keeps
going I do not know."[87] Nearby gloomed the tomb of John C. Calhoun; at
his death in 1850, the city had been draped in black bunting, some of it later
made into a cape for Dr. Ryngo, the doctor to the dead of Bennett's story.

And Bennett came to realize that it just might as well have been the
funeral of the doctor to the dead he had attended. Although Heyward, good
to his word, had passed the manuscript onto John Farrar, he had declined
to publish it.[88] That had not hurt the author's feelings unduly, but within
six months, with the attack on Pearl Harbor and the coming of the Second
World War, he realized there might be no future for *The Doctor*. With the
world occupied with history in the making, would there be any interest in
an odd tale from another century?

## CHAPTER 21

# The Day of The Doctor to the Dead

THE WAR CHANGED CHARLESTON: the wharves were ruled off limits, Marines protected the Cooper River Bridge, and no one could carry a camera to any nearby beach. Susan was busy with the rationing board; Laura Bragg served on the cost of living panel of the war prices board, and she heard from one of her "Chinese boys," now a general, in 1943. Shortages of sugar forced Onslow Candy Company to shut its doors; grocery stores closed, and restaurants changed their menus. Cars, with no replacement tires, were marooned on jacks. Debutantes had to come together for one major debut instead of having separate functions and parties, and for the first time in sixty years the Citadel cadets had to face breakfast without grits. The housing shortage was so acute that the merchant marine took over two of the city's greatest mansions (the literary history–entwined Villa Margherita and the house where the members of the renaissance had gathered for one last time, in a tribute to Wendell Willkie); the Navy commandeered the Fort Sumter Hotel; garbage was not picked up; teachers left their jobs; and gangs of unruly teenagers ruled the streets. Gardens, parked cars, and hotel lobbies were filled with sleeping women—girlfriends, wives, and mothers who had come to the city to see their men off or take them back; thousands of wounded soldiers were brought in on hospital ships; British troops snapped to attention when St. Michael's bells rang "America": to them, it was "God Save the King."

Many Charlestonians pitched in. Alice Smith and her sister entertained service men, some of whom slept on cots in the drawing room. The Bennetts fixed up an apartment in the back of their house to help with the shortage of housing. One Charleston lady volunteered to entertain the injured and sick, but when two soldiers, one black and one white, were deposited on her doorstep, she panicked. (Entertaining blacks was still taboo; Federal Judge J. Waties Waring would get stones tossed through his Meeting Street windows for doing that in the late 1940s.) She saved the situation by greeting the men on her side piazza—not in her house but on her property. In a great mansion on East Bay Street, one Charlesto· aristocrat refused to believe that his house had been hit by lightning; Hitler has sent a bomb over, he swore, to kill him personally.[1]

Bennett tried as he could to make light of things, but he sank into a general depression as the world turned to darkness. There were "hideous noon-day" blasts from St. Michael's Church steeple; blackouts were called but street lights stayed on; some people could not hear the sirens; others ignored them, staying on the streets.[2] Bennett tried feebly to keep his *Doctor to the Dead* from being one of the war's earliest fatalities.

Ever since Martha had lost the manuscript, he had revised, even revived it. To this he had added nearly all the other folktales he had stumbled upon in the early years of the century; he knew now he was too old to produce one tale per volume, as he had foreseen in the "Bat Series." Now it was to be a collection of all he had found, with "The Doctor" being the title piece.

Once Farrar and a few others had turned it down, Bennett, for the first time in is life, secured the service of literary agents Russell and Volkening (agents to, among others, William Butler Yeats). Although Diamard Russell was highly encouraging and respectful of Bennett's manuscript, which went "the complete rounds of publishing houses," every one turned it down. Each gave the same reason; "there can be nothing in this collection at present for themselves [the publishers], us, or you," his agents told him. "But . . . bring it back when the WAR IS OVER," they said.[3] All editors assured him they would then be glad to reevaluate the manuscript.

Dorothy Heyward was having a similar sort of problem with a play about blacks she had been brought in to fix; its author, Howard Rigsby, had been called up into service, and his play about blacks in the military needed help. "Time is of the very essence. In a few short months, the negro has leapt some tall hurdles, making my play that was timely a year ago, seem like something by Thomas Nelson Page," she wrote of the drama first called *New Georgia;*[4] when that island was liberated she gave the play a name that was to become more famous for someone else, *South Pacific.* (She'd also toy with the situation of blacks and whites in the military as a prologue to her Denmark Vesey play, *Set My People Free.*)

Old ideas about blacks were undergoing a radical change, and in a few

years, the works of writers of the renaissance would pay the price. So many
works of these elite whites rested on the depiction of blacks; some had been
sympathetic, even radically so, in the 1920s, but in the 1940s and '50s all
became suspect and were facilely lumped together with Joel Chandler Harris
and tar baby. Their books would be dismissed, unread by the upcoming
socially conscious literary critics.

*Porgy* was forgotten (although the opera began its rise to world wide fame
through the Cheryl Crawford revival in 1942; she, unfortunately, also started
the process of removing DuBose Heyward's name from it). In the same vein,
Warner Brothers studios started a campaign to change the name of Folly
Beach, where Gershwin had worked, to "Gershwin Isle" to help promote a
Gershwin film biography.[5] Supplanting Porgy were characters like Chalmers
Murray's hero in his novel *Here Come Joe Mungin.* Mungin, in the charged
words of the dust-jacket copy, is "a hard-headed, loose-limbed black giant
who sweats and wenches and fights his way" to become the shape of things
to come.[6] No crippled beggar trying to snatch a brief hour of happiness is
he; instead he's a sort of Crown triumphant, a force like a hurricane, dam-
aging itself and all around him. Having created him, Murray would never
be able to close his hands around another character again; none of his other
novels, all dealing with whites, would ever reach print. A similar fate held
true for Richard Coleman, a novelist on the Charleston fringe. He published
his novel of blacks, *Don't You Weep, Don't You Moan* in 1935; he'd write short
stories, one adapted as part of a Bing Crosby and Ingrid Bergman film,
another taking place in a Charleston whorehouse. He'd gain great notoriety,
hiding under the pseudonym Edward Twig, in a debunking piece: "Charleston: The Great Myth," published in the *Nation* in 1940. He'd befriend Flan-
nery O'Connor and teach some of the rising Charleston newcomers, such as
novelist and playwright Patricia Colbert Robinson, but he'd never produce
another sustained piece of fiction.[7]

The most noteworthy Charleston writer after the war would be the one
Bennett had doubted all along: Josephine Pinckney. Her phenomenally successful *Three o'Clock Dinner,* and all her forthcoming works, would center on
entirely white casts. Robert Molloy, Charleston-born but living in the New
York City area, would become a best-selling writer, too, focusing his gentle
and loving satire on Charleston's interconnected Catholic families; he'd be a
friend to all things Charleston, even showing characters in his second novel

reading Pinckney's *Three o'Clock Dinner;* like Pinckney and historical novelist Katherine Drayton Mayrant Simons, he would concentrate on white characters only.[8]

When many had begun writing in the 1920s, the African American had been down so many rungs on the social ladder that writers, if they used the stereotypes of the day, did not "damage" themselves using them. But now with the transformation and the demand for civil rights, white Charlestonians were not so secure in their relations with blacks; it did not help that one of their class, Judge Waties Waring, as a federal judge, opened up the all-white Democratic primary to blacks and angered many. Once they had viewed the Negro with *noblesse oblige;* they had deigned to lift a cripple like Porgy, but swearing, fist-swinging, demanding-to-be-heard Joe Mungin made them nervous. Glenn Allan would try to keep the stereotype alive in his "Boysi" stories; Dorothy Heyward would be conflicted in *Set My People Free* and *South Pacific;* within a few years, Charleston writers would no longer look across the "color line" and into the "sordid courts and alleys" as had Heyward and Bennett; they'd stay entirely in the parlors and piazzas.

The 1950s would bring a new writer to the city, or its outskirts, at least. Once an international banker, diplomat, and member of the Algonquin Round-Table set, Paul Hyde Bonner, retiring to Summerville, would produce sophisticated novels of finance, diplomacy, and social life in international settings; only his *Art of Llewellyn Jones* would feature the city. In his sports writing, he'd use the low country and even Dorothy Parker and other New York literati. And the most noted poet in town, the Pulitzer Prize–winning George Dillon, though a member of the Poetry Society, would rarely break his publishing silence living in Charleston.

Bennett had an inkling of the changes in the wind; he knew he had outlived his time. His last attendance at a Poetry Society function in 1938 had been embarrassing; he was too deaf to hear what was being said—only Englishman Peter Gething enunciated well enough for him to hear, but, sadder still, no one realized who he was. Only Paul Smith and secretary Joan Williman pressed forward to greet him.[9] During the war, the society discontinued all large public gatherings; the working group of interested writers still met, as it had for years, mostly due to efforts of Charleston Library Society director and Poetry Society member Arabella Mazyck, called "Bumptious Belle" behind her back by Sam Gaillard Stoney.[10]

"For many years," Bennett wrote in tribute,

Miss Arabella . . . has opened her house . . . once every month during the winter season, and been hostess to . . . those who try to write verse, . . . who succeed, and . . . those who find pleasure and aid in mutual criticism of their work. Arabella has never relied upon her "feminine charm" to allure the masculine; but her common-sense and unfailing hospitality have made her service to the poetry-writing group a . . . rather unusual thing; and the group has maintained its meetings for reading and criticism without a break for fifteen years or so, and still continues. Among its members are quite a number of faculty from the Citadel's English Department, whose wives, grown half-amused at themselves, half-jealously of Arabella's perennial entertainment of their spouses . . . have organized themselves into a wives' resentful-protective-and-sympathetic Contract Bridge Club, which meets every night their husbands go to Miss Mazyck's for intellectual stimulus and mutual wrangling. And, that its intention shall not be misinterpreted, the ladies have called their retaliatory organization "The ARABELLA MAZYCK CARD CLUB." [11]

Despite Mazyck's continuing generosity and zeal, the glory days of the Poetry Society had passed. "Sam Stoney is the only chap in town who can talk shop with me," Bennett lamented, referring to those knowledgeable of Charleston's past, including its literary history.[12] Stoney had organized a series of lectures on the Poetry Society and the renaissance as a course at the College of Charleston in 1939, giving further proof that the era had passed and could now be spoken on with authority.

Stoney asked Bennett to speak to the class. In preparing his notes, he looked over his past and told his family that

while that pleasant confraternity of Heyward, Allen and I, with Mom giving us supper and sitting on the side lines, lasted, it was most companionable. When that broke, from the mutual jealousy of those two lads, and their departure on separate paths, the last real fraternity ended. The meetings of P. Gething, A. Sprunt, and H. Sass promised pleasure, but petered out. . . . And there has been no fellowship since among the "literati" of Charleston. Sam Stoney vows that selfishness and a desire to stab one another in the back prevents all comradeship. . . . More than ever I realize what a companionship I enjoyed with Harry [Bennett], Jack [Appleton], and Jo [Russell Taylor], and M[artha] T[rimble] B[ennett] as my devoted encourager and perfect critic. I think life offers such friendship but once and then destroys the pattern. . . . The One-for-all and all-for-one ideal has vanished from the map. Hail and farewell! [13]

Also gone was much of Bennett's own enthusiasm for things; "incomplete dreams and unfinished efforts ride my heart like an obsession," he wrote in the early 1940s, "and I find no escape except in working; . . . cramped with an idea, I move. I go here and there; I meet and part with 'he and she' or chat with 'him and her.' But . . . within I . . . am a chaos of incomplete dreams and altered plans. Someday I'll find my way out, and then if land be still at liberty and spring still green, I'll see what there is left of me can do with idleness and sweet converse."[14]

"Sometimes a complete panorama of my life flashes across my memory like a moving picture; and I see it all, the griefs, the hardships, the toil; its little moments of success, . . . its hours of despair; the high parts in the sunlight, and dark, shadowed valleys of discouragement; . . . but I dare not let that keen swift instrument, my mind, dwell upon that panorama of the past, nor stare into the future, so I go on working."[15]

He wanted to finish the story of his father's life, but he had problems. "The plain fact is, when I began this book, this BUCKHORN JOHNNY, I was many a year younger, and of fancy buoyant," he acknowledged. "It is unnecessary to say why I have, again and again, been compelled to set the story aside. . . . I have been interrupted; but the years have rolled on uninterruptedly."[16] He no longer could muster the focus to keep the book as accurate as he wanted and to have it double as local history of the places his father had been. His years of wanting to produce "honest, hope-I-may-die-if-this-is-not-true history" had led him to the "ruinous habit of meticulous accuracy in statement, language and presentation." Now he had to give it up and go for imaginative fiction only. "So, if . . . discrepancies appear between what I try to write and what Father set down for me in his brief and fragmentary memoirs, pray pass them up as an unavoidable difference and forgive the variation," he asked of his family.[17]

Next, an acute and disfiguring case of dermatitis on his hands caused his skin to flake off and kept him from writing. And his daughter Susan was treated shabbily and abandoned by a man she had fallen in love with, a man whom Bennett had encouraged but misjudged; sorely grieved, he asked his daughter's apology. To escape, and because he had lost most of his hearing ("When a man's hearing fails, he is shut out of the life of them he loves most"), he sat alone most nights reading detective or "defective stories," as he called them;[18] "by determinedly fixing my distressed attention upon the piffling text, I . . . prevent the intrusion upon my heart of bitterness and

wrath at the astounding folly and madness of mankind."[19] As he had in
World War I, he found himself prey more and more often to his "Scottish"
melancholy. "The blues will come when your body is weary and your mind
distressed," he had warned his son, on the eve of his wedding to Leonora
Stack in Wilmington, North Carolina, on June 1, 1939.[20]

John's job and his preparation for military service took him out of town;
Lee, as Leonora was called, settled in Mount Pleasant, and Bennett went
by bus to visit. On one of his trips, he rose to give a woman his seat, but
she, trousered, returning home from work in a factory, looked him up and
down and, seeing his age and fragility, told him (as others laughed) that if
any one needed to sit, it was he.[21] Bennett was amused at this but a bit
perplexed by the droves of new people who had moved to town and did not
know him. Yet when the visiting author Millard Brand came to town and
asked in a bookstore about Charleston writers to meet, he was directed to
John Bennett.

Bennett welcomed him in; as for others, "I told him that Herbert Sass
was probably down Jeremy Creek, Edisto; Alex Sprunt in Louisiana for the
Audubon Society; Sam Stoney in Kentucky; DuBose Heyward dead; Clem
Ripley probably in California; . . . Hervey Allen permanently in Maryland;
Miss Jo Pinckney probably out of town, and . . . that Peter Gething was
selling stocks and bonds; Archie Rutledge on his plantation."[22]

Bennett often wanted to leave himself. "I wish I was upon a green hillside
in the old Middle-western State of Ohio, with a silver-gray boled beech tree
behind me," he dreamed, "and the Scioto Valley laid out before me like a
pattern for boyhood paradise! I've lived in Charleston longer than I lived in
Chillicothe; but I am still occasionally, particularly at the fall of the year, . . .
so homesick for Ohio I could walk the floor and weep, if it were not so
gauche for a man to exhibit his emotions so flagrantly."[23]

He did that only with a few friends—one being Jim Gittman. "This
morning," he wrote him,

as I came down by St. John's Cathedral, I met upon the concrete sidewalk, feebly
endeavoring to advance to kindly earth, a common earth worm, dying in that futile
search . . . to continue its pitiful existence. . . . And that worm, to me, in its hopeless,
futile adventure toward certain extinction . . . seems to me to represent better than
any other simile the precarious, petty life of mankind. Poor, futile dubs. . . .

The plain cold truth is when we think it over at three o'clock in the morning . . . that neither we, nor anything mortal matters anything at all. . . . Why then all our pother? When compared with the incredible immensity of space and infinite nothingness?[24]

Perhaps he had expressed it more succinctly in his poem "In a Rose Garden" some fifty years before. "A hundred years from now, dear heart," he had written, "we shall not care at all."

He could find nothing in religion to console him. "I suppose I am an agnostic, a heathen, a heretic, an outlaw and outcast. I regret that; but I cannot believe the incredible artifice which has gone into the structure of every creed. The incredibility of nature and the universe serves me for awe, for wonder, and for trust and hope."[25] And concerning hope, he wrote, "The most cogent argument for eternal life and our immortality is the little time here given for friendship; that a thing so fine, so full of satisfaction to a hungry heart, should be so brief . . . and vanish like a fog, forever, is an appeal to unreason."[26] And for these friends, to honor and achieve their hopes for him, he met other challenges.

In 1940, for his "mental equals," the children of Charleston, he became honorary godfather of the Children's Room that was named for him in the Charleston Free Library;[27] for years he would give out diplomas for the summer reading program to white children in the garden of the main library, a cotton planter's, and later a mayor's, mansion; he'd do the same thing for the black children at the inferior Dart Hall branch. In 1944 he wrote happily that "our diploma-presentations made history . . . the *Evening Post* printing immediately beneath and in conjunction with the . . . white children . . . the names of all the negro children . . . the first time in the history of the Charleston press that such a thing has been done. What a small thing . . . yet how much it means."[28]

The separate libraries did not trouble him as much as the incredible disparity between the two facilities; he was infuriated over the gross inequality of schools, too. Children became more and more important to him in these years. The cruelties in Europe hit home, as well; he made his strongest statements against anti-Semitism, calling it "an offense against God," and castigated some Charlestonians for their "rudeness and snobbishness" for refusing to speak to people of "Jewish appearance" vacationing in High Hampton.[29] Sadly he noted that Ludwig Lewisohn, one of the first to alert

America to the Nazi's anti-Jewish policies, had lectured in a synagogue in Charleston, saying, "Any Jew today who doesn't give Zionism his vote is guilty of the blood of his people"; only about sixty-five people had turned up to listen in spring 1943.[30]

Standing up for a feared and hated minority—the dispossessed black children of Charleston—Bennett took a politically unpopular stand. (Etcher and painter Elizabeth O'Neill Verner took a small stand on black issues, too: she stopped the city from removing the black women who sold flowers on the street, "I need them for models," she said, and she thought them a good advertisement for the colorful ways of the old city.)[31] Bennett had no motivation of self-interest when his fighting spirit, long dormant, revived. He grew angry reading an article in the paper in July 1945 that said that the city's board of education had given up the task of seeking accreditation for Burke, the only public black high school in the city. (There were two other black high schools on the peninsula; Avery and Immaculate Conception *were* accredited but private.) The lack of accreditation meant that Burke graduates had a poorer education and had to take special tests before being accepted into college.

It seemed grossly unfair: the city had a large black population, and there were thirty-seven towns and cities in the state with accredited high schools. It angered others, too: Robert F. Morrison, president of the Negro Young Men's Christian Association, called for a mass public meeting in the Morris Street AME Church, Friday evening, July 6.

Dishearteningly, only about fifty people attended, mostly black but with some whites; an interracial committee, including Bennett's niece by marriage, Mrs. Albert Simons, was charged to draw up a petition for accreditation. Three people charged with presenting this to the school board were chosen: Bennett, the Reverend R. E. Brodgen of the Emanuel AME Church, and Morrison, who had called the meeting. Many obviously remembered the role that Bennett had played in the First World War, for he was the only white person on the committee.

The three met with the school board, but when nothing came of it, Bennett then "decided to bring the thing into the open light."[32] He wrote an "Appeal to Justice and Reason," which the *News and Courier* published as "An Appeal for an Accredited Negro High School" on July 15, 1945. William Watts Ball, editor, had been forced to publish it, though it conflicted with his own beliefs; Bennett was too well-known to ignore, and Ball, Bennett believed, grew angry at his meddling, sounding off sourly and enviously that Bennett was an "S.O.B. who writes what he god-damn pleases."[33]

Bennett presented his argument logically, showing that nearby Mt. Pleasant and Summerville had accredited schools; the fact that Charleston "had more negro inhabitants than any other city in South Carolina [but] no free public accredited high school" he called "inexpedient, unwise and unjust." To those who said Negroes were poorer, paid less taxes, and so should get less, Bennett countered that providing blacks with better educations would raise their salaries and thus their taxes; he also appealed to those who had fought for freedom in Europe by referring to the American ideal of equality for all. It was nonsense to believe (as some said they did) that accrediting the city school would bring in a flood of blacks from the country.

Not just relying on the school board members to read his appeal in the paper, Bennett sent a copy of it to all seven of them, "requesting their earnest attention to the matter."[34] It seemed to work, for within a week, the board appointed a committee to investigate accreditation. When school opened in the fall, however, there was still no definite progress. Bennett went to Burke and wrote of what he saw there for the *News and Courier,* which again reluctantly published it.

He started in on the good aspects of the building but soon brought up its history; it had been built forty years before for two hundred to three hundred students, but the current student body numbered twelve hundred. There were not enough teachers or classrooms, no auditorium or cafeteria to accommodate the students; the heating was inadequate, the makeshift classrooms open to the elements. The poor drainage on this site, once a potter's field, made it a health hazard. "One only had to go see," he wrote, "to be convinced" of the impossibility of administering a school in the building.[35]

Suddenly the *News and Courier* endorsed Bennett. Ball did not believe in free schools for either blacks or whites, but he frightened the population with the thought that the blatant inequality between the white and black schools could play into the hands of the "agitators for mixed schools" to create a cry for integration; "separate but equal" was his plea. (J. Waties Waring would later call a halt to that by equating segregation with "per se inequality.")[36]

After the paper switched tactics, Bennett followed up with a letter to the school board members; the needed work came quickly, for word of state accreditation came by December 15. Those finishing by June would be the first class to receive a diploma from the state of South Carolina. The *News and Courier* published an article commending Bennett for his efforts.[37]

The victory was pleasant but, banging on his typewriter, Bennett grew disgusted that although he had put out some branches and borne fruit in Charleston, his tap root nevertheless was back in Ohio. "If I were a single man, and had not a wife, family and residence here, I'd go back to Chillicothe so fast that my trail would resemble a comet's tail trailing over the mountains."[38]

In fact, he thought more and more of his hometown in these years as he did work for the Ross County Historical Society, which was housed in his uncle's house. A few years earlier, its director had requested the native son to research the Indian chief Blue Jacket, who had started his life as Marmaduke van Sweringen; one of Bennett's forebears, Sweringen had renounced his birthright to be adopted by the Shawnees. Scholars in Ohio and the Midwest called Blue Jacket a Native American, nevertheless, which Bennett knew to be both untrue and ridiculous; he rose to the occasion to honor his town and family and to correct a historical inaccuracy. His monograph was published by the Ross County Historical Society in 1943.[39] Tales from his collection *The Doctor to the Dead* were published in the *Yale Review* and the *Negro Digest* in the same year, too.[40]

But something even more important to Bennett was happening in the field of writing and publishing, and it became the one consistently bright spot in the war years; he noted, with glee, that his son and namesake, John Henry van Sweringen Bennett, had become interested in writing. "In the latter 1880s and through the 1890s, Jack Appleton, Joe Taylor, Harry B[ennett] and I worked together with immense pleasure and mutual benefit over our literary ventures," he wrote; "in 1918−19−20, etcetera, again, with Hervey Allen and DuBose Heyward, young and untried aspirants, . . . I had a few years of most agreeable contact." This era "did not lack much in comparison with Wm Gilmore Simms, Paul Hamilton Hayne, Henry Timrod, etc.," he believed. Then "once more with Peter Gething, Herbert Sass, and Alex Sprunt, I played the ancient warrior, and lent such advice as I could to those hopeful youths, and I might describe these three eras as Golden, Silver-Plated, and Tin. But a bit, and a good bit of the GILDED AGE has returned in the immense pleasure of watching my own son take up, with every evidence of no small ability, the pen which my fingers, soon or late, may lay aside."[41] "It would amuse me if the puppy out-ran the old dog," he wrote to a friend.[42]

Having completed the rough draft of a novel in 1941, his son John could go no further as he left his forestry job to wait for his induction into the Army; every publisher he showed it to replied that its pace was too leisurely and that it was not sufficiently exciting. Bennett and his son started the rewriting together. "It is an odd experience, and most agreeable to be talking professional shop with one's own boy, an experience I am much enjoying."[43] He sighed to himself, "Age has its compensations," adding, "it needs them."[44]

When his son was called up to service, Bennett volunteered to take on the rewriting and editing, which the younger man had only half finished. "Somebody had to lend him a hand who knows what [a] manuscript must be and [how] a tale must run, where chaotic paragraphs belong, and how to check on the discrepancies which inevitably occasion such hurried revision." So he tended to his son's manuscript, putting *Buckhorn Johnny* aside once more, for "the boy's work is more important than mine; he is starting out and I am headed for home."[45]

Contacting his own agent about taking on his son's rewritten book, Bennett wrote, "let me dovetail the rewrite and that latter half of the original draft, scanning . . . for any excess dialect . . . and rewriting a page or two."[46] Whatever he did (and Bennett's exact contribution to the text is hard to determine) worked.[47] For when the manuscript was sent back out, it sold. And it was he who proofed the galleys and added punctuation.

The publishers were right in billing this a tale of the Civil War more in line with Stephen Crane than Margaret Mitchell.[48] The story is rough and, like its feuding characters, unkempt but compelling; in an era prior to and during the Civil War "poor white" swamp clans fight each other, the Yankees, the tough economic times, and the hardness and futility of swamp life. It is action-packed and raw, featuring scenes of great violence and brutality. It keeps up a dynamic pace (although the latter half is still slower than the first) and contains much to make a reader wonder how much is the elder Bennett's. The character of the "Dutchman," for instance, is at first ridiculed for being a "nigger lover," and one wonders if it could be a disguised self-portrait. But the stark, cruel treatment given him, and the low nature of his wife causes one to stop seeking comparisons; furthermore, it seems impossible for Bennett to have written such bloody scenes, there being only suggestions, no graphic depictions, in his earlier writings. The touches of humor, however, and the book's visual quality, as well as its depictions of everyday activities such as cooking, washing, and cleaning, could owe something to him. And some rhythms, such as the repetitive lines in chapter 29 of death stalking, seem so reminiscent of crescendoing scenes from *Peyre Gaillard* and *Barnaby Lee* that they argue strongly for Bennett's editing.

A view of the Civil War more different from Heyward's *Peter Ashley* or Sass's *Look Back to Glory* could not be found. They had viewed the past as something roseate, far removed in time; the Bennett version was much truer to life, and though historically accurate, it was, in fact, based on life in the twentieth century. For the younger Bennett had drawn his characters from life, as his father had. Even more, he took the characters his father had pointed out to him; years earlier, the elder Bennett had suggested that the incredible antics of Sabb Cumbee and his family in the Hell Hole Swamp area of Berkeley County might be the stuff of a novel. Coming upon moonshiners and murderers working as a forester in the same exact area, his son had taken his father's advice, turning "Hell Hole" into "Big Hole" and Sabb Cumbee to Bass Crombie.[49] To further reduce the chance of recognition (and revenge from the Cumbees), John moved his characters back in time to the Civil War and west to Alabama.[50]

*So Shall they Reap* was published in 1944 to consistently good reviews; the fact that it had been written by a young man (John Bennett III was how he styled himself on the title page), and was about poor whites instead of Charlestonians, apparently kept natives from chastising both it and him. Bennett was thrilled for his son, and kept his contributions to his work (whatever they were) out of the public eye. This was happiness enough, he felt, to see his son emulating him, but then his own writing was soon to be cause for celebration.

Word came from Martha that she had just found the version of *Doctor to the Dead* that had been misplaced in Chillicothe. It had been pushed aside and behind furniture by the carelessness of a cleaning woman, she believed; she returned it to him happily. Bennett then compared the original to the rewritten version and blended the best of each. He wrote Hervey Allen of this fortuitous recovery, and as soon as the war was finished, Allen, who had earlier been instrumental in the publishing of *Madame Margot*, told his publisher, Stanley Rinehart, of the manuscript. Rinehart directed one of his firm's representatives to call for the work; and that is how *The Doctor to the Dead* was resurrected. Rinehart accepted it immediately.

Due to the shortage of paper, Bennett condensed the version of "Madame Margot" and had to forego having the correct type of coated paper stock needed to artfully reproduce the etching he had done in 1924 to serve for the frontispiece. It was scheduled for publication in March 1946 but was delayed until May 23rd, a few days after his eighty-first birthday.

Critics were delighted with it, many struck by the manner Bennett had chosen to render his tales. "The method by which these legends are told is . . . a certain convention," he knew; "a legend, not being a natural story, cannot be told in a naturalistic way without losing the effect of marvel, strangeness [and] grotesquery." That is why, as in *Margot*, he had worked toward "a mysterious control of effect by [a] careful, deft, exact, and deliberate" choice of words.[51]

Bennett had gathered information for the title tale "from a hundred sources [including] several older physicians, court records, [the] probate office, newspaper notices, a Lady of Charleston [and] Francis Nipson, who knew the Doctor personally."[52] Dr. Henry Charles Rynker, son of the College of Charleston gatekeeper before the Civil War, had grown morbid after his rejection from Charleston society. He grew odder with each passing year; women would cross the street to avoid the contagion of passing his house,[53] the burnt foundations of which Bennett measured; superstitious folk told stories about him when he was seen riding only at night with women who would vanish in the morning.

"The Doctor to the Dead," which in some ways can also be read as Bennett's symbolic revival of the dead literary tradition of Charleston, was one of the tales that, along with "Margot," had gotten him in trouble with the Charleston ladies in 1908. Another one he told at that same time was also included here—the story "The Black Constable," based on a real-life prototype, John Domingo; so death-resistant was he that a generation later another Charleston writer would revive Bennett's Domingo and use him as the basis of a novel.[54]

Of all the others in the book, Bennett believed the most important to be "The Death of the Wandering Jew," a variation on the story that had haunted various cultures and centuries. "Wandering Jew" was the name given by antebellum Charlestonians to an old misanthrope who, like Timon of Athens, lived in the elements and was often seen penciling what people took to be Hebrew on the sidewalks on Hasell Street, site of both a synagogue and a Catholic church. Another version of the story, which Bennett did not publish, included the old man's return from death; many reported seeing him wearing an iron crown in nearby St. George's Winyah Parish. "Charleston had completely forgotten the strange old man" by the time Bennett had come to town in the late 1890s. He had tracked down an old man who as a little boy had followed the strange little burial party to the cemetery, where fifty or so years later he showed Bennett "the sunken spot in the abandoned burying ground" at Rykersville and said, "There lies the man who was known throughout town as the Wandering Jew." [55]

Critics lauded Bennett for his dramatically charged writing, for his mingling of the profound and homely, and for his fantastic inventiveness. "These stories, macabre and always grotesque, are highly poetic and imaginative," raved the *New Yorker*. The critic marveled at the "charnel house feeling, mingling the ghostly with the homely," and the "magic of the language"; he compared Bennett's fabulous subjects and prose to *Seven Gothic Tales* by Isak Dinesen.[56]

The reviewer of the *Chicago Sun* added, "The collection . . . of folktales of Old Charleston proves that the hand of the seasoned maestro has lost none of its cunning or versatility," [57] and Robert Molloy praised Bennett in the *New York Times* for "the fastidious simplicity of his prose." He ended by calling Bennett the "dean of Charleston's writing fraternity." [58] Bennett was moved and gladdened by the triumph; adding to the joy were the birth of another daughter to Jane and the birth and christening of his son's child, also named John.

It was another generation being born and another generation meeting John Bennett through his writings; his previous books had appeared in the 1920s. When writer Harriette Kershaw Leiding had encouraged him back in 1911 to publish his folktales, he had laughed and "told her they are to be printed [only] in the New Jerusalem Free Press Millennium I, and afterward collected in the Angelic Pamphlet and distributed among the collect." [59]

But here they were printed, and praised, not just in New York but back in the city of the tales' origin.

Writing in the *South Carolina Historical and Genealogical Magazine*, Sam Stoney Jr. noted that "Mr. Bennett has at last given us these long-expected stories. Found at the turn of the century when the *on dit* of the ante-bellum times had fermented into fable and folklore, they have the strength and mellowness of properly aged wine. Like over-kept Madeira, they and the likes of them have faded in the more literate but less believing times that have followed. We can be thankful that Mr. Bennett bottled them at their prime and, more so, that he has now put them on our tables."[60]

More acclaim came when the public came to listen to Stoney and Josephine Pinckney discuss the book at the Charleston Free Library; the room was not just filled to capacity but overflowed. The local press covered the success like a valedictory. Bennett wrote Pinckney gratefully that the reception finally "wiped away the remnant of bewildered indignation which attended my public indictment forty years ago, as a damned Yankee writer who dared to suppose that the ladies of Charleston could possibly be interested in malodorous narrative dredged from the silurian depths of the town."[61]

He had been ahead of his time, but lived to see himself vindicated. Time had been cruel, then kind, but suddenly it came at him again, cruelly and vengefully. After The Doctor's success in May 1946, the years pounced on him with a terrible swiftness; his health deteriorated quickly. "I am not physically fit to undertake absence from these immediate surroundings," he wrote a friend in August of that year; a scant two years before he had been nimble enough to climb to the roof of 37 Legare Street and inspect wind damage to the chimneys.[62] "I am too deaf to engage in any but direct individual conversations; and dread that . . . incessant need to repeat, 'I beg your pardon, what was that? . . .' At the close of an evening's pleasant, familiar chitchat, I am in a dumb fury of weariness and disappointment."[63]

Unlike the patients of The Doctor to the Dead, he bowed to the inevitability that awaited him. "You may carve for my epitaph . . . 'Let the Old Gentleman Rest; He's Earned it.'" This he had written years earlier in jest, but now he meant it.[64] Yet characteristically he thought not of himself but of his family: "It is my hope not to grow irascible, crabbed and difficult in my family's life as I slip down the long hill."[65]

PART FOUR

# Winter

CHAPTER 22

# *An Epitaph*

I'm tired of Smith, Brown, and Jones
Who say they wish no line above
Their cast-off bones!

So Bennett wrote in his poem "I Want an Epitaph," published in 1927.
"Of many a life-long friend," he continued, he was "unforgetful and unfor-
got." [1] Nearly deaf, over eighty, almost blind in one eye, and suffering various ailments, he nevertheless kept up a cheerful façade for these friends
and his family, despite the troubles he was having. "I am having one fright-
ful time with a bunch of complicated chapters right in the middle" of
*Buckhorn Johnny,* he wrote; that "and family affairs, the world's worry, and
personal obnoxiousness due to advancing years make the composition of
light-hearted fun and nonsense more difficult than . . . of yore," he wrote to
a friend. And that reminded him of a funny story. Just a few days before, a
youngster had come to him with a telegram from his childhood friend Will
Poland, back in Chillicothe, commemorating the antics they had shared on
those Fourth of July celebrations eons ago in the "happy days of yore."
"Where, what, when and why was 'yore'?" the puzzled telegraph boy had
asked. "I sometimes wonder, myself," Bennett laughed, "looking back on the
incredible gaiety of youth." [2]

Continuing on with the manuscript he thought, "When it shall come
time that I perceive the truth to be that I shall never finish the work, . . . and
have accepted it, then perhaps I shall have both rest and . . . peace. . . . But
never until then." [3] He wrote his sister Martha in August 1947,

I find I need to rest frequently, to stretch out an hour or so, at almost any time, to
gather up energy and determination to get up and go about the task that waits. . . .

263

Morning is my poorest time for adventure into action. . . .

I gain substance as the day runs by; and afternoon often finds me ready and willing to get on with incompleted work, and, from time to time, lends a living sparkle to the ashes of intention. It is a grind, as you know . . . but for us there is only one course: to go on, to persevere, to work, and to hope. . . .

Instead of life growing simpler as we grow old, it seems only to grow more complex.

For me, Jane, her life and the future of her children; Jack's life, his little son, and his hopes and dreams of authorship; Sue's future, all these are with me always, involving my deep responsibility.

And, at my side, the toil of time, for her, as for me, having to be paid, goes Susan. I hate to see Time take its toll from all who are near and dear.

And with them, you, dear, finest, best and truest sister man ever had. God bless, guard and keep you now and ever more, amen.[4]

So he went on, but in August 1947 he collapsed. The following October he wrote, "The great depression has not yet left my mind nor the accompanying exhaustion of body. To get up in the morning to face the unprofitable day takes every ounce of will I possess." But he kept at it. "For the sake of my family and friends I manage somehow to keep a reasonably smiling face, and . . . a . . . serenity I do not feel. To add anxiety to the lives of those about us who have . . . perplexities of their own . . . is not according to Hoyle." He chose not "to parade one's own depression of mind and body."[5]

The depression was now the greatest he had ever experienced, for he acknowledged sadly, "I have been compelled . . . to abandon my effort to complete the book upon which I worked so long and with such bright hope, and to give up my dream of achieving a piece of writing that should crown . . . the fifty years of my life in the South."[6] There would be no *Buckhorn Johnny*.

It is hard to assess the manuscript he left; his wife Susan, typing it up after his death, lost some of its order and destroyed the original. What one sees are flashes of wonderful scenes, but all narrative drive is lost in the meandering lives of minor characters wandering in chapters that are aimless and prolix. He had lost all thread of the drama, the means of connecting the various pieces, but he went on making patches with no thought of creating a quilt. Susan Bennett thought that he failed because he could not picture his parents' love life, but that diagnosis seems amiss, for much of the action and text does not even happen in Chillicothe where John Briscoe Bennett and Eliza Jane McClintick met.

The giving up of his manuscript was perhaps his greatest disappointment; it came so late in life, when he was so weak, and its shadow was so deep, that it seemed he could never come out from its darkness. He had hoped at one point he could pass it, like a torch, to his son, who would finish the manuscript, but Jack, married now, was busy with another novel, based partially on the research Bennett had done on the Revolutionary War decades before. The working title was *Before the Tumult,* and Bennett, when he could focus at all, helped his son instead of dwelling on his own project.

He knew he did not have much time left. "If when the end comes, that which I set out to do is still undone, pray remember, friend, that, in one way or another, though by wrong roads, I did my best; and prithee, comrade on the way, make me an epitaph saying, 'Here lies a Man Who Did His Best despite well knowing It Was Not Enough.' You see, I make . . . frank confession. I am, when all is said and done, a very simple personality, grown somewhat cynical, but, keeping still, some sense of simple . . . honor, to temper the bitterness of long years of work and disappointment." [7]

There was another collapse in 1948; in November his son wrote, "He has been ill for over a year, has lost the use of his right hand, and partially of his legs. Fortunately, his mind is clear, and his spirits amazingly good, considering." Though ill, he could still keep up the pretense of happiness for his family. "His trouble is [his] years, pernicious anemia, and general arthritis. There is not hope of recovery, or even improvement. All of us here do the best we can from day to day." [8] But with his persistence, he rallied. "The invincible will to live," as he had said of his mother, "the will to live and not to die; a frail body which seemed from long acquaintanceship with pain to have formed a habit of resisting death" also worked for him. [9]

His laugh, though not last, sounded once again.

With the start of the 1950s, he got better. He continued writing articles for the *News and Courier* on numerous subjects, such as DuBose Heyward, Sammy Smalls and Porgy, and other bits of local history. The editors, realizing his fragility, wished him well on his eighty-eighth and ninetieth birthdays. He was not seen on the streets anymore, "his silvery hair and brisk walk . . . [once] a welcome sight to countless friends on the streets of Charleston," [10] but he was still handsome, with the "chiselled profile of a cameo." [11]

Visitors came to him instead. In 1951, he helped Frank Durham with his dissertation on DuBose Heyward, eventually to be published as the first biography of the man who wrote *Porgy*.[12] "So we once more, 'lent a hand,'" he noted happily.[13] The same year the University of South Carolina Press released a new edition of *Madame Margot* in two different bindings. Interviewed on his birthday in 1953, he presented well. His eyes behind gold-rimmed glasses were still bright and astonishingly blue; they, and the color of the shirts he had worn to set off his coloring, had been responsible for his nickname "The Blue Man."[14] Nobody in Charleston remembered or thought of him as being melancholy. "My son," he said at the interview, "has written a historical romance of South Carolina about 1765. I'm helping him with his history. It's carefully tied in with the events of the tale and is most intricate. He made the spider web, and now I'M stuck in it."[15]

In June 1956 his sister Martha was invited to a program at the Ross County Historical Society and wept with surprise at the ceremonies, complete with a message from the governor, in which the entire Bennett family was lauded for all its gifts to the town of Chillicothe; in 1966 a building on the Chillicothe Campus of Ohio University would be named for the family.[16]

Bennett had written Martha of a Charleston editorial listing him as "'one of the most thorough going Charlestonians.' Being a *Chillicothean* in a strange land," he felt, "it was . . . up to me to make myself respected . . . and to prove . . . that a 'damnyankee from Ohio' could take just such a position in a town . . . 'dubious of foreigners,' Northerners in particular." Despite that, he told her, "I have always preserved my old rubber-stamp address: 'John Bennett, of Chillicothe,' and have much amused my acquaintances in the post-office by back-stamping my letters with that memorial."[17]

Despite his age and the pain of arthritis, he still worked.

Some mornings . . . utterly unrested by the night's effort at sweet repose, I feel like throwing up the sponge; but some perpetual, persistent, bullheaded stubbornness refuses to give over the effort to do what I have determined by God's grace, to do: to finish the historical emendations and revisions in my boy's book.[18]

He was still also handling his business correspondence. In April 1956 he agreed to reduced royalties for *Barnaby Lee*, still in print, and upon whose profits he had married fifty-four years before. (He had refused to allow

editions of his works recast with easier words for modern readers, however.)
"For once—at least—I have remembered not to forget," he wrote on a card
he gave to his wife Susan on the last birthday of hers he witnessed.[19]

On Valentine's Day he was more loquacious. "Dear Old Lady," he wrote,

> I have told you how I first saw you, waving your hand to Col. Appleton as you
> walked past Mrs. Appleton's flower-bed on your way up the hill to cottage row. I
> have told you also of punching a hole in a penny for you. You stood at my right
> hand as I did so. That was a long time ago. I thought you the most interesting girl
> I had ever known. Those two incidents are as fresh in my mind as though it were
> yesterday. *You are still standing at my right hand* and are still the most interesting woman
> I have ever known.[20]

Never could he forget his love for her and her willingness to cast her lot
in with his, a struggling young man from Ohio come to the strange antique
city. In September 1956 he was at work on his son's book; he had Christmas
with his family and died December 28.

DuBose Heyward and Hervey Allen had died years before.[21] Yates Snowden, Walter Mayrant, Francis Nipson, Caesar Grant, Ned Jennings, and
others were all gone too. Only Martha, still living at 76 West Second Street,
was left of his family. The Southern literary renaissance and the Charleston
movement were things of the past, being written about by scholars and
graduate students. Yet children were still charmed by *Master Skylark*; his tales
of nonsense and silhouettes betrayed no bitterness.

Two cities, Chillicothe and Charleston, had been changed by him. Those
he had encouraged and brought along had won prizes, contributed works
like *Anthony Adverse* and *Porgy and Bess.* Countless others had felt his comfort
and kindness, had laughed and been touched and helped and moved to
gladness. With time, he would be lauded for his contributions as storyteller,
historian, linguist, artist, folklorist, and social activist. "A hundred years
from now, dear heart . . . It will not matter," he had written once, but his
contributions *did* matter; his works *did* last: his cities showed his handiwork,
and one hundred years after its original appearance, *Master Skylark* was still in
print; *The Doctor to the Dead* was republished and scholars and writers continue
to consult his notes and build articles and books and knowledge on the
scraps he collected and left.[22] All attest to the achievements of the "real and
original" John Bennett.[23]

Yet the fact that brought him the greatest satisfaction was the one he expressed again and again, stated most earnestly perhaps in a work he attributed to his alter ego, Alexander Findlay McClintock,

> *Write on my gravestone:*
> *Without Education, this Man studied Friendship*
> *And in that was Erudite, Wealthy and Glad.*
> *You who have any more*
> *Pause here for a Moment.*[24]

And those who do, those who come upon his grave in Charleston's Magnolia Cemetery see carved on his own modest stone, not those words, but others of utter simplicity:

> *John Bennett*
> *1865–1956*
> *son of*
> *Eliza J. McClintick and John H. B. Bennett*

With the noting of those names it was as if a dream had passed and he was back in the place of his birth: Chillicothe, Ohio, where he had first known happiness.

# Notes

The vast majority of papers by and about John Bennett are in the collections of the South Carolina Historical Society in Charleston. The Bennett materials are so vast that locating a particular item can often be challenging. As the archivist for the collection, I followed the original order that had been started by Bennett himself or his family. This entailed filing materials in a number of different series: there is, for example, a series called professional correspondence, a series called personal correspondence, a series of family letters, etc. In some of my footnotes, I have stated in which series a particular letter may be found. The term "John Bennett to his family" refers to the series of "Sunday Budgets," those multipage letters sent in carbon to various family members and friends around the globe, although some individual letters to his wife and other close family members are filed in that series as well. As for his reminiscences, they are grouped by subject: general reminiscences of various episodes from his life, reminiscences of Charleston, and of the Poetry Society. Because he was such a reviser, often the same episode, event, or thought can be found in dozens of slightly varying versions. The following abbreviations are used in the notes:

DHP    DuBose Heyward Papers
JBP    John Bennett Papers
RCHS    Ross County Historical Society, Chillicothe, Ohio
SCHS    South Carolina Historical Society
SCL    South Caroliniana Library, Columbia, South Carolina

## Introduction

1. "Distinguished Charleston Author Dies," *Charleston (S.C.) Evening Post*, 31 December 1956.

2. *Charleston News and Courier*, 18 December 1956.

3. Douglas Street, "John Bennett," in *Dictionary of Literary Biography* 42 (1985): 83; Cornelia Meigs et al., *A Critical History of Children's Literature* (New York: Macmillan, 1953), 391.

4. John Bennett, "Story of Forgotten Bells, Sacrificed to Confederate Guns," *Charleston News and Courier,* 12 December 1937.

### Prologue

1. John Bennett to his family, 10 August 1941, JBP, SCHS. Bennett calls him "Millard" Brand. A native of New Jersey, Brand wrote novels and poetry and was co-author of the screenplay for *The Snake Pit.* He became an editor at Crown Publishers.

2. John Bennett's notes for a lecture to the P.T.A., Autobiographical papers, JBP, SCHS.

### CHAPTER 1. *Buckhorn Johnny*

1. Bennett family genealogical papers, JBP, SCHS.

2. *Buckhorn Johnny* typescript, JBP, SCHS. Bennett family genealogies disagree on the order of names. Sometimes Bennett's father is noted as John Henry Briscoe Bennett; at other times it is John Briscoe Henry Bennett. He is called "John Briscoe" here to more easily differentiate him from his sons John and Henry.

3. *Buckhorn Johnny* typescript, JBP, SCHS. The basis for the story of Buckhorn Johnny is present in many of Bennett's letters. See his letter to George C. Tyler, 10 January 1925, JBP, SCHS; and the letter to his family, 21 August 1927 (page 5), regarding his grandmother's marriage to Hilary Talbot, JBP, SCHS. Bennett also told other versions of the tale that contradict the version told here.

4. *Buckhorn Johnny* typescript, JBP, SCHS.

5. *Buckhorn Johnny* typescript, JBP, SCHS.

6. *Buckhorn Johnny* typescript, JBP, SCHS.

7. *Buckhorn Johnny* typescript, JBP, SCHS. In an alternate version, Bennett states that Thomas ran away from the family while still in Virginia.

8. This appears to be the way Bennett planned to tell the story, but real life seems to have been different. Family genealogies show that Laura was not totally separated from the family, but rejoined them in Chillicothe and married Anvil James, a kinsman.

9. *Buckhorn Johnny* typescript, JBP, SCHS.

10. John Bennett to I. Jenkins Mikell, 20 April 1923, JBP, SCHS.

11. *Buckhorn Johnny* typescript, JBP, SCHS.

12. "Dr. James Woodrow spent his boyhood in Chillicothe, Ohio and remembered my father as a 'handsome, dashing, popular young man.' I met him in Charleston in the winter of 1898–99 at Maj. A. T. Smythe's home. . . . Woodrow Wilson himself visited the home of Mr. Thos. Woodrow, in Chillicothe, several times when

I was a boy." Annotation by Bennett on page 63 of Scrapbook Incidental History of Charleston, JBP, SCHS. Woodrow Wilson's mother lived in Chillicothe.

13. John Bennett to James I. McClintock, 29 January 1945, JBP, SCHS.

14. John Bennett to Susan Smythe, n.d. (ca. March 1899), JBP, SCHS.

15. Reminiscences of John Bennett, JBP, SCHS.

16. Reminiscences of John Bennett, JBP, SCHS.

17. John Bennett, *Master Skylark: A Story of Shakspere's Time* (New York: The Century Company, 1897), 17.

18. Bennett repeated this story over and over again in his correspondence; but his father's obituary in the Chillicothe *News Advertiser* on 23 March 1903 states that he saved all his stock and was in business ten days later. Bennett did correct and question many parts of the obituary, however (JBP, SCHS).

19. Reminiscences of John Bennett, JBP, SCHS.

20. According to a Bennett genealogy the children were: Thomas James (1849–52), Elizabeth McClintick (1851–52), Anna McClintock (1853–55), Alice, William van Sweringen (1858–61), Margaret Evans (1860–61), Henry Holcomb, John, and Martha Trimble.

CHAPTER 2. *Yore*

1. Reminiscences of John Bennett, JBP, SCHS.

2. Reminiscences of John Bennett, JBP, SCHS.

3. Reminiscences of John Bennett, JBP, SCHS. This story, as well as many of Bennett's childhood reminiscences, appears in "John Bennett of Chillicothe," by Janie M. Smith in the *Horn Book Magazine* 19, no. 6 (November–December 1943), 427–34. The article was reprinted and also appeared as "John Bennett of Charleston" in the February ca. 1944 program of the Carolina Art Association. A letter Bennett wrote describing his early school years is printed in Amelia Hydell, *School Desk Memories of Chillicothe's John Bennett* (Chillicothe: Dave Webb Private Press, 1940).

4. Janie Smith, "The Young John Bennett," typescript in the vertical file of the Charleston County Public Library (ca. 1937).

5. Reminiscences of John Bennett, JBP, SCHS.

6. John Bennett to J. W. Raper, 8 December 1945, JBP, SCHS.

7. Reminiscences of John Bennett, JBP, SCHS.

8. John Bennett to his family, 7 February 1937, JBP, SCHS.

9. From fragments of a biographical essay Bennett wrote about himself, in the third person, for a publisher (JBP, SCHS).

10. Reminiscences of John Bennett, JBP, SCHS.

11. Reminiscences of John Bennett, JBP, SCHS.

12. Reminiscences of John Bennett, JBP, SCHS.

13. John Bennett to Frank P. O'Donnell, 18 Nov. 1925, JBP, SCHS. This remarkable letter of fifteen legal-sized, single-spaced typed pages was written in response to the request from O'Donnell, of Chillicothe, for biographical information on Bennett to report to the town's "Current Topics Club." It is a valuable source of information on Bennett's life and how he viewed those events. The letter was published in the Chillicothe papers, but all the quotes are from the typescript letter.

14. Bennett to O'Donnell, 18 Nov. 1925.

15. John Bennett on Biographical Request form for the A. N. Marquis Company, JBP, SCHS. See also Janie Smith's article "The Young John Bennett" about the FBS. On this same form, Bennett listed "The Wednesday Nighter" meetings in Charleston, a reference to his literary "fanging sessions" with DuBose Heyward and Hervey Allen.

16. "Perry Bowsher was hanged for [the] brutal murder of two old people. His body was exhumed by the doctors of the town and carefully dissected in a vacant room in the vast unoccupied upper floor of the Clinton House. His skull was taken possession of by one of the surgeons engaged in the exhumation; the remainder of his skeleton was spread to bleach and to be picked clean of all shreds of integument by the ants, upon a shed-roof in the back yard of Dr. Jonath B. Scearce's office and home. I have never known who took them but the smaller bones of hands and feet soon disappeared. . . . The smaller bones of the skeleton continued to vanish, until there remained only the greater bones of the skeletal frame. I took a basket, climbed the back fence, crossed the ice-house roof to the shed, and carried off all the remaining portions of Perry Bowsher. The thigh-bones appeared on[c]e in public, in connection with a skull borrowed from Dr. Wm. Waddle, and photographed for their grisly intent as a centerpiece in a group photograph of our boys' club, the F.B.S. That was their one and only appearance. . . . For, after a very brief possession and study as intriguing samples of human anatomy, I buried the poor devil's remains in our backyard, at 76 West Second [S]treet, about where my sister later had a war-garden, just beyond our seckel pear tree, and there to this day, and the future, the bones of that misguided fellow remain, slowly returning to their original elements, earth to earth and dust to dust" (Reminiscences of John Bennett, JBP, SCHS).

17. John Bennett, "John Bennett Recalls Days Passed Beneath the Sycamores Along the West Bank Beaches of the Scioto," *Chillicothe (Ohio) News Advertiser*, 4 March 1926.

18. Bennett, "John Bennett Recalls Days Passed Beneath the Sycamores."

19. Reminiscences of John Bennett, JBP, SCHS. "I began . . . at a kindergarten conducted for the neighborhood children, by Miss Anna Welsh. . . . Willy Poland attended, my earliest friend; before our mutual memory recalls the event, Willy and I were found paddling happily together in a large mud puddle in the street; the

paddling that followed was not so happy; but it cemented our lifelong friendship to an unbreakable and unchanging bond."

20. Reminiscences of John Bennett, JBP, SCHS.

21. Reminiscences of John Bennett, JBP, SCHS.

22. John Bennett to J. T. Gittman, 12 Sept. 1945, JBP, SCHS.

23. Reminiscences of John Bennett, JBP, SCHS.

24. Reminiscences of John Bennett, JBP, SCHS.

25. Reminiscences of John Bennett, JBP, SCHS. He'd use the maxim of every dog having its day again in *Barnaby Lee* (New York: The Century Company, 1902), 10.

26. John Bennett, "What a Free Library Did for a Bunch of Small Town Boys," *Charleston News and Courier*, 21 December 1941.

27. Bennett told the story of this relic numerous times, in interviews, published and unpublished reminiscences, and letters (Reminiscences of John Bennett, JBP, SCHS).

28. John Bennett wrote this as a letter to a young child; various other drafts are also in the reminiscences of John Bennett, JBP, SCHS. The story of his illness and his convalescence is also covered in some detail in Janie Smith, "An Author and Children in the South," *The Horn Book* 18, no. 2 (March–April 1942), 83–87.

29. John Bennett to E. Y. Chapin, 17 Nov. 1932, JBP, SCHS.

30. Bennett to Chapin, 17 Nov. 1932.

31. Bennett to O'Donnell, 18 Nov. 1925.

32. Bennett to O'Donnell, 18 Nov. 1925.

33. Bennett to O'Donnell, 18 Nov. 1925.

34. Reminiscences of John Bennett, JBP, SCHS.

35. Reminiscences of John Bennett, JBP, SCHS.

CHAPTER 3. *The Black Arts*

1. John Bennett to Frank P. O'Donnell, 18 Nov. 1925, JBP, SCHS.

2. "Went to work as a reporter on [Ross County] Register, under Will Waddle, City Editor, O. B. Chapman, Proprietor, June 4, 1883." Annotation by John Bennett in scrapbook called "Beginnings" 1, JBP, SCHS.

3. Born in Lynn, Massachusetts, in 1859, Lummis soon after this time with Bennett went west, where he founded and edited *Out West Magazine* and was librarian at the Los Angeles Public Library. Bennett was to see him again in 1924, before Lummis's death in 1928.

4. Reminiscences of John Bennett, JBP, SCHS.

5. Reminiscences of John Bennett, JBP, SCHS.

6. Interview by author with John Bennett's daughter, Susan Bennett, 11 November 1977.

7. Reminiscences of John Bennett, JBP, SCHS (21-129-01). See also a clipping in scrapbook "Beginnings" 2, JBP, SCHS. "Entered the school Nov. 1st 1883. It closed on March 14, 1884." Annotation by JB on clipping.

8. Bennett to O'Donnell, 18 Nov. 1925, JBP, SCHS. For a drawing by John Bennett showing where he stayed in "Major Wm E. Strong's house, Maplewood, Ohio," see Beginnings scrapbook 56, JBP, SCHS.

CHAPTER 4. *Cold Courage: Famous to Myself*

1. Reminiscences of John Bennett, JBP, SCHS.

2. Reminiscences of John Bennett, notes for talk to Library Institute Workers, JBP, SCHS.

3. "To give him as much happiness and as much intimate knowledge of what I am doing & of the friends who come, is, of course, the main object of my life" (Martha Trimble Bennett to Susan Smythe Bennett, 22 November 1953, JBP, SCHS).

4. Reminiscences of John Bennett, JBP, SCHS. Elsewhere, in a letter to his wife (21 July 1913), Bennett noted that she suffered "from things never to happen and her own timidity" (JBP, SCHS).

5. Reminiscences of John Bennett, JBP, SCHS. In the sentimental prose of the day, he wrote of their rapprochement, "I remember the night I met him on the old turnpike, in an agony of doubt, galloping into the hills to make sure I was not lying somewhere there in the night, injured and unable to make my way home. [Bennett had gone to a nearby town and his horse had thrown him.] I remember . . . how my throat choked as he called out through the dark, 'Is that you, Johnny? . . . 'Never again from that day to the end did a doubt of his . . . devotion . . . shadow our regard for one another." This "mutual admiration and confident trust . . . made . . . both our lives better . . . and we rejoiced in each other's achievements . . . as we trudged on, as he . . . said, with the tinge of romance which sweetens life, so, 'On our way to Heights that are Higher.'"

6. Reminiscences of John Bennett, JBP, SCHS.

7. "Began work as a reporter on the Daily News May 8th, 1884 under E. D. Alberti; Rufus Putnam, Proprietor, Hon. John. H. Putnam, 1st U.S. Consul-General to Honolulu, 'General Mentor.'" Annotation by JB in Beginnings scrapbook 2, JBP, SCHS.

8. Reminiscences of John Bennett, JBP, SCHS.

9. Reminiscences of John Bennett, JBP, SCHS.

10. Reminiscences of John Bennett, JBP, SCHS.

11. Reminiscences of John Bennett, JBP, SCHS.

12. Reminiscences of John Bennett, JBP, SCHS.

13. Reminiscences of John Bennett, JBP, SCHS.

14. Reminiscences of John Bennett, JBP, SCHS.

15. Reminiscences of John Bennett, JBP, SCHS.

16. "My hat was full of holes"—John Bennett to Susan Smythe, 8 December 1900. Descriptions of turning hats, inking seams, etc. are among the reminiscences of John Bennett, JBP, SCHS.

17. Reminiscences of John Bennett, JBP, SCHS. This fragment is entitled "Resemblances, January 1, 1900, Chillicothe."

18. Reminiscences of John Bennett, JBP, SCHS.

19. This anecdote was published in a variety of formats, with different names, such as Billy Wiggers; Bennett contributed it in one format to a young cadet at The Citadel Military College of South Carolina in Charleston when the cadet, Bill Geer, asked him for a contribution. See *The Shako*, autumn 1934. According to his letter of 30 June 1929, the politician's name was Willis Wiggins (JBP, SCHS).

20. "Tom Gordon: Or the Haps and Mishaps of a Boarding School Boy," by "Bee Jay," began in Burton Stevenson's *Boy's Own* magazine in December 1886; it was published monthly until June when the notice "Owing to the serious illness of the author . . . we are obliged to go to press without it" appeared; it continued again in August and finished in November. See the Beginnings scrapbook, JBP, SCHS. Earlier in 1883, according to an annotation in the Beginnings scrapbook 3, he "sent 'Kiah the Case' to Frank Tousey of Tousey & Small's Publishing House in September 1883. My first attempt at a 'novel'—a dime novel at that. Rejected promptly—how lucky!" (JBP, SCHS).

21. Reminiscences of John Bennett, JBP, SCHS.

22. John Bennett to John Briscoe Bennett, 13 October 1898, JBP, SCHS.

23. John Bennett to John Briscoe Bennett, 24 March 1896, JBP, SCHS.

24. John Bennett to John Briscoe Bennett, 13 October 1898, JBP, SCHS.

25. Reminiscences of John Bennett, JBP, SCHS. It is labeled "SOMEWHERE, SOMEHOW, SOMEDAY: How a Well-Known Author Meant to Become an Artist, but Turned out a Writer" (JBP, SCHS).

26. Reminiscences of John Bennett, JBP, SCHS. This rival paper was run by George Tyler, the father of his boyhood friend George C. Tyler. Bennett treated the competition between the two papers lightheartedly in "How the Howler Rushed the Growler: A Comical Tragedy," *New York Journalist*, 13 December 1890; "Learning to Write" notebook 108½, JBP, SCHS.

27. Reminiscences of John Bennett, JBP, SCHS.

28. Reminiscences of John Bennett, JBP, SCHS.

29. Reminiscences of John Bennett; also John Bennett to Frank P. O'Donnell, 18 November 1925, JBP, SCHS.

30. Reminiscences of John Bennett, JBP, SCHS. See T. R. Waring papers, box 5, SCHS. In gathering information for Bennett's obituary, Waring noted that Bennett went to inspect a real-estate development and wrote an article saying it was no good. The ensuing wrath of the backer caused him to be fired. Also an article in the *Columbia (S.C.) State*, 5 January 1931, in John Bennett's Work notebook B, page 82, JBP, SCHS, states "Being ousted from his editorial position by capitalists whom the paper had opposed, Mr. Bennett went to Columbus, Ohio." Also, *Charleston News and Courier*, 11 December 1938.

CHAPTER 5. *"The Fragrance of Success"*

1. "This is the first story I ever sold to a magazine. . . . In fact it was the first piece of fiction outside newspaper 'stuff.' I felt fame and fortune were at the door" (annotation by JB in "Learning to Write" scrapbook 133, JBP, SCHS). It was accepted 28 September 1889, paid for in January of the following year, and apparently not published until 1891. See *New York Times Book Review*, 7 Feb. 1937, and John Bennett to his family, 21 Feb. 1937. According to Bennett, it was reprinted as no. 31 of "Choice Selections for Reading and Recitation" or "One Hundred Choice Selections" by the Penn Publishing Company, ca. 1897.

2. Beginnings scrapbook 15, JBP, SCHS. He won it in May 1889.

3. From the masthead of *Light* magazine (Beginnings scrapbook 33, JBP, SCHS). Confusing matters is the fact there was another magazine by the name of *Light* associated with Bennett. It was the small Chillicothe magazine first called *Boy's Own*, edited by his friend and associate Burton Stevenson, which had published Bennett's first serial, "Tom Gordon," in its pages. Bennett did the design for the masthead of *Light*, ca. 1889, which he noted was his first photo-engraved drawing; he also contributed poetry to it. See Beginnings scrapbook 10, 15, JBP, SCHS.

4. See article clipped from unknown publication, Work notebook B, page 3, JBP, SCHS.

5. John Bennett to Frank P. O'Donnell, 18 November 1925, JBP, SCHS.

6. This paraphrases some miscellaneous reminiscences of Bennett. "Roost" is mentioned in several of his reminiscences and letters and in the brochure "The Flag Goes By," by Henry Holcomb Bennett, John Bennett, and Martha Trimble Bennett (Chillicothe, Ohio: Ross County Historical Society, 1956).

7. One of his early drawings, "Abijah's Fourth of July," was reprinted in *Modern Maturity* magazine in the June–July issue of 1966; and "The Snake Charmer's Tale," carrying the date of "[18]96" was reprinted on page 83 of "The City and Country

American Elsewhen Almanac" of 1979. Several of his later silhouette designs have also been used by Piccolo Spoleto and South Carolina Historical Society publications. In a letter to Frank P. O'Donnell, Bennett wrote, "Jokes I perpetrated then [1890s] I still see going the rounds, and verses [I see] sold and resold to newer editors ignorant of what has been beyond the few years of their youth" (18 Nov. 1925, JBP, SCHS).

8. Reminiscences of John Bennett, JBP, SCHS.

9. Reminiscences of John Bennett, JBP, SCHS.

10. John Bennett to his family, 31 October 1937, JBP, SCHS.

11. "Darn your old cocaine bottle, Jack, I like you" (Jack Appleton to John Bennett, 30 October 1893, JBP, SCHS).

12. "I visualize much of all that I write. . . . I would rather draw than write, and hence SEE first what I then endeavor to express in words" (John Bennett to Nellie [Ward?], 16 October 1920, JBP, SCHS).

13. A copy of the poem, reprinted in an Oregon newspaper, is in the Beginnings scrapbook 50, JBP, SCHS. According to Bennett, it was first printed in 1892, then reprinted in the *National Humane Review* in 1931 and *The Cat in Verse*, ed. Carolyn Wells and Louella Everett (Boston: Little Brown, 1935). See also the "Early Works" scrapbook 66, JBP, SCHS. In the Boston *Transcript*, 30 April 1932, Bennett noted that the cat was based on his cat Dennis. "He was my companion by day, my alarm clock in the morning, and a curiously interested, unobservant and unintrusive spectator of my cartoon work upon my drawing table, where he would sit motionless for hours." Bennett used the poem again in "Queen Kitty-Cat," published in *The Electric Spark*, Early Works scrapbook 106, JBP, SCHS.

14. "That was the first time the idea had occurred to me that I might possibly do something better than newspaper work" (John Bennett to cousin Dorothy Bishop, 30 December 1938, JBP, SCHS). Bennett told this anecdote in similar ways countless times, including in his letter to O'Donnell, 18 November 1925, JBP, SCHS.

15. Quoted in Cornelia Meigs et al., *A Critical History of Children's Literature* (New York: Macmillan, 1953), 284.

16. In many of his reminiscences, Bennett said "The Barber" was the first piece sold, but "How Little Peter Won a Kingdom" was purchased in Feb. 1891, to appear in February 1893, with illustrations by Daniel Beard. "The Barber of Sari-Ann," with illustrations, was accepted 19 June 1891; it was revised, at the request of the editors, to be used in the November issue. Bennett was asked if he had anything else. "The Knight, The Yeoman, and the Fair Damosel" was purchased November 1891. The verse "Ye Most Veracious Tale" was sent before October 1891; "Ben Ali, the Egyptian," with fifteen silhouettes, was received 3 Feb. 1892, and accepted 17 Feb. 1892. "A Persian Columbus" was accepted 10 June 1892; "Granger Grind (and Farmer

Mellow)," with words and music, was accepted 5 January 1893; "It Wasn't That Kind," with two silhouettes that were revised by request, was rejected in Feb. 1893; "Abijah's Fourth of July" was bought 12 June 1893; "Fritz the Master Fiddler" was accepted in July 1893; "The Pig-tail of Ah Lee Ben Loo" was accepted 29 December 1893; "Three Wise Owls" was accepted in June 1896; "The Snake Charmer" was accepted in August 1896 (*St. Nicholas* correspondence, JBP, SCHS).

17. Bennett recounted numerous times how he came to write the poem, but perhaps the most honest and complete one is contained in a letter he wrote to Yates Snowden, 1 November 1932, published in *Two Scholarly Friends*, a collection of the two men's correspondence ably edited by Mary Crow Anderson (Columbia: University of South Carolina Press, 1993). It is one of the few references to the broken love affair of his that prompted it: "She was, indeed, an Experience, rather than an individual . . . a young ideal whose pedestal had crumbled into the dirt. . . . The taste was pretty bitter." He began it on the back of an envelope and reworked the phrase from an older song, "'A Hundred Years Hence,' a sardonic and cynical piece of verse, which, if memory serves me rightly, had wide popularity at and after the close of the 18th century, in England and America." Bennett's father often quoted it "in moments of catastrophe."

18. Bennett to O'Donnell, 18 Nov. 1925, JBP, SCHS. Others also set it to music, including Paul Ambrose, published by Arthur Schmidt in 1914. McCoy's was in 1910 and Mrs. Bond's in 1915. In 1942, copyright was released and it was set to music again by Lewis M. Isaacs. Mrs. Bond also set Bennett's later poem "Today" to music, and it was recorded on record, as was "In a Rose Garden." Earlier poems of his were set to music, as well. His "Tell Mother I Am Coming Home" and his "In the Dear Long Ago" were set to music in 1893 by Cincinnati composer W. T. Church and published by the John Church Co. (Beginnings scrapbook 47, JBP, SCHS).

19. Yates Snowden, before meeting Bennett personally, would reprint the poem in the Charleston paper under the title "In a Charleston Rose Garden." Bennett's fiancée would point out Snowden to him the first time they saw each other.

20. Again, Bennett would frequently list all the publications that reprinted it, with and without his permission. One list is in his Work notebook B, page 92, JBP, SCHS; another is in his correspondence with Carrie Jacobs Bond, JBP, SCHS. One edition it appears in is the thirteenth and centennial edition of Bartlett's *Familiar Quotations* (Boston: Little, Brown, 1955), 810. The work was so well known it was often pirated and spoofed, as C. L. Edson did in "Nothing Really Matters": "A thousand years from now, dear heart / The world will never know / Whether I took a shave today / Or let my whiskers grow" (*Rhymes & Circuses* [Charleston: Southern Printing and Publishing Co., 1924], 26). Edson syndicated a newspaper

column from Charleston and included a tribute to the city in his anonymous autobiography, *The Great American Ass* (New York: Brentano's, 1926).

21. Bennett to O'Donnell, 18 November 1925, JBP, SCHS.

22. An unidentified clipping in the Beginnings scrapbook, page 40, JBP, SCHS, notes that the volume "is illustrated by representations of skeletons, bones, implements, and ornaments found in the mounds." Bennett notes it was his first book illustration; he was paid $210. "*The Critic* called my work careful and conscientious; *The Art Amateur* found fault with my criticism on bone carving." He further noted, "Winter of '91–2, Morehead offered me artist and photographer's position on expedition to Arizona, New Mexico pueblos and cliff-dwellings for the 'Illustrated American.' Declined. Expedition failed in the field. Was subsequently offered position as field photographer and draughtsman with expedition to Yucatan; declined; expedition broke down, with several deaths from jungle fever."

23. Fremont Arford, "Ohio Notes," *Western Journalist*, undated clipping in "Beginnings" scrapbook 32, JBP, SCHS.

24. *The (New York) Journalist*, vol. 17.5, 15 April 1893 ("Beginnings" scrapbook 48, JBP, SCHS).

25. John Bennett to Jack Appleton, 26 February 1894, JBP, SCHS. Most of the letters quoted here are carbons of typescripts Bennett kept. This one to Appleton is an original typescript, so I have assumed it was not sent.

26. Bennett to Appleton, 26 February 1894.

27. Bennett to Appleton, 26 February 1894.

28. Bennett to Appleton, 26 February 1894.

29. John Bennett to Alexander Lawton, 2 April 1917, "L" correspondence, JBP, SCHS.

30. Reminiscences of John Bennett, JBP, SCHS.


CHAPTER 6. *A Transcendent Word*

1. John Bennett to Yates Snowden, 30 August 1927. Published in Mary Crow Anderson, *Two Scholarly Friends* (Columbia: Univ. of South Carolina Press, 1993), 256–57. There is another reason to doubt some of the veracity of this tale—he passes this visit off as his first one to the Appletons; but from his own notes, correspondence, and correspondence of the Appletons, it is obvious that Bennett first went to the mountains of West Virginia in the summer of 1893; he wrote Appleton the very dejected letter in February of 1894 quoted at length in the previous chapter. The following summer he went back, and it was this second visit that he seems to be describing here. Perhaps, looking back over the years, he combined the two summers, recollecting that his first visit brought on the dramatic

change. Some of the following quotes are from the first summer he spent at the Springs.

2. Bennett to Snowden, 30 August 1927.

3. Bennett to Snowden, 30 August 1927.

4. Jane H. Pease and William H. Pease, *A Family of Women: The Carolina Petigrus in Peace and War* (Chapel Hill: University of North Carolina Press, 1999).

5. The *Chillicothe Daily News* carried the following item under the head "This is a Pair of Jacks": "Mr. Jack Bennett left on the southbound N & W Friday night for Salt Sulphur Springs, W. Va., where he will be the guest of his friend, Mr. Jack Appleton. Mr. Appleton met Mr. Bennett at Fort Spring . . . and the two, with characteristic humor, sent a telegram to this city, reading, 'We have met the enemy and they are ours. The two Jacks.'" Undated, but ca. 1893 clipping in Beginnings scrapbook 50, JBP, SCHS.

6. John Bennett to Martha Trimble Bennett, 28 July 1893, JBP, SCHS.

7. John Bennett to John Briscoe Bennett, 6 August 1893, JBP, SCHS.

8. John Bennett to Martha Trimble Bennett, 28 July 1893, JBP, SCHS.

9. Bennett to Snowden, 30 August 1927.

10. Bennett to Snowden, 30 August 1927.

11. In the same letter to Yates Snowden, Bennett wrote that the *Independent* published it in 1892; wanting to share the lyric with others, Snowden often reprinted the poem on a broad sheet and passed on the information that it was published in that year. (He also reprinted it in 1929, if not before.) But Bennett was obviously faulty in his memory; the poem was not accepted by the *Independent* until 13 November 1894 and not published until 1895 (Beginnings scrapbook 52, JBP, SCHS).

> His feet are winged with living flame,
> These are the hills the Lord hath made
> That men may fear him, unafraid.
> Up through the gateway of the skies
> Their purple slopes of peace arise
> Like sunlit paths to paradise.
>
> Range after range in grand accord
> They stand like altars of the Lord,
> Mute Sinais of divine decree,
> Whose silent heights shall ever be
> A decalogue of life to me.
>
> For from them faith doth fill like dew
> As well on Gentile as on Jew;

And through their calm rolls up a cry
Of distant valleys chanting high:
"The King of Kings is Passing By."

The Lord hath left His secret place;
The heavens veil His dazzling face;
The waters are before Him bowed;
And on the mountains, hoary-browed,
The herald thunder shouts aloud.

"The Lord is walking in His world
With banner-clouds of storm unfurled;
His feet are winged with living flame,
And trumpet-winds abroad proclaim
The deathless glory of His name!"

Arise, my soul, from trouble free!
The best of life is yet to be.
The Lord thy God is living still;
The valley yet shall find the hill
Up which a way awaits thy will!

Arise, my soul, confiding stand
Within the hollow of His hand
Who was before the Earth and Sea,
Is now, and evermore shall be
The Lord of All Infinity.

12. Reminiscences of John Bennett, JBP, SCHS.

13. John Bennett quoted in the *Columbia (S.C.) State*, 9 July 1922. See Work notebook C, 10, JBP, SCHS.

14. See chapter 4, note 5, for a description of their reconciliation.

15. John Bennett to Susan Appleton, 1 October 1932, JBP, SCHS.

16. Reminiscences of John Bennett, JBP, SCHS.

17. Reminiscences of John Bennett, JBP, SCHS.

18. "Joseph Russell Taylor, later head of the English Department of the Ohio State University, a short, fair, plump, natural-born comedian . . . played 'Uncle Tom.' The savage part of Simon Legree . . . was taken by Jack Appleton, a handsome, talented, lovable . . . lad . . . the very opposite of the original brute. . . . Clad in immaculate white linen, armed with a slender riding crop, he produced a howl

of delight by his presentation. . . . Henry Bennett . . . gave a unique interpretation of Topsy. . . . 'Little Eva' was played by Charles Smith of Boston . . . six feet tall with a fine black moustache" (newspaper clipping in Work notebook C, 61–62, JBP, SCHS).

19. John Bennett to Martha Trimble Bennett, 28 July 1893, JBP, SCHS.

20. Reminiscences of John Bennett, JBP, SCHS.

21. He referred to his dying but dauntless friend in an annotation in his Learning to Write scrapbook 129, JBP, SCHS.

22. It was printed first in the first *Year Book of the Poetry Society of South Carolina.* It also was included in various editions of Bartlett's *Familiar Quotations,* and in the early 1920s it was attributed to Berton Brawley, a newspaper poet whose verses were syndicated in newspapers around the country. (See the *Charleston News and Courier* 3 December 1922 article in Work notebook B, 29, JBP, SCHS.) Bennett acidly commented that Brawley did not deny the attribution to him. Others, such as Bennett, wrote in to say it was not so. The comment about his motto is in one of his reminiscences.

23. Reminiscences of John Bennett, JBP, SCHS.

24. The Ross County Historical Society issued a pamphlet on Flag Day, 14 June, 1956, to commemorate Henry Holcomb Bennett's most famous poem. John Bennett wrote a small essay on its origin, and his sister, Martha Trimble Bennett, wrote a small essay on its author. Bennett wrote, "I remember . . . how he composed it, entire, lying on the day-bed, the old 'lounge' in Mother's room; how he rose quickly, went directly up to 'the Roost,' and after quite a while came down, a bit dishevelled with intense production and singularly simple and direct creation, and handed me the first typed draft for my criticism, with one or two suggested verbal alterations already noted in pencil by himself."

25. Reminiscences of John Bennett, JBP, SCHS.

CHAPTER 7. *Master Skylark*

1. See chapter 5, note 16. "The publication of 'The Barber of Sari Ann' in November 1891, brought a request; 'We are tempted to ask if you have not on your table something of a similar sort, with or without silhouettes, which you could send immediately for use in December or January St. Nicholas. We should be glad to see any funny verses or pictures you may have ready to submit without delay" (Reminiscences of John Bennett, JBP, SCHS).

2. Reminiscences of John Bennett, JBP, SCHS.

3. W. F. Clarke to John Bennett, 6 June 1896, *St. Nicholas* correspondence, JBP, SCHS.

4. According to Bennett's daughter Susan, Henry Holcomb Bennett was en-

gaged once for a year; Alice was engaged for thirteen years. Martha Trimble Bennett was never engaged. Interview with Susan Bennett, 11 November 1977.

5. Martha Trimble Bennett to John Bennett, 21 April 1895, JBP, SCHS.

6. John Bennett to "My dear Miss Dixie [Ancrum]," 16 November 1932, JBP, SCHS.

7. John Bennett, *Master Skylark: A Story of Shakspere's Time* (New York: The Century Company, 1897), 55–56.

8. Reminiscences of John Bennett, JBP, SCHS.

9. John Bennett to Frank P. O'Donnell, 18 Nov. 1925, JBP, SCHS.

10. Bennett, *Master Skylark*, 2.

11. Bennett to "My dear Miss Dixie [Ancrum]," 16 Nov. 1932.

12. Reminiscences of John Bennett.

13. John Bennett to George C. Tyler, 10 January 1925, JBP, SCHS.

14. Bennett to "My dear Miss Dixie [Ancrum]," 16 Nov. 1932.

15. John Bennett to John Briscoe Bennett, 27 October 1896, JBP, SCHS.

16. Reminiscences of John Bennett, JBP, SCHS.

17. Thomas Beer, *The Mauve Decade* (New York: Alfred A. Knopf, 1926); see the chapter on "American Magazines": "Buried in St. Nicholas, you'll find John Bennett's 'Master Skylark,' half artifice, half sentiment, which children followed from month to month, doting on Gaston Carew's ferocious, unmoral swagger, but not caring a rap about Master Skylark who smelled as though he'd been playing in Mrs. Frances Hodgson Burnett's nursery, until he got home-sick and became real, asking the red-haired queen, after his song had pleased her, to send him home" (228).

18. Reminiscences of John Bennett, JBP, SCHS.

19. John Bennett to his family, 24 September 1944, JBP, SCHS.

20. *Publishers Weekly*, 19 Oct. 1935. See John Bennett to his family, 27 October 1935, JBP, SCHS. Reginald Birch's illustrations for the "May Day Play" chapter of *Master Skylark*, along with Bennett's prose, are included in the tribute book to Birch, *Reginald Birch: His Book*, ed. Elisabeth Hamilton (New York: Harcourt, Brace, 1939). Included are incidents from *Little Lord Fauntleroy*, *The Little Princess*, and other selections by Frank Stockton, Tudor Jenks, Ogden Nash, W. S. Gilbert, and Edward Lear.

21. Reminiscences of John Bennett, JBP, SCHS.

22. Bennett, *Master Skylark*, 272.

23. Bennett, *Master Skylark*, 264.

24. Bennett, *Master Skylark*, 264.

25. Scratch copy of letter of John Bennett to Spencer Mapes, JBP, SCHS. Bennett was responding to Mapes's request for biographical information on Mary Mapes Dodge.

26. "You are now thirty years of age," A. W. Drake wrote him. "You have already put in two years of hard work and struggle, and have managed to squeeze out a living. Wouldn't it be worth your while to make one final effort? Suppose you threw away two years in trying to do what you want to do? That is, come to New York and study in the Art Students' League and learn your trade" (A. W. Drake to John Bennett, Century correspondence, JBP, SCHS). Later he wrote, "Your work . . . is not only promising, but wonderful when I read your account of how most of it has been done. . . . It is remarkable—not that you have done so well, but that you have done it at all" (A. W. Drake to John Bennett, 10 December 1894, Century correspondence, JBP, SCHS).

27. John Bennett to John Briscoe Bennett, 24 March 1896, JBP, SCHS.

28. Bennett wrote of these episodes in a variety of places. See the draft copy of his letter to Spencer Mapes (JB biography file, JBP, SCHS). On 26 July 1895, he had a letter from the Century Company saying, "Let us see [the] Shakespeare story as soon as finished." He sent a piece of it to New York by 9 September 1895. A 26 March 1896 letter from the Century Company enclosed a check for $400 for the first half of the payment; an earlier check for $100 had apparently been a previous advance. The second installment was slated for December (Century correspondence, JBP, SCHS).

29. The letter admitting him is in Beginnings scrapbook 54, JBP, SCHS.

30. Information about the League is from "Training of Women Breadwinners, No. 1," an article by Seddie Boardman Aspell in *Woman's Magazine*, January 1896 (mostly unpaginated), 55–56, 61.

31. Bennett to O'Donnell, 18 November 1925.

32. John Bennett to John Briscoe Bennett, 21 September 1897, JBP, SCHS.

33. John Bennett to his family, 1 March 1925. The quote comes from a postscript to his daughter Susan, apparently to help her deal with her homesickness while away at school at Dana Hall in Wellesley, Mass.

34. John Bennett, letter to his family, 16 April 1944, JBP, SCHS.

35. Seddie Boardman Aspell, "Training of Women Breadwinners, No. 1," *Women's Magazine*, January 1896, 61.

36. "Was at the Art Students' League, New York, with Rollin Kirby, of the N.Y. World, and Valentine Kirby, Pennsylvania State Director of Arts, then known as 'Big' and 'Little Kirby.'" Reminiscences of John Bennett, apparently from a draft for promotional material drawn up by JB for Longmans Green and Co, publisher of *The Pigtail of Ah Lee Ben Loo* (JBP, SCHS).

37. "At the close of his first year at the League, [Rollin Kirby] came to me in great distress. His father had written him to come home, and give up the foolish idea of becoming a writer. SKYLARK was running in *St. Nicholas*, and I was supposed to be 'a person of some importance.' He begged me to write his father, assuring

him that Rollin had genuine talent and well-based hopes of a future financially sound, if but permitted to continue his studies. I wrote such a letter—to give the boy a chance. Rollin returned to New York glowingly happy, to continue his study" (John Bennett to his family, 8 October 1944, JBP, SCHS; see also Bennett to his family, 18 December 1927). Kirby later began to correspond with Bennett again in the 1920s and visited him in Charleston.

38. Reminiscences of John Bennett, JBP, SCHS.

39. John Bennett to his family, 19 September 1937, JBP, SCHS.

40. John Bennett to his family, 19 September 1937.

41. John Bennett to his family, 28 February 1937, JBP, SCHS.

42. Reminiscences of John Bennett, JBP, SCHS.

43. John Bennett to his family, 28 February 1937, JBP, SCHS.

44. John Bennett to John Briscoe Bennett, 24 March 1896, JBP, SCHS.

45. Draft copy of letter from John Bennett to Spencer Mapes, JBP, SCHS.

46. Bennett, *Master Skylark*, 379.

47. John Bennett to Ron McKissick, 19 May 1925 (see Skylark and Pigtail scrapbook 16). The date was 5 June 1896, according to the date on the drawing Bennett made of his desk the day the book was finished. Continuing on in his letter to McKissick, Bennett noted, "I made a pen drawing, next day, of the table, the bookcase and the typewriter as they stood on the completion of those paragraphs, a thunderstorm without preventing my sketching out of doors." As for those final maudlin thirty-seven lines, Bennett noted, "There was a law suit won before lower and upper court in Pennsylvania by the quotation of that paragraph by the pleading attorney . . . in the case of the loss of an only son by a widowed mother (John Bennett to Louella Everett, the compiler of Bartlett's *Familiar Quotations* and editor of books of verse, 12 October 1937). Bennett's typewriter, a Remington number 2, was later taken apart by one of his nephews eager to see how it worked; it never worked again. It is part of the collections of the Charleston County Public Library.

48. *Chicago Tribune*, 4 October 1897.

49. *Boston Daily Advertiser*, 3 October 1897.

50. *Cincinnati Commercial Tribune*, 3 October 1897.

51. "Jack" Condell as an identifying "point" and error in the first edition, and notes by Bennett on how to tell a first edition from others, appear in a letter of John Bennett to John M. Stevens, 11 January 1934, JBP, SCHS. The "first-first" (first edition, first state), as Bennett called it, has a drab front cover, with a Reginald Birch drawing of Shakespeare and the boy, with Shakespeare's coat of arms. The second state is "apple-green cloth, diapered design red-and-white Tudor roses; title in panel at top . . . red-and-gold."

52. Reminiscences of John Bennett, JBP, SCHS.

53. Hogan's introduction is part of the paperback Airmont Classic Series (CL 92) "specially selected . . . from the immortal literature of the world" (New York: Airmont Publishing Company, 1965), 10, 12.

54. Douglas Street, "John Bennett," in *Dictionary of Literary Biography* 42 (1985), 83.

55. Meigs, *Critical History*, 390–91.

56. See the 1928 *Year Book of the Poetry Society of South Carolina* (Columbia: The State Company, 1928), 66: "The Century Company, N.Y., being asked by the American Library Association to name the juvenile book on their list which has been most popular through the years, gave that place to Bennett's *Master Skylark*."

57. "'Master Skylark,' John Bennett's well known story for young people has been selected as one of the '100 Best Books From All Time' by McCall's Magazine. The national magazine named the Charleston author's book in its November issue" (*Charleston News and Courier*, 12 December 1956).

58. Jacob Blanck, *Peter Parley to Penrod: A Bibliographical Description of the Best-Loved American Juvenile Books* (New York: R. R. Bowker, 1956), 104.

59. John Bennett to John Briscoe Bennett, 27 October 1896, JBP, SCHS (21-137-07).

60. Bennett to O'Donnell, 18 November 1925. In another letter, Bennett noted that this next book "was written, at order of the Century Company to be 'an American story of Romance, as near the times of my first book as might be'" (John Bennett to Walter Mitchell, 24 August 1921, JBP, SCHS).

61. Bennett to O'Donnell, 18 November 1925.

62. John Bennett to Susan Smythe, 9 November 1897, JBP, SCHS.


CHAPTER 8. *"I Am Glad People Like Me"*

1. John Bennett to Yates Snowden, 5 December 1921, JBP, SCHS. This letter, apparently, is not included in Mary Anderson's *Two Scholarly Friends*.

2. L[ouisa]. S. M[cCord]., review of *Uncle Tom's Cabin, or Life among the Lowly*, by Harriet Beecher Stowe. *Southern Quarterly Review*, January 1853, 82.

3. "The regiment of damn Yankees from my native town were provost-guard in the devastated capital; and my cousin, on the march, was quartered in the Mc-Cord House at Ft. Motte, Lang-Syne, passant guardant—and *didn't burn the house*" (John Bennett to Yates Snowden, 10 September 1931, quoted in Mary Crow Anderson's *Two Scholarly Friends*, 295).

4. Bennett was paid $7.00 for the two watercolors and $0.50 for the initials. He comments on finding his old invoice for this in a letter to his family, 18 November 1927, JBP, SCHS.

5. *Charleston News and Courier*, 24 November 1894. The clipping is preserved in a scrapbook, JBP, SCHS.

6. John Bennett to Major Augustine Smythe, 9 December 1894, JBP, SCHS. One can see the marks made on this letter by the newspaper workers who copied it.

7. Susan Smythe to John Bennett, 2 March 1899, JBP, SCHS.

8. John Bennett to Susan Smythe, 2 May 1899, JBP, SCHS.

9. Undated (ca. 1925) clipping from unidentified newspaper. Titled "Confessions," the article is a letter by DuBose Heyward to Miss [Fanny?] Butcher regarding his favorite book, JBP, SCHS, file number 21-05-02.

10. John Bennett to Susan Smythe, dated "Tuesday," JBP, SCHS.

11. John Bennett to Susan Smythe, 9 November 1897, JBP, SCHS.

12. Reminiscences of John Bennett, JBP, SCHS. In a letter to a child, he wrote, "When a doctor is giving one . . . horrid things to take, it is not easy to pretend that you are having a most interesting and exciting time way back in 1664." John Bennett to "Miss Catherine," 30 October 1901, JBP, SCHS.

13. Bennett noted this gas poisoning in numerous biographical letters and reminiscences, but never stated its cause. It is likely it came from a poorly ventilated apartment in New York City; all those he mentioned in his letters and reminiscences were grim from his descriptions. See the letter of John Bennett to "Cimiotti," 12 April 1943, JBP, SCHS: "After leaving New York that last Spring, under contract to write a second serial story for 'St. Nicholas,' I contracted a gas poisoning over in 6th Ave, [and] was ordered south for the winter." And see the letter of John Bennett to "Miss Constance" Griffiths, 3 April 1935: "Dr. Maria Norris, one of the frequenters of Mackinac, . . . ordered me south for the winter, following a case of gas-poisoning in New York."

14. John Bennett's reminiscences of Charleston, JBP, SCHS.

15. Bennett often mentioned the tenth as being the date he arrived: "On 10 Nov. 1898, I landed in Charleston," he wrote to his family on 28 November 1937 (JBP, SCHS). But Susan Smythe, on 2 November 1899, wrote a letter to him that day and said it was the anniversary of his arrival (JBP, SCHS).

16. John Bennett's reminiscences of Charleston, JBP, SCHS.

17. "Queerest and oddest" is quoted from John Bennett's reminiscences of Charleston, JBP, SCHS. "Pathetic beauty" is from "Grotesque Old Charleston," by John Bennett, published in *The Reviewer*, July 1922, 556.

18. John Bennett to Miss Triplett, 20 November 1898, JBP, SCHS.

19. John Bennett to Miss Silliman, 27 November 1898, JBP, SCHS.

20. John Bennett, "Grotesque Old Charleston," *Reviewer*, July 1922, 553.

21. Bennett, "Grotesque Old Charleston," 552.

22. See James, *The American Scene*. The best discussion of James in Charleston is in an article on Owen Wister's stay there, including Henry James's visit with him: "Owen Wister: Champion of Old Charleston," by Julian Mason, published in the

*Quarterly Journal of the Library of Congress* 29, no. 3 (July 1972), 162–185. There is no mention in Bennett's papers that they ever met.

23. John Bennett to Miss Triplett, 20 November 1898, JBP, SCHS.

24. Bennett, "Grotesque Old Charleston."

25. John Bennett's reminiscences of Charleston, JBP, SCHS.

26. Susan Smythe to John Bennett, 2 November 1899, JBP, SCHS.

27. John Bennett's reminiscences of Charleston, JBP, SCHS.

28. John Bennett to Miss Silliman, 27 November 1898, JBP, SCHS.

29. Henry James, *The American Scene* (New York: St. Martin's Press, 1927), 300.

30. *Charleston News and Courier*, 30 April 1902, 5. See note 22 to this chapter, above. The connections between Wister and another Charleston writer, DuBose Heyward, are interesting. Wister dedicated his book *Lady Baltimore* to S. Weir Mitchell, who was the Philadelphia physician and writer who diagnosed Heyward with polio. A former Charlestonian, Caroline Sinkler, paid for Heyward's visit to Philadelphia to consult Mitchell; she was the basis for the "Eliza La Heu" character in Wister's *Lady Baltimore*, and Heyward dedicated his second novel, *Angel*, to her.

31. John Bennett's reminiscences of Charleston, JBP, SCHS.

32. John Bennett's reminiscences of Charleston, JBP, SCHS. In her review of *Uncle Tom's Cabin*, Louisa McCord had also made comments about how "Yankees" talked, saying of Mrs. Stowe: "She makes her Southern ladies and gentlemen talk rather vulgar Yankee-English" (*Southern Quarterly Review*, January 1853, 107). When Bennett died, an editorial in the *Charleston News and Courier* of 30 December 1956 (page 8A) noted that "he never lost his Ohio accent." Also quoted in Mary Crow Anderson's *Two Scholarly Friends*, 332.

33. John Bennett's reminiscences of Charleston, JBP, SCHS.

34. John Bennett to Miss Triplett, 20 November 1898, JBP, SCHS. Years later, John Bennett and his wife Susan would try unsuccessfully to interest a publisher in publishing the letters the major wrote from the steeple.

35. John Bennett's reminiscences of Charleston, JBP, SCHS.

36. Bennett's reminiscences of Charleston, JBP, SCHS.

37. Bennett's reminiscences of Charleston, JBP, SCHS.

38. *Charleston News and Courier*, 11 June 1946. Clipping in Work notebook A, page 78, JBP, SCHS.

39. John Bennett's reminiscences of Charleston, JBP, SCHS. Bennett, much later, liked to point out the fact that he was not, after all, a "Yankee," despite his birth in Ohio. When South Carolina historian Yates Snowden learned of Bennett's very Southern ancestry, he wrote him, "You are no more damnyankee than I am" (27 June 1926, quoted in Mary Crow Anderson's *Two Scholarly Friends*, 235).

40. John Bennett's reminiscences of Charleston, JBP, SCHS.

41. John Bennett's reminiscences of Charleston, JBP, SCHS. Referring to the Charleston Club, he would much later recall it as "a collection of quaint . . . fossils of the PALEOZOIC AGE, which played penny whist, read London papers, and viewed its vanishing [wine] cellars with anguish" (John Bennett to his family, 13 March 1927).

42. John Bennett's reminiscences of Charleston, JBP, SCHS.

CHAPTER 9. *The Story of Barnaby Lee*

1. John Bennett to Miss Silliman, 27 November 1898, JBP, SCHS.

2. Wilky James participated in the assault on Charleston in July 1863 and was wounded, then taken back to Newport to recover. The 55th Massachusetts was sent to reinforce the 54th, of which James's brother Bob was a member; the 55th participated in the attack on Fort Wagner in August. In September, the Confederates abandoned the fort. From *Henry James: The Young Master*, by Sheldon Novick (New York: Random House, 1996), 91.

3. See chapter 7, note 61.

4. John Bennett, *Barnaby Lee* (New York: The Century Company, 1902), 18, 19.

5. Bennett, *Barnaby Lee*, 12.

6. Reminiscences of John Bennett, JBP, SCHS.

7. Bennett, *Barnaby Lee*, 280.

8. "I have not told anyone else, but tell you, his [van Sweringen's] daughter's real name was Elizabeth: I called her Dorothy because I had fallen in love with that name: yet Elizabeth is as lovely and perhaps a bit statelier; and if I were writing the book again to-day, I'd call her Elizabeth" (John Bennett to Jane Shaffer, 24 April 1923, JBP, SCHS).

9. Bennett to Shaffer, 24 April 1923.

10. "An Interesting Experiment" is an eight-page stapled pamphlet with "From the Sign of THE WANDERERS" as a return address. It contains extracts from the forthcoming novel, describes van Sweringen and Bennett's literary experiment, has an image (of van Sweringen?), comments on *Master Skylark*, and sports the maxim, "There is no need to wait for a ship to come in if you have sent no ship out." A masted ship in front of the moon is associated with the sign of the Wanderers. Bennett apparently put it out, and the Century Company, delighted with it, used it for promotional purposes.

11. In a letter to his family dated 15 January 1928, Bennett referred to a pamphlet

he devised to advertise the book; it was sent to van Sweringens all over the country to attract their interest (JBP, SCHS).

12. John Bennett to Susan Smythe, 1 June 1899, JBP, SCHS.

13. Reminiscences of John Bennett, JBP, SCHS.

14. Bennett, *Barnaby Lee*, 346.

15. Bennett, *Barnaby Lee*, 411–17, passim.

16. Bennett, *Barnaby Lee*, 453–54.

17. Notes by Bennett, Century Company correspondence, JBP, SCHS.

18. Reminiscences of John Bennett, JBP, SCHS.

19. John Bennett to Frank and Nettie Taylor, 23 March 1922, Ross County Historical Society.

20. John Bennett to Frank P. O'Donnell, 18 November 1925, JBP, SCHS.

21. John Bennett's description of Mrs. Dodge staying in town to read his manuscript is taken from his scratch copy of a letter to Spencer Mapes, 20 February 1937, JBP, SCHS. The quotes he attributes to her are from his letter to Frank P. O'Donnell, 18 November 1925.

22. John Bennett to "Dear Father and dear people," 5 June 1900, JBP, SCHS.

23. Bennett to "Dear Father and dear people," 5 June 1900.

24. W. F. Clarke to John Bennett, 15 November 1901, JBP, SCHS.

25. Blanck, *Peter Parley to Penrod*, 116.

26. See clippings in Work notebook A, 11, JBP, SCHS.

27. *Critic*, April 1903, Unidentified clipping labeled by John Bennett, scrapbook number 21-175-2, JBP, SCHS.

28. Quoted in the *Charleston Sunday News*, 25 January 1903.

29. Concerning the film version, Bennett noted that he sold rights to the Thomas A. Edison Company on 26 October 1916 for $375. He reported that the film was made but never released; Edison didn't think it would be successful (*Barnaby Lee*, Century Company correspondence, JBP, SCHS). As for the later offer from the magazines, he noted, "About twenty years ago, one of the pulp magazines of adventure asked me to do a series of short stories based upon the dramatic character, Gerrit van Sweringen, the Man from Troublesome Corner" (John Bennett to Jay E. Sweringen, 14 March 1941, JBP, SCHS). He declined since he was busy with other projects. See letter of Arthur Hoffman of *Adventure* magazine to John Bennett, 9 May 1922, JBP, SCHS.

30. Bennett, *Master Skylark*, 257.

31. John Bennett to Susan Smythe, 17 July 1899, JBP, SCHS.

32. John Bennett to Jack Appleton, 2 April 1927, JBP, SCHS.

33. Susan Smythe to John Bennett, 25 November 1899, JBP, SCHS.

CHAPTER 10. *"Love in Its Fullness, Replete"*

1. John Bennett to Susan Smythe, 8 May 1899, JBP, SCHS.

2. John Bennett to Susan Smythe, undated "Wednesday morning" (February 1899), JBP, SCHS. It is addressed to "My dear Miss Susan" and signed, "Very faithfully yours."

3. John Bennett, *The Treasure of Peyre Gaillard* (New York: The Century Company, 1906), 273. The descriptions of Bennett in the library of 31 Legare Street are from his reminiscences of Charleston, JBP, SCHS. A picture of this room and how it looked some years later appears in Albert Simons and Samuel Lapham, *The Octagon Library of Early American Architecture, Volume I: Charleston, South Carolina* (New York: The American Institute of Architects, 1927), 165.

4. Bennett, *Peyre Gaillard*, 274–76.

5. Susan Smythe to John Bennett, n.d. ("Tuesday 7 a.m." [ca. 1899]), JBP, SCHS. "I am hopelessly practical," she wrote him, saying she hid the feelings that others did not think she had; "practical people are not necessarily devoid of sentiment. They hide it. . . . What dreaming they may indulge in, is done in private" (Susan Smythe to John Bennett, 25 November [1899], JBP, SCHS).

6. Bennett, *Peyre Gaillard*, 276.

7. John Bennett to Susan Smythe, "Saturday morning," dated by its envelope as 4 February 1899, JBP, SCHS.

8. John Bennett to Augustine Smythe, Monday, 6 February 1899, JBP, SCHS. "Your note was handed to me just as I was leaving the house on my way to your office, to see you or await your coming there. I therefore take time here but to say that I will do as I had intended, and more quickly that it is your wish. I will be at your office at 9:30 o'clock, or as soon thereafter as possible, and await your pleasure."

9. John Bennett to Susan Smythe, 19 February 1899, JBP, SCHS.

10. "I went, Friday evening, to call at Capt. Pinckney's, and had a very pleasant evening. There were two ladies, whose names I did not catch, of course, in the introduction, but they insisted on mentioning 'Master Skylark, that famous book,' and I roared very softly. As usual we read Thomas Hardy, Hall Caine and all their confreres completely out of the sanctuary of honest literature, leaving only a few such great men as Will Shakespere [sic], Alfred Tennyson, Robert Browning, William Molen and John Bennett to respectability and permanence" (John Bennett to Susan Smythe, Sunday afternoon, 26 February 1899, JBP, SCHS).

11. John Bennett to Susan Smythe, 5 March 1899, JBP, SCHS.

12. John Bennett to Susan Smythe, Tuesday morning, 7 March [1899], JBP, SCHS.

13. John Bennett to Susan Smythe, n.d. [March 1899], JBP, SCHS. The comments about his ship coming in are on a sheet he pasted to this letter.

14. John Bennett to Susan Smythe, 14 March 1899, JBP, SCHS.

15. John Bennett to Yates Snowden, 18 July 1926, quoted in *Two Scholarly Friends,* 238.

16. John Bennett to Susan Smythe, 8 May 1899, JBP, SCHS.

17. Years later as Susan compiled material on her family, she did the same for John Bennett. Though he was called an "Ohio Yankee," he had considerable Southern family, other than Beale; his uncle Isaac Trimble was a Confederate General at Gettysburg, and another ancestor of his had lived in Charleston after the Revolutionary War and had been in business with a member of the Stoney family, into which the Smythes had married by the time Bennett came to Charleston.

18. John Bennett, *Barnaby Lee* (New York: The Century Company, 1902), 453–54.

19. John Bennett to Susan Smythe, 19 February 1899, JBP, SCHS.

20. Yates Snowden to John Bennett, 18 May 1924, quoted in *Two Scholarly Friends,* 208.

21. Susan Smythe to John Bennett, 30 April 1899, JBP, SCHS.

22. John Bennett to Susan Smythe, n.d. (ca. May 1899), JBP, SCHS.

23. Susan Smythe to John Bennett, n.d. (late May 1899), JBP, SCHS. The Whaley house ultimately stood empty for years and was eventually remodeled, taking off all the ostentatious elements that so riled Susan Smythe. The Rodgers mansion is so large that it eventually became a Masonic Hall, later the headquarters of an insurance company, and then a hotel.

24. Susan Smythe to John Bennett, 26 November 1899, JBP, SCHS.

25. Dawson had taken up the Southern cause, fought for the Confederacy and became one of the most eloquent voices of the city during the political tumult of reconstruction. He received a papal award for helping to abolish dueling in the south; his death and the acquittal of his murderer, following the still practiced code of honor (no white man being convicted for the death of another if they fought over an issue involving one or another's honor) was a bitter pill for his family to swallow. Dawson's life and role in Charleston is detailed in E. Culpepper Clark's *Francis Warrington Dawson and the Politics of Restoration: South Carolina: 1874–1889* (Tuscaloosa: University of Alabama Press, 1980). His son became an expatriate writer who lived the rest of his life in Paris. See Dale B. J. Randall's *Joseph Conrad and Warrington Dawson: The Record of a Friendship* (Durham, N.C.: Duke University Press, 1968). A fictionalized account of the Dawson murder was written by Charleston novelist Robert Molloy, *An Afternoon in March* (Garden City, N.Y.: Doubleday, 1958).

26. Susan Smythe to John Bennett, 26 November 1899, JBP, SCHS.

27. The "body-servant" is mentioned in a letter of John Bennett to Joe and Esther Taylor, 6 February 1901, JBP, SCHS. Description of the house and depredations on local property are present in John Bennett's letters to Master Galen New-

man, 21 September 1914, and to Gadsden C. Zimmerman, 6 December 1920, JBP, SCHS.

28. Bennett to Joe and Esther Taylor, 6 February 1901, JBP, SCHS.

29. Susan Smythe to John Bennett, 14 December 1899, JBP, SCHS.

30. The women's building is the only building remaining in Charleston; it was the Lowndes Grove plantation, now at the end of Gordon Street in Charleston. All other buildings built on the then vacant land were temporary structures, dismantled after the Exposition.

31. The president was polite and apparently sat down for the meal. Owen Wister, hearing of this, was quite angry at Mrs. Simonds; when he came to write a biography of his friend Roosevelt, he included this anecdote in his manuscript, although he did not name her. Despite the fact that he highly praised Charlestonians for their politeness and their reserve, he did not practice it; in the first edition of his work, he wrote of Daisy Simonds that she was "allied to Charleston by her marriage which, I had been told . . . was a distinct mesalliance for her husband, even though he did sit among the very elect. She had married him for his money. . . . At a proper time after their union, she had produced a baby: but it wasn't her own" (Owen Wister, *Roosevelt: The Story of a Friendship, 1880–1919* [New York: Macmillan, 1930], 100). Once the books reached the stores, Daisy Simonds, remarried and now Mrs. Crittendon Calhoun, apparently threatened a lawsuit; the publisher of the biography withdrew the books, and so those few that have survived are quite rare. The more common copies of the book show that Wister rewrote the episode as a paean to Charleston.

After this event, Roosevelt would have some further accounts with Charleston writers; he'd challenge Wister on his portrayal of Charlestonians and their attitudes toward blacks in his book *Lady Baltimore;* and in Africa, on safari, he'd run into another Charleston writer, Warrington Dawson, son of the editor of the *Charleston News and Courier* mentioned in note 25 above.

32. The house that Daisy Simonds had built for her, and in which she entertained Roosevelt, also came to play a part in Charleston literary history. After the death of her husband, she opened it as a guest house, and many famous writers such as Sinclair Lewis, Gertrude Stein, and others would stay here over the years. Called "The Villa Margherita," the house would be mentioned in Charleston novelist Ludwig Lewisohn's *The Broken Snare* as the Villa Mercedes; Sinclair Lewis would call it by its real name in his novel *Main Street,* having his heroine Carol Kennicott seek solace there; and it would figure in much less distinguished literature such as Leslie Ford's 1940 mystery novel, *Road to Folly.* The house today is half the original size and is a private residence.

33. As if to counter Wister's version of the episode, Daisy Breaux Simonds Cal-

houn published her own version of her life, called *Autobiography of a Chameleon* (Washington, D.C.: The Potomac Press, 1930). John Bennett, tongue in cheek, obviously aware of the true story, referred to the author as "an entertainer of Presidents," noting that in her book "many a vivacious legend acquires unanticipated serenity; and many an audacious anecdote is very gently told" (*Year Book of the Poetry Society of South Carolina* (Columbia: The State Company, 1930), 48.

34. John Bennett to his son John H. Bennett, 26 May 1939, JBP, SCHS. The occasion of this confession was his son's own marriage, looming in a few days. "I do not know how wise you are as to the intricacies and difficult relations of a married life," he wrote. "I presume you are as wise as a decent young fellow should be. I know you are not as experienced as those who have frequented bawdy houses think themselves." He told of his own difficulties and told his son he was ordering him a book on the subject.

35. He published "A Revival Sermon at Little St. John's" in the August 1906 issue of the *Atlantic Monthly*, 256-68.

36. See his comment in Work notebook B, 34, JBP, SCHS. Also: "I am perhaps . . . the only person south of Mason & Dixon's Line who heard the first paid concert given by the Fisk Jubilee Singers in Chillicothe, Ohio, 1871. I was just six years old: I recall the event clearly, and remember, also clearly, how the Dunlap household, assisted by Ada Laird's wailing also, sang spirituals every night for a year after (John Bennett to his family, 21 April 1940, JBP, SCHS).

37. Susan Smythe had already collected sixty by November 1899 and was planning to get more from her acquaintance, the writer Annie Colcock (Susan Smythe to John Bennett, 25 November 1899, JBP, SCHS).

38. Jane Hunter to John Bennett, 10 January 1939, JBP, SCHS; see also Jane Edna Hunter, *A Nickel and a Prayer* (n.p.: Elli Kani Publishing Company, 1940), 35.

39. John Bennett to John Briscoe Bennett, n.d. ("Back River, Wednesday evening," ca. May 1901), JBP, SCHS.

40. Reminiscences of John Bennett, JBP, SCHS.

41. Bennett's mother did not like the name Eliza and forbade him to use it to name his daughter (interview with Martha Bennett Stiles, Jane McClintock Bennett's daughter, 15 April 1999).

42. Bennett, *Peyre Gaillard*, 276.

CHAPTER 11. *Charleston's Adopted Son and His Treasure*

1. John Bennett to Yates Snowden, 21 January 1925, quoted in *Two Scholarly Friends*, 220.

2. The date of the article is 5 May 1895. In it, he noted, "The last Charlestonians

to follow in the footsteps of their forefathers . . . to the quaint old fashioned resort were Mr. Augustine Smythe and his family in the summer of 1894." Yates Snowden brought about another appearance in the local press, republishing Bennett's poem, "In a Rose Garden," as "In a Charleston Rose Garden" in the paper as well.

3. The title is "Souvenir Calendar, 1902, Charleston, SC." It is approximately legal sized, and the cover, with panels of St. Michael's Church, and palmetto trees and garlands of roses, is printed in a bluish color. John Bennett's name is nowhere mentioned on the publication, but it is evident it is his work from the typical overpainting and his correspondence.

4. The two sites associated with African American history include the "training school for colored nurses" on Cannon Street and the Zion Presbyterian Church, "erected 1850, by gentlemen of Charleston, for a negro congregation; still maintaining." Bennett did make some mistakes in the calendar, confusing Magazine and West Streets.

5. For convincing his mother-in-law, see Work notebook B, 48, JBP, SCHS. For information on the Carolina parakeet, see article in the *Chillicothe News-Advertiser,* quoted in the *Charleston News and Courier,* 14 May 1908, Work notebook B, page 5.

6. Bulletin of the Charleston Museum, volume 5, number 1, January 1904. The Museum expressed its gratitude for Bennett turning up an 1828 advertisement showing that the Museum had transferred from Chalmers Street to the Medical College on Queen Street.

7. For Bennett as a trustee of the Library Society, see the *Charleston News and Courier* article of 10 June 1903, Work notebook B, page 4, JBP, SCHS.

8. Interview of Bill Geer by Harlan Greene, Chapel Hill, N.C., Good Friday, March 1997.

9. *Charleston News and Courier,* 2 April 1905.

10. John Bennett, "George Herbert Sass," in *The Library of Southern Literature* (Atlanta: The Martin and Hoyt Company, 1909), 10:4661–86. Bennett would help his son Herbert Ravenel Sass with many of his writing projects, particularly *Look Back to Glory.* Bennett himself would be included in *The Library of Southern Literature.* See Ellison A. Smyth Jr., "John Bennett," *The Library of Southern Literature,* 1:323–43.

11. "Blue Man": interview with John Bennett's daughter Susan, 11 November 1977. As for the "vivid" color of his clothes, he wrote, "You remember my blue cotton coolie cloth suits? And that I was the first gent, to trod the stately streets of Charleston in so 'vivid' a color—unless a workman in overalls would count?" (Bennett to his family, 22 October 1939, JBP, SCHS). He writes, "King McDowell, first; and I second, were the pioneer hatless men on the streets" in the same letter.

12. Correspondence of John Bennett and Thornwell Jacobs, 1904, JBP, SCHS. It may be the book published by the Taylor-Trotwood Publishing Company of Nash-

ville in 1908 as *The Law of the White Circle.* The novel, with nearly identical women characters, one white and one mulatto, concerns race riots in Atlanta where Jacobs was the founder of Oglethorpe University. Although Jacobs declares in his introduction that the "object of his book is not to call the negro a 'black brute' and the Aryan a 'white angel,'" he nevertheless does exactly that. Its premise is fear of miscegenation, and although Jacobs was apparently a moderate in his day, the racism of his novel is vicious. Yet it sets in context some of the problems Bennett would soon encounter in Charleston (see chapter 12), and it shows how atypical and truly less racist Bennett's own writings were. He referred to Thornwell Jacobs much later in a letter to his family of 11 February 1940, JBP, SCHS; in this reference it does not seem to match the novel. When he read it in 1915, he called it a "miserable" book (John Bennett to Susan Bennett, 11 July 1915, JBP, SCHS).

13. Edwin Augustus Harleston to his wife, Eloise. Edwin Augustus Harleston papers, SCHS.

14. John Bennett to Susan Smythe Bennett, 28 September 1904, JBP, SCHS.

15. There are many references in Bennett's letters implying the lower social ranking afforded to Jewish families. He made the ranking clear in a letter to his family on 3 January 1937, noting, "Mrs. [Huntington] Hartford gave a party, a New Year's assembly, fancy dress, half a thousand invitations, to her house on her plantation at Wando; quite a grand smash of the New Year. Now Mrs. Hartford, while a widow of the A & P [family fortune], and wealthy as a mince pie, is by birth one half Pollitzer, a party [sic] Jewess, and has never been wholly accepted or received socially, not that the Pollitzers are not all right; but that they never had been any part of 'society' here" (21-142-13, JBP, SCHS).

16. There are numerous mentions of Jews in Bennett's letters, some slightly derogatory, some neutral, some complimentary. The fact that he noted the Jewishness of his friends is indicative of his using it as a definition. Stereotypical mentions of Jews as usurers appear both in *Master Skylark* and in *The Treasure of Peyre Gaillard.*

17. Wister describes with some wit how Henry James, keeping a "tryst" with him in Charleston in early 1905, listened to the opening chapters and then begged him to change the name of the city; see Wister's introduction to *Lady Baltimore* in his collected works: *The Writings of Owen Wister* (New York: Macmillan, 1928), viii–ix.

18. Lewisohn set his novel *The Broken Snare* partly in Charleston, although he called it Queenshaven. He also used that name for the city in the first volume of his biography, *Upstream. The Case of Mr. Crump,* his best-known novel (which is certainly autobiographical), is set partly in Charleston, as well, but it is called Charleston. Both novels deal with sex outside of marriage.

19. For a discussion of this episode in Lewisohn's life, see Ralph Melnick's two-volume biography of Lewisohn, *The Life and Work of Ludwig Lewisohn* (Detroit: Wayne

State University Press, 1998). Melnick mentions Bennett a few times, getting his name wrong once and confusing him with his son.

20. "He was personally obnoxious to my friends at Ohio State University, while they very thoroughly appreciated his intelligence," Bennett wrote W. W. Ball in a letter postmarked Charleston, 5 April 1934 (Perkins Library, Duke University). Bennett was writing Ball to say he agreed with Ball's editorial on Lewisohn. In a letter to his family on 2 March 1930, Bennett wrote of Lewisohn, "Barnett Elzas [Rabbi of Beth Elohim] told us some Jewish gossip concerning Ludwig Lewisohn, the brilliant obnoxious Jewish critic and writer, who, deserting his first wife, who married him when he was nobody, has gone abroad with, and there, somehow, married an affinity, and so dares not return, being undivorced; that he once applied for a place as a Unitarian minister in Pennsylvania! and that but for his really brilliant and scholarly mind he is karacterles [sic]. At Ohio State University he was deemed one of the most brilliant minds on the faculty, but personally IMPOSSIBLE. He endeavors to believe, or so professes, that religious and racial prejudice prevents welcome among people of quality. He apparently found Vienna not warm, and has removed to the Metropolis of all volatile essences, delightful or otherwise, Paris." The 1929 *Year Book of the Poetry Society of South Carolina* contains a pleasant reference to him; but the 1930 *Year Book* reprints an unflattering mention, perhaps the only such tidbit reproduced in all the years of its publishing. It quoted Henry Bellaman's comment on Lewisohn's *Israel*. Bellaman, a South Carolina novelist and poet and influence on Julia Peterkin, wrote, "Lewisohn is always provocative. One may not like him (and I hasten to enroll myself in that ever-growing majority), and may detest the strain of propaganda that mars all of his writing; but there is no denying that he is a man of important talent. But how mortally tired one becomes of his concern with sex, with his cries from the housetops, his endless defense mechanisms instead of the able invention he is really capable of bringing to his writing! No one cares now whether a writer be Jewish, Gentile, or Chinese. He must be an artist; and Lewisohn has forgotten how to be an artist." He was, however, asked to address the Poetry Society in January 1939 and did. Bennett praised his lecture then.

It is ironic to note that although Lewisohn tried to forget his Jewish ancestry at one time, he ultimately became one of the foremost of America's Zionists, was one of the first to warn Jews of the danger of Adolph Hitler, and became a founding faculty member of Brandeis University. It may be that his being constantly identified as a Jew by Charlestonians and others ultimately led him to embrace his identity.

21. Lewisohn would seek his fortune elsewhere. In New York, once he started on the writing life, he'd be championed by the likes of Theodore Dreiser, and he'd join the expatriates in Paris in the 1920s, but he'd never break free from the spell of

Charleston. His *The Case of Mr. Crump* was championed by Thomas Mann, who wrote an introduction to it; Sigmund Freud called it a masterpiece. Other than the opera of *Porgy and Bess*, based on the novel *Porgy*, this may be the most famous book ever to come out of Charleston. Except for the plaque on a house he lived in on Calhoun Street, the city has forgotten him utterly.

22. Reminiscences of John Bennett, JBP, SCHS.

23. Reminiscences of John Bennett, JBP, SCHS.

24. Comment on Clarke, Reminiscences of John Bennett, JBP, SCHS. The description of the plot, John Bennett to "54 children, Georgia Avenue School," 15 November 1930, JBP, SCHS.

25. Reminiscences of John Bennett, JBP, SCHS. "Tom Churchyard was to have been a graphic by-character in an historical tale describing the life of the Wandering players during the year of their banishment or exile." John Bennett to W. R. Benét, 17 March 1923, *Saturday Literary Review* correspondence, JBP, SCHS.

26. John Bennett to John Briscoe Bennett, 10 August 1896, JBP, SCHS. The letter also mentions *Buckhorn Johnny*.

27. John Bennett to his family, 12 September 1937, JBP, SCHS.

28. Reminiscences of John Bennett, JBP, SCHS. "I have always believed that I might have done a sequel which would have stood upon its own base as a story independent of, though a sequel to, the original tale." John Bennett to John Williams, 7 February 1942, D. Appleton-Century correspondence, JBP, SCHS.

29. *Charleston News and Courier* article on Bennett's lecture "The Spiritual Songs of the Old Plantation," given before the fourth annual midwinter meeting of the Charleston City Union of Women's Clubs, February 1903. See Work notebook B, 39, JBP, SCHS.

30. Oliver Ditson Company to John Bennett, 11 March 1908, JBP, SCHS. According to his entry in *Who's Who in America* in 1908, Bennett gave lectures on "Plantation Folk Music," "Primitive African Communal Balladry in America," and "The Growth of Music Illustrated by Southern Negro Songs." He also corresponded with the Century Company about the possibility of such a book. Ironically, years later, the 1928 *Year Book of the Poetry Society of South Carolina* would note that the Oliver Ditson Company had recently published "an arrangement of the old Charleston negro fishing fleet folk-song, *Hi, oh! New-Born Babe!* by Harvey Gaul, organist of the Church of the Ascension, Pittsburgh, words and air from the folk-song collection of Mr. and Mrs. John Bennett, of this city" (63).

31. John Bennett to Jane Hunter, 12 January 1939, JBP, SCHS.

32. John Bennett to his family, 27 June 1937, JBP, SCHS. His "all American, or almost all-American voice" was attributed to his being "born and raised in Ohio, with Michigan, New York, and Southern experience, a student of English usage and enunciation, resident more than twenty years in Charleston."

33. John Bennett to his family, 17 October 1937, JBP, SCHS.

34. On lending the manuscript to Tudor Jenks, see John Bennett to Susan Smythe Bennett, 8 July 1903, JBP, SCHS; Booker Washington to John Bennett, 26 December 1903, JBP, SCHS. Bennett answered him saying he would send a book to the Tuskegee Library.

35. The novel is described in the letters of John Bennett to Susan Smythe Bennett of 11 September 1904, 25 September 1904, and others of the period (JBP, SCHS).

36. A copy of "Tudo" is clipped in Newspaper notebook 125. "A Carolina Christmas Story" is in the Learning to Write scrapbook 125, JBP, SCHS. According to a letter to his wife (2 September 1931, JBP, SCHS), "Tudo and Crook Fang" was turned down by *St. Nicholas Magazine* for not being true, although apparently it was; Rollin Kirby, whom Bennett had known at the New York Art Students' League, paid $60 for it for the *Criterion*.

37. "A Revival Sermon at Little St. John's" was published in the *Atlantic Monthly* 98, no. 2 (August 1906), 256–68. Bennett planned to include this in his spiritual book, as well, and got permission to do so (Work notebook B, 80, JBP, SCHS).

38. Bennett, "A Revival Sermon at Little St. John's," 267–68.

39. See Harlan Greene, "'The Little Shining Word': From Porgo to Porgy," *South Carolina Historical Magazine* 87, no. 1 (January 1986), 75–81. In one of her Gullah tales she told in the lobby of the Francis Marion Hotel, which she named, she presented a story of a black girl in her family with a doll from Africa named Porgo. Heyward apparently got the title for his character and novel from this, for Porgo is what he first called his book and his character. He changed it to Porgy; and his mother later changed the name of the character in her Gullah tale to Gobo.

40. In a letter to his family, Bennett wrote, "Sam Stoney has written home to his Mother, asking her to tell him from whom he got the stories in *Black Genesis*, from Gran, Daddy Pompey, Maum Di, Davy Gourdin, retold of course by his elders from the ancients. I did not tell Loula to inform Sam where he got 'How Buh Rabbit God Bud Dee Eye-Water'; it is an African tale which I myself introduced many years ago for the amusement of the young at Back River; was adopted as one of the cycle relating to Buh Rabbit's adventures rivalling God in smartness, and, I suppose, will remain a 'genuine' South Carolina folk-tale until the end of time. But it isn't; I mark it here. It is an African tale adapted to Buh Rabbit by the undersigned to entertain the children, and was never in South Carolina until I fetched it in. Yet after all, what difference does it make; the work is built on mis-statements and waxes fat on them."

41. John Bennett to Gadsden C. Zimmerman, 6 December 1920, JBP, SCHS.

42. John Bennett, *The Treasure of Peyre Gaillard* (New York: The Century Company, 1906), 46–47.

43. John Bennett to Gadsden C. Zimmerman, 6 December 1920, JBP, SCHS.

44. John Bennett would eventually abandon that manuscript and then burn it. "The best detective story ever written by an American author," he immoderately confided to Yates Snowden, once no one could disprove him. John Bennett to Yates Snowden, 2 December 1924, JBP, SCHS. This is quoted in *Two Scholarly Friends*, 213.

45. Bennett, *Peyre Gaillard*, 28.

46. Bennett, *Peyre Gaillard*, 5.

47. John Bennett, quoted in biographical sketch of him by Sarah Cassells Davis, 13, JBP, SCHS.

48. Bennett, *Peyre Gaillard*, 28.

49. John Bennett to Gadsden C. Zimmerman, 6 December 1920, JBP, SCHS.

50. Bennett, *Peyre Gaillard*, 136.

51. Susan Smythe to John Bennett, n.d. (late May 1899), JBP, SCHS.

52. The attribution to the Drayton family of the treasure legend is in John Bennett's letter to Gadsden C. Zimmerman, 6 December 1920, JBP, SCHS, which is the best single source for the origins of the book. "Just at the time the story was completed a message was telephoned the author, informing him that a workman was digging a ditch following an old drain, and had unearthed a huge crock filled with stale and ancient grease, and that when it was melted a bundle of handsome silver spoons was revealed, marked with a crest" of the McCrady family" (Work notebook A, 21, JBP, SCHS).

53. Bennett, *Peyre Gaillard*, 212. Bennett, while mainly respectful of his black characters, does, however, pick up the same stereotypes employed by Poe, and almost all writers following Poe to his own time, showing blacks as loyal, strong, but childlike and fearful. It is the one place in his writings that Bennett appears to be derivative; it does not show up elsewhere in his later published works, but it does appear every now and then in his letters.

54. Bennett, *Peyre Gaillard*, 96.

55. See *Darkey Sermons From Charleston County Composed and Delivered by John Palmer Lockwood, Alias Rebrin Isrel Manigo* (Columbia, S.C.: The State Company, 1925). It is a posthumous publication copyrighted by Leize F. B. Lockwood, with an introduction by Yates Snowden.

56. Bennett, *Peyre Gaillard*, 212.

57. Bennett, *Peyre Gaillard*, 235.

58. Bennett, *Peyre Gaillard*, 255.

59. Bennett, *Peyre Gaillard*, 288–90.

60. Bennett, *Peyre Gaillard*, 264.

61. See letter of John Bennett to Tiffany & Co., 2 December 1905, JBP, SCHS. In regard to using James Allen & Co., see the letter of John Bennett to J. P. Stroud, 23 November 1932, JBP, SCHS.

62. John Bennett to George C. Tyler, 27 January 1925, JBP, SCHS. He apparently

wrote this scene 11 July 1906; see his letter to his wife of that date, JBP, SCHS. On the next day, he wrote her, "Mark it down, this is the first time I have written a book this way, and the first time I have written a love scene."

63. The full title is *The Treasure of Peyre Gaillard, Being an Account of the Recovery, on a South Carolina Plantation, of a Treasure, which had Remained Buried and Lost in a Vast Swamp for Over a Hundred Years. Containing the strange history of Peyre Gaillard, Judas Gay, his man, and the Double Cryptogram; the surprising narrative of My Uncle Peter John; and the Myths, Legends and History of that Ancient Mansion, Indigo House, Blue Hill Plantation, St. Jude's Parish, Santee. Arranged by John Bennett, after the MS narrative by Buck Guignard, Esq. In the French Manuscript entitled, "Le Monticule de Jude."*

64. The *New York Times* review of 8 December 1906 is in 21-175-02, JBP, SCHS.

65. In the first paragraph on that page Tom and Jack are talking about the memoranda on the back of a document; in the next, there is a switch to a money-lender in Georgetown; and in the next paragraph, it is the narrator talking again. The running title "The Last Straw" seems to belong to a chapter that would have begun with the segue to the money lender; the earlier pages in the chapter are more about Jack trying to solve the riddle; and the chapter is titled "Jack Sets Himself to Solve the Riddle, and I Go On a Wild-Goose Chase."

66. He attributes it to "St. Gelais *Chronicle*, of July 12, 1906" (*Peyre Gaillard* 363–64).

67. All these articles are in Bennett's Work notebook A, 18, JBP, SCHS. The quotes are used in Century Company advertisements for the book (Work notebook A, 18, JBP, SCHS).

68. Ludwig Lewisohn to John Bennett, 27 Oct. 1906, JBP, SCHS.

69. See the *Charleston News and Courier* article of 6 January 1907, Work notebook A, page 23, JBP, SCHS. After saying it is "the greatest South Carolina novel . . . written," Wauchope notes that Bennett "has applied to the long novel Poe's theory of the cryptogram or ratiocinative tale, and at the same time has complicated and successfully elaborated [Robert Louis] Stevenson's perfect system for conducting plot." The local paper gave *Lady Baltimore* a less than positive review, taking Wister to task for presenting the city as a ghost town obsessed with the past instead of a modern place for business, which is how the booster editors of the paper liked to portray the city. "It is a libel upon this community," the reviewer wrote of this depiction, "a travesty on truth. If it had been written with the intention of doing injury to a people whose courtesy he conceded, whose bravery he affects to admire, over whose memories he gushes, the author could not have carried out so malevolent a purpose with greater artistic skill" (*Sunday News* [*and Courier*], 15 April 1906).

70. *Charleston Evening Post*, 24 Dec. 1906, JBP, SCHS.

71. *New York Times Saturday Review of Books*, 8 December 1906.

72. *Outlook*, 24 November 1906, Work notebook A, JBP, SCHS.

73. According to a small typescript scrap in Bennett's papers, the epigrams trans-

lated as "I shall record a remarkable event, which is new . . . and untold by the lips of another" (Horace); "But if anyone shall think fit to cavil, because not only wild beasts, but even trees speak, let him remember that we are disporting in the language of fable" (Phaedrus); "And it is pleasant to play the fool on proper occasion" (Horace).

74. See *Charleston News and Courier* article of 11 December 1938; see also John Beaufain Irving, *A Day on Cooper River*, ed. Louisa Cheves Stoney (Columbia, S.C.: R. L. Bryan Company, 1969), 21.

75. John Bennett to Gadsden C. Zimmerman, 6 December 1920, JBP, SCHS. The cover design, signed "DD," was from an artist associated with "Decorative Designers." For more information on this group, see "American Trade Bindings and Their Designers, 1880–1915," by Charles Gullans and John Espey in *Collectible Books: Some New Paths*, ed. Jean Peters (New York: R. R. Bowker, 1979), 32–67.

76. *New York Evening Post*, 8 December 1906, JBP, SCHS.

77. Bennett explains the photographs in his letter to Gadsden C. Zimmerman, 6 December 1920. For a mention of William Abrams, born 1823, see Bennett's note on Work notebook A, page 26, JBP, SCHS.

78. Reminiscences of John Bennett, JBP, SCHS. While most copies of the book have red covers with the dark-green designs by DD, some copies are in green cloth with gothic arched and interlocked designs with thorns, with the title stamped in gold. They do not appear to be the British edition but perhaps just a later binding, since the spine also carries the stamp of the Century Company.

79. John Bennett to Miss Elizabeth B. Heyward, 24 April 1929, JBP, SCHS.

80. Bennett, *Peyre Gaillard*, 362.

81. Bennett, *Peyre Gaillard*, 362–63.

82. Bennett noted to Grace MacPherson, "My people were Virginians, from the Eastern Shore Tidewater, and Shenandoah Valley. They came early to America, the first in 1607; when there were but 32 people in the Virginias, two of them were my family ancestors: we have been a long time in America. My father's people were English; my mother's Scotch. There is also a strain of Huguenot French, of sound Holland Dutch in our makeup" (JBP, SCHS).

CHAPTER 12. *"A Brilliant . . . Execution"*

1. John Bennett minimized the differences in their names from the very beginning. Just after his son's birth (the boy would be called "Jack" as Bennett himself had been), Bennett sent Yates Snowden a note announcing the dual arrival of the year of 1907 and John Bennett Junior (John Bennett to Yates Snowden, [n.d.], South Caroliniana Library; reprinted in *Two Scholarly Friends*, 17).

2. Speaking of W. F. Clarke's role in the book, Bennett noted that he "suggested to the Century Company that 'Peyre Gaillard's Treasure' might give them an adventure story for publication that year; they had none. . . . they therefore declined it for *St. Nicholas*, for which I had written it, and had me rewrite much of it, introduce the famous 'love interest,' and so saved themselves the cost of the story as a serial in *St. Nicholas* . . . which I darn well needed. I told them I needed immediate money. So they allowed me $600 advance royalty, which they deducted from the first year's book sales" (John Bennett to his family, 12 September 1937, JBP, SCHS).

3. "Some day a South Carolina–printed edition with glossary of facts and notes," he had written to Yates Snowden (14 December 1920, JBP, SCHS); and "A South Carolina edition has been considered to be annotated and briefly and amusingly appendixed with the legends and facts upon which the story is based . . . with an actual sketch or photograph of 'Indigo House,' and architect's plans of it, for the amusement of the curious," he wrote to Henrietta R. Palmer (20 April 1925, JBP, SCHS), as she planned to use an extract from the novel for a book of Southern sketches. Palmer's book appeared as *In Dixie Land: Stories of the Reconstruction Era by Southern Writers* (New York: The Purdy Press, 1926), with a chapter of Bennett's describing Pompion swamp.

4. John Bennett to Augustine Smythe Jr., 14 January 1907, JBP, SCHS.

5. John Bennett to his family, 1 October 1939, JBP, SCHS. The *Chillicothe News and Advertiser* of 29 November 1907 drew attention to the 1908 prospectus for *Harper's Magazine*, to contain an article by Bennett on "What is Voodooism?" It was also to have compilations of Negro songs with a collaboration by his wife. See Work notebook B, 5, JBP, SCHS.

6. It appeared in the October 1908 issue, 332–47; and the January 1909 issue, 39–52. His corrections regarding the October issue appear in his letter to Susan Smythe Bennett, 8 November 1908, JBP, SCHS.

7. In the letter to the editor clipped in Work notebook A, 27 (JBP, SCHS), Bennett credits "Maum Araminta Tucker" for telling it to him. Her name is mentioned in the published version of it (*The Doctor to the Dead*, 1946); and Bennett, in an extra-illustrated edition of the volume that he made for friends (which the University of South Carolina Press reprinted in 1995), tipped in a photograph of her in front of the chapter, between pages 222 and 223. In Work notebook C, 57, however, Bennett notes that the story was told to him by D. E. Huger Smith (JBP, SCHS).

8. John Bennett to the Editor, 5 February 1907, published 12 February 1907, 21-175-2, 28, JBP, SCHS.

9. John Bennett, *The Doctor to the Dead* (New York: Rinehart & Co., 1946), vii–ix.

10. John Bennett to Janet Clapper, 19 December 1945, *Doctor to the Dead* correspondence, JBP, SCHS.

11. Reminiscences of John Bennett. Bennett included a picture of Mayrant in his

extra-illustrated editions; it is reprinted in the Univ. of South Carolina Press version, between pages xxvi and xxvii.

12. Typed comments by Bennett; miscellaneous loose notes in his materials on superstition and folklore, JBP, SCHS.

13. The best source for Francis W. Dawson and his vacillation on the "Negro question" is E. Culpepper Clark's excellent book, *Francis Warrington Dawson and the Politics of Restoration: South Carolina, 1874–1889* (Tuscaloosa: University of Alabama Press, 1980.)

14. Typed comments by Bennett; miscellaneous loose notes in his materials on superstition and folklore, JBP, SCHS.

15. Bennett, *The Doctor to the Dead*, x.

16. Bennett, *Peyre Gaillard*, 29.

17. Bennett, *The Doctor to the Dead*, xiv.

18. Nipson is listed as "health detective" in the Charleston City Directories and is mentioned in Leon Banov's *As I Recall: The Story of the Charleston County Health Department* (Columbia, S.C.: R. L. Bryan Company, 1970), 5. Nipson died about this time. See the letter of John Bennett to Susan Smythe Bennett, 12 September 1907, JBP, SCHS. Nipson sold slaves before the Civil War.

19. Bennett, *The Doctor to the Dead*, vii.

20. For a history of the FeeJee Mermaid, see Lester D. Stephens's "The Mermaid Hoax: Indications of Scientific Thought in Charleston, South Carolina in the 1840s," *Proceedings of the South Carolina Historical Association*, 1983, 45–55. Bennett did not make the link with this event and the mermaid riot.

21. Bennett, *The Doctor to the Dead*, xi.

22. Bennett quoted by Kitty Ravenel in "John Bennett's Legends Caused Uproar in 1908," *Charleston News and Courier*, 10 February 1946.

23. Elmina Eason remembered a Mrs. Burgess, who had been told to cross the street as a child to avoid the house and the shadow it cast; interview with Harlan Greene, 10 November 1976.

24. The description of the street is from *The Doctor to the Dead*, 110–11; the chemise is from page 112.

25. "Now" (Perhaps) "It Can Be Told." An article by John Bennett in the *Columbia (S.C.) State*, 5 January 1930.

26. Reminiscences of John Bennett, dated 1904, JBP, SCHS.

27. "Now" (Perhaps) "It Can Be Told."

28. *Charleston Evening Post*, 20 February 1908.

29. *Charleston Evening Post*, 20 February 1908.

30. She quotes Stowe on such themes, whites marrying blacks, octoroons, quadroons, etc. "Uncle Tom's Cabin," review by L. S. M., *Southern Quarterly Review*, New series, vol. 8, no. 13 (January 1853), 81–120.

31. Owen Wister quotes a letter to him from Roosevelt in his book *Roosevelt: The Story of a Friendship* (New York: Macmillan, 1930), 255. Referring to Charlestonians, he states, "They shriek in public about miscegenation, but they leer as they talk to me privately of the colored mistresses and colored children of the white men whom they know."

32. *Charleston Evening Post*, 20 February 1908.

33. John Bennett to his family, 24 March 1940, JBP, SCHS.

34. John Bennett to his family, 24 March 1940; *The Doctor to the Dead*, 112.

35. John Bennett to his family, 24 March 1940.

36. *Charleston Evening Post*, 20 February 1908.

37. John Bennett to his family, 4 July 1915, JBP, SCHS. The film was only slated to show in Charleston for two days (and did), according to the advertisements in the newspapers. Extra hours were observed at the Majestic Theatre to accommodate the hundreds who went to see the "Sensational Drama of Thrilling Love and Royal Intrigue" (*Charleston News and Courier*, 3 July 1915). A few decades later, Bennett would remark that the novel was burned in Edgefield, South Carolina. John Bennett to family, 2 February 1930, JBP, SCHS.

38. *Charleston Evening Post*, 20 February 1908.

39. *Charleston News and Courier Sunday Times*, 1 November 1908.

40. John Bennett to his family, 15 October 1935, JBP, SCHS.

41. John Bennett to John Farrar, 15 March 1940, *The Doctor to The Dead* correspondence, JBP, SCHS.

42. *Charleston Evening Post*, 20 February 1908. According to a note of John Bennett (item 21-175-4, 7), the writers of the cards of protest were Mrs. Octavus Roy Cohen and Miss Clelia Porcher.

43. Reminiscences of John Bennett, JBP, SCHS.

44. His letters are full of such references, long and short, over the years. On 20 August 1939, in a letter to his family, he mentions the winter "long ago, when I was left bewildered upon a peak in Darien, as lonely after that onslaught as Robinson Cruse on his island. . . . I was, I think, for many a day, the loneliest man mentally on the face of the earth; and the shock was deadening. . . . I think no man of any character or spirit can ever be serene at heart after such an unexpected and unwarranted assault in the community where it occurred. I have been happy here, in many ways, and reasonably content; but have never forgiven the town for that unjust attack by a few fools . . . which seemed to paralyze the opinion of the rest of the intelligent community, even of my friends, and left me feeling like a pariah dog in the streets of Benares or Calcutta" (JBP, SCHS). On 10 March 1940, he picked up the theme again, listing the tales he told that day and continuing, "It is perhaps harsh to say, but it is certain that those who found that talk 'foul,' discovered that foulness in their own imaginations, and not in my address. To be sure I did use the

word 'harlot' and referred to a woman's 'chemise,' and had found the stories among the negroes" (JBP, SCHS).

## CHAPTER 13. *The Prayer of the Brave*

1. John Bennett to Susan Smythe, 7 August 1899, JBP, SCHS.

2. Lewisohn's letter appeared in the *Charleston News and Courier*, 9 November 1908, following Harris's, which appeared on the eighth. A friend of Bennett's did consider defending him in a letter to the local press. Charles Henry White, a colleague from the Art Students' League, wrote him, "I would have given everything I possess to have heard your lecture that made you famous in a day. . . . As a matter of fact I had a letter all ready to be mailed to the Charleston paper, in your defense" (3 January 1909, JBP, SCHS). Afraid it would show Bennett "in a false light," White wrote, "I tore it up but *am really* sorry that I could not have sent it on."

3. *Charleston Evening Post*, 21 February 1908.

4. Years later, Bennett wrote, "The reception I received so dismayed me that I laid the whole collection aside, since I had made, and wished to make, my home here. I was accused by both the local press and by contributed cards of protest from ladies of the city of having gone to the sewer for my subject and wallowed in its filth; and that to deliver such a collection of narratives before so cultured and refined an audience was an insult to the women of Charleston. . . . Until that generation had passed away and more liberal minds made up my public here, and possibly elsewhere, I forbore to set the collection in shape for submission to a publisher." John Bennett to John Farrar, 15 March 1940, JBP, SCHS.

5. Reminiscences of John Bennett, JBP, SCHS (this seems to date from 1907). He continues, "If not, and that is God's dispensation, not mine, I should like her to know, yet without my telling, that at least in patient endurance, and determined endeavor, her husband has played a man's part, not whining, but trying to do, daily, weekly, yearly, through misery, and in hearty despite of weakness and what may truly be described as woe of body."

6. He had mentioned being "cocaine-poisoned" to his fiancée in a letter to her on 5 July 1901 (JBP, SCHS). Interviewed on 11 November 1977, his daughter Susan Bennett stated that he was addicted and spent several winters at Flat Rock in these years breaking himself of it.

7. John Bennett to Susan Smythe Bennett, 11 April 1909, JBP, SCHS.

8. Tudor Jenks to Susan Smythe, 31 March 1909, JBP, SCHS. Bennett was too depressed to correspond with Jenks. Susan answered and wrote letters for him.

9. Connor copyrighted a dramatic version of the play on 20 January 1903. Bennett had granted him the right to do so for a private presentation of the play, not to make money. See letter of John Bennett to the Century Company, 18 Nov. 1902.

Burrill's description of the Connor version is in his letter to John Bennett, 12 January 1909, JBP, SCHS.

10. John Bennett to Edgar White Burrill, 12 March 1909, JBP, SCHS.

11. Reminiscences of John Bennett, JBP, SCHS.

12. Reminiscences of John Bennett, JBP, SCHS. This typed fragment is dated 15 February 1911.

13. Reminiscences of John Bennett, JBP, SCHS.

14. Common sense, thrift, and the ability to invest well were some of Susan Bennett's strengths. "She likes to straighten out erring bankers and tell them how to run their banks, and does!" Bennett once wrote. "Of course she should have been a financier and practical business manager" (John Bennett to his family 10 February 1924, JBP, SCHS). This wasn't just her husband's opinion; others sought out her advice on many topics. One was the etcher Alfred Hutty who, torn between different ways of producing art and making a living (his wife, it was said, would sell his paintings before he finished them), sought advice on this from Susan Bennett (John Bennett to his family, 16 March 1924, JBP).

15. John Bennett to Edgar White Burrill, 12 March 1909, JBP, SCHS.

16. John Bennett to Yates Snowden, 5 May 1915, quoted in *Two Scholarly Friends*, 74.

17. Bennett referred to his commitment to Macmillan constantly in his correspondence, but there is no contract or contractual papers from Macmillan in his papers at the South Carolina Historical Society. The firm brought out a four-volume history of South Carolina by Edward McCready in these years.

18. Reminiscences of John Bennett, JBP, SCHS.

19. Much of the research he turned up in these years he did not use himself, although other researchers using his collection have benefited from it. His finding of a mention of a particular synagogue in Charleston provided one scholar with the basis for an article: Solomon Breibart, "Two Jewish Congregations in Charleston, S.C., before 1791: A New Conclusion," *American Jewish History* 69 (1980): 360–63. The author, finding the reference in Bennett's papers, informed Breibart. Another researcher used Bennett's finding on Arthur Hugh Clough in an article published in the *South Carolina Historical Magazine* in January 1997 (SCHM 98, no. 1, page 58, note 1). Various books on South Carolina history over the years make mention of using the Bennett papers. And in 1997 a novel, *The Root of All Evil* by David Farrow (Charleston: Wyrick & Co.), used a true-life character Bennett saved for posterity. *The Doctor to the Dead* itself was used as the basis for a play for the arts festival Spoleto in the 1980s (handbill, author's collection). In 2000, Pam Durban cited her use of John Bennett's papers and referred to the mermaid riot in her novel *So Far Back*.

20. Bachman was a Charleston clergyman who hosted Audubon for his visit to Charleston. Bachman also collaborated with Audubon on some of his publications,

and two of his daughters married two of Audubon's sons. The quote is from the *Charleston News and Courier,* dated March 1911 by Bennett; see Work notebook B, 14, JBP, SCHS.

21. Bennett would work with Bragg on many projects over the years; his correspondence often contains snide comments about her. He did not believe she was the authority on poetry she believed herself to be; he disagreed with many things and decisions she made regarding the Poetry Society of South Carolina. "Of course, Laura Bragg has her enemies," he once wrote, "but marrain [sic] on them—they are doing nothing. She *does* things (John Bennett to his family, 16 April 1925, JBP, SCHS). For an excellent appraisal of Laura Bragg as a new woman and her influence on the museum field and Charleston, see Louise Allen, *Laura Bragg: A New Woman Practicing Progressive Social Reform as a Museum Administrator and Educator,* Ph.D. diss., 1997, University of South Carolina.

22. *Charleston News and Courier,* March 1911 (see note 20, above). Although the newspaper gave him credit for discovering the date, Laura Bragg did not, perhaps causing another reason for tension between them (see note 21, above). An article under her editorship gives credit to Miss Ellen FitzSimons of the Charleston Library Society for finding a manuscript journal of meeting minutes that established the date (*Charleston Museum Quarterly* 1, no. 1 [first quarter 1923], 3).

23. Tudor Jenks to John Bennett, 17 February 1911, JBP, SCHS. Jenks refers specifically to the Partisan War.

24. Arthur Schlesinger to "Dear good old Dr. Bennett," 3 January 1915; John Bennett to his wife, JBP, SCHS.

25. Reminiscences of John Bennett, JBP, SCHS.

26. John Bennett to Susan Smythe Bennett, 1 September 1913, JBP, SCHS.

27. Bennett to Susan Smythe Bennett, 1 September 1913.

28. John Bennett to Susan Smythe Bennett, 8 August 1911, JBP, SCHS.

29. Bennett asked Yates Snowden if he knew of any other life class in South Carolina before this (John Bennett to Yates Snowden, 24 April 1916; published in *Two Scholarly Friends,* 89). For an article announcing the establishment of the class, see *Charleston Evening Post,* 9 March 1915.

30. Bennett gives his impression of Bissell and Alice Smith and others in the letter mentioned in note 29, above. Paul Bissell later sent Bennett some of his professional work. See his comments in Work notebook B, 19–20, JBP, SCHS.

31. Bennett quoted in the *Savannah Morning News,* 2 January 1927.

32. John Bennett to Jane Judge, 15 October 1926, Georgia Poetry Society correspondence, JBP, SCHS. A *Charleston News and Courier* article of December 1915 noted this; see Work notebook B, 15. As for the Academy of Music's use of his silhouette on the piper, he noted, "Jean Flinn, hoping to make a livelihood from publishing theatre programs, etc., offered $10 prize for the best design submitted as cover for

her program. Those submitted were impossibly bad. She appealed for assistance and I lent her the [design]" (see Work notebook B, 16, JBP, SCHS). Earlier, in 1901, Bennett had lent a silhouette design of his *St. Nicholas Magazine* tale, "How Cats Came to Purr," for the Charleston Art Club. See the *Charleston News and Courier* article of 15 March 1901 in Work notebook B, 3.

33. Tudor Jenks helped with the contract and came up with the compromise title, "Master Skylark: (Will) Shakespeare's Ward." See Burrill/*Master Skylark* papers, JBP, SCHS.

34. See note 9, above. Miss Emily J. Dyer of Newton, Massachusetts, made an adaptation of it for use in grammar schools, and it was presented in May 1913 (undated June 1913 letter of John Bennett to his wife, JBP, SCHS). Bennett worked with her, possibly thinking the Century Company would publish it (John Bennett to his wife, 29 June 1913, JBP, SCHS). Bennett also gave rights to Mr. S. J. Synott to produce it at Detroit College and later at St. Xavier College, Cincinnati (Bennett to Century Company, 30 Nov. 1908, JBP, SCHS). Anna May Irwin Lutkenhaus adapted it too, and a version for the use of elementary schools in New York City was published by the Century Company, ca. 1914, after it was presented. (Lutkenhaus was the director of the dramatic club of Public School 15, Borough of Manhattan, for whom she prepared the adaptation and presented it twelve times.)

35. Bennett's 2 June 1918 letter describing one of the trips to Flat Rock in "Betsy" is published in "Hi-Ho, Betsy," with an introduction by Claude Henry Neuffer, in *South Carolina History Illustrated* 1, no. 2 (May 1970), 37–43.

36. Reminiscences of John Bennett, JBP, SCHS.

37. John Bennett to George C. Tyler, 10 January 1925, JBP, SCHS. Later to Tyler (11 May 1936), he explained further, "It proved impossible for me to go to England to check up the wild statements and misstatements of our native fabricators, and in the end I threw up the whole contract as one too great for me to correct." In a letter to Wessen, Susan Smythe Bennett wrote that his work "was stopped when he found out that all the Headquarters papers which were taken by the British in 1780, and . . . kept sealed all this time, had just been opened in the British War Office. The index of them was several large volumes" (Literary estate papers, JBP, SCHS).

38. John Bennett to Yates Snowden, 10 September 1931, JBP, SCHS.

39. Reminiscences of John Bennett, JBP, SCHS.

40. Very little of the drafts survived, but there are some notes by Bennett. In a letter of 5 September 1911 he wrote his wife, "I think the next book I write will be something in the nature of a pseudo-biography, as human as I can make it, historical to be sure, or it will be that Arabian Nights' adventure of the young Scotch factor of Charleston, SC, circa 1804–1805." To his wife on 1 July 1915, he wrote of a work with the Gritty Cameron heroine; the work used Scottish dialect, took place in Scotland and in America, and had a character nicknamed "Auld Scratch."

41. John Bennett to Alice Bennett, 23 April 1917, JBP, SCHS.

42. John Bennett to Joe Taylor, 29 December 1916, JBP, SCHS.

43. "*The Huguenot*," 1915, in unidentified, undated clipping scrapbook 21-175-6, 124, JBP, SCHS.

44. John Bennett to Henry Holcomb Bennett, 29 April 1917, JBP, SCHS. Bennett appears to have copied this letter to his brother to keep in his own files.

45. John Bennett to Susan Smythe Bennett, 25 June 1917, JBP, SCHS.

46. John Bennett to Susan Smythe Bennett, 22 June 1917, JBP, SCHS.

47. John Bennett to Susan Smythe Bennett, 25 June 1917.

48. John Bennett to Susan Smythe Bennett, 24 April 1919, JBP, SCHS.

49. It seems likely that Bennett, so allied to all cultural events in the city, would have attended the play, especially with the participation of his nephew and brother-in-law. In a letter to his wife on 20 June 1915, Bennett had mentioned seeing at her sister Loula's, "the young folk there singing." Among them were Jack Matthew, Austin (Augustine) Smythe, DuBose Heyward, and Samuel G. Stoney Jr. They were singing the same scene from *Lucia di Lammermoor* that had inspired Bennett to finish the pivotal scene in *Master Skylark*.

50. Undated (ca. 1925), unidentified clipping, JBP, SCHS. The article reproduces a signature and image of DuBose Heyward in his letter to Miss [Fanny?] Butcher regarding a book he wished he had written.

51. In a letter to his wife of 21 June 1915, Bennett mentions seeing Heyward about insurance for their silver and jewelry (JBP, SCHS). In 1910 there was a series of eight dory races each Thursday for eight weeks. In one race there was A. T. Smythe Jr., skipper, C. P. Means, and John Bennett; in a second race, in dory number 4, was Smythe and Bennett again and T. Grange Simons Jr. (*Charleston News and Courier*, 19 May 1910, Work notebook B, 9 and 11, JBP, SCHS). In a race on 26 May 1910, in boat number one were W. Lindsay Smith, E. Pettigrew Verner, and E. DuBose Heyward, coxswain (*Charleston News and Courier*, Work notebook B, 10, JBP, SCHS).

52. John Bennett to Susan Smythe Bennett, 18 June 1917, JBP, SCHS.

53. John Bennett to Susan Smythe Bennett, 2 April 1918, JBP, SCHS.

54. John Bennett to Susan Smythe Bennett, "Wednesday [April] 3d, 1918," JBP, SCHS.

55. John Bennett to Susan Smythe Bennett, 4 April 1918, JBP, SCHS. Referring to Dr. Huldah Prioleau, he continued, "Dangerous she could be; not if handled with any consideration whatever." He seemed to share the prejudice of others of his time and class in believing of the "trouble makers," "*It's the yellow men!*" The mulatto "Sportin' Life" causes much of the trouble in DuBose Heyward's *Porgy*; and Gilly Blutton, also a mulatto, is the chief villain in Heyward's *Mamba's Daughters*.

56. John Bennett to Susan Smythe Bennett, 17 April 1918, JBP, SCHS.

57. John Bennett to Susan Smythe Bennett, 4 April 1918, JBP, SCHS.

58. John Bennett to Susan Smythe Bennett, 2 April 1918, JBP, SCHS.

59. *Charleston News and Courier,* 12–13 May 1919. See also Herbert Shapiro, *White Violence and Black Response: From Reconstruction to Montgomery* (Amherst: University of Massachusetts Press, 1988), 148.

60. John Bennett's notes for his four-minute speeches, JBP, SCHS.

61. Dr. Huldah J. Prioleau to John Bennett, JBP, SCHS.

62. John Bennett to Walter Wilbur, 27 January 1919, JBP, SCHS.

63. This tale of the 1886 earthquake hitting during a church revival ceremony on Edisto Island Bennett eventually illustrated with silhouettes and published in the April 1920 issue of the short-lived *Southern Review* published in Asheville, North Carolina. According to Bennett's letter to I. Jenkins Mikell of 14 November 1922, JBP, SCHS, Bennett got Williams's permission to retell it and publish it. He said the same thing to Yates Snowden in a letter of 9 April 1920, when Snowden inferred that Bennett had "stolen" the story. Mikell reprinted it in his autobiographical book *The Rumbling of the Chariot Wheels* (Columbia, S.C.: The State Co., 1923), 148–52. It was also republished in Nell Graydon's *Tales of Edisto* (Columbia, S.C.: The R. L. Bryan Co., 1955), 105–7. Of the Chaos Club itself, Bennett wrote that Pinckney had founded it "for discussion of all unanswerable questions" (John Bennett to his family, 21 May 1944, JBP, SCHS).

64. John Bennett to his family, 31 October 1937, JBP, SCHS.

65. Reminiscences of John Bennett, JBP, SCHS.

66. John Bennett to Walter Wilbur, 27 January 1919, JBP, SCHS.

67. John Bennett's reminiscences of Charleston, JBP, SCHS.

68. John Bennett to his family, 9 September 1917, JBP, SCHS.

69. DuBose Heyward, *Porgy* (New York: George H. Doran Company, 1925), 11.

70. John Bennett to his family, "Communiqué Extraordinaire," 1 September 1918, JBP, SCHS. Writing of old Charleston to Yates Snowden, he noted, "It is disappearing, side-street life and all, with distressing rapidity to those who care for the quaint, the queer, the *outré* and the grotesque, and for beauty in ruin, loveliness *perdue*" (John Bennett to Yates Snowden, n.d. [25 July 1918?], JBP, SCHS).

71. John Bennett to Martha Trimble Bennett, 15 May 1918, JBP, SCHS.

72. John Bennett to his family, 8 February 1918, JBP, SCHS.

73. John Bennett to Martha Trimble Bennett, 22 January 1916, JBP, SCHS.

74. Bennett to Martha Trimble Bennett, 15 May 1918.

75. Bennett to Martha Trimble Bennett, 15 May 1918.

76. John Bennett to Yates Snowden, 22 December 1919, Yates Snowden papers, South Caroliniana Library, University of South Carolina.

77. John Bennett to Jack Appleton, 28 August 1921, JBP, SCHS.

78. John Bennett to Nellie [Ward?], 16 October 1920, JBP, SCHS,

79. Richard Ellmann, *Oscar Wilde* (New York: Alfred A. Knopf, 1988), 197.

80. John Bennett to "Elizabeth," 7 March 1921, *Madame Margot*/Family correspondence, JBP, SCHS.

81. John Bennett to his family, 24 July 1917, JBP, SCHS. He wrote that he was going to start in on the legends on June 30; on July 13 he wrote, "I then trimmed some wisteria, washed my hands, changed my clothes, and proceeded to slice Madame Margot into strings, for reshaping; you know my method." He finished the first draft on July 18.

82. John Bennett, *Madame Margot: A Grotesque Legend of Old Charleston* (New York: The Century Company, 1921), 3.

83. John Bennett to Yates Snowden, 14 December 1920, quoted in *Two Scholarly Friends*, 159.

CHAPTER 14. *"We Have Waked . . . the Slumbering"*

1. *New York Evening Sun*, 4 May 1906.

2. *Charleston News and Courier*, 30 April 1906. The article begins, "The following is a thoughtful and interesting address delivered by Mr. John Bennett of this city, before the Columbia [sic] Art Association of Charleston." It was, no doubt, the Carolina Art Association.

3. *Charleston News and Courier*, 30 April 1906.

4. Dale Rosengarten, *Row upon Row: Sea Grass Baskets of the South Carolina Lowcountry* (Columbia, S.C.: McKissick Museum, University of South Carolina, 1986), 29. She notes that Clifford Legerton began marketing sea grass, or sweetgrass, baskets made by local African Americans in 1916.

5. Martha Severens and Charles L. Wyrick, *Charles Fraser of Charleston: Essays on the Man, His Art and His Times* (Charleston, S.C.: The Carolina Art Association, 1983), plates 13, 19, 27, and others.

6. William Gilmore Simms to James Lawton, 11 September 1830, quoted in Mary Simms Oliphant, Alfred Taylor Odell, and T. C. Duncan Eaves, eds., *The Letters of William Gilmore Simms, Vol. 1 (1830–44)* (Columbia: University of South Carolina Press, 1952), 5.

7. Ludwig Lewisohn, *Cities and Men* (New York: Harpers and Brothers, 1927), 81. Lewisohn refers to the rumors about Timrod and his wife having a "touch of the tar brush" in "South Carolina: A Lingering Fragrance," *Nation* 115, no. 2975 (12 July 1922), 36.

8. Lewisohn, *Cities and Men*, 83–84.

9. John Bennett to Yates Snowden, 23 June 1922. Published in *Two Scholarly Friends*, 174.

10. John Bennett's appreciation and assessment of Barton Grey was published in the *Charleston Sunday News (and Courier)*, 2 April 1905.

11. Lewisohn, *Cities and Men*, 85.

12. The best source on Beatrice Ravenel is Louis Rubin's essay in *The Yemasee Lands: Poems of Beatrice Ravenel* (Chapel Hill: University of North Carolina Press, 1969). The calling of the Witte girls half wits is from an interview with Laura Mary Bragg by the author (Harlan Greene). In her copy of *Cavalier and Courtier Lyricists: An Anthology of Seventeenth-Century Minor Verse*, ed. W. H. Dircks (London: Walter Scott, n.d.), which she signed and dated 1893, Beatrice Witte marked a poem that punned on her name. She marked Thomas Randolph's "The Poet":

*From witty men and mad*
*All Poetry conception had.*
*No sires but these will Poetry admit:*
*Madness or wit.*
*This definition poetry doth fit:*
*It is witty madness or mad wit.*
*Only these two poetic heat admits:*
*A witty man or one that's out of's wit. (114)*

Collection of the author.

13. Other writers also wrote of Charleston in these and earlier years. The early realist author John DeForest, a Union veteran, set his *Bloody Chasm* in Charleston in 1867; he became one of the first to suggest the binding up of sectional differences by marrying off his Charleston heroine to a visiting Yankee. The prolific E. P. Roe used the city in *The Earth Trembled* to commemorate the 1886 earthquake. Other authors snatched their heroes or heroines away from the lurid horror of miscegenation, as Genie Stoval did in *The Son of Carolina* (1876); and other novelists, such as Elisabeth Carpenter Satterthwait in *A Son of the Carolinas*, used the great hurricane of 1893 as a setting.

Janie Screven Heyward, in *Wild Roses* (New York and Washington: The Neale Publishing Company, 1905), published a poem about her son DuBose. She rented out rooms to boarders in a house on Sullivan's Island called "Tranquillity," and she often sold copies of her book to her boarders. See also Mary Weston Fordham, *Magnolia Leaves*, intro. by Booker T. Washington (Charleston: Walker, Evans and Cogswell, 1897); Annie T. Colcock, *Margaret Tudor: A Romance of Old St. Augustine* (New York: Frederick A. Stokes Co., 1901); Annie T. Colcock, *Her American Daughter* (New York and Washington: The Neale Publishing Company, 1905); and Theodore D. Jervey, *The Elder Brother* (Washington and New York: The Neale Company, 1905).

14. John Bennett's notes to his lecture on South Carolina literature, delivered at the College of Charleston, 21 July 1939, JBP, SCHS.

15. Bennett's lecture notes, 21 July 1939, JBP, SCHS. For more on Billy Molen, see A. S. Salley's article on him in the *Columbia (S.C.) State Magazine*, 1 January 1952; Frank Gilbreth's mention of him is in his book *Ashley Cooper's Doing the Charleston* (Charleston: The Post and Courier, 1993), 64–65. See also Basil Hall's article in the *Charleston Evening Post*, 24 September 1958, and the poem on him in Arthur Jervey Stoney, *A Miscellany of Doggerel Rhymes*, ed. Emmett Robinson (Charleston, S.C.: Nelson's Southern Printing, 1964). The book is unpaginated. The poem "The Torch of Billy Molin [sic]" is the last in the book, number 90. Several of Molen's broadsides are in various collections in the South Carolina Historical Society. A William M. Molen, author and poet, is listed living at the rear of 12 Wentworth in the Charleston city directory of 1894. Various addresses are given over the years.

16. John Bennett to Charles Henry White, 26 December 1907, JBP, SCHS. Cited in Martha Severens, *The Charleston Renaissance* (Spartanburg, S.C.: Saraland Press, 1998), 48.

17. Alice R. Huger Smith and D. E. Huger Smith, *Twenty Drawings of the Pringle House on King Street, Charleston, SC* (Charleston: Lanneau's Art Store, 1914). The same authors collaborated on *The Dwelling Houses of Charleston* (Philadelphia: J. B. Lippincott Company, 1917).

18. An undated clipping in a scrapbook in the DuBose Heyward papers, SCHS, documents his Confederate Memorial Day activities; it is pasted in with materials dating it to around 1917. Janie Heyward published an ode to the Confederate dead in her book *Wild Roses*. Heyward's "Aftermath: To One Killed in Action" was published in the first yearbook of the Poetry Society of South Carolina. It is identified with Edward L. Wells in the version published in his *Skylines and Horizons* (New York: Macmillan, 1924), 53.

19. John Bennett's February 1922 annotation to a letter to him from Hervey Allen, 21 July 1922, JBP, SCHS. Continuing it, Bennett wrote, "He dreams of making money out of poetry, I fear. I will not say it cannot be done, but it isn't often."

20. *The Year Book of the Poetry Society of South Carolina* (Columbia, S.C.: The State Company, 1928), 6.

21. John Bennett to Anton [Wright], 12 October 1919, JBP, SCHS.

22. In a letter to his family on 30 July 1939, JBP, SCHS, Bennett recounts Hervey Allen's falling out with principal Walter Mitchell over smoking on campus. The superintendent of Charleston High School, Robert V. Royall, asked Allen if he smoked; he blushed and said yes. Royall was, Bennett said, aware of the episode and wanted to see if Allen would tell the truth. In a letter to Walter Mitchell (20 July 1921, JBP, SCHS) Bennett made recommendations to better the school that were adopted; he then withdrew his son for Phillips Andover, 26 July 1921, JBP, SCHS.

23. Bennett's lecture notes, 21 July 1939, JBP, SCHS.

24. John Bennett's letter to the *Charleston News and Courier* published 26 February 1929.

25. Both Allen and Heyward worked with Bragg. She often claimed credit for introducing them, but her successor at the museum, director E. Milby Burton, wrote a note saying his mother had introduced them. See his note in his copy of Hervey Allen's *Action at Acquila,* author's collection. Allen himself says that Heyward sought him out and introduced himself to Allen, naming a literary friend they had in common (John Bennett); see Hervey Allen, *DuBose Heyward: A Critical and Biographical Sketch* (New York: George H. Doran Company, n.d. [ca. 1926]). Oddly enough, this small nineteen-page pamphlet was reprinted in an edition of 150 copies by the Folcroft Press in 1970.

26. John Bennett to "The Infants & Others," 3 August 1924, JBP, SCHS.

27. Photographs of Heyward invariably show him hiding his right hand (he was left-handed). Some Doris Ulman photos do show his withered hand, and in the Emmett Robinson papers at the Charleston County Library there is one image that shows how shockingly skeletal his arm and hand truly were. Hervey Allen noted the following for an introduction to *Porgy:* "I might also say, although you will appreciate that it is a somewhat delicate reference, that I think DuBose was attracted to the character of Porgy because Porgy was a cripple, and so was DuBose. When Heyward was a young boy, he had a terrible attack of infantile paralysis and only those who knew him well understood how marvelously he handled himself and how well he concealed his twisted body. Undoubtedly into the making of *Porgy* went that personal understanding that enabled DuBose to tell his tale with passionate sympathy." Allen also goes on to tell his memory of Heyward writing the book in *Great Short Novels: An Anthology,* ed. Edward Weeks (New York: The Literary Guild of America, 1941), 562. Heyward died the previous year.

28. Bennett's lecture notes, 21 July 1939, JBP, SCHS.

29. Bennett's lecture notes, 21 July 1939.

30. The quote comes from a letter to his wife dated 21 January 1913, JBP, SCHS; he implied similar feelings regarding his writing career elsewhere as well.

31. Bennett's lecture notes, 21 July 1939.

32. Bennett often claimed credit for alerting Allen to Poe's presence in Charleston; Allen thanked him for his information on Poe in Charleston in *Israfel: The Life and Times of Edgar Allan Poe* (New York: The George H. Doran Co., 1926). Allen further acknowledged the importance of Bennett in the project, and his thanks, by sending his mentor a signed, boxed, and numbered set (no. 2 of 250) of the limited edition published for the Edgar Allan Poe Shrine.

33. John Bennett to Jack Appleton, 17 October 1925, JBP, SCHS.

34. Reminiscences of John Bennett, JBP, SCHS.

35. John Bennett's speech before the Carolina Art Association, *Charleston News and Courier,* 30 April 1906, JBP, SCHS.

36. John Bennett to William Watts Ball, 1 December 1921, Perkins Library, Duke University.

37. DuBose Heyward,, *Peter Ashley* (New York: Farrar and Rinehart, 1932), 316. The poem is "Chant for an Old Town" in his *Skylines and Horizons* (New York: Macmillan, 1924), 65–71.

38. *Year Book of the Poetry Society of South Carolina for 1921*, 17.

39. His short story "The Ghost of the *Helen of Troy*" has a local setting. See Frank Durham, *DuBose Heyward: The Man Who Wrote Porgy* (Columbia: University of South Carolina Press, 1954), 17–18.

40. Reminiscences of John Bennett, JBP, SCHS.

41. John Bennett to "Dear, dear Heart" (Susan Bennett), 1 August 1920, JBP, SCHS.

42. John Bennett, speech to the Carolina Art Association, *Charleston News and Courier*, 30 April 1906. JBP, SCHS.

43. John Bennett to "Dear, dear Heart" (Susan Bennett), 1 August 1920, JBP, SCHS.

44. John Bennett speech to the Carolina Art Association, 30 April 1906, *Charleston News and Courier*, JBP, SCHS.

45. John Bennett to Susan Smythe Bennett, 2 August 1920, JBP, SCHS.

46. *Porgy* in dramatic form went to London, where royalty was in attendance. According to Laura Bragg, Dorothy Heyward wore a backless dress and forgot to wear appropriate lingerie. Just after the Heywards left London, an invitation arrived inviting them to Buckingham Palace.

47. Laura Bragg, interview by author, 2 November 1976.

48. John Bennett to his family, 15 August 1921, JBP, SCHS.

49. John Bennett to DuBose Heyward, 22 August 1921, DHP, SCHS.

50. Louise Allen, *Laura Bragg*, 137.

51. Her June 1920 copy, for instance, contains the signatures, Mr. & Mrs. John Bennett, East Flat Rock, N.C.; Helen von Kolnitz, visiting in New London, Conn.; Josephine Pinckney summering in Gloucester, Mass.; Hervey Allen, with his family in Pittsburgh, Pa.; DuBose Heyward at his house Orienta, outside Hendersonville, N.C.; and Elizabeth Myers, back in Charleston. Author's collection, gift of Laura Mary Bragg.

52. Laura Bragg, interview by author, 2 November 1976. When it was impossible, she said, to have not heard of him, she sent him a volume of Eliot's poems, and Heyward confessed his ignorance.

53. Laura Bragg often told stories of how Heyward loved Josephine Pinckney and how Pinckney, Bragg, and others conspired to get all of Pinckney's beaux married to other women so Pinckney could have a career. She said at one time that seven men had proposed to Josephine, and she and her friends worked to marry them to seven other women. Pinckney, according to Bragg, told her that she would never have a life of her own if she married Heyward. Amy Lowell, in a letter to Pinckney dated 21 June 1924 (Harvard University), inferred that she thought Hervey Allen was in love with Pinckney.

54. John Bennett to his family, 5 September 1921, JBP, SCHS.

55. Even as late as 1935, before an honorary degree was given to her, the *Charleston News and Courier* (2 April 1935, 10) called Pinckney "writer of verse since 1918."

56. Bennett's sister Martha was always sympathetic and deferential to her older brother. In later life, she'd say that one of her reasons for living on in the old house in Chillicothe was to give him pleasure and keep intact the home of his memories.

57. John Bennett to his family, 12 September 1921, JBP, SCHS.

58. Bennett's lecture notes, 21 July 1939.

59. The date for the appearance of the book is from Fred Hobson, *Mencken: A Life* (New York: Random House, 1994), 213. In a letter dated July 1921 to "Dear Heart" (his wife), JBP, SCHS, Bennett wrote, "That chap Mencken seems to have been scalding Charleston, somewhere: Beatrice R.[avenel] has replied rather vitriolic[ally], in the *State;* and T. Waring written him, personally—astonishing vivacity in Tom—this Mrs. Wolseley [sic] . . . speaks with bluntness concerning the exploitation of the Charleston symphony orchestra, apropos Mencken's critique, which I have not seen and know not where it was printed. As I make out, he said they could not play a symphony, and if they did, who would come to hear them play it? Cruel." The woman in question was a Mrs. W. W. Woolsey, who lived at 68 Meeting Street, an early member of the society, as the first yearbook of the Poetry Society attests. She ran into Bennett and had a copy of *The Double Dealer* in her hand. That fact that she took the article about the South and the lack of good symphony orchestras as a deliberate attack on Charleston life and its musical abilities is quite telling.

60. Bennett's lecture notes, 21 July 1939. The date was eighteen years to the month after his hearing of the Mencken diatribe, see note 59, above.

61. Rules of the "Courting, Wooing and Matrimonial Society," ca. 1915, are present in a scrapbook in the DuBose Heyward papers, SCHS. Heyward participated in the publication of a small pamphlet that, at first glance, appears to be a memorial published on someone's death. It is titled "In Memoriam—John Douglas Matthew, 1885–1916." It is a jest, published by the "Brotherhood of Sir Galahad, Lodge of Sorrow," remarking on Matthew's passing from bachelorhood into "a wedded state." In one section there is the question, "What is the duty of every true and loyal brother?" The answer is "To love God, fear women, and elude the net of matrimony." Collection of the author.

62. Frank Durham mentions this in his dissertation, *DuBose Heyward, the Southerner as Artist: A Critical and Biographical Study*, Columbia University, 1953, 47. He had an idea for a film script set on local themes in 1917, but it never was taken up by anybody, it seems.

63. John Bennett's lecture to the Carolina Art Association, *Charleston News and Courier*, 30 April 1906.

64. Amy Lowell to Josephine Pinckney, 21 January 1925, Harvard University Libraries.

65. John Bennett to Susan Smythe Bennett, 11 August 1921, JBP, SCHS.

66. "As you know, I did not start it or engage but from love of the two boys" (John Bennett to Susan Smythe Bennett, 11 January 1923, JBP, SCHS).

67. John Bennett to Susan Smythe Bennett, 13 April 1925, JBP, SCHS.

68. Sunday *Charleston News and Courier,* 26 December 1920.

69. Durham, *DuBose Heyward,* 57.

70. Bennett's lecture notes, 21 July 1939.

71. John Bennett to his family, 2 June 1929, JBP, SCHS.

72. DuBose Heyward, *Mamba's Daughters* (Garden City, N.Y.: Doubleday, Doran & Company, 1929), 120. "Poetry should be left to undernourished, anemic . . . people unfitted for other things in life," Dorothy Heyward wrote in *The Pulitzer Prize Murders* (New York: Farrar and Rinehart, 1932), 78.

73. John Bennett to Susan Smythe Bennett (about Gordon Miller), 13 April 1925, JBP, SCHS.

74. John Bennett to Laura Bragg, 11 January 1921, JBP, SCHS.

75. Annotation by John Bennett on his notes for this speech, JBP, SCHS.

76. *Year Book of the Poetry Society of South Carolina for 1921* (Charleston, 1921), 8.

77. *Attention to all members is called to the fact that they are members of the Society, and not yearly subscribers. All members appearing on the list for the current year will therefore be considered as members and liable for dues for the ensuing year, unless their resignations are in the hands of the Secretary by the date of the annual meeting.* Undated "Important Notice to Members" from Secretary DuBose Heyward, kept by Laura Bragg in her copy of the *Year Book of the Poetry Society of South Carolina for 1921.* Author's collection.

78. John Bennett to Carl Sandburg, 21 February 1921. JBP, SCHS.

79. A quote from the *Bulletin of the Poetry Society of American for May 1921,* 8, quoted in the *Year Book of the Poetry Society of South Carolina for 1921,* 9.

80. *Year Book of the Poetry Society of South Carolina for 1921,* 8, 22.

81. *Year Book* (1921), 14–16. It is in the essay "The Worm Turns: Being in Some Sort a Reply to Mr. H. L. Mencken." Although unattributed in the published form, the author's copy of the yearbook has the essay signed by Allen.

82. *Year Book* (1921), 15.

83. *Year Book* (1921), 6. It continues, "And as *our prime object* we shall strive to work toward the eloquent vocal expression of our own part of the United States in any poetic form which carries the message that a poet's inspiration urges him to convey" (7).

84. *Year Book* (1921), 12. Winners would include Elizabeth Malcolm Durham (1922), who would publish a volume of poetry later (*The Prices of Wisdom*); Beatrice Ravenel and Elizabeth Miles would put up a fight against awarding the Skylark

Prize to "Malcolm Durham," the name under which the poem *"La Belle Vie"* was submitted. They thought it the product of a callow young man affecting "a French blase and sardonic pose" about a woman's passion and devilishness. Bennett liked it and fought for the award, and later crowed with delight when he found out "Malcolm Durham" was the pseudonym of a married woman taking classes under Yates Snowden. John Bennett to Susan Smythe Bennett, 1 September 1922, JBP, SCHS.

85. *Year Book* (1921), 13.

86. It was number 9 in the series.

87. *Year Book* (1921), 43

88. John Bennett to Mary Sinton Leith, 31 March 1925, Virginia Poetry Society correspondence, Poetry Society correspondence, JBP, SCHS. Others also noted the aptness of Bennett's silhouette and poem in regard to the society. Katherine Drayton Mayrant Simons titled her history of the Poetry Society "If Any Man Can Play the Pipes," and closing it she wrote, "In discussing the Poetry Society of South Carolina, it is impossible either to begin or end without notice of John Bennett, poet, novelist, non-fictioneer, and founder. The frontispiece he did for our first year book could well be our motto" (*South Carolina Magazine* 14, no. 9 [Sept. 1951], 9, 21–22).

89. John Bennett to Mrs. MacDowell, 28 April 1921, papers relating to Hervey Allen, JBP, SCHS.

90. John Bennett to Susan Smythe Bennett, 11 August 1921, JBP, SCHS.

## CHAPTER 15. *"The Golden Age"*

1. John Bennett to Bertha Gunterman, 20 May 1928, JBP, SCHS. The "furor" quote is from an article in the *Columbus (Ohio) Enquirer,* 31 October 1926. Gunterman, in turn, wrote an article about Bennett called "The Astrologer's Tower," *The Horn Book* 4, no. 3 (Aug. 1928), 63–70.

2. John Bennett, *Madame Margot: A Grotesque Legend of Old Charleston* (Charleston, 1933), [xvi]. Bennett took the unbound sheets of the 1921 Century Company edition, bound an appendix to it with roman numerals on its pages (except for the very last, following page xv), stamped "Charleston, 1933" on the copyright page, and called the book a Charleston edition.

3. John Bennett to Jack Appleton, 28 August 1921, JBP, SCHS.

4. John Bennett to DuBose Heyward, 23 August 1920, DuBose Heyward papers, SCHS.

5. John Bennett, *Madame Margot: A Grotesque Legend of Old Charleston* (New York: The Century Company, 1921), 4–5.

6. DuBose Heyward, *Porgy* (New York: George H. Doran Co., 1925), 11.

7. Bennett, *Madame Margot*, 3, 6, 15–16, 19–20, 21, 26, 27. This "touch of irregularity" in Gabrielle, Bennett leaves no doubt, is her "drop" of Negro "blood."

8. Bennett, *Madame Margot*, 34–35.

9. Bennett, *Madame Margot*, 41–42, 43, 45–46, 47.

10. Bennett, *Madame Margot*, 48–50.

11. Bennett, *Madame Margot*, 50–51, 52, 57, 59, 61.

12. Bennett, *Madame Margot*, 64–67.

13. Bennett, *Madame Margot*, 81, 82, 84–85, 86, 88, 89–90.

14. Bennett, *Madame Margot*, 97–98, 101, 102, 106, 107–8, 109, 110.

15. Hervey Allen's review of *Madame Margot, Charleston Evening Post*, 26 November 1921. Allen's review is perhaps one of the best on the book, and in it he refers to Beatrice Ravenel's "feminine" review.

16. John Bennett to William Watts Ball, 1 December 1921, Ball papers, Perkins Library, Duke University.

17. John Bennett to Susan Smythe Bennett, 18 August 1920, JBP, SCHS.

18. John Bennett to Hervey Allen, 22 June 1921, JBP, SCHS.

19. Bennett to Allen, 22 June 1921.

20. John Bennett to Susan Smythe Bennett, 1 September 1921, JBP, SCHS.

21. *Charleston Sunday News (and Courier)*, 4 December 1921.

22. *Springfield (Mass.) Union*, 1 January 1922.

23. John Bennett to William Watts Ball, 10 December 1921, William Watts Ball papers, Perkins Library, Duke University.

24. Beatrice Ravenel's review appeared in the *Columbia (S.C.) State* on 20 November 1921 and noted that "Mr. Mencken will like this book very much." She compared Bennett to George Washington Cable and James Branch Cabell. "I have seen Mrs. R personally," Bennett wrote W. W. Ball; "she seemed to think it extraordinary I should not have taken umbrage" (John Bennett to William Watts Ball, 1 December 1921, William Watts Ball papers, Perkins Library, Duke University). "Mrs. R's critique in the STATE persuaded many to read the book." In another letter to Ball, he wrote of "Mistress Beatrice uncovering the damn-Yankee concealed beneath the Freudian complex of our plot" (23 January 1922, William Watts Ball papers, Perkins Library, Duke University). Bennett attributes the quote to Heyward in his letter to William Watts Ball of 1 December 1921.

25. His doggerel poem, "A Reaction to 'Madame Margot' and Grotesque Charleston by John Bennett," is poem number 35 in the collection of his poems edited by Emmett Robinson, *A Miscellany of Doggerel Rhymes by A. J. S.* (Charleston: Nelsons' Southern Printing Company, 1964). Stoney also has a poem (no. 36) on Josephine Pinckney's *Three o'Clock Dinner* and ends his collection (no. 90) in a tribute to William Molen.

26. The book was passed to Robinson by Whitall, who was an expert, collector of his works, and an author of a bibliography of Robinson's poetry (Edwin Arlington Robinson to John Bennett, 15 January 1922, JBP, SCHS).

27. *Charleston Evening Post,* 27 November 1921.

28. John Bennett to his family, 8 November 1925, JBP, SCHS.

29. His review was published in the *New York Evening Post,* 24 December 1921. See Work notebook A, 49, JBP, SCHS.

30. John Bennett to Elizabeth B. Heyward, 24 April 1929, requests for biographical information, JBP, SCHS.

31. *The Year Book of the Poetry Society of South Carolina* (Columbia: The State Company, 1926), 42–43. Bennett probably wrote this paragraph; the quote is in quotation marks in the yearbook, quoting apparently from the letter from the translator/publisher or from Bennett. Bennett planned to use his reviewer article on the alleys and byways of "Grotesque Old Charleston" for an introduction. The title would have been *Signora Margot, Groteska Legendo.*

32. "I should much like to hear from him in regard to his proposal for 'Madame Margot.' Mrs. Mignon Ziegfeld, Flo Ziegfeld's sister-in-law, has already approached me on this topic of possible dramatization" (John Bennett to McDavid Horton, 22 August 1923, Poetry Society correspondence, JBP, SCHS). Bennett's presentation copy to Mignon Ziegfeld is in the author's collection.

33. John Bennett to Frank P. O'Donnell, 18 November 1925, JBP, SCHS.

34. John Bennett to William Watts Ball, 23 January 1922, William Watts Ball papers, Perkins Library, Duke University.

CHAPTER 16. *"Your Affections Have Betrayed You"*

1. John Bennett to Susan Smythe Bennett, 11 August 1921, JBP, SCHS.

2. John Bennett to Susan Smythe Bennett, 3 September 1922, JBP, SCHS.

3. Bennett to Susan Smythe Bennett, 3 September 1922.

4. Bennett quotes the letter from Gaul at length in his letter to Susan Smythe Bennett, 12 September 1921, JBP, SCHS.

5. John Bennett to Susan Smythe Bennett, 6 September 1922, JBP, SCHS.

6. For a good description of the various levels of meetings and criticism, see John Bennett's letter to Mrs. Paschall Strong, 12 May 1926, JBP, SCHS. The system worked so well that DuBose Heyward used a similar method (ca. 1938), when with Rockefeller Foundation funding he instituted a playwriting group at the Dock Street Theatre; instead of producing poets, the Charleston group now wanted to produce playwrights.

7. *Columbia (S.C.) State,* 21 May 1922.

8. The best source on Peterkin is Susan Williams, *A Devil and a Good Woman, Too: The Lives of Julia Peterkin* (Athens: University of Georgia Press, 1997).

9. Bellaman was obviously aware of many facets of Peterkin's life and the odd intense relationship she had with her father, a physician, who cut off the gangrenous toes of the plantation foreman that triggered Peterkin to write *Black April*. Powerful and manipulative doctors dominate Bellaman's *King's Row*; one pursues an incestuous relationship with his daughter, and another needlessly amputates the legs of a man to keep his daughter from marrying him.

10. "He taught me how to train myself to write," Lewisohn wrote of the character he called Ferris; "he gave me generously of his time." But, Lewisohn noted, he had been ruined by gentility. "Since art means passion and since all passion has a touch of wildness, he was ever too much of a gentleman to be an artist. Not with his mind and heart, but with his unconquerable tribal self he always loved something else—a quiet manner, reserve of speech, an aristocratic nose [none of which Lewisohn had]—a little better than he loved truth or beauty" (Ludwig Lewisohn, *Up Stream: An American Chronicle* [New York: Boni & Liveright, 1922], 82–83).

11. Heyward at one point in his career said that the story behind "Gamesters All" really happened; he was walking along the docks of Charleston, heard a shot, and saw a black man running. The man was hit and fell dead at his feet (Theatre Guild publication, DuBose Heyward papers, SCHS). The poem was so well known that Margaret Widdemer, a lecturer in 1925 at the Poetry Society, would entertain people at a party with a parody of it (John Bennett to his family, 18 January 1925, JBP, SCHS).

12. Lowell leaving Magnolia Gardens is referred to in her letters to Josephine Pinckney and also in S. Foster Damon's *Amy Lowell: A Chronicle; with Extracts from her Correspondence* (Boston: Houghton Mifflin, 1935), 597. The biography also notes on the same page that Lowell was puzzled by Charlestonians not inviting her to dinner.

13. John Bennett to James Henry Rice, 30 March 1922, James Henry Rice papers, Perkins Library, Duke University.

14. *The Year Book of the Poetry Society of South Carolina, 1922* (Charleston: The Carolina Press, 1922), 53.

15. John Bennett to his family, 3 September 1922, JBP, SCHS.

16. John Bennett to his family, 16 January 1938, JBP, SCHS.

17. The "map" comment is from John Bennett to J. T. Gittman, October 1938, JBP, SCHS. The description of McClintock is from *The Year Book of the Poetry Society of South Carolina, 1922*, 52.

18. Bennett to Gittman, October 1938.

19. John Bennett to DuBose Heyward and Hervey Allen, 22 August 1921, JBP, SCHS.

20. His poems included "In a Rose Garden," "The Abbot of Derry," "The Song

of the Spanish Main," "Love Has Forsaken You: A Dirge," "The Wandering Minstrel's Song," and "The Piper's Song." See Jean Wright Gorman and Herbert S. Gorman, eds., *The Peterborough Anthology: Being a Selection from the Works of the Poets Who Have Been Members of the MacDowell Colony* (New York: Theatre Arts, Inc., 1923).

21. John Bennett to Susan Smythe Bennett, 11 September 1922, JBP, SCHS.

22. John Bennett to Mary Elizabeth Pratt, 13 June 1941, JBP, SCHS.

23. John Bennett to Susan Smythe Bennett, 2 September 1922, JBP, SCHS.

24. John Bennett to Susan Smythe Bennett, 1 September 1922, JBP, SCHS.

25. Bennett to Susan Smythe Bennett, 1 September 1922.

26. This event could not have been celebrated, and Heyward could not have written a play on it, if John Bennett had not discovered the date of the Museum's founding when he was researching the Revolutionary War history of South Carolina.

27. "DuBose Heyward's wife . . . looks so exactly like DuBose that on one occasion she was jestingly but successfully presented as his twin sister" (John Bennett to his family, 3 February 1924, JBP, SCHS).

28. John Bennett to Susan Smythe Bennett, 1 September 1922, JBP, SCHS.

29. John Bennett to Susan Smythe Bennett, 5 September 1922, JBP, SCHS.

30. See the *Carolina Chansons* contract in the DuBose Heyward papers, SCHS. At least one scholar has misinterpreted this clause of Heyward and Allen buying books to mean that the Macmillan Company demanded Allen and Heyward help pay for publishing. Heyward was quite a businessman and would, with his publisher's help, create a "Carolina Edition" of *Angel*, his second novel, which he would market himself.

31. Hervey Allen to John Bennett, 19 June 1922, JBP, SCHS.

32. John Bennett to James Henry Rice, 30 March 1922, James Henry Rice papers, Perkins Library, Duke University.

33. John Bennett to William van R. Whitall, 5 April 1922, JBP, SCHS.

34. Laura Bragg, interview by author, 4 August 1976. Bragg also noted that Bennett was used by Heyward.

35. John Bennett to William van R. Whitall, 4 April 1922, JBP, SCHS.

36. John Bennett to his family, 16 April 1925, JBP, SCHS.

37. John Bennett recommended Rex Fuller's novel manuscript to John Farrar (John Bennett to his family, 19 April 1925, JBP, SCHS) and praised his poetry in the 1922 *Year Book of the Poetry Society of South Carolina* (52); in the fall of 1923, however, Fuller's "financial accounts were so peculiarly entangled that he could not explain a deficiency but by saying that many checks had blown out his window" (John Bennett to his family, 2 March 1924, JBP, SCHS).

38. According to *The Year Book of the Poetry Society of South Carolina for 1925*, "By courtesy of Messrs. Harpers Bros., publishers of Hervey Allen's *Earth Moods*, the

award of the Blindman Prize to Keen Wallis, of Missouri, was broadcast from New York through the entire United States the night the announcement of the award was made in the Society here" (*The Year Book of the Poetry Society of South Carolina, 1925* [Columbia, S.C.: The State Company, 1925], 49). In 1926, Ruth Manning Sanders of Cornwall, England, won the award, and the Dial Press published her book-length poem. This was the last year the Blindman Prize was awarded; van R. Whitall had funded the prize, even after Allen left town, only because of his fondness and respect for John Bennett. (See letter of John Bennett to Susan Smythe Bennett, 25 October 1925, JBP, SCHS: "My good wife reminded me that van R. Whitall continued his $250 Blindman Prize . . . mainly because of my membership in it, and on condition that I represent the Society on the board of judges in that contest.")

39. See Frank Durham, *DuBose Heyward: The Man Who Wrote Porgy* (Columbia: University of South Carolina Press, 1954), 28–29.

40. *The Year Book of the Poetry Society of South Carolina, 1923* (Columbia: The State Company, 1923), 83. See also Durham, *DuBose Heyward*, 27–28.

41. John Bennett to Yates Snowden, 19 April 1923, SCL, reprinted in *Two Scholarly Friends*, 197. Commenting on it to Heyward he wrote, "It has simply ruined my entire year's work so far. So much for the service of the Public, which doesn't care a hang! Never again for me, lad!" (John Bennett to DuBose Heyward, 23 May 1921, DuBose Heyward papers, SCHS).

42. John Bennett to his family, 21 July 1921, JBP, SCHS.

43. John Bennett to his family, 22 February 1925, JBP, SCHS.

44. John Bennett to William van R. Whitall, 7 May 1923, JBP, SCHS.

45. John Bennett to Walter Wilbur, 27 January 1919, JBP, SCHS.

46. John Bennett to Josephine Pinckney, 19 July 1923, JBP, SCHS.

47. It may be that Josephine Pinckney "inherited" some of Bennett's ill will from her mother, Camilla. Bennett felt Camilla had been rude and cold to him for years; he talks about his "stately" relations with Mrs. Pinckney in his letter to his family, 31 July 1927, SCHS, and chides Josephine for neglecting her duties at the Poetry Society, "not what a 'Pinckney' should do" (John Bennett to his family, 3 July 1927, JBP, SCHS). Bennett passed along the cruel comment often meted out to Mrs. Pinckney, "Camilla the Gorilla" or "Madame Gorilla," in a letter to his family, 26 November 1927, JBP, SCHS. The author Harry Hervey, in his 1942 novel *The Damned Don't Cry* about a love affair across social class lines, would base a Savannah society matron on Camilla Pinckney, even appropriating the term "Camilla the Gorilla" to describe her. Josephine Pinckney and Harry Hervey were good friends.

48. *The Year Book of the Poetry Society of South Carolina, 1923* (Columbia: The State Company, 1923), 16.

49. Reminiscences of John Bennett, JBP, SCHS.

50. John Bennett to Alfred Hutty, 18 May 1923, JBP, SCHS.

51. *The Year Book of the Poetry Society of South Carolina, 1925* (Columbia: The State Company, 1925), 50. The etching was published as a frontispiece to the yearbook of that year. It later served as a model for the frontispiece in a published version of his collection *The Doctor to the Dead* in 1946. War-time shortages of paper prevented the use of coated stock, which would have allowed a truer reproduction of the original. It is reproduced in Martha R. Severens, *The Charleston Renaissance* (Spartanburg, S.C.: Saraland Press, 1998), 37.

52. Fed up with the goings-on in that building, many whites in the neighborhood sent a petition to the city council of Charleston, on 23 May 1922, about the building "commonly known as CABBAGE ROW." They wrote that the "tenement is unquestionably used by many of its occupants as a bed or assignation house" and that "while the fleet was here a special detail of TWO provost guards were [sic] kept in the vicinity . . . and from time to time these guards were joined by their Superior Officers." The signers requested that the house, a "menace to public Health and Morals," be closed to Negro tenants. DuBose Heyward was a resident of the neighborhood but, tellingly, did not sign it (Miscellaneous manuscripts, SCHS). The role of the provost guard in keeping sailors from the premises is mentioned in John Bennett's letter to his family of 30 November 1924, JBP, SCHS.

53. Bennett's speaking activities are noted in *The Year Book of the Poetry Society of South Carolina, 1924* (Columbia, S.C.: The State Company, 1924), 78. For a list of materials purchased for Alice Smith, see John Bennett to his son, 24 December 1923, JBP, SCHS.

54. John Bennett to Joe Taylor, 23 June 1924, JBP, SCHS.

55. John Bennett to Joe Taylor, 1 January 1924, JBP, SCHS.

56. Bennett to Joe Taylor, 1 January 1924.

57. Bennett notes this on a letter from the Winthrop Literary Society dated 18 October 1923, which he answered in Manila a month later (Requests for biographical information, JBP, SCHS).

58. *Buckhorn Johnny* MS, chapter 5, page 3, JBP, SCHS.

59. John Bennett to his family, 24 September 1944, JBP, SCHS. Also in his reminiscences, Bennett wrote, "Charles F. Lummis, of Pasadena, California, the author, for whom the great caracole tower of the Southwest Museum is named, was editor when John Bennett was cub-reporter; they parted for forty years; neither forgot the other. They met, unheralded, in Los Angeles. 'Lummis!' said one. One returning glance: 'By the god! It's Jack Bennett!' said Lummis, and they fell on each other's necks, actually" (JBP, SCHS).

60. John Bennett to his family, 3 February 1924, JBP, SCHS. Laura Bragg often told the story that Dorothy Heyward wanted to touch up the gray in her hair before the wedding, but it turned out much darker than expected, so much so that DuBose Heyward did not recognize her, passing her on the street in New York, just before

their wedding. As for Pinckney, she would suffer romantic disappointment within a year. In a letter to Amy Lowell of 16 September 1924 in the Harvard University Libraries, Pinckney wrote that she was in love with a young man. She confessed this to him, and he said he suspected as much. He said he wasn't ready for marriage; Pinckney suggested he elope with her, but "he was too moral for that." It seems that this man was Dick Wigglesworth; one of the reasons he gave for not marrying was that he was afraid of some sort of insanity that ran in his family. (See Pinckney's letter to Amy Lowell, 7 October 1924, Harvard University Libraries.)

61. Emily Clark, *Innocence Abroad* (New York: Alfred A. Knopf, 1931), 238.

62. *Nancy Ann* was the play that won the Harvard Prize and gained her entry into the MacDowell Colony, where she met Heyward. The play was produced on Broadway, constantly rewritten for the star, Francine Larrimore, and failed. It was produced by many a stock company, including one that came to Charleston and played at the Academy of Music, again failing dismally. "Dorothy and DuBose," Bennett wrote, "were all day yesterday at the theatre, advising and directing the minor details; the text as supplied from New York, having no stage directions attached. Dorothy, pulling a wry face, says that she has had difficulty in recognizing her own child in the form offered for stock company work: twelve characters have been totally eliminated, and four others squashed into two, and one masculine character suddenly transformed into feminine, or the reverse, I forgot now which. We [Bennett, Susan, and Mr. and Mrs. Alfred Hutty] are to be a 'box party' in tux's" (John Bennett to his family, 22 February 1925). Alicia Rhett, later to be "discovered" in Charleston and to play in the film *Gone with the Wind,* played in another production of *Nancy Ann* produced in Charleston by the Thalians (*Charleston Evening Post,* 23 February 1935).

63. John Bennett to Dorothy and DuBose Heyward, 10 August 1924, JBP, SCHS.

64. See typescript of Karen Greene's book, *Porter-Gaud School: The Next Step* (Easley, S.C.: The Southern Historical Press, 1982). Her interviews, nearly sixty years after the fact, contained gossipy mentions of the fact but were cut out and not published (SCHS).

65. Josephine Pinckney noted her suspicions regarding Aunt May to Amy Lowell in a letter of 5 June 1924 (Harvard University Libraries).

66. Pinckney notes in the letter above that Allen did say he looked forward to a big city but gave no reason for leaving. In a letter to Lowell on 10 August 1924 (Lowell papers, Harvard University Libraries), she writes that Heyward has heard nothing about the affair they discussed; he refused to believe the story being circulated and said he would contact Mr. Waring about it.

67. Karen Greene, interview by author.

68. Laura Bragg, interview by author; also confirmed in Gene Waddell interview with Laura Bragg, 6 May 1976.

69. This is the story Pinckney told to Amy Lowell in a letter of 7 October 1924. In a letter of 16 September 1924, before she got this version, she noted to Lowell that Mr. Waring warned her to keep her communication with Allen a secret; and the Reverend William Way, who was convinced of the worst about Allen, told her not to communicate with him at all (Lowell papers, Harvard University Libraries).

70. In early 1935, Heyward's publishers came to town with their wives; Heyward invited Hervey Allen to come, too, since they were also Allen's publishers. Hervey, he suggested, could stay out at Heyward's house "Follywood"; Heyward suggested that Allen not look up Bennett, since he had become a hermit, and because his wife Suso (a nickname for Susan) monopolized him (DuBose Heyward to Hervey Allen, 29 January 1935, DuBose Heyward papers, SCHS). Whether he meant it or not, or was trying to keep Allen from being seen by others, is hard to tell. None of the contemporary articles mentioned Allen, and a later one (*Charleston News and Courier*, 12 February 1936) discussed how a number of others connected to Heyward and Allen were also published by Farrar and Rinehart. Allen apparently did come, and was glimpsed by someone who knew him, which forced Heyward to make up a story to appease Bennett (DuBose Heyward to Hervey Allen, 2 March [1935], DuBose Heyward papers, SCHS).

71. Allen telephoned Bennett and said he would be there very soon for a visit. "Hervey and Anne, Mary Anne, Marcia and Dickey [their children], chauffeur and nurse all rolled up the door in [their] spacious chariot, dark blue . . . and for an hour's lapse [there] was hurrying conversation and gathering together of broken threads. If we had but earlier notice we should have delighted in keeping them for lunch; but what we had wouldn't stretch out to that limit. Hervey is tremendous, and [is] growing too heavy, a truly huge chap. Anne is charming: intensely blond. The children are slender to thinness, very pale, tall . . . perilously anemic" (John Bennett to his family, 8 January 1939, JBP, SCHS).

72. Josephine Pinckney to Amy Lowell, 3 April 1925, Lowell papers, Harvard University Libraries; Amy Lowell to Josephine Pinckney, 21 January 1925, Lowell papers, Harvard University Libraries. Lowell also notes, as she did in a letter of 21 June 1924 to Pinckney, that van R. Whitall was an unhealthy influence on Allen; Bennett, ironically, wrote to Whitall in April 1922 (JBP, SCHS), saying Lowell was an unwholesome influence on Allen and his poetry.

73. John Bennett to his family, 24 February 1929, JBP, SCHS. His article "Henry Allen Here, Not Hervey Allen" appeared in the *Charleston News and Courier*, 26 February 1929, and served as a long tribute to Allen and his years in Charleston; he also quoted from an Allen letter to prove that he was indeed in Bermuda.

Harry Hervey lived for awhile in Charleston, with his mother, and apparently entertained lavishly; having traveled in the Far East, he interested Laura Bragg in Angkor Watt. He set one of his novels, *Red Ending*, in Charleston and gave a typescript of it to Josephine Pinckney; it is a tale similar to Pinckney's later *My Son and Foe*, and it is one of the few works ever to picture Charleston as decadent and smothering, not picturesque and quaint.

74. John Bennett to his family, 27 March 1927, JBP, SCHS.

75. John Bennett in the *Charleston News and Courier*, 26 February 1929. (This is from the same article mentioned in note 73, above.)

76. Hervey Allen to Susan Smythe Bennett, 24 May 1924, JBP, SCHS.

77. John Bennett to Susan Smythe Bennett, 28 May, 1924, JBP, SCHS.

### CHAPTER 17. Porgy *vs.* Buckhorn Johnny

1. It depicted, Bennett noted, "Heyward in the Bow with the Lyre, Allen in the stern with the torch, Bennett at the oars, with the high hat." Concerning it, he wrote, "I have in my possession a small cartoon of three men in a boat which represents a vessel with the head of Pegasus for [a] prow, DuBose Heyward standing in the bow, carolling to the music of a lyre; Hervey Allen at the helm, guiding the craft, with the flaming torch of genius in his hand; and myself at the oars with spectacles and 'high hat' propelling the boat, signed below by the three of us, autographed officially at the 'launching of the Poetry Society, A.D. 1920. . . .' There is in it more than an ironical, touch of humor . . . and that was its purpose. There seemed something of jocularity in the whole affair. We had PUT IT ACROSS. . . . I wonder if the so-called lights of other 'eras' looked at themselves with the same sardonic eye" (Reminiscences of John Bennett, JBP, SCHS). Bennett notes that he made photographic copies of it for Anne Allen, Hervey Allen's wife. In celebration of the Poetry Society's sixtieth anniversary, Bennett's grandson John Bennett made souvenir reproductions of the drawing (Sunday edition of the *Charleston News and Courier* and the *Charleston Evening Post*, 1 February 1981).

2. John Bennett to his family, 26 October 1924, JBP, SCHS. Josephine Pinckney wrote Amy Lowell about her assessment of DuBose Heyward leaving his job for writing: "DuBose has with noble recklessness given up his insurance business in spite of a delicate wife. He made a bit of money this past year lecturing and he expects to make a business of it next year" (5 June 1924, Lowell papers, Harvard University Libraries).

3. John Bennett to DuBose Heyward, 28 October 1924, JBP, SCHS.

4. John Bennett to his family, 1 August 1924, JBP, SCHS.

5. John Bennett to his family, 2 June 1924, JBP, SCHS.

6. John Bennett to his family, 15 April 1925, JBP, SCHS.

7. John Bennett to his family, 26 October 1924, JBP, SCHS.

8. Bennett to his family, 26 October 1924.

9. John Bennett to his family, 15 March 1925, JBP, SCHS.

10. John Bennett to his family, 12 April 1925, JBP, SCHS.

11. A miscellaneous note in DuBose Heyward's manuscript for *Peter Ashley*, DuBose Heyward papers, SCHS.

12. Harlan Greene, "The Little Shining Word: From Porgo to Porgy," *South Carolina Historical Magazine* 87, no. 1 (January 1986), 75–81. "Hell-bent": DuBose Heyward to John Bennett, 28 July 1924, JBP, SCHS.

13. John Bennett to his family, 1 August 1924, JBP, SCHS.

14. John Bennett to his family, 2 November 1924, JBP, SCHS.

15. John Bennett to his family, 30 November 1924, JBP, SCHS.

16. John Bennett to his family, 7 December 1924, JBP, SCHS.

17. Bennett to his family, 7 December 1924.

18. Bennett to his family, 7 December 1924.

19. Josephine Pinckney to Amy Lowell, 21 December 1924, Lowell papers, Harvard University Libraries.

20. Bennett to his family, 7 December 1924.

21. Bennett to his family, 7 December 1924. In another episode involving Susan Bennett, food, and the novel just a year later, the Bennetts gave a party where Susan "served cassava wavers toasted, rolled double, and buttered with tea, and a confection or cake of her own recipe: chocolate, raisins, and chopped nuts, with a little flour, etc., which for DuBose's pleasure, she named 'Porgies'" (John Bennett to his family, 17 January 1926, JBP, SCHS).

22. John Bennett to DuBose Heyward, 6 December 1924, JBP, SCHS

23. John Bennett to Jack Appleton, 17 October 1925, JBP, SCHS. He wrote in that letter that "Heyward can't punctuate any better than a private secretary or a stenographer in a boiler factory."

24. John Bennett to his family, 22 February 1925, JBP, SCHS.

25. Thomas Petigru Lesesne, *Landmarks of Charleston* (Richmond: Garrett & Massie, 1939), 101. "His last days were tragedy. It would spoil a reading of *Porgy* to discuss him at length."

26. *Baltimore Sun*, 10 March 1929.

27. In a letter to his family (31 October 1926, JBP, SCHS), he noted, "Everyone in Charleston remembers the lame negro who rode a-begging through the streets in a goat-cart, the prototype of DuBose Heyward's Porgy. He disappeared from the street and cart two years ago; one rumor said dead, the other in the penitentiary for murder. The quaint facts are that he flourishes still and is old and fat and infinitely disreputable. He was arrested for the shooting of a negro woman in one of the kennels of our slums; was found guilty; but the penitentiary said they could do nothing with him, crippled as he was; for gracious sake, don't send him up here! The chain-gang said we cannot employ him anywhere; he will be a vicious idler [and] a dangerous incubus, pray don't send him to us; so the judge paroled him

under a suspended sentence during good behavior, not knowing what else to do with him; and retiring to his property, which he had amassed by successful mendacity and mendicancy, he now prospers as proprietor of one of the worst joints in Charleston; I suppose that for him is good behavior!" There's no way of telling how Bennett got this information. The legal record suggests that he just shot at a woman but did not hit her and then was not "nol-processed"; some hand has notated on the legal documents that he "can't be located by police." If any of this information of Bennett's is true, it is ironic; for in the novel and play and opera, blacks are shown to be abused by the vagaries of white men and their justice system. This would be an escape from it. No matter what the source of the information, it appears to be the last recorded sighting of Sammy Smalls. All sources seem to suggest that he died by the early to mid-1920s. Dorothy Heyward discusses having never been able to see him, and the local legend he became, in her introduction to DuBose Heyward, *Porgy* (New York: Bantam Books, 1953).

28. John Bennett to Susan Smythe Bennett, 13 April 1925, JBP, SCHS.

29. John Bennett to his family, 5 June 1927, JBP, SCHS.

30. Bennett to his family, 13 April 1925.

31. John Bennett to his family, 19 April 1925, JBP, SCHS.

32. John Bennett to his family, 1 February 1925, JBP, SCHS.

33. John Bennett to his family, 4 April 1926, JBP, SCHS.

34. John Bennett to his family, 22 February 1925, JBP, SCHS.

35. John Bennett to his family, 15 April 1925, JBP, SCHS.

36. John Bennett to his family, 16 April 1925, JBP, SCHS.

37. John Bennett to his family, 13 April 1925, JBP, SCHS.

38. John Bennett to his family, 17 May 1925, JBP, SCHS.

39. The full title is "Just Out: An Appendix to the Complete Works of John Bennett. Sensational Details of the Author's Inner Life; Intimate, Private and Personal. Material Never Heretofore Brought to Light." Referring to the physicians who took care of Bennett, the spoof notes "This Appendix has been brought in small and compact form, by Messrs. Robert Wilson and Robert S. Cathcart. . . . The cuts by Dr. Cathcart are distinguished for their directness and simplicity."

Mary Crow Anderson, in *Two Scholarly Friends* (261), does realize it is a jest but assumes Snowden wrote it, since he had it printed. It does state, however, that thirty copies were printed "without the consent of the author." It does bear the date May 1925 on it, although the photograph reproduced in it bears the date of August 1927. To complicate it further, Bennett annotated at least one copy ("To Chas. Mills," author's collection), dating it from the hospital in May 1925. This copy also contains Bennett's corrections of typographical errors. This author has found the small spoof cataloged as a true appendix to Bennett's work in at least one Charleston Library.

40. *Charleston News and Courier,* 28 May 1925

41. John Bennett to William van R. Whitall, 4 June 1925, JBP, SCHS.

42. *The Year Book of the Poetry Society of South Carolina, 1925* (Columbia, S.C.: The State Company, 1923), 15.

43. John Bennett to his family, 23 May 1926, JBP, SCHS.

44. John Bennett's letter of resignation to the Poetry Society of South Carolina, 8 June 1925, JBP, SCHS.

45. John Bennett to family, 1 August 1924, JBP, SCHS.

CHAPTER 18. *"Changed by the Years"*

1. John Bennett to DuBose Heyward, 6 January 1926, JBP, SCHS.

2. John Bennett to DuBose Heyward, 28 October 1924, JBP, SCHS.

3. Reminiscences of John Bennett, JBP, SCHS.

4. John Bennett to Hervey Allen, 25 March 1927, JBP, SCHS.

5. John Bennett to his family, 3 March 1929, JBP, SCHS.

6. John Bennett to his family, 17 July 1927, JBP, SCHS.

7. There is a letter from W. F. Clarke of the Century Company to Bennett about a book of short stories and poems, dated 5 May 1896, even before the publication of *Skylark.* On 28 November 1906 (*Peyre Gaillard* correspondence, JBP, SCHS) the Century Company wrote saying, "We await with interest your volume of Silhouette Stories." But by 13 April 1907 the Century Company seemed to be at a loss as to how to market such a book; they felt the market had changed so radically with the cheap use of color and photographs that silhouettes were not viable. As late as 1915 the correspondence reflects that they thought such a book would be a losing proposition. In a letter to Spencer Mapes of 20 February 1937 (Biographical file, JBP, SCHS), Bennett notes that Mrs. Dodge was eager for it, but it was turned down "for unknown reasons." The book's ultimate success, Bennett felt, proved Mrs. Dodge's superior judgement.

8. Reminiscences of John Bennett, JBP, SCHS.

9. John Bennett to Yates Snowden, 23 [month?] 1907, published in *Two Scholarly Friends,* 19.

10. Reminiscences of John Bennett among promotional materials written by Bennett to promote the book, JBP, SCHS. For a list of those silhouettes he recut, see Bennett's letter to Berta Gunterman, 6 March 1928, JBP, SCHS.

11. Reminiscences of John Bennett, JBP, SCHS.

12. Reminiscences of John Bennett, JBP, SCHS.

13. Reminiscences of John Bennett, JBP, SCHS.

14. It is interesting to note that the word "Mamba" is used several times in Bennett's *The Treasure of Peyre Gaillard,* with which Heyward, no doubt, was familiar.

15. Bennett describes Gething taking his brother's body from the barbed wire in a letter to his family, 4 September 1927, JBP, SCHS.

16. John Bennett to his family, 20 February 1927, JBP, SCHS.

17. John Bennett to his family, 21 August 1927, JBP, SCHS.

18. Bennett mentions "the Chinese boys," as they were called in Charleston, throughout his letters in the mid- to late 1920s. See also Louise Allen's dissertation on Laura Bragg. There are some unpublished photographs of Bennett, others, and the Chinese boys in the South Carolina Historical Society; see Jian Li, "A History of the Chinese in Charleston," *South Carolina Historical Magazine* 99, no. 1 (January 1998), 34–65. The image on page 63 shows Laura Bragg with the Chinese boys at her house outside Charleston, although the location is misidentified in the caption. There was, apparently, some muttering in Charleston about the white Laura Bragg being seen with the Chinese; Bennett thought the *Charleston News and Courier* was being malicious when it printed a story about a Chinese boy being forced to attend a segregated black school in Mississippi, but he also objected to the rumor that Bragg might want to make the boys members of the Poetry Society. "This, too, is a faux pas: there are too many who take offense" (John Bennett to his family, 16 October 1927, JBP, SCHS). For more on Bragg and one of the Chinese boys, see note 53, below.

19. John Bennett to his family, 10 April 1927, JBP, SCHS.

20. John Bennett to his family, 22 April 1928, JBP, SCHS.

21. John Bennett to his family, 6 November 1927, JBP, SCHS.

22. John Bennett to his family, 18 December 1927, JBP, SCHS.

23. Bennett mentions the appearance in *The Year Book of the Poetry Society of South Carolina, 1928* (71), commends Gething's story on pages 59 and 66, but does not mention his contributions.

24. John Bennett to his family, 31 January 1926, JBP, SCHS: "Several citizens ran to speak to Jo Hergesheimer and be spoken to: I did not; being a modestly arrogant person myself: If he wants to speak to me, let him be introduced."

25. *The Year Book of the Poetry Society of South Carolina, 1928* (Columbia, S.C.: The State Company, 1928), 68. Ferber is mentioned the previous year.

26. John Bennett to his family, 18 March 1928.

27. Bennett mentions taking notes for them in his letter to his family, 9 October 1927, JBP, SCHS.

28. It is included in *The Cat's Compendium,* ed. Ann Currah (New York: The Meredith Press, 1969).

29. Clippings and advertisements regarding *The Pigtail of Ah Lee Ben Loo,* JBP, SCHS.

30. *New York Herald Tribune,* 4 February 1929, 54. Benét's comment was in the

*Saturday Literary Review* of 29 September 1928 (*Skylark* and *Pigtail* scrapbook, 88, JBP, SCHS).

31. Reminiscences of John Bennett, JBP, SCHS.

32. "Years ago," Bennett wrote, "I did a set of designs for a manufacturer of correspondence paper for young people" (Bennett to J. M. Friedman, 11 September 1935, Art correspondence, JBP, SCHS).

33. The 1931 *Year Book of the Poetry Society of South Carolina* announced, "The Wychwood suburban community development company, of Wychwood, New Jersey, by personal arrangement of its President Arthur Rule, with Longmans, Green & Co., and its author, will incorporate in the permanent architectural schemes of the suburb, exclusively residential, designs, in wrought-iron gates, grilles, barriers, weather vanes, and stained glass leadings, derived from the silhouette illustrations of John Bennett's . . . *The Pigtail of Ah Lee Ben Loo*, by the architect-designer, Bernhardt E. Muller" (30). A book was published showing the designs and houses (collections of South Carolina Historical Society), but by 1936 or so, with various lawsuits, it appears that the company no longer had the rights to Bennett's illustrations.

34. Bennett did the cover designs for the four final volumes of the "Three Guardsmen" books in the series called The Years Between. See his letter to his family, 18 October 1928, JBP, SCHS, and other letters in this time period. The books, translated from the French of Paul Feval and M. Lassez, were *The Mysterious Cavalier, Martyr to the Queen, The Secret of the Bastille*, and *The Heir of Buckingham.*

35. He did the cover designs and front board stampings for *Laguerre: A Gascon of the Black Border* (Columbia, S.C.: The State Company, 1924) and *With Aesop Along the Black Border* (Columbia, S.C.: The State Company, 1924).

36. John Bennett to Frank and Nettie Taylor, 15 July 1929, RCHS.

37. He was elected to honorary membership in the Alpha Chapter of the University of South Carolina in May 1928. He wrote Yates Snowden on 11 May 1928 about it, assuming Snowden had something to do with it (published in *Two Scholarly Friends*, 261).

38. John Bennett to his family, 17 January 1926, JBP, SCHS.

39. John Bennett speculated on the intervention of Hervey Allen in his letter to his family of 12 June 1927, JBP, SCHS, and mused on Pinckney's reaction to Cullen in his letter to his family of 15 January 1928, JBP, SCHS.

40. "The book is factitious; as art, only artifice: *Porgy* seemed to be strange and genuine; I think it was, and will remain. *Angel* cannot. Yet I hope it may have popular and heavy sale, to put DuB. on a sound and comfortable . . . basis" (John Bennett to his family, 24 October 1926, JBP, SCHS). It did sell well and make Heyward money, despite the fact that he lost out on selling it as a magazine serial; the editors balked at a scene in which he dramatized a hypocritical religious scene (John Bennett to his family, 14 March 1926, JBP, SCHS). "DuBose and I are a pair," he wrote his family

on 15 September 1939 (JBP, SCHS), "nothing I have done quite reaches the popularity of 'Nick Attwood.'" Similarly, Heyward had never outmatched his *Porgy*. "But nothing I have done quite reaches the depth of DuBose's *Angel* thus far."

41. DuBose Heyward to John Bennett, JBP, SCHS. His letter to his family, 12 June 1927, quotes it and describes their tour of the city.

42. John Bennett to Miss Bailey, 24 May 1941, JBP, SCHS.

43. The first quote is from the same letter in note 41, above; the second is from John Bennett to Josephine Pinckney, 7 June 1927, JBP, SCHS.

44. John Bennett to his family, 14 August 1927, JBP, SCHS.

45. John Bennett to his family, 11 September 1927, JBP, SCHS.

46. John Bennett to his family, 9 October 1927, JBP, SCHS.

47. John Bennett to Yates Snowden, 5 January 1927, JBP, SCHS. A letter of that date is published in *Two Scholarly Friends*, but does not have that line in it.

48. John Bennett to Joe Taylor, 23 November 1928, JBP, SCHS.

49. John Bennett to his family, 25 April 1926, JBP, SCHS. The book was printed both in London (Ernest Benn Limited, 1927) and New York (Dial Press, 1927). The American version (printed in Britain) calls it "The BLINDMAN PRIZE for 1926" on the dust jacket. Once discontinuing the Blindman, Whitall endowed a scholarship at the MacDowell Colony.

50. John Bennett to his family, 13 January 1929, JBP, SCHS.

51. John Bennett to his family, 12 May 1929, JBP, SCHS.

52. Bennett to his family, 12 May 1929.

53. Jennings, "being urged, did a fantastic dance, masked with a silver woman's face," Bennett wrote his family (20 April 1924, JBP, SCHS), but later he wrote them of Jennings, "I wish he would cut out the capering and posturing and so-called interpretive BLAH" (6 March 1927). In the same letter he noted the presence of the dancers Ruth St. Denis and Ted Shawn in town and how he also disliked them. On 13 March 1927 he wrote to his family (JBP, SCHS) that Laura Bragg and Mr. Hu, one of the Chinese boys, went to the St. Denis/Shawn performance and that it was improper.

54. John Bennett to his family, 12 May 1929, JBP, SCHS.

55. Bennett to his family, 12 May 1929.

56. John Bennett to his family, 12 April 1925, JBP, SCHS.

57. Schuler Livingston Parsons, *Untold Friendships* (Cambridge, Mass.: The Riverside Press, 1955), 136–37.

58. John Bennett to his family, 15 December 1929.

59. John Bennett to G. T. Gittman, 17 February 1934, JBP, SCHS.

60. Reminiscences of John Bennett, with typescript comments of Martha Trimble Bennett, JBP, SCHS.

CHAPTER 19. *"The Real John Bennett"*

1. Reminiscences of John Bennett, JBP, SCHS.

2. Concerning one of them, he wrote, "George Wauchope says his . . . son-in-law Bob Bass plans to 'do a LIFE of ME.' God of Our Fathers . . . preserve me from my friends! If anyone proposes to do a LIFE of ME, I shall have to, perforce, be fool enough to do it myself, to prevent greater folly. There is little enough to write about in my life of interest or importance, save the curious course from THERE to HERE, which has its amusing spots" (John Bennett to his family, 19 February 1939, JBP, SCHS). Five years later he noted, "I have, again and again, by this and that urgency, been requested to write my personal reminiscences or biography. Had the latter part of my life not been so unproductive, I might have been tempted to do so" (John Bennett to his family, 9 July 1944, JBP, SCHS).

3. John Bennett to his family, 23 May 1937, JBP, SCHS.

4. John Bennett to his family, 24 March 1941, JBP, SCHS.

5. John Bennett to his family, 27 April 1930, JBP, SCHS.

6. *Birmingham News Herald*, 27 January 1929, see Work notebook B, 69, JBP, SCHS.

7. *Pittsburgh Sunday Post*, 24 April 1921, see Work notebook B, 32–33, JBP, SCHS. Harvey Gaul also set one of Bennett's collected spirituals to music (*Year Book of the Poetry Society of South Carolina*, 63), and also took interest in Ned Jennings when he attended Carnegie-Mellon.

8. *Charleston News and Courier*, 20 May 1931.

9. From Bennett's article "Now" (Perhaps) "It Can Be Told," published in the *Columbia (S.C.) State*, 5 January 1930.

10. Many Charlestonians, according to Laura Bragg, found the episode of a white man carrying a black woman's suitcase quite shocking. Heyward himself, she said, had done a similar thing (interview by author, 17 August 1976). Bragg claimed that the original of Mamba was a cook who worked for her. Bennett at one point worried over Heyward having to write for money; he felt, he wrote Snowden, that Heyward had the true gift, but might have to desert it for immediate gain (30 August 1927, published in *Two Scholarly Friends*, 258). Many thought Heyward was deliberately being sensational. Bennett also explained why, when representatives of Heyward's publisher were in town, no one seemed overly enthusiastic over *Mamba*. "He seemed a little surprised to find DuBose's *Mamba* rather slightingly mentioned here among professional Charlestonians, who feel compelled by position to condemn departure from tradition" (John Bennett to his family, 3 March 1929, JBP, SCHS).

11. Laura Bragg spoke of this, and many others commented on how Mrs. Hutty, like Mrs. Hollister in the novel, drove Hutty to produce salable materials while he wanted to pursue art. Many quoted the story that Hutty came back to finish an oil

painting only to discover that his wife had sold it. Ironically, Hutty provided art for the book's dust jacket.

12. John Bennett to his family, 18 April 1925, JBP, SCHS.

13. John Bennett to his family, 27 November 1927, JBP, SCHS.

14. John Bennett to his family, 25 October 1928, JBP, SCHS.

15. John Bennett to his family, 2 February 1930, JBP, SCHS. He noted that the "*News & Courier* . . . protests editorially that Mrs. Julia Peterkin has NEVER, no NEVER, experienced the slightest maladversion or unpleasant criticism of her books in Carolina, but per contra, proud, immediate, universal acclaim. Which is another lie, of course."

16. John Bennett to his family, 6 October 1929, JBP, SCHS.

17. John Bennett to his family, 21 September 1930, JBP, SCHS.

18. On 28 June 1936, in a letter to his family (JBP, SCHS), Bennett noted that Rutledge was being criticized for faking his nature stories and that Peter Gething had written an angry letter to *Bird Lore* about it; Bennett said it was "quite a small sensation here not to Archie's repute." A year later he wrote, "Archie Rutledge, the only real sentimental survivor of the past idyllic plantation age, has been given, unanimously, a pension by Mercersburg Academy, which enables him to retire from teaching and to devote himself to writing. Now, ye gods, attend! Henceforth we will see tomes of rather sweet-scented, and rather futile verse, and volumes of reminiscences and woodland experiences, gilded and metamorphosed beyond nature. Archie says he 'will now have time to roam the woods and creeks of his beloved lowcountry'" (John Bennett to his family, 23 May 1937, JBP, SCHS). He wondered if Rutledge "had sense . . . or is just a plain conceited fool" in a letter to his family on 28 May 1939 (JBP, SCHS) and also said that Archie, "as poet is one of the washouts of his native state, and as a nature writer, pushes Munchausen in veracity" (John Bennett to his family, 16 January 1938).

19. Herbert Ravenel Sass, "Mixed Schools/Mixed Blood," *Atlantic*, November 1956, 45–49.

20. "Now" (Perhaps) "It Can Be Told," *Columbia (S.C.) State*, 5 January 1930.

21. *The Year Book of the Poetry Society of South Carolina, 1930* (Columbia: The State Company, 1930), 54.

22. The Spiritual Society would tour the eastern seaboard, and its singers, including DuBose Heyward, would sing before President Roosevelt eventually; the concerts continued on in the Charleston tourist season for years.

23. Augustine Smythe et al., eds. *The Carolina Low-Country* (New York: Macmillan, 1931), vii.

24. In a letter of 18 June to his family (JBP, SCHS), Bennett said he had seen a circular going the rounds saying the book would contain an article on spirituals by John Bennett; the book would contain work by "representative authors and

artists . . . who have either been born and reared in lower Carolina or who have lived most of their lives here," a condition that would allow him in but disallow Dorothy Heyward and Alfred Hutty. Bennett says in this letter that he will not contribute because it will not pay.

25. "While it is the fashion to press books by and about the American negro, his music and song, South Carolina has had her negro poet: J. P. Brownlee, of Anderson, whose small pamphlet of poems, *Ripples*, was published, 1914, by the Cox Co., of Anderson" (*The Year Book of the Poetry Society of South Carolina, 1926* [Columbia: The State Company, 1926], 55).

26. "I am sorry not to do what Mammy says she would like," Bennett wrote his family (22 June 1930, JBP, SCHS), stating here that he thought it should be done by natives only.

27. John Bennett to his family, 17 August 1930, JBP, SCHS.

28. *The Year Book of the Poetry Society of South Carolina, 1931* (Columbia: The State Company), 32.

29. John Bennett, "Protest of an Old Timer" (New York: The Marchbanks Press, 1930). The letter originally appeared in the *Saturday Review of Literature* on 26 July 1930.

30. "McClintock Protests Right of Privacy as to His Address," the *Columbia (S.C.) State*, 1 April 1934. Beneath the clipping of this article in his scrapbook, Bennett has written, "Good-bye, Alex McClintock!" (JBP, SCHS). At least one fan did write McClintock to praise his work. The letter came back to the fan stamped "No Such Post Office in State." Bennett eventually got the letter and dutifully pasted it in his scrapbook.

31. John Bennett to DuBose Heyward, 26 July 1930, JBP, SCHS.

32. John Bennett to his family, 6 September 1931, JBP, SCHS.

33. John Bennett to his family, 4 May 1930, JBP, SCHS.

34. John Bennett to "Frances," 8 February 1937, Unidentified series, JBP, SCHS.

35. John Bennett to Frank and Nettie Taylor, 5 January 1934, RCHS.

36. John Bennett to his family, 20 May 1934, JBP, SCHS.

37. Reminiscences of John Bennett, JBP, SCHS.

38. "Don Adumbras and the Dragon" was published in *St. Nicholas Magazine* in September, October, and November 1934.

39. In some he tipped in a photograph of the ruins of Margot's cottage as he had photographed it in the early part of the century; to the end of the appendix "I added my autograph . . . and for my own amusement and puzzlement of buyers . . . stamped each and every volume with my personal seal" (John Bennett to Lancelot Harris, 14 January 1934, College of Charleston archives).

40. John Bennett to his family, 17 June 1934, JBP, SCHS.

41. John Bennett to Esther Taylor, 4 May 1933, JBP, SCHS.

42. He had long before toyed with the idea of compiling his bits of philosophy into a volume called "Proverbs of an Unpopular Philosopher." The manuscript is in the Ross County Historical Society in Chillicothe, Ohio.

43. Reminiscences of John Bennett, JBP, SCHS.

44. Reminiscences of John Bennett, JBP, SCHS.

45. John Bennett to Frank and Nettie Taylor, 6 June 1927, JBP, RCHS.

46. John Bennett to Susan Appleton, 23 January 1933, JBP, SCHS.

47. John Bennett to his family, 24 October 1943, JBP, SCHS.

48. John Bennett to J. W. Raper, 8 December 1945, JBP, SCHS.

49. Reminiscences of John Bennett, JBP, SCHS.

50. John Bennett to Frank and Nettie Taylor, 5 January 1934, RCHS. "I suppose if I could sell letters I should be enormously wealthy," he wrote another friend. "I like to write letters to friends; writing books is not a gift with me, but an accomplishment of long wrestling with stubborn words" (John Bennett to George C. Tyler, 29 January 1934, JBP, SCHS).

51. The only years in this era that he did not send out an original silhouette Christmas card were 1932 and 1943. In 1943, the Bennetts sent out a penny post card with a poem on it.

52. He went on to say in the same letter that after he left Chillicothe and sent letters back, he found many postal workers could not decipher the name of the town. So he kept improving his handwriting (John Bennett to Philip Hinkle, 28 September 1943, RCHS).

53. J. T. Gittman to John Bennett, 17 November 1934, JBP, SCHS.

CHAPTER 20. *"A Life . . . Not a Career"*

1. John Bennett to his family, 6 November 1927, JBP, SCHS.

2. John Bennett to Joe Taylor, 12 May 1932, JBP, SCHS.

3. The earlier name for the novel is mentioned in *The Year Book of the Poetry Society for South Carolina, 1931* (Columbia: The State Company, 1931), 31. At one point in this era, Bennett forgave Heyward for saying something about him much earlier; it was published in a literary column in 1924, mentioned by Bennett in a letter to Snowden of 2 December 1924. "I have forgiven Heyward for saying that I have a Chippendale outlook on life; what in God's name he meant by that, I'll never know" (John Bennett to Herbert Ravenel Sass, 16 August 1933, JBP, SCHS).

4. John Bennett to his family, 15 May 1938, JBP, SCHS.

5. John Bennett to his family, March 1931, JBP, SCHS.

6. John Bennett to Grant Shepherd, 31 May 1933, JBP, SCHS. Shepherd was an-

other friend of Bennett's who moved to Charleston and wrote a book of memoirs, called *The Silver Magnet.* Bennett wrote a foreword for it, but it was not included in the published work.

7. John Bennett to his family, March 1931, JBP, SCHS.

8. John Bennett to his family, 12 June 1932, JBP, SCHS.

9. John Bennett to Grant Shepherd, 31 May 1933, JBP, SCHS.

10. John Bennett to Hervey Allen, 6 November 1933, JBP, SCHS.

11. Herbert Ravenel Sass to John Bennett, 12 February 1933, JBP, SCHS.

12. Herbert Ravenel Sass to John Bennett, 31 October 1933, JBP, SCHS.

13. John Bennett to his family, 11 May 1933, JBP, SCHS.

14. John Bennett to Arthur Rule, 21 May 1931, Wychwood correspondence, JBP, SCHS.

15. John Bennett to his family, May 1940, JBP, SCHS.

16. John Bennett to his family, 18 June 1939, JBP, SCHS.

17. John Bennett to his family, 18 February 1940, JBP, SCHS.

18. John Bennett to his family, 20 May 1934, JBP, SCHS. And once Sass, "our perennial shedder of gore," began to get his stories accepted again, his editors were more insistent on controlling content. He had to stop the "Mormon-like accumulation" of new wives for his character Captain Africa in each story (John Bennett to his family, 22 October 1937, JBP, SCHS).

19. John Bennett to his family, 1 July 1934, JBP, SCHS.

20. John Bennett to his family, 17 June 1934, JBP, SCHS.

21. John Bennett to his family, 20 May 1934, JBP, SCHS.

22. John Bennett to his family, 1 July 1934, JBP, SCHS.

23. John Bennett to his family, 15 July 1934, JBP, SCHS.

24. John Bennett to his family, 13 October 1935, JBP, SCHS.

25. John Bennett to his family, 25 May 1930, JBP, SCHS.

26. John Bennett to his family, 27 July 1930, JBP, SCHS.

27. John Bennett to J. T. Gittman, 6 March 1934, JBP, SCHS.

28. John Bennett to his family, 13 February 1938, JBP, SCHS.

29. John Bennett to his family, 17 August 1930, JBP, SCHS.

30. John Bennett to his family, 5 December 1937, JBP, SCHS.

31. John Bennett to his family, 13 February 1938, JBP, SCHS.

32. Frances Frost to Josephine Pinckney, 19 January 1934, Josephine Pinckney papers, SCHS.

33. Note by Josephine Pinckney, Josephine Pinckney papers, SCHS.

34. John Bennett to his family, 17 June 1934, JBP, SCHS.

35. Katharine Anthony, "Charleston Portraits," *Yale Review*, April 1927, 567–80. Anthony describes a trip she took with Bennett and Laura Bragg, "The Museum

Lady," to Medway. Bennett describes the trip in a letter to his family, 28 March 1926, JBP, SCHS.

36. John Bennett to his family, 29 November 1925, JBP, SCHS. The Federal Bureau of Education listed forty books every child should read by the age of sixteen, including authors like Defoe, Alcott, Hawthorne, Mary Mapes Dodge, Twain, Walter Scott, Howard Pyle, Hugh Lofting, and John Bennett.

37. *Charleston News and Courier,* 18 December 1956.

38. Film rights were inquired after as early as 1914; there was a near sell in 1924 involving the dramatist who adapted the novel to a play, Edgar White Burrill; more interest came in 1927. Constance W. Wain claimed that Cecil B. De Mille was considering purchasing it for her son; Metro Goldwyn Mayer was said to be considering it for Jackie Cooper in 1934, and then for Freddie Bartholomew (see film correspondence, JBP, SCHS).

39. Reading *Whatever Goes Up: The Hazardous Fortunes of a Natural Born Gambler,* co-written with J. C. Furnas (Indianapolis: Bobbs Merrill, 1934), Bennett must have been struck with the ironic differences in their lives. Bennett, poor, had wanted to leave town to become an artist, but was compelled to stay and work as a newspaperman; Tyler was much wealthier. In fact, it was Tyler's father who had launched the rival press to Bennett's employer in the 1890s. The young Tyler kept running away from his wealth to be a tramp printer all over the country.

40. John Bennett to his family, 27 December 1936, JBP, SCHS.

41. John Bennett to Lucile Brown, 25 April 1951, *Skylark* play correspondence, JBP, SCHS. Regarding Breen, he wrote in another letter, "Lesser was ambitious. He had a boy with an exquisite voice, whom he advertised as 'Bobby Breen,' though as far from that nationality as East Side New York is from Ireland. . . . His racial characteristics were 'Italicized,' so to speak; though he was no Italian" (John Bennett to Sallie Tevis, 17 February 1947, Film correspondence, JBP, SCHS).

42. John Bennett to Susan Smythe Bennett, May 1940, JBP, SCHS.

43. John Bennett to his family, 8 February 1927, JBP, SCHS.

44. Bennett noted the editions the book went through; he wrote Gittman on 17 February 1934 (JBP, SCHS) that the first sold out, and a second edition was printed in 1929 just before the stock market fell; the second edition, he said, was sold illegally as remainders. In 1934 the publisher sold fourteen hundred sheets of the book to the Harlem Book Company in an edition similar to the first two, with slight differences in the color of the book cloth and no illustrated endpapers. A third printing came in May 1938, and the fourth was done in a smaller size and cheaper paper; there was a serious attempt to republish it as late as 1967, but it miscarried.

45. Louella Everett, editor of the volume, noted that stanza three of "God Bless You, Dear, Today," the "Piper" poem, stanza one of "Today," two lines from stanza

one and two lines from stanza three of "The Love of a Summer Day," four lines from stanza one and four lines from stanza four of "In a Rose Garden," four lines from one stanza, four from another, and the two final lines from "I Want an Epitaph," and five lines from "The Magnificat of the Hills" would be used (Louella Everett to John Bennett, 27 March 1935); then she decided to include a few lines from *Madame Margot* as well (27 February 1937, JBP, SCHS). The number and size of the quotations varied in the years from the 1930s to the 1960s.

46. *Familiar Quotations by John Bartlett* (Boston: Little, Brown, 1955), 949.

47. Reminiscences of John Bennett, JBP, SCHS.

48. John Bennett to his family, 20 February 1927, JBP, SCHS.

49. John Bennett to his family, 23 May 1943, JBP, SCHS.

50. John Bennett to his family, 23 October 1927, JBP, SCHS.

51. Reminiscences of John Bennett, JBP, SCHS.

52. John Bennett to his family, 29 May 1927, JBP, SCHS.

53. John Bennett to his family, 3 April 1927, JBP, SCHS.

54. John Bennett to his family, 30 April 1939, JBP, SCHS.

55. Reminiscences of John Bennett, JBP, SCHS.

56. John Bennett to his family, 4 April 1937, JBP, SCHS.

57. Reminiscences of John Bennett, JBP, SCHS.

58. John Bennett to his family, 1 August 1937, JBP, SCHS.

59. John Bennett to George C. Tyler, 5 May 1936, JBP, SCHS.

60. Reminiscences of John Bennett, JBP, SCHS.

61. Collection of the author. "Frustration is the flower which blooms most gaily in Time's Garden," he had written Yates Snowden, 2 December 1924, JBP, SCHS.

62. "Story of Forgotten Bells, Sacrificed to Confederate Guns, Is Told," *Charleston News and Courier*, 12 December 1937.

63. "Craftsman in Graphic Arts Is Visitor to the City," *Charleston Evening Post*, 30 March 1954.

64. John Bennett to his family, 28 February 1937, JBP, SCHS.

65. John Bennett to Milby Burton, 14 October 1938, JBP, SCHS.

66. John Bennett's annotation to his research notes of "Gullah vs. Angola" notebook, JBP, SCHS.

67. John Bennett to J. T. Gittman, October 1938, JBP, SCHS,

68. John Bennett's typescript annotation to his notes on "Where the Gullah Negro Came From," JBP, SCHS.

69. John Bennett to Jane Hunter, 12 January 1939, JBP, SCHS.

70. Reminiscences of John Bennett, JBP, SCHS.

71. John Bennett to his family, "Intermezzo" letter, 17 October 1928, JBP, SCHS.

72. *The Year Book of the Poetry Society of South Carolina, 1930* (Columbia: The State Company, 1930), 45. Bennett enumerated Heyward's *Porgy* and *Brass Ankle*, the stage

version of Julia Peterkin's *Scarlet Sister Mary*, Harry Hervey's stage adaptation of his novel, *The Iron Widow*, and Wilbur Daniel Steele's *When Hell Froze.*

73. Bennett referred to his role in the theater reconstruction in a letter to Will Poland, 17 December 1937, JBP, SCHS. *Life* magazine of 20 December 1937 shows the opening night audience, including Bennett (49). He and Susan can also be seen in the Rotogravure picture section of the *New York Times* of 5 December 1937; shot from the stage, the photo shows the Bennetts in the sixth row from the front, just above and to the right of the conductor's head.

74. John Bennett to his family, 25 February 1940, JBP, SCHS. Willkie's relationship to Charleston and the William Watts Ball dinner party is mentioned in John D. Stark, *Damned Upcountryman: William Watts Ball, A Study in American Conservatism* (Durham NC: Duke University Press, 1968), 194–97.

75. Bennett to his family, 25 February 1940, JBP, SCHS. Although Bennett tried to help get a book of his poems published, this never happened. He contributed to many magazines and anthologies, and his one novel, *Invincible Surmise*, was published in 1936.

76. Kitty Ravenel to Anna Wells Rutledge, 14 November 1943, Anna Wells Rutledge papers, SCHS.

77. John Bennett to his family, 16 January 1938, JBP, SCHS.

78. John Bennett to his family, 30 June 1940, JBP, SCHS.

79. Josephine Pinckney, *Hilton Head* (New York: Farrar and Rinehart, 1941), 230–31. Pinckney and DuBose Heyward started on the book together. Pinckney "came to him with all her Henry Woodward material and suggested they collaborate. They set out to work, and after 3 or 5 strong, almost violent, sessions, Jo took her opus under her arm and went home. It was amusing because they were always such good friends" (Dorothy Heyward to T. R. Waring, 9 October 1960, T. R. Waring papers, SCHS). And if there was any tension between Josephine Pinckney and Irita van Doren over Willkie, it must have evaporated quickly; in April 1945 van Doren chaired a committee of the Southern Authors award (the other members were Burton Rascoe and William Bridgewater), and they passed over Charlestonian Robert Molloy's *Pride's Way* and Richard Wright's *Black Boy*, among others, to award the prize to Pinckney's *Three o'Clock Dinner.*

80. Wendell Willkie to Josephine Pinckney, Josephine Pinckney papers, SCHS.

81. John Bennett to his family, 25 February 1940, JBP, SCHS.

82. John Bennett to his family, 11 April 1937, JBP, SCHS. In the same letter Bennett mentions how good Rhett is in the local production of "Lady Windemere's Fan." There are photographs of her in that production in the Emmett Robinson papers, Charleston County Public Library.

83. The only physical reminder of Maugham in the low country apparently is the mailbox bearing his name given to the Beaufort County Library. See "Maugham

Began Writing Classic Near Beaufort," *Charleston News and Courier,* 17 December 1965; and "Maugham's Mail Box Given to Beaufort Library," *Charleston News and Courier,* 31 December 1954.

84. She spoke in Charleston on 13 February 1935. Frank Gilbreth wrote the next day in the *Charleston News and Courier* that the audience "never was entirely sure whether it was listening to a genius or a humorist." He wrote, too, that she was to speak on the difference between poetry and prose, "but, at the conclusion of her lecture, few people in the audience were sure what the difference is." Glenn Allan ridiculed her lecture as well in his letter to John Bennett, JBP, SCHS.

85. "Novel in Danger, Lewisohn Claims," *Charleston News and Courier,* 3 March 1936.

86. John Bennett to his family, 2 May 1936, JBP, SCHS. The local papers also were skeptical. Frank Gilbreth, who had raised his critical eyebrows over Stein, said the paintings made him "jittery" and gave him "what is commonly known as the willies" ("Art Gazers Recall Columbus, Too Smart to Twit Unknown," *Charleston News and Courier,* 8 March 1936). Alfred Hutty went on record with "Simply an expression of radicalism," and Josephine Pinckney said, "Stimulating. I want to see them again" ("Guggenheim Modern Art Show, Biggest in US, Opens," *Charleston News and Courier,* 2 March 1936).

87. John Bennett to his family, 23 June 1940, JBP, SCHS.

88. Farrar had written Bennett that he wanted to see it almost immediately after the dinner in February when Heyward brought up the subject. In May he turned it down. "There is one consolation about Farrar & Rinehart's inability to see the book as possible for them and that is I shall not be under obligation to DuB Heyward for placing the book. I think I shall be able to do, or hope I shall, in spite of the all-consuming WAR" (John Bennett to his family, 12 May 1940, JBP, SCHS).

CHAPTER 21. *The Day of* The Doctor to the Dead

1. All references are from John Bennett's letters to his family, JBP, SCHS: Bridge, 21 July 1940; Alice Smith, 10 August 1941; Laura Bragg, 13 February 1943; Merchant Marine, 6 Gibbes St, 28 March 1943; Onslow Candy Co., grocery stores closing, navy wives, in cars, parks, lobbies, 13 April 1943; Ludwig Lewisohn's speech, waterfront off limit, 16 May 1943; Merchant Marine in Villa M., 13 June 1943; garbage, teachers, unruly children, 27 June 1943; cars on jacks, 25 July 1943; lightning on high battery, 1 August 1943; no grits, 22 August 1943; debutantes, 24 October 1943; black and white soldiers, 7 May 1944; Fort Sumter Hotel, 21 May 1944; British at attention, 11 June 1944; cameras on beach, 18 June 1944; war wounded from hospital ships, 15 October 1944.

2. Noon-day blasts: John Bennett to his family, 10 September 1944; ineffectual blackouts: John Bennett to his family, 20 June 1943, JBP, SCHS.

3. John Bennett to Hervey Allen, 27 December 1944, JBP, SCHS.

4. Dorothy Heyward to Dorothy DeJaggers, July 1942, Dorothy Heyward papers, DHP, SCHS.

5. "Meeting at Folly Tomorrow on Making Name Gershwin," *Charleston News and Courier*, 25 June 1945; "Folly's Name Unanimously Upheld in Vote," *Charleston News and Courier*, 27 June 1945.

6. Chalmers S. Murray, *Here Come Joe Mungin* (New York: G. P. Putnam Co., 1942), dust jacket copy.

7. Coleman would later tell others that in despair he had buried a novel manuscript no publisher would publish; years later when one did inquire of it, Coleman said he went to dig it up, but it had vanished. On 7 January 1940, Coleman, again under the name "Twig," had a letter published in the *Charleston News and Courier* regarding his *Nation* article.

8. Most of Molloy's novels, except for *Uneasy Spring*, would use Charleston somewhat, even if primarily set in New York City.

9. Reminiscences of John Bennett, "FORUM MEETING OF MAY 20, 1938," dated the following day, JBP, SCHS. He continued on, "I conclude that while I am glad to observe that the Society is very much alive, and that many young folks are carrying it on successfully by their own efforts undisturbed by the old, this will be for me the last meeting I shall attend. If so few note my presence at all, and I can hear nothing, I get no pleasure myself, and give little to others; it is reasonable to think that the days of my usefulness to the Society except to give the Skylark prize, or, if asked, to act as judge, are done."

10. John Bennett to his family, 19 April 1944, JBP, SCHS.

11. John Bennett to his family, 3 October 1943, JBP, SCHS.

12. John Bennett to his family, 30 April 1939, JBP, SCHS.

13. John Bennett to his family, 18 June 1939, JBP, SCHS.

14. John Bennett to J. T. Gittman, 14 February 1942, JBP, SCHS.

15. John Bennett to J. T. Gittman, 13 May 1942, JBP, SCHS.

16. John Bennett to J. T. Gittman, 19 September 1941, JBP, SCHS.

17. John Bennett to his family, 27 August 1939, JBP, SCHS.

18. Reminiscences of John Bennett, JBP, SCHS.

19. John Bennett to J. T. Gittman, 27 February 1943, JBP, SCHS.

20. John Bennett to his son, 21 May 1939, JBP, SCHS.

21. John Bennett to his family, 3 October 1943, JBP, SCHS.

22. John Bennett to his family, 10 August 1941, JBP, SCHS.

23. John Bennett to his family, 19 September 1943, JBP, SCHS.

24. John Bennett to J. T. Gittman, 10 March 1941, JBP, SCHS.

25. Reminiscences of John Bennett, JBP, SCHS.

26. John Bennett to Rabbi Isaac Marcuson, 8 March 1945, JBP, SCHS.

27. John Bennett to his family, 30 April 1939, JBP, SCHS.

28. John Bennett to his family, 13 August 1944, JBP, SCHS.

29. Offense: John Bennett to his family, 18 April 1943; High Hampton: John Bennett to his family, 3 October 1943, JBP, SCHS.

30. John Bennett to his family, 18 April 1943, JBP, SCHS.

31. Martha Severens, *The Charleston Renaissance* (Spartanburg, S.C.: Saraland Press, 1998), 94.

32. Annotation by John Bennett in his scrapbook, JBP, SCHS, 53 (item number 21-175-6).

33. Reminiscences of John Bennett, JBP, SCHS.

34. Annotation by John Bennett in his scrapbook, JBP, SCHS, 54.

35. "The Case for Accrediting Burke High School," *Charleston News and Courier*, 30 September 1945.

36. The best source on Waring is Tinsley E. Yarborough, *A Passion for Justice: J. Waties Waring and Civil Rights* (New York: Oxford University Press, 1987).

37. "As to the Burke School," *Charleston News and Courier*, 2 October 1945.

38. Reminiscences of John Bennett, JBP, SCHS.

39. "Blue Jacket: War Chief of the Shawnees" was published by the Ross County Historical Society in Chillicothe in 1943 and republished in 1978. It was written, he noted, "in the main of material I had picked up here and there during the past fifty years . . . for the amusement of my original and acquired families, to which I added some substantial backgrounding for the sake of perspective and comprehension and to tie the man into the web of American history" (John Bennett to Hervey Allen, 12 Jan. 1944). Bennett also noted that Hervey Allen "has based the first volume of his six volume historical romance, recently published," on Blue Jacket (John Bennett to "Cimiotti," 12 April 1943, Miscellaneous correspondence, JBP, SCHS). The volume in question would be *The Forest and the Fort*.

40. They appeared in the summer number of the *Yale Review* for 1943 and in the September 1943 issue of the *Negro Digest*. After publication in book form, individual tales would be reprinted in magazines such as *In Short, Everybody's Digest,* and *Encore Magazine*.

41. Reminiscences of John Bennett, JBP, SCHS. Regarding the "Golden Age," Bennett wrote, "Carry on, son. Had you been there, you would have been one . . . of that bunch of Cheerful Idiots, each of us who worked his best to do stuff that would stand the critical test of quality and honest labor, in the hope that someday, in something, he might do, as R. L. Stevenson wrote, 'Something that would last, JUST FOR FUN'" (John Bennett to his son, 13 June 1943, JBP, SCHS).

42. John Bennett to John Slocum, 28 March 1941, *Doctor to the Dead* correspondence, JBP, SCHS.

43. John Bennett to J. T. Gittman, 10 March 1941, JBP, SCHS.

44. Reminiscences of John Bennett, JBP, SCHS.

45. John Bennett to J. T. Gittman, 14 February 1942, JBP, SCHS.

46. John Bennett to Henry Volkening, 23 February 1942, JBP, SCHS.

47. The correspondence apparently is the only clue, since many of the early rewrites of the manuscript no longer survive; it is worthy of noting that none of the other literary manuscripts that his son sent out over the years were ever published.

48. The publisher's remarks appear between the free end sheets and the half title (John Bennett III, *So Shall They Reap* [New York: Doubleday, Doran and Company, 1944]). John Henry van Sweringen Bennett dedicated it "To My Wife *and* My Dad."

49. "Jack will be amused, and readers of *So Shall They Reap* entertained and enlightened by the arrest, hearing and condemnation of old Sabb C. Cumbee, 'veteran of two decades' of night-hunting, moon-shining, murder, feuding and miscellaneous violations of the law, State and Federal, in Berkeley County. Old Sabb was fined $1,000 and sentenced to a year in the Federal Pen, or Berkeley County jail; the jail sentence was suspended on condition that the fine be paid within 24 hours. As we all know, old Sabb Cumbee was simply transmogrified into big Bass Crombie in Jack's narrative, and Hell Hole Swamp changed to 'Big Hole' for masking purposes. . . . Old Sabb was familiarly known as 'King of Hell Hole Swamp'" (John Bennett to his family, 28 May 1944, JBP, SCHS).

50. Bennett noted the origins of many things in his letter to editor Bucklin Moon, 4 August 1943, JBP, SCHS.

51. Reminiscences of John Bennett, JBP, SCHS.

52. Text from Bennett interview on WTMA, JBP, SCHS.

53. On 10 November 1976, in an interview with the author, Elmina Eason recalled that she knew someone whose mother had made her cross to the other side of the street before passing it.

54. David Farrow, *The Root of All Evil* (Charleston: Wyrick and Company, 1997).

55. "That was in 1906 and Morgan Varnert, the boy who watched, was old then. He has been dead for twenty years. They are all gone, everyone of those from whom I gathered my brief harvest, white and black" (John Bennett, interview by Dorothy Quick, *East Hampton Star*, 3 October 1946, JBP, SCHS).

56. *New Yorker*, 25 May 1946. See Work notebook A, 71, JBP, SCHS.

57. Jack Conroy in the *Chicago Sun*, 26 May 1946.

58. *New York Times*, 2 June 1946. See Work notebook A, 77.

59. John Bennett to Susan Smythe Bennett, 29 July 1911, JBP, SCHS.

60. *South Carolina Historical and Genealogical Magazine* 47, no. 4 (October 1946), 127–28.

61. John Bennett to Josephine Pinckney, 15 June 1946, JBP, SCHS.

62. John Bennett to J. T. Gittman, 19 August 1946, JBP, SCHS. In his letter to his family of 22 October 1944, Bennett wrote about repairing the storm damage on his roof, JBP, SCHS.

63. John Bennett to J. T. Gittman, 19 August, 1946, JBP, SCHS.

64. John Bennett to his family, 28 May 1939, JBP, SCHS.

65. John Bennett to J. T. Gittman, 19 August 1946, JBP, SCHS.

CHAPTER 22. *An Epitaph*

1. "I Want an Epitaph," *Saturday Review of Literature*, 23 July 1927.

2. John Bennett to J. T. Gittman, 12 July 1946, JBP, SCHS.

3. Reminiscences of John Bennett, JBP, SCHS.

4. John Bennett to Martha Trimble Bennett, 8 July 1947, JBP, SCHS.

5. John Bennett to J. T. Gittman, 30 October 1947, JBP, SCHS.

6. Bennett to J. T. Gittman, 30 October 1947.

7. Bennett to J. T. Gittman, 30 October 1947.

8. John Henry van Sweringen Bennett to Henry Volkening, 6 November 1948, JBP, SCHS.

9. Reminiscences of John Bennett, JBP, SCHS.

10. "John Bennett," *Charleston News and Courier*, 30 December 1956.

11. E. A. M., "Writers of Today in South Carolina," *Columbia (S.C.) State*, 25 March 1934.

12. Frank Durham, *DuBose Heyward: The Man Who Wrote Porgy* (Columbia: University of South Carolina Press, 1954). Durham thanks Bennett in his forward (viii).

13. John Bennett to his family, 23 April 1951. JBP, SCHS.

14. Susan Bennett (daughter), interview by author, 11 November 1977.

15. "Creator of 'Master Skylark' Is 88 Today and Still Busy," *Charleston News and Courier*, 17 May 1953.

16. "Flag Day Program Carries Surprise," *Charleston News and Courier*, 14 June 1956; "Everyone is Surprised at Tribute to Bennetts," *Chillicothe Gazette*, 11 June 1956; "At Ohio University: Building is Named for John Bennett," *Charleston News and Courier*, 21 December 1966.

17. John Bennett to Martha Trimble Bennett, 31 May 1953, JBP, SCHS.

18. Bennett to Martha Trimble Bennett, 31 May 1953.

19. John Bennett to Susan Smythe Bennett, n.d., JBP, SCHS.

20. John Bennett to Susan Smythe Bennett, n.d., JBP, SCHS.

21. Hervey Allen died in 1948.

22. For a partial list of works based on Bennett's research, see note 19 of chapter 13.

23. John Bennett to his family, 15 July 1937, JBP, SCHS.

24. "Here Sleep Companions Who Never Forgot," published with mistakes in the *Columbia (S.C.) State,* 1 March 1931, over the name Alexander Findlay McClintock. For the correct version, see folder number 21-115-12, JBP, SCHS.

# Bibliography of Works by John Bennett

"Tom Gordon: The Haps and Mishaps of a Boarding School Boy." *Boy's Own* 1, no. 1, 2, 3, 4, 5, 6, 8, 10, 11, 12 (December 1886–November 1887).

"How the Howler Rushed the Growler: A Comical Tragedy." *New York Journalist*, 13 December 1890.

"Black Art." *St. Nicholas Magazine* 18, no. 12 (October 1891): 952–56.

"The Barber of Sari-Ann." *St. Nicholas Magazine* 19, no. 1 (November 1891): 60–64.

"How the Church was Built at Kehoe's Bar." *Washington, D.C., Home Journal*, 1891.

"Ye Olde-Tyme Tayle of ye Knight, ye Yeo-manne, and ye Faire Damosel." *St. Nicholas Magazine* 19, no. 3 (January 1892): 209–14.

"Out of the Waste-Basket." *Newspaperdom* 1, no. 2 (April 1892): 1–2.

"Ben Ali the Egyptian." *St. Nicholas Magazine* 19, no. 9 (July 1892): 696–700.

"The Persian Columbus." *St. Nicholas Magazine* 20, no. 2 (December 1892): 146–50.

"The Press Club Banquet at Red Hoss." *New York Journalist* 16, no. 14 (17 December 1892): 3–4.

"Little Peter and the Giant: A Fable of the Old Fashioned Sort." *St. Nicholas Magazine* 20, no. 4 (February 1893): 261–68.

"Granger-Grind and Farmer Mellow." *St. Nicholas Magazine* 20, no. 6 (April 1893): 472–73.

"Abijah's Fourth of July." *St. Nicholas Magazine* 20, no. 9 (July 1893): 673.

"Fritz the Master Fiddler." *St. Nicholas Magazine* 20, no. 12 (October 1893): 939–943.

"The Pigtail of Ah Lee Ben Loo." *St. Nicholas Magazine* 21, no. 6 (April 1894): 530–34.

"Jack and I: Charming Letters from an Artist at the Old Salt." *Charleston Sunday News (and Courier)*, 25 November 1894.

"The Magnificat of the Hills." *Independent* 47, no. 2422 (2 May 1895): 30.

"An Old Fashioned Mecca: Times When Charlestonians Went on Pilgrimages." *Charleston Sunday News (and Courier)*, 5 May 1895.

"To the Robin That Sings at My Window." *St. Nicholas Magazine* 22, no. 8 (June 1895): 619–620.

"The Hills of Ross." *St. Nicholas Magazine* 22, no. 9 (July 1895): 774–775.

"Hans the Otherwise." *St. Nicholas Magazine* 22, no. 12 (October 1895): 1016–1023.

"In a Rose-Garden." *Chap-Book* 3, no. 10 (1 October 1895): 389–90.

"Week Days in Dolly's House." *St. Nicholas Magazine* 22, no. 1 (November 1895): 80–81.

"Jimmy Croly's 'Coo-operative Thanksgiving Dinner.'" *Independent* 48, no. 2452 (28 November 1895): 31–32.

"The Love of a Summer Day." *Chap-Book* 4, no. 5 (15 January 1896): 240–41.

"The Love of a Summer Day: Waltz Song." Verse by John Bennett. Music and Refrain by J. A. Clarke. San Francisco: Zeno Mauvais Music Co., 1896.

"His Father's Price." *St. Nicholas Magazine* 23, no. 7 (May 1896): 536–544.

"Whitey Durkin's Baby Farm." *Independent* 48, no. 2485 (16 July 1896): 27–29.

"The Three Wise Owls." *St. Nicholas Magazine* 23, no. 12 (October 1896): 992.

"Master Skylark: A Story of Shakspere's Time." *St. Nicholas Magazine* 24, no. 1 (November 1896): 3–13; no. 2 (December 1896): 106–15; no. 3 (January 1897): 202–14; no. 4 (February 1897): 283–92; no. 5 (March 1897): 370–78; no. 6 (April 1897): 471–80; no. 7 (May 1897): 545–55; no. 8 (June 1897): 622–32; no. 9 (July 1897): 717–27; no. 10 (August 1897): 808–18; no. 11 (September 1897): 897–909; no. 12 (October 1897): 986–98.

"A Tiger Tale." *St. Nicholas Magazine* 24, no. 6 (April 1897): 508–509.

"God Bless You, Dear, To-Day." *Chap-Book* 7, no. 5 (1 July 1897): 125.

"The Ingenious Little Old Man." *St. Nicholas Magazine* 24, no. 11 (September 1897): 917.

"The Skylark Song." *St. Nicholas Magazine* 24, no. 11 (September 1897): 962–63.

"The Proud Miss O'Haggin." *St. Nicholas Magazine* 24, no. 12 (October 1897): 1004.

"Ye Very Ancient Ballad of ye Lily Mayden and ye Lyttel Taylor-Boye." *St. Nicholas Magazine* 25, no. 1 (November 1897): 35–39.

*Master Skylark: A Story of Shakspere's Time.* (Illustrated by Reginald B. Birch). New York: Century Co., 1897.

"A Jest of Little John." *St. Nicholas Magazine* 25, no. 3 (January 1898): 228–232.

"The Song of the Spanish Main." *Chap-Book* 8, no. 4 (1 January 1898): 171.

"Under the Rose-Leaves, under the Rose." *Chap-Book* 8, no. 5 (15 January 1898): 211.

"The Story of Barnaby Lee." *St. Nicholas Magazine* 28, no. 1 (November 1900): 2–12; no. 2 (December 1900): 159–69; no. 3 (January 1901): 253–260; no. 4 (February 1901): 352–59; no. 5 (March 1901): 432–40; no. 6 (April 1901): 544–53; no. 7 (May 1901): 622–29; no. 8 (June 1901): 738–44; no. 9 (July 1901): 796–803; no. 10 (August 1901): 916–24; no. 11 (September 1901): 976–83; no. 12 (October 1901): 1093–98; vol. 29, no. 1 (November 1901): 63–70; no. 2 (December 1902): 166–69; no. 3 (January 1902): 260–65; no. 4 (February 1902): 351–59; no. 5 (March 1902): 447–54; no. 6 (April 1902): 530–38.

"The Snake Charmer's Tune." *St. Nicholas Magazine* 28, no. 5 (March 1901): 431.

"The Robin's Song." *St. Nicholas Magazine* 28, no. 7 (May 1901): 619.

"How Cats Came to Purr." *St. Nicholas Magazine* 29, no. 12 (October 1902): 1094–99.

*Barnaby Lee* (Illustrated by Clyde O. De Land). New York: Century Co., 1902.

*An Interesting Experiment.* [Promotional pamphlet for *Barnaby Lee.*] The Sign of the Wanderers, [1902].

*Souvenir Calendar: Charleston—1902.* Charleston: Daughters of the Confederacy, 1902.

"Monsieur M. and Monsieur N: A Hysterical Romance." *Criterion*, September 1903, 33–34, 47.

"The Skylark's Song." Words by John Bennett. Music by Dudley Buck. Cincinnati: John Church Co., 1903.

"Bobby's Newspaper." *St. Nicholas Magazine* 30, no. 3 (January 1903): 241–47.

"'Slave Tags' for Tourists." *Sunday News (and Courier)*, 3 May 1903.

"Tudo and Crook-Fang: The Story of a Desperate Fight between a Cooter and a Moccasin." *Criterion*, February 1904, 17–22.

"A Grammatical Dispute." *St. Nicholas Magazine* 31, no. 10 (August 1904): 882–83.

"A Carolina Christmas Story." *Criterion*, December 1904, 21–25

"A Penny a Day." *St. Nicholas Magazine* 32, no. 5 (March 1905): 454–55.

"A Tiger Tale." Verse by John Bennett. Music by Grace Wilbur Conant. Boston: G. Schirmer, Jr., 1906.

*The Treasure of Peyre Gaillard.* New York: Century Co., 1906.

"The Art Treasures of Europe." [Erroneous title to Bennett's lecture to "the Columbia (sic) Art Association."] *Charleston News and Courier*, 30 April 1906.

"A Revival Sermon at Little St. John's." *Atlantic Monthly* 98, no. 2 (August 1906): 256–268.

"The Views of Many Readers: Mr. John Bennett Replies to Certain Criticisms of His Novel, *The Treasure of Peyre Gaillard*—That 'Mermaid Riot.'" (*New York Times Saturday Review of Books*), *New York Times*, 26 January 1907.

"The Incredible in Literature." *New York Evening Post*, 12 February 1907.

"Ye Ballad of Scullion Jack." *St. Nicholas Magazine* 35, no. 2 (December 1907): 154–58.

"Mr. Bennett's Lecture." *Charleston Evening Post*, 21 February 1908.

"Gullah: A Negro Patois." *South Atlantic Quarterly* 7, no. 4 (October 1908): 332–47; vol. 8, no. 1 (January 1909): 39–52.

"George Herbert Sass." In *The Library of Southern Literature*, ed. Edwin Anderson Alderman and Joel Chandler Harris, vol. 10 (Atlanta: Martin and Hoyt Company, 1909), 4661–4686.

"Little Jack Trimble." *Confederate Veteran* 18, no. 10 (October 1910): 473–4.

"Master Skylark." In *Dramatizations of School Classics: A Dramatic Reader*, ed. Mary A. Laselle, 144–160. Boston: Educational Publishing Co., 1911.

"A Hundred Years from Now." Words by John Bennett. Music by Carrie Jacobs-Bond. Chicago: Bond Shop, 1914.

"A Hundred Years from Now." Words by John Bennett. Music by Neal McCay. New York: Waterson, Berlin & Snyder, 1914.

"In a Rose Garden." Words by John Bennett. Music by Paul Ambrose. Boston: Schmidt, 1914.

*Master Skylark: A Dramatization of the Book by John Bennett, Prepared for the Use of Elementary Schools in New York City,* by Anna May Irwin Loutkenhaus. New York: Century Co., 1914.

*Songs Which My Youth Sung.* Charleston: Daggett Printing Co., 1914. [A pamphlet published to secure copyright of "In a Rose Garden," "God Bless You, Dear, To-Day!," "Her Answer: But Just To-Day," "The Love of a Summer Day," "The Abbot of Derry: A Round," "Over the Rose-Leaves: 'Suppose, Dear Heart, Suppose!'," "The Songs that My Mother Sung," "The Dear Long Ago," and "'Tis Done!"]

"The Accounting." *Harper's Weekly* 59, no. 3010 (29 August 1914): 203.

"Today." Words by John Bennett. Music by Carrie Jacobs-Bond. Chicago: Bond Shop, 1915.

"A List of Noncommissioned Officers and Private Men of the Second South Carolina Regiment of Foot." *South Carolina Historical and Genealogical Magazine* 16, no. 1 (January 1915): 25–33.

"Will Shakespeare, Star of Poets." *St. Nicholas Magazine* 43, no. 6 (April 1916): 481–90.

"A Business Men's Library: The Charleston Library's Effort to Lend a Hand in Building Up Local Prosperity." *Charleston News and Courier,* 8 April 1915.

"Old Plantation Songs: Spiritual Songs of the Old Plantation the Great Gift of the American Negro to the Folk-Song of America." *Chillicothe (Ohio) News-Advertiser,* 29 December 1916.

*Master Skylark: Or Will Shakespeare's Ward.* Dramatized by Edgar White Burrill. New York: Century Co., [1916].

"Revival 'Pon Top Edisto." *Southern Review* 1, no. 3 (April 1920): 22–23.

*Madame Margot: A Grotesque Legend of Old Charleston.* New York: Century Co., 1921.

"Literature's Loss to Law: Thoughts on 'Barton Grey.'" *Columbia (S.C.) State,* 4 June 1922.

"Grotesque Old Charleston." *Reviewer* 3, no. 4 (July 1922): 551–558.

"Madame Margot." [Later revised and reprinted as an appendix to the 1933 Charleston edition of the book and as an introduction to the 1951 edition.] *Literary Review, New York Evening Post,* 15 July 1922, 814. (Reprinted in the *Columbia (S.C.) State,* 23 July 1922.)

"To Edgar Allan Poe." *Columbia (S.C.) State,* 16 July 1922.

Review of *The Black Border* by Ambrose Gonzales, *Literary Review, New York Evening Post*, 9 December 1922, 287.

"Blythe Ned Holland: Writer and Singer of Sea Songs—A Carolina Dibdin." *Columbia (S.C.) State*, 24 December 1922.

"In Memoriam: William Packrow" and "The Wandering Minstrel's Song." In *The Year Book of the Poetry Society of South Carolina* 22, 26, Charleston: Carolina Press, 1922.

*Master Skylark.* (Illustrated by Henry Pitz). New York: Century Co., 1922.

"The Abbott of Derry," "In a Rose Garden," "Love Has Forsaken You: A Dirge," "The Piper's Song," "The Song of the Spanish Main," and "The Wandering Minstrel's Song." In *The Peterborough Anthology*, ed. Jean Wright Gorman and Herbert S. Gorman, 53–59. New York: Theatre Arts, Inc., 1923.

"Activities of the Past Year" and "Chilion: A Fantasy." In *The Year Book of the Poetry Society of South Carolina*, 1923, 14–18, 37. Columbia: State Company, 1923.

*Apothecaries' Hall: A Unique Exhibit at the Charleston Museum.* Charleston: Presses of Southern Printing and Publishing Co., 1923.

"Revival 'Pon Top Edisto." In *The Rumbling of the Chariot Wheels*, by I. Jenkins Mikell, 148–52. Columbia: State Company, 1923.

"The Abbott of Derry." *Literary Review, New York Evening Post*, 9 June 1923, 745.

"Proud Miss O'Haggin." *St. Nicholas Magazine* 51, no. 4 (February 1924): 365.

Review of *Folk Songs of the South*, ed. John Harrington and *Legends of Texas*, ed. J. Frank Dobie. *Saturday Review of Literature*, 16 May 1925.

"South Faces Literary Future of High Promise." *Charleston Sunday News (and Courier)*, 31 May 1925.

"John Bennett's Autobiography." *Chillicothe (Ohio) News-Advertiser*, 11, 12, 13, 14, 15, 16, 18 and 19 January 1926. (A printed version of John Bennett's autobiographical letter to Frank O'Donnell, 18 November 1925.)

"In Pompion Swamp" (from *The Treasure of Peyre Gaillard*). In *In Dixie Land: Stories of the Reconstruction Era by Southern Writers*, ed. Henrietta R. Palmer, 133–43. New York: Purdy Press, 1926.

*Pettigrew Verner: 1882–1925.* [Charleston, 1926.]

"John Bennett Recalls Days Passed Beneath the Sycamores along the West Bank Beaches of the Scioto." *Chillicothe (Ohio) News-Advertiser*, 4 March 1926.

"I Want an Epitaph." *Saturday Review of Literature* 3 (23 July 1927): 393.

"On Poe's Raven." *Saturday Review of Literature* 4 (10 September 1927): 103.

"Foreword: Apologia pro Vita Poetica" and "The Last Visitor." In *The Year Book of the Poetry Society of South Carolina*, 1928, 5–12, 43. Columbia: State Company, 1928.

*Just Out: An Appendix to the Complete Works of John Bennett.* [Spoof done in May 1925 to mark the removal of his appendix; printed by Yates Snowden] 1928.

*The Pigtail of Ah Lee Ben Loo: With Seventeen Other Laughable Tales and 200 Comical Silhouettes.*
New York: Longmans, Green & Co., 1928.

Review of *The House at Pooh Corner,* by A. A. Milne. *Saturday Review of Literature,*
10 November 1928.

"Henry Allen Here, Not Hervey Allen." *Charleston News and Courier,* 26 February
1929.

"A Symposium on Juvenile Reading." *Saturday Review of Literature,* 16 November 1929.

"Lieut. Samuel Boyer Davis." *Confederate Veteran* 37, no. 12 (December 1929): 450–52.

"'Now' (Perhaps) 'It Can Be Told.'" *Columbia (S.C.) State,* 5 January 1930; reprinted
in *Charleston News and Courier,* 21 January 1930.

"Negro Spirituals: What They Are, and How and Where They Got Their Name."
*Charleston News and Courier,* 4 May 1930.

"Trees, Parapets, and Gables." *Charleston News and Courier,* 11 July 1930.

*Protest of an Old Timer* (Letter to the Editor, *Saturday Review of Literature,* 26 July 1930,
14–15). New York: Marchbanks Press, 1930.

"The Result of Vanity." *St. Nicholas Magazine* 58, no. 6. (April 1931): 474.

"The Dead Pussy Cat." *National Humane Review,* May 1931, 10.

"Don Adumbras and the Dragon." *St. Nicholas Magazine* 60, no. 11 (September 1933):
511–514; no. 12 (October 1933): 566–69; vol. 61, no. 1 (November 1933): 9–12.

*Madame Margot: A Grotesque Legend of Old Charleston.* (With an appendix "Concerning
the Legend of Madame Margot.") Charleston, 1933.

"Hon. Billy Wiggers' Most Famous Speech." *Shako: The Literary Magazine of the Corps
of Cadets, The Citadel, The Military College of South Carolina* 3, no. 1 (autumn 1934): 3–4.

"The Abbot of Derry: Song for Voice and Piano." Words by John Bennett. Music
by Powell Weaver. New York: G. Schirmer, Inc. 1935.

"The Dead Pussy-Cat." In *The Cat in Verse,* ed. Carolyn Wells and Louella D. Everett, 250–51. Boston: Little, Brown and Co., 1935.

"When Chillicotheans Got a Case of 'Jitters.'" *Chillicothe (Ohio) News-Advertiser,*
21 August 1936.

"Youthful Reporter Jack Bennett 'Takes A Walk[,]' Makes Orator Shufflebottom
Famous." *Chillicothe (Ohio) News-Advertiser,* 29 May 1936.

"Bells of Charleston Were Sent to Melting Pot for Confederate Gun Metal."
*Charleston News and Courier,* 13 September 1936.

"'Cannon, More Cannon!' Confederacy Cried as Bells Were Sacrificed." *Charleston
News and Courier,* 20 September 1936.

"Bells Melted for Cannon as South's Star Set—St. Michael's Are Recast." *Charleston
News and Courier,* 27 September 1936.

"Story of Forgotten Bells, Sacrificed to Confederate Guns, Is Told." *Charleston News
and Courier,* 12 December 1937.

"Do You Know Your Charleston." *Charleston News and Courier*, 17 January 1938.

"The Fool's Defense." *St. Nicholas Magazine* 65, no. 10 (August 1938): 8–12.

"The May-Day Play" [from *Master Skylark*.] In *Reginald Birch: His Book*, ed. Elisabeth B. Hamilton, 95–106. New York: Harcourt, Brace and Co., 1939.

"Story of the Cow that Gave Black Milk." *Charleston News and Courier*, 21 September 1939.

"What a Free Library Did for a Bunch of Small Town Boys." *Charleston News and Courier*, 21 December 1941.

"In a Rose Garden." Words by John Bennett. Music by Lewis M. Isaacs. Boston: Boston Music Co., 1942.

*Blue Jacket: War Chief of the Shawnees Society.* Chillicothe, Ohio: Ross County Historical Society, 1943.

"Was it Charleston's Statue of William Pitt, or Not?" *Charleston News and Courier*, 18 April 1943.

"Charleston Folk Tales" ["All God's Children Had Wings"]. *Negro Digest* 1, no. 11 (September 1943): 33–36.

"Folk Tales from Old Charleston" ["All God's Children Had Wings," "The Measure of Grief," "The Enchanted Cloak," "Death and the Two Bachelors," and "Two Tales from Trapman Street Hospital"]. *Yale Review* 32, no. 4 (summer 1943): 721–740.

"The Side-Streets of Charleston, Forty Years Ago" [Recast from an article in *Reviewer*, vol. 3, no. 4 (July 1922), as a preface to *Legends of Old Charleston*]. *This November* Carolina Art Association Program. (November 1944): 10–15.

"First SC Paper Mill, 1806, Made Newsprint." *Charleston News and Courier*, 18 February 1945.

"Appeal for an Accredited Negro High School." *Charleston News and Courier*, 15 July 1945.

"The Case for Accrediting Burke High School." *Charleston News and Courier*, 30 September 1945.

*The Doctor to the Dead: Grotesque Legends and Folk Tales of Old Charleston.* New York: Rinehart and Co., 1946.

"Escort of the Dead." *Charleston News and Courier*, 21 July 1946.

"Fight to the Death of Snake and Cooter." *Charleston News and Courier*, 1 September 1946.

"Who Was Dicky Brux?" *Charleston News and Courier*, 1 September 1946.

"Riddle of Dinner Service Dug Up in Charleston Revived." *Charleston News and Courier*, 15 December 1946.

"Fritz the Master Fiddler." In *The Second St. Nicholas Anthology*, ed. Henry Steele Commanger, 87–91. New York: Random House, 1950.

*Madame Margot, a Legend of Old Charleston.* [With an introduction condensed from the 1933 Charleston edition]. Columbia: University of South Carolina Press, 1951.

"South Carolina Folk Tales: B'Rabbit and the Sweet-Potato Hills." *Charleston News and Courier,* 7 September 1951.

"South Carolina Folk Tales: How Buh Owl Got all the Meat and B'Rabbit and the Barkful Dog." *Charleston News and Courier,* 8 November 1951.

"The Army of the Dead" (From *The Doctor to the Dead*). In *South Carolina in the Short Story,* ed. Katherine M. Jones and Mary Verner Schlaefer, 110–113. Columbia: University of South Carolina Press, 1952.

*Master Skylark.* Adapted by Kathryn F. Mahoney and Laura E. Preble. (Illustrated by Mary F. Landrigan). New York: Globe Book Co., 1953.

"Revival 'Pon Top Edisto." In *Tales of Edisto* by Nell Graydon, 105–7. Columbia: The R. L. Bryan Co., 1955.

"Its Origin." [A history of Henry Holcomb Bennett's poem "The Flag Goes By."] In *The Flag Goes By: The Poem, Its Origin, Its Author.* John Bennett and Martha Trimble Bennett, Chillicothe: Ross County Historical Society, 1956.

*Master Skylark. A Story of Shakspere's Time.* New York: Airmont Publishing Co., 1965.

"Abijah's Fourth of July." *Modern Maturity* (June–July 1966): 33.

"How Cats Came to Purr." In *The Cat Compendium,* ed. Ann Currah, 93–100. New York: Meredith Press, 1969.

"Dear Everybody, Everywhere." (Letter of John Bennett, 2 June 1918, in "Hi-Ho, Betsy" by Claude Henry Neuffer). In *South Carolina History Illustrated* 1, no. 2 (May 1970): 36–43.

"The Army of the Dead," "The Little Harlot and Her Broken Pitcher," and "The Thirsty Dead," in *A Tricentennial Anthology of South Carolina Literature,* ed. Richard James Calhoun and John Caldwell Guilds, 405–414. Columbia: University of South Carolina Press, 1971.

*The Doctor to the Dead: Grotesque Legends and Folk Tales of Old Charleston.* Westport, Connecticut: Negro University Press, 1973.

"The Snake Charmer's Tune." *The City and Country Elsewhen Almanac,* 83. Brooklyn: Almanac/Everbe Press, 1979.

"The Remember Service." In *Dixie Ghosts,* ed. Frank D. Sherry Jr., Charles G. Waugh, and Martin H. Greenberg, 115–17. Nashville: Rutledge Hill Press, 1988.

*The Doctor to the Dead: Grotesque Legends and Folk Tales of Old Charleston.* Introduction by Thomas L. Johnson. Columbia: University of South Carolina Press, 1995.

"Madame Margot" and "The Wandering Minstrel's Song." In *Literary Charleston: A Lowcountry Reader,* ed. Curtis Worthington. Charleston: Wyrick & Co., 1996.

# Index

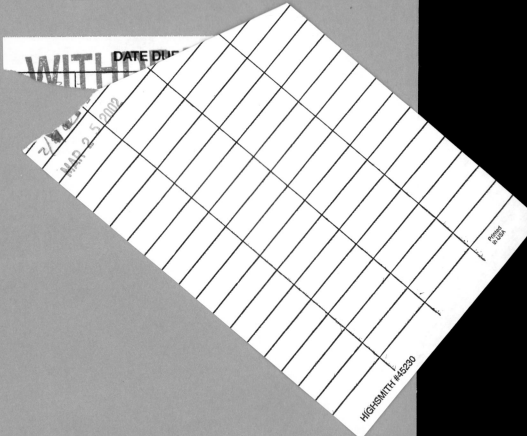